The Eighties

Other books by Gilbert T. Sewall

After Hiroshima: The U.S.A. since 1945 (coauthor)
Necessary Lessons: Decline and Renewal in American Schools

The Eighties

A Reader

Edited by Gilbert T. Sewall

PERSEUS BOOKS

Reading, Massachusetts

Many of the designations used by manufacturers and sellers to distinguish their products are claimed as trademarks. Where those designations appear in this book and Perseus Books was aware of a trademark claim, the designations have been printed in initial capital letters.

ISBN 0-7382-0035-2

Library of Congress Catalog Card Number: 98-87976

Perseus Books is a member of the Perseus Books Group

Cover design by Andrew Newman
Text design by Greg Johnson
Set in 10-point Veljovic by Vicki L. Hochstedler

1 2 3 4 5 6 7 8 9-DOH-0201009998
First paperback printing, October 1998

Find us on the World Wide Web at
http://www.aw.com/gb/

Contents

PART IV Hot and Cool

PART V The House of Intellect

PART VI The Movement of Culture

THE EIGHTIES

Preface

During the 1980s, I had the mixed fortune to observe the dazzle emanating from Manhattan and Los Angeles. The excesses were not hard to see: the BMWs and Mercedes station wagons parked all in a row at a Long Island polo match; the coke at Laguna and Aspen—and then in the Bronx; the investment bankers and, with even greater ambitions, the imagineers of the media and Hollywood—who by their extravagant example set about creating a new and luxe domestic universe for the rest of us.

As a writer and education critic, I was also observing radical changes going on about me in schools, in the humanities curriculum, and in juvenile behavior—not always subjects of burning interest to the zeitgeist generals of the day, but matters that provided ample chance to watch the advent of the culture wars up close. The emphasis on social and psychological forces beyond the individual's control—coupled with sixties-style hedonism—was leading to randy styles of mind and identity. *Be anything you want to be, do anything you want to do, as long as it doesn't hurt anybody.*

I lived in New York City where, in 1985, my neighbors—who had suddenly made it big in video—outfitted their three-year-old in neon orange day-glo togs and little red Lolita sunglasses. Not far away lived neighbor Monica, twenty-three years old and a self-described model. Monica had foregone the natural world. What had been considered sordid or unthinkable a generation ago was to Monica acceptable and even fashionable. The canons of knowledge and behavior that might have been prescribed by a parish priest or a high school English teacher had slipped to the margin long before Monica had reached the age of reason. Monica saw nothing peculiar, nothing degrading about partying all night downtown, then taking some uppers so she could spend her day modeling peekaboo tank tops at the Paramus Mall in suburban New Jersey. In California, about the same time, the scene was not much different. The "adults" were sending new signals. New lifestyles were leading to new situations, and a nine-year-old child chatted with her "single-parent" mother about mom's new boyfriend, whom the child had found naked in the bathroom that morning.

In geopolitics during the 1980s, the United States got lucky. Soviet opportunism at the beginning of the decade contrasted with its demise at the end. Civil life was another matter. Venerable sources of authority—notably family, schools, and churches—began to fold up with remarkable speed, abdicating to new forces—notably individual will and the entertainment industry. The distinction between reality and fantasy was fading out. Inner lives seemed to be emptied or emptying, anemic or flat. In this new and unanchored climate, gesture and frivolity insinuated themselves into areas of life where they had formerly been unwelcome. Fashion expanded its domain: to give a look, to measure worth, to tempt with luxury, to fill the hole of the spirit. A quest for amusements, or "entertainment," began to drive entirely new areas of American experience. In the querulous phrase of the eighties, "Are we having fun yet?" It was hard not to have fun during this flamboyant, party-driven decade, at least if you had a thick wallet. But below the surface sheen lurked intractable social problems and novel kinds of shamelessness that continue to haunt us today.

Some readers might think this collection gives a loaded or dire view of postmodernism and its creep into institutional life. I would respond that by the end of the eighties this counterculture, descended from changes in American intellectual life that were introduced in the sixties, demonstrated renewed force in the places where ideas are minted and ratified, not only in colleges but also in museums and foundations. Its assertive propositions, I would add, were often having a pernicious influence on the quality of intellect and knowledge, especially in history and the humanities. These new ideas had natural appeal, for they were fresh, clever, and often illuminating. But by 1980, they faced self-conscious resistance—some "liberal," some "neoconservative"—in the intellectual community. A number of older cultural critics had second thoughts about the sixties' vision of social justice and civic redemption. They were joined by younger writers who had come of age during the sixties and as a result had fresh insights about the eighties.

The eighties were a period of superb reporting and writing on cultural affairs. Magazines and journals congenial to the times appeared, from *Manhattan Inc., Spy,* and *7 Days* to the *American Spectator* and the *New Criterion.* Overall, I think, the "neocons" had better arguments and critiques of the culture, as they were not beholden to the *idées fixes* of the sixties. A skeptical response to liberal dogma and hip licentiousness seemed appropriate, to me at least. The cultural left was retreating into stock thought and rhetoric. It bristled and huffed. It exacted loyalty tests, accusing anyone chary of its agenda of "insensitivity," "monoculturalism," and worse. It had little clue as to the causes or solutions for mounting public concerns such as criminality, family breakdown, idiotized youth, and declining civility in daily life. (To be fair, neither did the nation's official political machinery, which was also at a loss for cures.)

The following collection does not dwell on the stock market crash, the Iran-Contra hearings, the Robert Bork nomination to the Supreme Court, or the fall of the Berlin Wall—all signal events of the decade. Instead, it emphasizes changing forms of expression, both public and private. Its subjects include lifestyle and subculture, exhibitionism and shamelessness, academic corruption, the lure of money, and spiritual hunger. Despite critical acclaim or intense reaction to these selections in the intellectual community, many works reprinted here circulated quite narrowly at the time of their publication. Some were later expanded into books, and, in a few cases, into best-sellers.

The selections explore ideational tensions in domestic affairs that have not been resolved and that ultimately may be unresolvable. I include some lapidary articles that raise profound cultural issues in highly original ways. I balance these with some jauntier writing of the day that illuminates ephemeral events that now seem emblematic of the times. As an ensemble, the book tries to capture the many sides of cultural and social change between 1978 and 1992, a period that seems increasingly distant from our own—but nonetheless heralds it.

I am indebted to James V. Capua and William T. Alpert of the William H. Donner Foundation, which provided special support to assemble the book, and to James Piereson, Caroline Hemphill, and Janice Riddell of the John M. Olin Foundation for their support over the years. I thank Peter A. Gilbert, Ralph Lerner, Constance Lowenthal, Robert Ferrell, Edwin J. Delattre, and Roger W. Smith for their diverse ideas, contributions, suggestions, and admonitions about the eighties and the rise of the culture wars. I am grateful for librarian Ernest Rubinstein's expertise with reference questions and periodical collections. Thanks go also to Pat Jalbert and Barbara Ann Starr for their assistance with the manuscript. Much credit goes to my agent John F. Thornton for his thoughtful editorial counsel and help as the anthology grew beyond a concept. Above all, I thank Stapley W. Emberling for her energy and skill with permissions, the manuscript, and production, and for her good nature, which made editing this collection a pleasure.

Revisiting the Eighties

Gilbert T. Sewall

In 1988, after the stock market had crashed but when Los Angeles real estate was still a bubble, a Morgan Stanley broker based in California could cackle over Easter lunch, "Only suckers work for less than $200,000 a year." The eighties were the "decade of greed," some critics asserted. But these critics were wrong—or at least incomplete—in their analyses. Money and the plutocratic impulse behind it were secondary, only symptoms of a profound cultural shift in the United States.

Between the inauguration of Ronald Reagan in 1981 and the Los Angeles riots eleven years later, Wall Street, Silicon Valley, and Hollywood thrust themselves upon us. The nation's skylines rose. The savings-and-loan industry expanded and then ruptured. The opening of Berlin and the fall of the Soviet Union brought the Cold War to an end and with it the chronic fear of Hot War, which was replaced by the fear of terrorism and nuclear blackmail. AIDS claimed almost 80,000 lives. The IBM PC and the Apple Macintosh began an ongoing personal computer and communications revolution. Fiber optics, satellites, cable television, transnational banking operations, automated teller machines, microwave ovens, compact discs, high-powered pharmaceuticals, and new medical technology came on the scene. (Even so, the 1986 *Challenger* explosion provided an endlessly televised reminder of human error and frailty in an age of technical miracles and scientific virtuosity.) Condominiums, shopping centers, and low-rise office complexes altered the American landscape, with loosely coupled cities and towns spreading over whole regions. Technology accelerated these exurban tendencies.

Amid the widening luxury, the nation's institutions, neighborhoods, and social habits faltered. It was not the trade deficit that bothered "normal" people on a day-to-day basis in the eighties, nor the possibility of new oil shortages or Japanese economic imperialism. It was the rising fear of the fiend lurking at the rest stop or at the shopping mall; the "homeless" crack addict, out of his mind and ready to kill; or New York art dealer Andrew Crispo. Pornography ("adult entertainment") of the rawest kind ("explicit") developed into a billion-dollar business, on display at the corner newsstand. Videocassette players, a luxury item for a few at the beginning of the eighties, were in more than 90 percent of U.S. households by the end of the decade. MTV influenced the young as profoundly as all of the nation's textbooks combined. Of the inner-city public schools, "we use comparative terms, but *outstanding* isn't one of them," said a New York City teacher in Tom Wolfe's 1987 novel, *The Bonfire of the Vanities*. "The range runs more from cooperative to life-threatening." It became harder and harder to pretend that, as a nation, we were steering the course.

Ideas and movements called *liberal* differed from older liberal imperatives. As Thomas B. Edsall of the *Washington Post* described it, an insurgency "concerned with the rights of the individual—with freedom from oppression, from confinement, from hierarchy, from authority, from stricture, from repression, from rigid rule-making, and from the status quo" had developed since the sixties. The nation had undergone a struggle between traditional values and a competing set of insurgent values, one that coincided with the rise of a black underclass, Edsall said. "This stigmatization as 'racist' or as 'in bad faith' of open discussion of values-charged matters—ranging from crime to sexual responsibility to welfare dependence to drug abuse to standards of social obligation—has for more than two decades created a *values barrier* between democratic liberals and much of the electorate."

For lifestyle radicals forged by the counterculture, the insurgency was more than okay—it was a secular crusade, a kind of reformation. The ideology of liberation made it okay to push low culture into high places, to demand new rules of cultural equivalency, to refuse to make—or invert—qualitative distinctions in the arts and letters. The insurgency sought coercive force of regulation and law, not least "affirmative action," to enforce its causes. The venerable political concept of an honorable opposition faded; to its opponents, Reaganism was a ridiculous or sinister political force. The great contradiction of the decade remains the consolidation of progressive power in culture and society despite the solid Reagan majority.

Cultural Politics

For the United States, the seventies had been an era of damaged self-image and unaccustomed economic insecurity. Following the American withdrawal from Vietnam in 1975, the country's self-confidence in international affairs waned. The Carter Administration seemed solicitous, even diffident, toward the Soviet Union and Third World. Around the globe, and perhaps more so in its own eyes, America seemed a "pitiful giant," as a revolutionary Iranian government debased and humiliated the Great Satan. In April 1979, the disastrous Desert One attempt to rescue American hostages in Tehran further eroded national confidence. Despite massive internal disorder, the Soviet Union gave the appearance of imperial confidence as its tanks rolled into Kabul, Afghanistan, that December. In *The Present Age* (1980), Norman Podhoretz wondered about future American will to fight for freedom in light of rising pacifist and anti-military sentiments. In 1980, interest rates were pushing 20 percent, the cost of living was increasing at a 13.5 percent annual rate, and gasoline shortages raised the specter of further economic insecurity in the future. By 1980, not surprisingly, the electorate sought a restoration of social stability and order, a return to the spirit of Eisenhower and the American Century.

When Ronald Reagan defeated Jimmy Carter in the November 1980 elections, few people outside the universities, the news establishments, and partisan circles of the Democratic Party were really surprised. Administration officials including Secretary of Defense Casper Weinberger, Secretary of State George Shultz, Attorney General William French Smith, Federal Reserve chairman Arthur Burns, and budget director David Stockman signaled collective determination (despite conflicting policy prescriptions) to reverse the nation's policies abroad and at home. Between 1981 and 1989, Reaganism sought to contain Soviet expansionism, comfort bourgeois culture, and remind the public of values that were dominant in the nation before the social disorders of the late sixties. In economic policy, the Republicans emphasized controlling inflation, lowering taxes for investors, deregulating industries, and shrinking federal domestic spending. The White House resorted to deficit spending (with the cooperation of Congress) to pay for rapid military buildup and to stimulate the economy. Public and private debt soared during the eighties, more evidence of the decade's *carpe diem* spirit.

To Republican advantage, McGovernism ruled the Democratic Party throughout the eighties, making isolationism, economic redistribution, group-based action politics, and individual empowerment the center of its political vision. In 1984, the "San Francisco Democrats" whom Jeane J. Kirkpatrick, ambassador to the United Nations, accused of a "blame America first" reflex at the 1984 Republican convention, held power on the Left. The Reagan/Bush ticket—employing the theme of "morning in America"—obtained 59 percent of the popular vote and captured 49 states, swamping the stolid Walter Mondale, Carter's Vice President and a former senator from Minnesota. Four years later, the hapless and mechanical Michael Dukakis was no match for George Bush. But Bush, cosseted among the rich and powerful, disconnected from domestic travail, was blind to what he called the "vision thing." Agile in foreign relations, he had zero feeling for America's quickened pulse and increasing moral panic in domestic affairs.

Through the Reagan and Bush years, the utopian view of social justice first articulated in the sixties remained forceful not only as slogans. End racism! Advance women's rights! Save the children! Clean up the environment! Identity politics took on new forms. The gay liberation movement remained outré before AIDS arrived in 1981. Then, as thousands of young men started to die, the disease exacted a huge toll, physical and psychological, especially in the arts community. Actor Rock Hudson died in 1985. Not so gradually, public attitudes toward this once taboo sexual orientation shifted. Black and feminist caucuses, followed by other groups, including the Hispanic, the Native American, and the disabled, insisted on high stakes of public feeling, a preferential standard. Many of the angriest demanded that putative social oppressors—white people, males, heterosexuals, and other people of "privilege"—confess their wrongdoing and atone for their sins.

Jesse Jackson, an enterprising veteran of the civil rights movement, ran for president in 1984 and again in 1988. In gaining millions of primary election votes, Jackson established his position as the chief spokesman for black Americans, calling for a Rainbow Coalition of disadvantaged and oppressed "peoples." In 1984, Jackson demanded that 30 million blacks be known collectively as "African Americans." Jackson's canny politics worked to cement racial consciousness and group divisions that earlier liberals in the civil rights movement had expected to disappear. In the 1980s, seeking increased self-esteem and racial pride among black children, radical Afrocentrists dismissed "white culture" as inherently evil and thus something to be avoided. By the late eighties, for a substantial fraction of the black population, imitating "white culture" was considered a form of cultural surrender.

Americans of all races may have revered Bill Cosby, Michael Jackson, and a number of black sports heroes. But white America's guilt over past racial injustice mixed increasingly with resentment over race-hustling, a rising sense of victimhood, and spreading anti-white feeling among blacks. Racial incidents were rising. By any measure, the black family was not doing well. By 1989, the black illegitimacy rate had risen to more than 60 percent. Many children—not only black—were growing up in squalor. Soaring crime rates cast a pall of fear throughout the land, having radical effects on urban life and national demography. There seemed little hope for a better future, and law-abiding Americans of all races began to wonder about the efficacy of public policy, the rule of law, and the ability of the nation to police itself in such a climate of violence.

The global ambitions of Soviet militarism escaped many people who condemned the Reagan Administration's renewed policy of containment—or who feared a "trigger happy" foreign policy. A post-sixties "peace movement" sputtered through the whole decade, allied to environmentalism. From Jonathan Schell's *The Fate of the Earth* (1982) to Bill McKibben's *The End of Nature* (1988)—as their titles indicated—apocalyptic tracts appeared on best-seller lists. In 1983, with great fanfare, ABC aired "The Day After," a remarkable drama featuring the nuclear destruction of Kansas City. The Bhopal, India, chemical explosion (1984), the Chernobyl nuclear contamination (1986), and the Exxon *Valdez* oil spill (1989) were disturbing events, as was the more subtle ecological deterioration of the Los Angeles basin. Acid rain, global warming, hazardous wastes, ozone depletion, and asbestos poisoning alarmed a rising share of the population. For the culturally ambitious, and for companies appealing to a certain mindset, politics and good public relations became indistinguishable: from Jackson Browne and No Nukes, to Ben and Jerry's, and Rain Forest Chic.

Boomers on the Make

The years after 1945 ushered in the most spectacular increase in birth rate in American history. The declining birth rate reversed itself, and between 1948 and 1953 the number of babies born in the United States shot up. After 1959, the birth rate began to drop sharply. The remarkably large and defined generation, born during the baby boom, came into adulthood and midlife during the eighties: It got married, had children, and made a living. But it had grown up in the sixties, an era of declining individual probity and increased social permissiveness. While many in it may have been voting Republican, this situational generation stood a long way from the Burkean ideals of community and tradition. It was too young to remember the former strength of those ideals in American life.

One aspect of the sixties—small is beautiful—lost its appeal. Beginning with the economic reversals of 1973 and 1974, American abundance and individual prosperity seemed more conditional than in previous decades. Despite rising environmental sensitivity, Less Is More changed to Getting Mine. Materialism came back in style, and money was suddenly very exciting. Gordon Gekko in Oliver Stone's hit movie *Wall Street* (1987) was the new kind of guy. The eighties were an era of five-hundred-dollar briefcases, power suits, and BMWs. In big cities and small, the money scene was no joke, and aggressive young urban professionals of a certain age—*thirtysomething*—were not at all lighthearted in their quest for cash. *Value added*, went the mantra of the day, and God help the older, more passive, old-school investment counselor who entrusted his future to client loyalty instead of his ability to cut a deal.

After the 1982 economic bounce and subsequent years of rapid economic growth, distinctions between winners and losers in the economy were glaring. Lawyers, bankers, accountants, computer and software manufacturers, bond brokers, realtors, and investors all benefited from high returns on capital and expanding paper assets. Arcane financial instruments (that only a few people could understand or access) allowed ambitious young bankers willing to work 80 hours a week to get very rich very fast.

Tom Wolfe's *The Bonfire of the Vanities,* the best-selling novel of 1987, captured the New York money scene with a winking eye as it chronicled the fall of Master of the Universe bond trader Sherman McCoy. Donald (*The Art of the Deal*) Trump appeared, doing deals, moving forward into public life with deranged energy and self-enchantment. Armed with high-yield bonds and other financial vehicles, cunning takeover artists perfected the leveraged buyout. "Greed is healthy," high-flying arbitrageur Ivan Boesky said at the University of California, Berkeley, business school in 1985. "You can be greedy and still feel good about yourself." Speculation of all kinds grew fevered and reckless. Real estate and stocks soared in value. Then, in October 1987, the stock market tanked, losing about one-fifth of its capitalization in one day. It took three long years for the party to wind down. By then, it looked as though Trump might go bankrupt. Boesky went to jail for insider trading, as did Kidder Peabody's former superstar, Martin Siegel; after a massive Securities and Exchange Commission investigation, so did Drexel Burnham Lambert's engineer of junk-bond-castles-in-the-air, Michael Milken. In 1990, Drexel, the most feared pirate company of the eighties, went out of business.

Debt—government, corporate, and consumer—greased the free-for-all. Starting in 1982, the Democratic Congress and the Republican White House jointly relaxed rules and increased federal protection for savings and loan (S&L) institutions, the nation's main agents of mortgage loans. Both sought to "help" local financial leaders and campaign contributors. Taking advantage of federal deregulation, hustlers flocked into the S&L business with borrowed capital, making shady investments and quick profits, especially in the fast-growing Sunbelt. Before the intrigue ended,

plunder by the rich and well-connected had gutted many S&Ls. Beset by
bad loans, S&L pyramids collapsed. Defaults were commonplace by the
late eighties. In July 1989, Congress established the Resolution Trust
Corporation to sell off failed thrifts' assets for pennies on the dollar and at
incredible taxpayer expense.

The cynical self-interest of wheeler-dealers, the attitude that only
suckers work for less than $200K, the stacked deck of big money—all
proved too remote for John and Mary Q. Public to care about. (The S&L
looting would have even less place in memory were it not for an Arkansas
S&L linked to the then-Governor Bill Clinton. After 1992, the Madison
Guaranty Trust affair provided a detailed and explicit case study of the
fast-and-loose financial and political dealings of the eighties.) America's
go-for-it presentism stood in sharp contrast to Japan's frugality and economic discipline. During the eighties, Japan's influence in global trade,
real estate, and art soared, and its influence on U.S. markets, including
bonds and currency, impressed and frightened Wall Street.

More Americans were living in castles or trailer parks, it seemed.
For the privileged, private-protection costs—gated communities, security
systems, and private schools—rose, indicators of decaying quality of life
beyond a few fortunate enclaves. North Central industrial cities like
Buffalo, Cleveland, Detroit, and St. Louis; the Mississippi Valley's farmers;
and the Oil Patch of Texas, Oklahoma, and Louisiana experienced economic reversals. The Sunbelt grew and prospered. Commercial real estate
syndicates fueled by plentiful real estate loans (from the S&Ls) remapped
whole regions such as Orange County, California, and Broward County,
Florida, expanding over grove and lowland farm to create the low-rise
sprawl of contemporary exurbia.

Los Angeles sold itself to dazzled, ingenuous observers as a reces-
sion-proof economy, a complex of aerospace, entertainment, finance, real
estate, tourism, international trade, and consumer markets. Were racial
turmoil, disorder and crime, declining air quality, and freeway saturation
troubling? Lighten up! After the 1984 Olympics, southern California
fueled itself on *Beach Life! Future Is Here! Pacific Rim*! fantasies. Ivy League
MBAs arrived in the Southland, the decade's new carpetbaggers. "They're
printing money in L.A.," one said.

In the rarified world of outer Sunset and El Temescal Canyon,
blessed by high air quality and a marine climate, a dreamy, filmic reconsideration of the good life was under way, setting a breezy style for a
nation. Moneyed L.A. seemed like Nietzsche's vision sprung to life, where
the Last Men and Last Women sought only the sun, spending their days in
body worship, clothed by Patagonia, drinking expensive bottled water. By

1988, when California's literary first couple, Joan Didion and John Gregory Dunne, decamped to Manhattan, it was obvious something was going very wrong in L.A. The city seemed intoxicated by itself and nonchalant about its problems. About then too came the Didionesque premonition: The rich and white in L.A. began to talk *sotto voce* about parts of town that looked like the Third World. They feared public disorder to come, as it did with the Los Angeles riots in May 1992, the death twitch of the eighties.

Hot and Cool

At the high end, yuppie taste was consciously upscale, openly ambitious, and even snobbish, rooted firmly in the prep schools and the Ivy League. The egalitarian rhetoric that flourished on campus in the sixties and seventies may have stirred a lot of these yuppies. They nonetheless embraced badges of status. Published in 1980, *The Official Preppy Handbook* sold 1.3 million copies. This peek-into-WASP-manners-and-Zagat-guide-to-aristo-reinvention spawned eighties-style tradition, patrimonies as purchasable as a Laura Ashley sheet, a Polo shirt, or braces by Brooks, in red silk, please. But it was all flashdance, a retro fantasy. In fact, nostalgia merchants—they ranged from Col. Oliver North to Ralph Lauren—were rewrapping venerable symbols and images from the past. These calculating souls were unsuccessful at creating anything more than an image or mood, however, for the movement of society was in a different direction. The genuine Anglo-American aristocratic model was going, going, gone, replaced by affectionate recreations in "Masterpiece Theatre" and *Chariots of Fire*.

In epicenters of Hotness—Melrose Avenue and Tribeca, Aspen and Sagaponack—Looking Good was what mattered. Herb Ritts, *echt* photographer of the eighties, mined dreams and desires, creating for his viewers the illusion of intimacy—a peek or a feel—with the ultrafamous and ultraglamorous: Nancy Reagan and Prince, Richard Gere and the Dalai Lama, celebrities all. And behind the curtain lurked dark genius Andy Warhol, whose linkage of art and glamour at the end of the sixties anticipated the eighties scene.

A number of moments in the decade tore away any lingering taste in matters carnal and sensate. If sex sold, why not go Triple X—or at least keep testing the edge of decency? In 1980, designer Calvin Klein gave us Brooke Shields and her jeans. *Vanity Fair*, revived in a tell-all format in 1983, created a tony version of the once-despised *Confidential* magazine. Carnival barker Robin Leach appeared, host of the television show

"Lifestyles of the Rich and Famous." Leering and poking, Phil Donahue was another pioneer of TV exhibitionism, opening doors formerly marked "private" every weekday afternoon for millions of mesmerized viewers. In 1987, the *National Enquirer* published photographs of presidential hopeful Gary Hart and Donna Rice aboard the *Monkey Business*, a "tabloid" act that may have changed presidential politics forever.

Dramatist Eric Bogosian, for one, provided a harrowing and comedic vision of the eighties' dark side, the new American vernacular. But the scene wasn't exactly funny. In 1982, actor John Belushi died of a drug overdose at Los Angeles' notorious Chateau Marmont hotel, and two years later, 28-year-old heir David Kennedy's drug-induced death in Palm Beach, Florida, also became the stuff of tabloids. Cocaine remained the decade's drug of choice, first among the mighty and then among the low. In centers of fashion, author *noir* Bret Easton Ellis later said, sexual ambiguity, club-hopping, and studied nihilism were of the moment. A sense of lost bearings—the thrill of decadence—permeated the giddy scene. "They read Hobbes, not Rousseau," said Tom Bethell of Los Angeles' gilded youth in 1981. (In fact, they were reading nothing at all.)

New temples appeared, beckoning to the spiritually restless. In New York City, during the autumn of 1983, the nightclub Limelight opened up in the former Episcopal nunnery and Church of the Holy Communion, built in 1850 in the Gothic style and brought up to date. That fall, night after night in lower Chelsea, limousines pulled up to deposit the A-List of the celebrity world. William Burroughs, Andy Warhol, and Shirley MacLaine cavorted in what had been, not long before, a sacred place. Much hipper than the bishops and their acolytes, bold icons of celebrity culture found the presence of cocaine in a former nunnery a deliciously modern thrill, and understood how very far fashion had come in erasing the moralities of the past. For the culturally correct, part of the fun was the affront, the *frisson*, the shudder.

The art and lit scene, especially in Manhattan, was never more showy. But there was one problem: The young and fabulous were generally of limited talent. Of what interest is Julian Schnabel today except perhaps as a case study of the eighties Celebrity Comet Phenomenon or the Madness of Crowds? Ann Beattie, Jay McInerney, Bret Easton Ellis, Susan Minot, and David Leavitt—let's not forget Tama Janowitz!—were everywhere, everywhere, promoting themselves with extraordinary self-confidence. By 1990, where had they all gone? Were they in detox? Were they writing screenplays in Jackson Hole? Were they dead?

Jean Stein and George Plimpton immortalized Warhol's first sacrificial lamb, Edie Sedgwick, in *Edie*, their 1982 literary sensation. The romance of flame-out, Sedgwick-style, persisted through the eighties. In 1987, at age 58, Warhol himself died from complications of a gallbladder operation. Warhol's protégé, downtown "Caribbean" painter Jean-Paul Basquiat, expired from a heroin overdose the following year. In early 1990, grafitti artist Keith Haring died of AIDS.

The House of Intellect

Among the young and privileged, frustration and disillusionment with society's failure to enact its highest ideals did not die in the seventies. Ideals first expressed by the New Left and counterculture ripened and matured. Some boomers built careers trying to make these ideals happen. Academics and publishers, editorial writers and makers of television dramas, and government officials and foundation executives discovered that prestige and power could flow from investigating newly discovered injustices, treating social problems, creating "meaningful" documentaries, or administering multimillion dollar grant programs. But even the most ambitious and aggressive of the postwar generation took time to reach positions of institutional control within education, media, religion, and law. Only in the eighties did the era of "tenured radicalism," in Roger Kimball's apt phrase, arrive.

Decoders, interpreters, and augurs of postmodernism gained new prestige in the nation's best colleges and universities. The effort to dissolve standards used to establish truth and assess aesthetic value for over two centuries moved through the humanities and other fields, leaving whole areas of the curriculum demoralized, or defanged, depending on one's viewpoint.

Advocates of multiculturalism, diversity, and group-based sensitivity demanded allegiance and revisions of content. Venerable authors and texts were decentered. In came Maya Angelou; out went Alexander Pope. New university courses, departments, lecture series and workshops, tenure procedures, and administrative rewards helped consolidate the influence of these concepts. Campus-based authorities appeared, ready to conduct inquisitions on errant students or faculty suspected of harboring forbidden views. In order to avoid the looming questions of value, long-established assumptions—poverty as a product of personal limitations, for example, or the superiority of Western ideas—grew unpopular and then unmentionable.

On campus, equivalency of culture and value were seminar games in the humanities that even modestly intelligent assistant professors and undergraduates could play with quite a degree of moral superiority. The "social construction of knowledge" became an intellectually *stylish* concept. Revisionism was hot. "Question Authority," commanded the popular broadside and bumper sticker that surfaced on college campuses nationwide in 1981. From Stanley Fish at Duke University to Cornel West at Yale, smooth operators on the Left gained immense prestige on and off campus. In the late eighties, ideological disputes and pitched protests rocked prominent campuses more violently than they had in twenty years. Campus discourse suddenly became less friendly and more adversarial than in the past. But unlike in the sixties, student and faculty animus did not center on American foreign policy or on individual rights. Instead, it was aimed at the content of the curriculum and culture.*

These challenges did not come without a fight. In 1987 the University of Chicago philosopher Allan Bloom published *The Closing of the American Mind*, a best-selling and influential book that became a pivot point in the culture wars. As had no one before him, Bloom explicated contemporary trends in the humanities. In particular, Bloom analyzed Nietzsche's thought and its vast influence on U.S. and European campuses during the previous quarter century. Radical theories advanced by a determined professional minority from the sixties onward, Bloom thought, had seized control of philosophy and the social studies. In the humanities, he argued, the erosion of objectivity, hostility to inherited texts and traditions, and a relativistic disposition were elements of an "intellectual crisis of the greatest magnitude, which constitutes the crisis of our civilization." Popular culture had corrupted many undergraduates and their tutors, Bloom added, scripting a dramatic vision of pandemonium.

On January 15, 1987, several hundred students and faculty members gathered at Stanford University to hear the Reverend Jesse Jackson speak and to show support for his "rainbow agenda," that is, quotas in campus admissions and teaching. What started as an ordinary protest, however, led to a much larger contretemps. The crowd marched across campus to present its demands to the Faculty Senate. Led by Jackson, the demonstrators began to cheer: "Hey, hey, ho, ho! Western Culture's got to go!" During the next year, Stanford University dismantled its freshman Western Civilization program under great internal and external scrutiny.

---

* For many years, "politically correct" (or "PC") had been used in Ivy League dining halls to describe—derisively—more-aware-than-thou collegiate lefties, vegans, and young compassion artists. I did not hear the phrase used in earnest until 1988, then by a young and very with-it *Rolling Stone* reporter.

Finally, William J. Bennett, the U.S. Secretary of Education, sensing opportunity, arrived on campus in April 1988 to make a pointed speech defending "the West." He was roundly criticized by educational leaders and editorial writers.

By 1987 and 1988, it had dawned on the reading public and a share of the intellectual community that sixties-style sentiments were winning a "war" over symbols, titles, and heroes, forcing basic changes in the ideas of the beautiful and the true, of value and virtue. Conservatives began to fight these changes in earnest. Correctly enough, the academic Left saw its program as being under siege. Inside the nation's most visible centers of knowledge, the culture wars smoldered, becoming the subject of news-magazine cover stories and talk shows.

The Movement of Culture

Christopher Lasch's *The Culture of Narcissism* (1979)—which is the first selection in this collection—was the most probing of several influential books published in the late seventies, whose authors were disturbed by a culture pursuing the untrammeled self to extremes. Lasch described a wary, wised-up, litigious society, where normative feeling and a sense of commonwealth ("middle class") were weakening, replaced by radical individualism and group identity ("subcultures"). A cinematic genre of the eighties—*The Big Chill; Hannah and Her Sisters; sex, lies, and videotape*—provided powerful portraits of malaise and ennui among the cosmopolitan, the well-educated, and the upwardly mobile. (Meanwhile, Rambo and Conan the Barbarian provided thrills for the mass market.)

In a climate of self-gratification and self-absorption, Lasch and others asserted, familiar governors of public and private life were losing their regulatory force. The "old rules" that had provided an orderly compass for politics, high and popular culture, and the discerning individual could no longer be expected to exert much influence or command much respect. The language of rights, victimhood, self-esteem, and empowerment was beginning to have drastic effects on the way millions of Americans thought and lived. Then, as now, a lot of people were traveling lighter, *No baggage, thank you.*

During the eighties, traditional religion faced external and internal affronts. It was open season on the Roman Catholic church. Here came the Sisters of Perpetual Indulgence, transvestite pseudo-nuns who did street theater in San Francisco. Here came Madonna, scampering across the television screen on MTV, rubbing her crotch for the cameras, crosses burning in the background. Protestant denominations—riven between traditionalists and insurgents within their ranks—were losing membership, stature, and even a sense of purpose. Meanwhile, energetic Christian fundamentalists were organizing politically, drawing millions of new adherents dismayed by the turns of radical secularism. Televangelists Jimmy Swaggart (whose taste ran toward prostitutes) and Tammy Faye Bakker (who preferred gaudy jewelry and false eyelashes) appeared as if from anti-religion's central casting office. In 1989, after spending $3.7 million in solicited donations for his Christian vacation theme park, Tammy's husband, Jim, was convicted and later jailed for fraud and conspiracy.

Some modern clerics were blasé about attacks on church-inspired morality. Or they welcomed them, delighted in them. We have no better example than the Reverend Lesley Northup of the Episcopal Church, featured on the front page of the *Washington Post* in December 1987. Headlined "A Need Examined, a Prayer Fulfilled: Unmarried Priest Bears Child by Artificial Insemination," the lengthy article detailed her search for sperm and subsequent self-insemination process. Northup, 40, was from a new school of clerics: the shock troops of alternative lifestyles. What made the Reverend Northup and her revelations so disturbing? It was not so much her unconventional practices; it was her abandonment of individual restraint, her apparent contempt for decorum and church dignity, her confusion of the pulpit and the Donahue show, her exhibitionism.

These new ways of acting out did not appear overnight. Writing in 1968, critic Irving Kristol had sensed the revolutionary nature of changing cultural modes around him: "Our world is being emptied of its ideal content, and the imposing institutional facade sways in the wind," he said. Kristol's unease about the lapsing moral authority of bourgeois institutions only prefigured the culture of the eighties. Twenty years after Kristol wrote, what had been a limited cultural revolution had altered the lives of all Americans of different generations, locales, and social levels. The quest for self-satisfaction, the decline of families and the rise of subcultures, violent crime, the reshuffling of knowledge, and spiritual confusion had altered everyday life. New—and unsated—appetites had cascaded onto Main Street, into the dreams and aspirations of plant managers, keyboard operators, and baby-sitters.

Not everyone bought in, of course. But by the end of the eighties, the culture-bound majority had noticed that while it was not looking, or while it had been trying to avoid open conflict with the outlandish, it had been robbed of comfortable values and verities. It realized that the twenty-year-long cultural revolution had not been a game nor had it been only of the imagination. The Reverend Northup was just one in a crowd of reformers and saints manqués trying to obtain a franchise on acceptable behavior by any means necessary. "What is sacred?" ordinary folk asked with increasing desperation in their hearts. It was then that the shooting in the culture wars began.

The eighties are of contemporary interest not only for what has recently passed but for their abundant legacy, which continues to inform the most vexing domestic issues in the nation today. The eighties arguments and counterarguments about the good life and the soul of the nation flow into the present, of course. Using the vocabulary of the eighties, educators, the media, and pop culture continue to do battle over what we as a nation and a people should be. The culture wars of the eighties have not ended, and they are destined to be with us for a long while to come. They are capable of producing further chaos in the nation's cultural identity and in individual lives. To understand their origins and impact on contemporary affairs, let's begin with the state of the culture at the close of the seventies.

Drawing by Ziegler from the *New Yorker*, 1979

PART I

Antecedents

From

The Culture of Narcissism
(1979)

Christopher Lasch

Lasch's pioneering critique identified an important and incompletely understood shift in the nation's temper after the end of the sixties. Self-referential
thinking and what Lasch called "the therapeutic sensibility" were gaining new
influence among the nation's educated elites. Lasch questioned what impact
this might have on the relationship between the individual and institutions such
as family and religion. The book was not solely about the "me decade," Lasch
said in 1990. It was instead an effort to "explore the psychological dimension
of long-term shifts in the structure of cultural authority."

A s the twentieth century approaches its end, the conviction grows
that many other things are ending too. Storm warnings, portents,
hints of catastrophe haunt our times. The "sense of an ending,"
which has given shape to so much of twentieth-century literature, now
pervades the popular imagination as well. The Nazi holocaust, the threat
of nuclear annihilation, the depletion of natural resources, well-founded
predictions of ecological disaster have fulfilled poetic prophecy, giving
concrete historical substance to the nightmare, or death wish, that avant-
garde artists were the first to express. The question of whether the world
will end in fire or in ice, with a bang or a whimper, no longer interests
artists alone. Impending disaster has become an everyday concern, so
commonplace and familiar that nobody any longer gives much thought to
how disaster might be averted. People busy themselves instead with survival strategies, measures designed to prolong their own lives, or programs guaranteed to ensure good health and peace of mind.

Those who dig bomb shelters hope to survive by surrounding themselves with the latest products of modern technology. Communards in the
country adhere to an opposite plan: to free themselves from dependence

on technology and thus to outlive its destruction or collapse. A visitor to a commune in North Carolina writes: "Everyone seems to share this sense of imminent doomsday." Stewart Brand, editor of the *Whole Earth Catalogue,* reports that "sales of the *Survival Book* are booming; it's one of our fastest moving items." Both strategies reflect the growing despair of changing society, even of understanding it, which also underlies the cult of expanded consciousness, health, and personal "growth" so prevalent today.

After the political turmoil of the sixties, Americans have retreated to purely personal preoccupations. Having no hope of improving their lives in any of the ways that matter, people have convinced themselves that what matters is psychic self-improvement: getting in touch with their feelings, eating health food, taking lessons in ballet or belly-dancing, immersing themselves in the wisdom of the East, jogging, learning how to "relate," overcoming the "fear of pleasure." Harmless in themselves, these pursuits, elevated to a program and wrapped in the rhetoric of authenticity and awareness, signify a retreat from politics and a repudiation of the recent past. Indeed Americans seem to wish to forget not only the sixties, the riots, the new left, the disruptions on college campuses, Vietnam, Watergate, and the Nixon presidency, but their entire collective past, even in the antiseptic form in which it was celebrated during the Bicentennial. Woody Allen's movie *Sleeper,* issued in 1973, accurately caught the mood of the seventies. Appropriately cast in the form of a parody of futuristic science fiction, the film finds a great many ways to convey the message that "political solutions don't work," as Allen flatly announces at one point. When asked what he believes in, Allen, having ruled out politics, religion, and science, declares: "I believe in sex and death—two experiences that come once in a lifetime."

To live for the moment is the prevailing passion—to live for yourself, not for your predecessors or posterity. We are fast losing the sense of historical continuity, the sense of belonging to a succession of generations originating in the past and stretching into the future. It is the waning of the sense of historical time—in particular, the erosion of any strong concern for posterity—that distinguishes the spiritual crisis of the seventies from earlier outbreaks of millenarian religion, to which it bears a superficial resemblance. Many commentators have seized on this resemblance as a means of understanding the contemporary "cultural revolution," ignoring the features that distinguish it from the religions of the past. A few years ago, Leslie Fiedler proclaimed a "New Age of Faith." More recently, Tom Wolfe has interpreted the new narcissism as a "third great awakening," an outbreak of orgiastic, ecstatic religiosity. Jim Hougan, in a book

[*Decadence: Radical Nostalgia, Narcissism, and Decline in the Seventies*] that seems to present itself simultaneously as a critique and a celebration of contemporary decadence, compares the current mood to the millennialism of the waning Middle Ages. "The anxieties of the Middle Ages are not much different from those of the present," he writes. Then, as now, social upheaval gave rise to "millenarian sects."

Both Hougan and Wolfe inadvertently provide evidence, however, that undermines a religious interpretation of the "consciousness movement." Hougan notes that survival has become the "catchword of the seventies" and "collective narcissism" the dominant disposition. Since "the society" has no future, it makes sense to live only for the moment, to fix our eyes on our own "private performance," to become connoisseurs of our own decadence, to cultivate a "transcendental self-attention." These are not the attitudes historically associated with millenarian outbreaks. Sixteenth-century Anabaptists awaited the apocalypse not with transcendental self-attention but with ill-concealed impatience for the golden age it was expected to inaugurate. Nor were they indifferent to the past. Ancient popular traditions of the "sleeping king"—the leader who will return to his people and restore a lost golden age—informed the millenarian movements of this period. The Revolutionary of the Upper Rhine, anonymous author of the *Book of a Hundred Chapters*, declared, "The Germans once held the whole world in their hands and they will do so again, and with more power than ever." He predicted that the resurrected Frederick II, "Emperor of the Last Days," would reinstate the primitive German religion, move the capital of Christendom from Rome to Trier, abolish private property, and level distinctions between rich and poor.

Such traditions, often associated with national resistance to foreign conquest, have flourished at many times and in many forms, including the Christian vision of the Last Judgment. Their egalitarian and pseudohistorical content suggests that even the most radically otherwordly religions of the past expressed a hope of social justice and a sense of continuity with earlier generations. The absence of these values characterizes the survivalist mentality of the seventies. The "world view emerging among us," writes Peter Marin, centers "solely on the self" and has "individual survival as its sole good." In an attempt to identify the peculiar features of contemporary religiosity, Tom Wolfe himself notes that "most people, historically, have *not* lived their lives as if thinking, 'I have only one life to live.' Instead they have lived as if they are living their ancestors' lives and their offspring's lives. . . ." These observations go very close to the heart of the matter, but they call into question his characterization of the new narcissism as a third great awakening.

᎗

The contemporary climate is therapeutic, not religious. People today hunger not for personal salvation, let alone for the restoration of an earlier golden age, but for the feeling, the momentary illusion, of personal well-being, health, and psychic security. Even the radicalism of the sixties served, for many of those who embraced it for personal rather than political reasons, not as a substitute religion but as a form of therapy. Radical politics filled empty lives, provided a sense of meaning and purpose. In her memoir of the Weathermen, Susan Stern described their attraction in language that owes more to psychiatry and medicine than to religion. When she tried to evoke her state of mind during the 1968 demonstrations at the Democratic National Convention in Chicago, she wrote instead about the state of her health. "I felt good. I could feel my body supple and strong and slim, and ready to run miles, and my legs moving sure and swift under me." A few pages later, she says: "I felt real." Repeatedly she explains that association with important people made her feel important. "I felt I was part of a vast network of intense, exciting and brilliant people." When the leaders she idealized disappointed her, as they always did, she looked for new heroes to take their place, hoping to warm herself in their "brilliance" and overcome her feeling of insignificance. In their presence, she occasionally felt "strong and solid"—only to find herself repelled, when disenchantment set in again by the "arrogance" of those whom she had previously admired, by "their contempt for everyone around them."

Many of the details in Stern's account of the Weathermen would be familiar to students of the revolutionary mentality in earlier epochs: the fervor of her revolutionary commitment, the group's endless disputes about fine points of political dogma, the relentless "self-criticism" to which members of the sect were constantly exhorted, the attempt to remodel every facet of one's life in conformity with the revolutionary faith. But every revolutionary movement partakes of the culture of its time, and this one contained elements that immediately identified it as a product of American society in an age of diminishing expectations. The atmosphere in which the Weathermen lived—an atmosphere of violence, danger, drugs, sexual promiscuity, moral and psychic chaos—derived not so much from an older revolutionary tradition as from the turmoil and narcissistic anguish of contemporary America. Her preoccupation with the state of her psychic health, together with her dependence on others for a sense of selfhood, distinguish Susan Stern from the kind of religious seeker who turns to politics to find a secularized salvation. She needed to establish an identity, not to submerge her identity in a larger cause. The narcissist differs also, in the tenuous quality of his selfhood, from an earlier type of American individualist, the "American Adam" analyzed by R. W. B. Lewis, Quentin Anderson, Michael Rogin, and by nineteenth-century observers like Tocqueville. The contemporary narcissist bears a superficial resemblance, in his self-absorption and delusions of grandeur, to the "imperial self" so often celebrated in nineteenth-century American literature. The American Adam, like his descendants today, sought to free himself from the past and to establish what Emerson called "an original relation to the universe." Nineteenth-century writers and orators restated again and again, in a great variety of forms, Jefferson's doctrine that the earth belongs to the living. The break with Europe, the abolition of primogeniture, and the looseness of family ties gave substance to their belief (even if it was finally an illusion) that Americans, alone among the people of the world, could escape the entangling influence of the past. They imagined, according to Tocqueville, that "their whole destiny is in their own hands." Social conditions in the United States, Tocqueville wrote, severed the tie that formerly united one generation to another. "The woof of time is every instant broken and the track of generations effaced. Those who went before are soon forgotten; of those who will come after, no one has any idea: the interest of man is confined to those in close propinquity to himself."

Some critics have described the narcissism of the 1970s in similar language. The new therapies spawned by the human potential movement, according to Peter Marin, teach that "the individual will is all powerful and totally determines one's fate"; thus they intensify the "isolation of the self." This line of argument belongs to a well-established American tradition of social thought. Marin's plea for recognition of "the immense middle ground of human community" recalls Van Wyck Brooks, who criticized the New England transcendentalists for ignoring "the genial middle ground of human tradition." Brooks himself, when he formulated his own indictment of American culture, drew on such earlier critics as Santayana, Henry James, Orestes Brownson, and Tocqueville. The critical tradition they established still has much to tell us about the evils of untrammeled individualism, but it needs to be restated to take account of the differences between nineteenth-century Adamism and the narcissism of our own time. The critique of "privatism," though it helps to keep alive the need for community, has become more and more misleading as the possibility of genuine privacy recedes. The contemporary American may have failed, like his predecessors, to establish any sort of common life, but the integrating tendencies of modern industrial society have at the same time undermined his "isolation." Having surrendered most of his technical skills to the corporation, he can no longer provide for his material needs. As the family loses not only its productive functions but many of its reproductive functions as well, men and women no longer manage even to raise their children without the help of certified experts. The atrophy of older traditions of self-help has eroded everyday competence, in one area after another, and has made the individual dependent on the state, the corporation, and other bureaucracies.

Narcissism represents the psychological dimension of this dependence. Notwithstanding his occasional illusions of omnipotence, the narcissist depends on others to validate his self-esteem. He cannot live without an admiring audience. His apparent freedom from family ties and institutional constraints does not free him to stand alone or to glory in his individuality. On the contrary, it contributes to his insecurity, which he can overcome only by seeing his "grandiose self" reflected in the attentions of others, or by attaching himself to those who radiate celebrity, power, and charisma. For the narcissist, the world is a mirror, whereas the rugged individualist saw it as an empty wilderness to be shaped to his own design.

In the nineteenth-century American imagination, the vast continent stretching westward symbolized both the promise and the menace of an escape from the past. The West represented an opportunity to build a new society unencumbered by feudal inhibitions, but it also tempted men to throw off civilization and to revert to savagery. Through compulsive industry and relentless sexual repression, nineteenth-century Americans achieved a fragile triumph over the id. The violence they turned against the Indians and against nature originated not in unrestrained impulse but in the white Anglo-Saxon superego, which feared the wildness of the West because it objectified the wildness within each individual. While celebrating the romance of the frontier in their popular literature, in practice Americans imposed on the wilderness a new order designed to keep impulse in check while giving free rein to acquisitiveness. Capital accumulation in its own right sublimated appetite and subordinated the pursuit of self-interest to the service of future generations. In the heat of the struggle to win the West, the American pioneer gave full vent to his rapacity and murderous cruelty, but he always envisioned the result—not without misgivings, expressed in a nostalgic cult of lost innocence—as a peaceful, respectable, churchgoing community safe for his women and children. He imagined that his offspring, raised under the morally refining influence of feminine "culture," would grow up to be sober, law-abiding, domesticated American citizens, and the thought of the advantages they would inherit justified his toil and excused, he thought, his frequent lapses into brutality, sadism, and rape.

Today Americans are overcome not by the sense of endless possibility but by the banality of the social order they have erected against it. Having internalized the social restraints by means of which they formerly sought to keep possibility within civilized limits, they feel themselves overwhelmed by an annihilating boredom, like animals whose instincts have withered in captivity. A reversion to savagery threatens them so little that they long precisely for a more vigorous instinctual existence. People nowadays complain of an inability to feel. They cultivate more vivid experiences, seek to beat sluggish flesh to life, attempt to revive jaded appetites. They condemn the superego and exalt the lost life of the senses. Twentieth-century peoples have erected so many psychological barriers against strong emotions and have invested those defenses with so much of the energy derived from forbidden impulses that they can no longer remember what it feels like to be inundated by desire. They tend, rather, to be consumed with rage, which derives from defenses against desire and gives rise in turn to new defenses against rage itself. Outwardly bland, submissive, and sociable, they seethe with an inner anger for which a dense, overpopulated, bureaucratic society can devise few legitimate outlets.

The growth of bureaucracy creates an intricate network of personal relations, puts a premium on social skills, and makes the unbridled egotism of the American Adam untenable. Yet at the same time it erodes all forms of patriarchal authority and thus weakens the social superego, formerly represented by fathers, teachers, and preachers. The decline of institutionalized authority in an ostensibly permissive society does not, however, lead to a "decline of the superego" in individuals. It encourages instead the development of a harsh, punitive superego that derives most of its psychic energy, in the absence of authoritative social prohibitions, from the destructive, aggressive impulses within the id. Unconscious, irrational elements in the superego come to dominate its operation. As authority figures in modern society lose their "credibility," the superego in individuals increasingly derives from the child's primitive fantasies about his parents—fantasies charged with sadistic rage—rather than from internalized ego ideals formed by later experience with loved and respected models of social conduct.

The struggle to maintain psychic equilibrium in a society that demands submission to the rules of social intercourse but refuses to ground those rules in a code of moral conduct encourages a form of self-absorption that has little in common with the primary narcissism of the

imperial self. Archaic elements increasingly dominate personality structure, and "the self shrinks back," in the words of Morris Dickstein, "toward
a passive and primeval state in which the world remains uncreated,
unformed." The egomaniacal, experience-devouring, imperial self regress-
es into a grandiose, narcissistic, infantile, empty self: a "dark wet hole," as
Rudolph Wurlitzer writes in *Nog*, "where everything finds its way sooner
or later. I remain near the entrance, handling goods as they are shoved in,
listening and nodding. I have been slowly dissolving into this cavity."

Plagued by anxiety, depression, vague discontent, a sense of inner
emptiness, the "psychological man" of the twentieth century seeks neither individual self-aggrandizement nor spiritual transcendence but peace
of mind, under conditions that increasingly militate against it. Therapists,
not priests or popular preachers of self-help or models of success like the
captains of industry, become his principal allies in the struggle for compo-
sure; he turns to them in the hope of achieving the modern equivalent of
salvation, "mental health." Therapy has established itself as the successor
both to rugged individualism and to religion; but this does not mean that
the "triumph of the therapeutic" has become a new religion in its own
right. Therapy constitutes an antireligion, not always to be sure because it
adheres to rational explanation or scientific methods of healing, as its
practitioners would have us believe, but because modern society "has no
future" and therefore gives no thought to anything beyond its immediate
needs. Even when therapists speak of the need for "meaning" and "love,"
they define love and meaning simply as the fulfillment of the patient's
emotional requirements. It hardly occurs to them—nor is there any reason why it should, given the nature of the therapeutic enterprise—to
encourage the subject to subordinate his needs and interests to those of
others, to someone or some cause or tradition outside himself. "Love" as
self-sacrifice or self-abasement, "meaning" as submission to a higher loyalty—these sublimations strike the therapeutic sensibility as intolerably
oppressive, offensive to common sense and injurious to personal health
and well-being. To liberate humanity from such outmoded ideas of love
and duty has become the mission of the post-Freudian therapies and particularly of their converts and popularizers, for whom mental health
means the overthrow of inhibitions and the immediate gratification of
every impulse.

The Adversary Culture
of Intellectuals
(1979)

Irving Kristol

This lengthy essay first appeared in *Encounter,* a small London-based journal of opinion. It later came to be regarded as a "neoconservative manifesto." Defending bourgeois culture, democratic capitalism, and reason against the "adversary culture" whose conquest of the nation's universities and cultural institutions was only then beginning to become evident, Kristol became the leader of a new political movement.

No sooner did the late Lionel Trilling coin the phrase "adversary culture" than it became part of the common vocabulary. This is because it so neatly summed up a phenomenon that all of us, vaguely or acutely, had observed. It is hardly to be denied that the culture that educates us—the patterns of perception and thought our children absorb in their schools, at every level—is unfriendly (at the least) to the commercial civilization, the bourgeois civilization, within which most of us live and work. When we send our sons and daughters to college, we may expect that by the time they are graduated they are likely to have a lower opinion of our social economic order than when they entered. We know this from opinion poll data, we know it from our own experience.

We are so used to this fact of our lives, we take it so for granted, that we fail to realize how extraordinary it is. Has there ever been, in all of recorded history, a civilization whose culture was at odds with the values and ideals of that civilization itself? It is not uncommon that a culture will be critical of the civilization that sustains it—and always critical of the failure of this civilization to realize perfectly the ideals that it claims as inspiration. Such criticism is implicit or explicit in Aristophanes and Euripides, Dante and Shakespeare. But to take an adversary posture toward the ideals themselves? That is unprecedented. A few writers and thinkers of a heretical bent, dispersed at the margins of the culture, might do so. But culture as a whole has always been assigned the task of, and invariably accepted responsibility for, sustaining and celebrating those values. Indeed, it is a premise of modern sociological and anthropological theory that it is the essence of culture to be "functional" in this way.

Yet ours is not. The more "cultivated" a person is in our society, the more disaffected and malcontent he is likely to be—a disaffection, moreover, directed not only at the actuality of our society but at the ideality as well. Indeed, the ideality may be more strenuously opposed than the actuality. It was, I think, Oscar Wilde who observed that, while he rather liked the average American, he found the ideal American contemptible. Our contemporary culture is considerably less tolerant of actuality than was Oscar Wilde. But there is little doubt that if it had to choose between the two, it would prefer the actual to the ideal.

The average "less cultivated" American, of course, feels no great uneasiness with either the actual or the ideal. This explains why the Marxist vision of a radicalized working class erupting into rebellion against capitalist society has turned out to be so erroneous. Radicalism, in our day, finds more fertile ground among the college-educated than among the high school graduates, the former having experienced more exposure to some kind of adversary culture, the latter—until recently, at least—having its own kind of "popular" culture that is more accommodating to the bourgeois world that working people inhabit. But this very disjunction of those two cultures is itself a unique phenomenon of the bourgeois era, and represents, as we shall see, a response to the emergence, in the nineteenth century, of an "avant-garde," which laid the basis for our adversary culture.

Bourgeois society is without a doubt the most prosaic of all possible societies. It is prosaic in the literal sense. The novel written in prose, dealing with the (only somewhat) extraordinary adventures of ordinary people, is its original and characteristic art form, replacing the epic poem, the lyric poem, the poetic drama, the religious hymn. These latter were appropriate to societies formally and officially committed to transcendent ideals of excellence—ideals that could be realized only by those few of exceptional nobility of character—or to transcendent visions of the universe wherein human existence on earth is accorded only a provisional significance. But bourgeois society is uninterested in such transcendence, which at best it tolerates as a private affair, a matter for individual taste and individual consumption, as it were. It is prosaic, not only in form, but in essence. It is a society organized for the convenience and comfort of common men and common women, not for the production of heroic, memorable figures. It is a society interested in making the best of this world, not in any kind of transfiguration, whether through tragedy or piety.

Because this society proposes to make the best of this world, for the benefit of ordinary men and women, it roots itself in the most worldly and common of human motivations: self-interest. It assumes that, though only a few are capable of pursuing excellence, everyone is capable of recognizing and pursuing his own self-interest. This "democratic" assumption about the equal potential of human nature, in this limited respect, in turn justifies a market economy in which each individual defines his own well-being, and illegitimates all the paternalistic economic theories of previous eras. One should emphasize, however, that the pursuit of excellence by the few—whether defined in religious, moral, or intellectual terms—is neither prohibited nor inhibited. Such an activity is merely interpreted as a special form of self-interest, which may be freely pursued but can claim no official status. Bourgeois society also assumes that the average individual's conception of his own self-interest will be sufficiently "enlightened"—that is, sufficiently farsighted and prudent—to permit other human passions (the desire for community, the sense of human sympathy, the moral conscience, etc.) to find expression, albeit always in a voluntarist form.

It is characteristic of a bourgeois culture, when it exists in concord with bourgeois principles, that we are permitted to take "happy endings" seriously (" . . . and they lived happily ever after"). From classical antiquity through the Renaissance, happy endings—worldly happy endings—were consigned to the genre of Comedy. "Serious" art focused on a meaningful death, in the context of heroism in battle, passion in love, ambition in politics, or piety in religion. Such high seriousness ran counter to the bourgeois grain, which perceived human fulfillment—human authenticity, if you will—in terms of becoming a good citizen, a good husband, a good provider. It is, in contrast to both prebourgeois and postbourgeois *Weltanschauungen,* a *domestic* conception of the universe and of man's place therein.

This bourgeois ideal is much closer to the Old Testament than to the New—which is, perhaps, why Jews have felt more at home in the bourgeois world than in any other. That God created this world and affirmed its goodness; that men ought confidently to be fruitful and multiply; that work (including that kind of work we call commerce) is elevating rather than demeaning; that the impulse to "better one's condition" (to use a favorite phrase of Adam Smith's) is good because natural—these beliefs were almost perfectly congruent with the worldview of postexilic

Judaism. In this worldview, there was no trace of aristocratic bias: Everyman was no allegorical figure but, literally, every common person.

So it is not surprising that the bourgeois worldview—placing the needs and desires of ordinary men and women at its center—was (and still is) also popular among the common people. Nor is it surprising that, almost from the beginning, it was an unstable worldview, evoking active contempt in a minority, and a pervasive disquiet among those who, more successful than others in having bettered their condition, had the leisure to wonder if life did not, perhaps, have more interesting and remote possibilities to offer.

The emergence of romanticism in the middle of the eighteenth century provided an early warning signal that, within the middle class itself, a kind of nonbourgeois spiritual impulse was at work. Not antibourgeois; not yet. For romanticism—with its celebration of noble savages, *Weltschmerz*, passionate love, aristocratic heroes and heroines, savage terrors confronted with haughty boldness and courage—was mainly an escapist aesthetic mode as distinct from a rebellious one. It provided a kind of counterculture that was, on the whole, safely insulated from bourgeois reality, and could even be tolerated (though always uneasily) as a temporary therapeutic distraction from the serious business of living. A clear sign of this self-limitation of the romantic impulse was the degree to which it was generated, and consumed, by a particular section of the middle class: women.

One of the less happy consequences of the women's liberation movement of the past couple of decades is the distorted view it has encouraged of the history of women under capitalism. This history is interpreted in terms of repression—sexual repression above all. That repression was real enough, of course; but it is absurd to regard it as nothing but an expression of masculine possessiveness, even vindictiveness. Sexual repression—and that whole code of feminine conduct we have come to call Victorian—was imposed and enforced by women, not men (who stand to gain very little if *all* women are chaste). And women insisted on this code because, while sexually repressive, it was also liberating in all sorts of other ways. Specifically, it liberated women, ideally if not always actually, from their previous condition as sex objects or work objects. To put it another way: All women were now elevated to the aristocratic status of *ladies*, entitled to a formal deference, respect, consideration. (Even today, some of those habits survive, if weakly—taking off one's hat when greeting a female acquaintance, standing up when a woman enters the room, etc.) The "wench," as had been portrayed in Shakespeare's plays, was not dead. She was still very much to be found in the working and lower classes. But her condition was not immutable; she, too, could become a lady—through marriage, education, or sheer force of will.

The price for this remarkable elevation of women's status was sexual self-restraint and self-denial, which made them, in a sense, owners of valuable (if intangible) property. It is reasonable to think that this change in actual sexual mores had something to do with the rise of romanticism, with its strong erotic component, in literature—the return of the repressed, as Freud was later to call it. For most of those who purchased romantic novels, or borrowed them (for a fee) from the newly established circulating libraries, were women. Indeed they still are, even today, two centuries later, though the romantic novel is now an exclusively popular art form, which flourishes outside the world of "serious" writing.

This extraordinary and ironical transformation of the novel from a prosaic art form—a tradition that reached its apogee in Jane Austen—to something radically different was itself a bourgeois accomplishment. It was made possible by the growing affluence of the middle classes that provided not only the purchasing power but also the leisure and the solitude ("a room of one's own"). This last point is worth especial notice.

It is a peculiarity of the novel that, unlike all previous art forms, it gains rather than loses from becoming a private experience. Though novels were still occasionally read aloud all during the romantic era, they need not be and gradually ceased to be. Whereas Shakespeare or Racine is most "enchanting" as part of a public experience—on a stage, in daylight—the novel gains its greatest power over us when we "consume" it (or it consumes us) in silence and privacy. Reading a novel then becomes something like surrendering oneself to an especially powerful daydream. The bourgeois ethos, oriented toward prosaic actualities, strongly disapproves of such daydreaming (which is why, even today, a businessman will prefer not to be known as an avid reader of novels, and few in fact are). But bourgeois women very soon discovered that living simultaneously in the two worlds of nonbourgeois "romance" and bourgeois "reality" was superior to living in either one.

The men and women who wrote such novels (or poems—one thinks of Byron) were not, however, simply responding to a market incentive. Writers and artists may have originally been receptive to a bourgeois society because of the far greater individual freedoms that it offered them; and because, too, they could not help but be exhilarated by the heightened vitality and quickened vivacity of a capitalist order with its emphasis on progress, economic growth, and liberation from age-old constraints. But, very quickly, disillusionment and dissent set in, and the urge to escape became compelling.

From the point of view of artists and of those whom we have come to call "intellectuals"—a category itself created by bourgeois society, which converted philosophers into *philosophes* engaged in the task of critical enlightenment—there were three great flaws in the new order of things.

First of all, it threatened to be very boring. Though the idea of ennui did not become a prominent theme in literature until the nineteenth century, there can be little doubt that the experience is considerably older than its literary expression. One can say this with some confidence because, throughout history, artists and writers have been so candidly contemptuous of commercial activity between consenting adults, regarding it as an activity that tends to coarsen and trivialize the human spirit. And since bourgeois society was above all else a commercial society—the first in all of recorded history in which the commercial ethos was sovereign over all others—their exasperation was bound to be all the more acute. Later on, the term "philistinism" would emerge to encapsulate the object of this sentiment.

Second, though a commercial society may offer artists and writers all sorts of desirable things—freedom of expression especially, popularity and affluence occasionally—it did (and does) deprive them of the status that they naturally feel themselves entitled to. Artists and writers and thinkers always have taken themselves to be Very Important People, and they are outraged by a society that merely tolerates them, no matter how generously. Bertolt Brecht was once asked how he could justify his Communist loyalties when his plays could neither be published nor performed in the USSR, while his royalties in the West made him a wealthy man. His quick rejoinder was: "Well, there at least they take me seriously!" Artists and intellectuals are always more respectful of a regime that takes their work and ideas "seriously." To be placed at a far distance from social and political power is, for such people, a deprivation.

Third, a commercial society, a society whose civilization is shaped by market transactions, is always likely to reflect the appetites and preferences of common men and women. Each may not have much money, but there are so many of them that their tastes are decisive. Artists and intellectuals see this as an inversion of the natural order of things, since it gives "vulgarity" the power to dominate where and when it can. By their very nature "elitists" (as one now says), they believe that a civilization should be shaped by an *aristoi* to which they will be organically attached, no matter how perilously. The consumerist and environmentalist movements of our own day reflect this aristocratic impulse, albeit in a distorted way: Because the democratic idea is the only legitimating political idea of our era, it is claimed that the market does not truly reflect people's prefer-

ences, which are deformed by the power of advertising. A minority, however, is presumed to have the education and the will to avoid such defor-
mation. And this minority then claims the paternalist authority to
represent "the people" in some more authentic sense. It is this minority
which is so appalled by America's "automobile civilization," in which
everyone owns a car, while it is not appalled at all by the fact that in the
Soviet Union only a privileged few are able to do so.

In sum, intellectuals and artists will be (as they have been) restive in
a bourgeois-capitalist society. The popularity of romanticism in the century after 1750 testifies to this fact, as the artists led an "inner emigration" of
the spirit—which, however, left the actual world unchanged. But not all
such restiveness found refuge in escapism. Rebellion was an alternative
route, as the emergence of various socialist philosophies and movements
early in the nineteenth century demonstrated.

Socialism (of whatever kind) is a romantic passion that operates
within a rationalist framework. It aims to construct a human community
in which *everyone* places the common good—as defined, necessarily, by
an intellectual and moral elite—before his own individual interests and
appetites. The intention was not new—there is not a religion in the world
that has failed to preach and expound it. What was new was the belief that
such self-denial could be realized, not through a voluntary circumscrip-
tion of individual appetites (as Rousseau had, for example, argued in his
Social Contract) but even while the aggregate of human appetites was
being increasingly satisfied by ever-growing material prosperity. What
Marx called "utopian" socialism was frequently defined by the notion that
human appetites were insatiable, and that a self-limitation on such
appetites was a precondition for a socialist community. The trouble with
this notion, from a political point of view, was that it was not likely to
appeal to more than a small minority of men and women at any one time.
Marxian "scientific" socialism, in contrast, promised to remove this conflict between actual and potentially ideal human nature by creating an
economy of such abundance that appetite as a social force would, as it
were, wither away.

Behind this promise, of course, was the profound belief that modern
science—including the social sciences, and especially including scientific
economics—would gradually but ineluctably provide humanity with
modes of control over nature (and human nature, too) that would permit
the modern world radically to transcend all those limitations of the
human condition previously taken to be "natural." The trouble with imple-
menting this belief, however, was that the majority of men and women
were no more capable of comprehending a "science of society," and of

developing a "consciousness" appropriate to it, than they were of practicing austere self-denial. A socialist elite, therefore, was indispensable to mobilize the masses for their own ultimate self-transformation. And the techniques of such mobilization would themselves of necessity be scientific—what moralists would call "Machiavellian"—in that they had to treat the masses as objects of manipulation so that eventually they would achieve a condition where they could properly be subjects of their own history making.

Michael Polanyi has described this "dynamic coupling" of a romantic moral passion with a ruthlessly scientific conception of man, his world, and his history as a case of "moral inversion." That is to say, it is the moral passion that legitimates the claims of scientific socialism to absolute truth, while it is the objective necessities that legitimate every possible form of political immorality. Such a dynamic coupling characterized, in the past, only certain religious movements. In the nineteenth and twentieth centuries, it became the property of secular political movements that sought the universal regeneration of mankind in the here and now.

The appeal of any such movement to intellectuals is clear enough. As intellectuals, they are qualified candidates for membership in the elite that leads such movements, and they can thus give free expression to their natural impulse for authority and power. They can do so, moreover, within an ideological context, which reassures them that, any superficial evidence to the contrary notwithstanding, they are disinterestedly serving the "true" interests of the people.

But the reality principle—*la force des choses*—will, in the end, always prevail over utopian passions. The fate of intellectuals under socialism is disillusionment, dissent, exile, silence. In politics, means determine ends, and socialism everywhere finds its incarnation in coercive bureaucracies that are contemptuously dismissive of the ideals that presumably legitimize them, even while establishing these ideals as a petrified orthodoxy. The most interesting fact of contemporary intellectual life is the utter incapacity of so-called socialist countries to produce socialist intellectuals—or even, for that matter, to tolerate socialist intellectuals. If you want to meet active socialist intellectuals, you can go to Oxford or Berkeley or Paris or Rome. There is no point in going to Moscow or Peking or Belgrade or Bucharest or Havana. Socialism today is a dead end for the very intellectuals who have played so significant a role in moving the modern world down that street.

In addition to that romantic-rationalist rebellion we call socialism, there is another mode of "alienation" and rebellion that may be, in the longer run, more important. This is romantic antirationalism, which takes a cultural rather than political form. It is this movement specifically that Trilling had in mind when he referred to the adversary culture.

Taking its inspiration from literary romanticism, this rebellion first created a new kind of "inner emigration"—physical as well as spiritual—in the form of "bohemia." In Paris, in the 1820s and 1830s, there formed enclaves of (mostly) young people who displayed *in nuce* all the symptoms of the counterculture of the 1960s. Drugs, sexual promiscuity, long hair for men and short hair for women, working-class dress (the "jeans" of the day), a high suicide rate—anything and everything that would separate them from the bourgeois order. The one striking difference between this bohemia and its heirs of a century and a quarter later is that to claim membership in bohemia one had to be (or pretend to be) a producer of "art," while in the 1960s to be a consumer was sufficient. For this transition to occur, the attitudes and values of bohemia had to permeate a vast area of bourgeois society itself. The engine and vehicle of this transition was the "modernist" movement in the arts, which in the century after 1850 gradually displaced the traditional, the established, the "academic."

The history and meaning of this movement are amply described and brilliantly analyzed by Daniel Bell in his *The Cultural Contradictions of Capitalism* (1976). Suffice it to say here that modernism in the arts can best be understood as a quasi-religious rebellion against bourgeois sobriety, rather than simply as a series of aesthetic innovations. The very structure of this movement bears a striking resemblance to that of the various gnostic-heretical sects within Judaism and Christianity. There is an "elect"—the artists themselves—who possess the esoteric and redeeming knowledge (*gnosis*); then there are the "critics," whose task it is to convey this gnosis, as a vehicle of conversion, to potential adherents to the movement. And then there is the outer layer of "sympathizers" and "fellow travelers"—mainly bourgeois "consumers" of the modernist arts—who help popularize and legitimate the movement within the wider realms of public opinion.

One can even press the analogy further. It is striking, for instance, that modernist movements in the arts no longer claim to create "beauty" but to reveal the "truth" about humanity in its present condition. Beauty is defined by an aesthetic tradition that finds expression in the public's "taste." But the modern artist rejects the sovereignty of public taste, since truth can never be a matter of taste. This truth always involves an indictment of the existing order of things, while holding out the promise, for those whose sensibilities have been suitably reformed, of a redemption of the spirit (now called "the self"). Moreover, the artist himself now becomes the central figure in the artistic enterprise—he is the hero of his own work, the sacrificial redeemer of us all, the only person capable of that transcendence that gives a liberating meaning to our lives. The artist—painter, poet, novelist, composer—who lives to a ripe old age of contentment with fame and fortune strikes us as having abandoned, if not betrayed his "mission." We think it more appropriate that artists should die young and tormented. The extraordinarily high suicide rate among modern artists would have baffled our ancestors, who assumed that the artist—like any other *secular* person—aimed to achieve recognition and prosperity in this world.

Our ancestors would have been baffled, too, by the enormous importance of critics and of criticism in modern culture. It is fascinating to pick up a standard anthology in the history of literary criticism and to observe that, prior to 1800, there is very little that we would designate as literary criticism, as distinct from philosophical tracts on aesthetics. Shakespeare had no contemporary critics to explain his plays to the audience; nor did the Greek tragedians, nor Dante, Racine, and so forth. Yet we desperately feel the need of critics to understand, not only the modern artist, but, by retrospective reevaluation, all artists. The reason for this odd state of affairs is that we are looking for something in these artists—a redeeming knowledge of ourselves and our human condition—which in previous eras was felt to lie elsewhere, in religious traditions especially.

The modernist movement in the arts gathered momentum slowly, and the first visible sign of its success was the gradual acceptance of the fact that bourgeois society had within it two cultures: the "avant-garde" culture of modernism, and the "popular culture" of the majority. The self-designation of modernism as avant-garde is itself illuminating. The term is of military origin, and means not, as we are now inclined to think, merely the latest in cultural or intellectual fashion, but the foremost assault troops in a military attack. It was a term popularized by Saint-Simon to describe the role of his utopian-socialist sect vis-à-vis the bourgeois order, and was then taken over by modernist innovators in the arts. The avant-garde is, and always has been, fully self-conscious of its hostile intentions toward the bourgeois world. Until 1914, such hostility was as likely to move intellectuals and artists toward the romantic Right as toward the romantic Left. But Right or Left, the hostility was intransigent. This is, as has been noted, a cultural phenomenon without historical precedent.

And so is the popular culture of the bourgeois era, though here again we are so familiar with the phenomenon that we fail to perceive its originality. It is hard to think of a single historical instance where a society presents us with two cultures, a "high" and a "low," whose values are in opposition to one another. We are certainly familiar with the fact that any culture has its more sophisticated and its more popular aspects, differentiated by the level of education needed to move from the one to the other. But the values embodied in these two aspects were basically homogeneous: The sophisticated expression did not *shock* the popular, nor did the popular incite feelings of revulsion among the sophisticated. Indeed, it was taken as a mark of true artistic greatness for a writer or artist to encompass both aspects of his culture. The Greek tragedies were performed before all the citizens of Athens; Dante's *Divine Comedy* was read aloud in the squares of Florence to a large and motley assemblage; and Shakespeare's plays were enacted before a similarly mixed audience.

The popular culture of the bourgeois era, after 1870 or so, tended to be a culture that educated people despised, or tolerated contemptuously. The age of Richardson, Jane Austen, Walter Scott, and Dickens—an age in which excellence and popularity needed not to contradict one another, in which the distinction between "highbrow" and "lowbrow" made no sense—was over. The spiritual energy that made for artistic excellence was absorbed by the modernist, highbrow movement, while popular culture degenerated into a banal reiteration—almost purely commercial in intent—of "wholesome" bourgeois themes.

In this popular literature of romance and adventure, the "happy ending" not only survived but became a standard cliché. The occasional unhappy ending, involving a sinful action (e.g., adultery) as its effectual cause, always concluded on a note of repentance, and was the occasion for a cathartic "good cry." In "serious" works of literature in the twentieth century, of course, the happy ending is under an almost total prohibition. It is also worth making mention of the fact that popular literature remained very much a commodity consumed by women, whose commitments to the bourgeois order (a "domestic" order, remember) has always been stronger than men's. This is why the women's liberation movement of the past two decades, which is so powerfully moving the female sensibility in an antibourgeois direction, is such a significant cultural event.

In the last century, the modernist movement in the arts made constant progress at the expense of the popular. It was, after all, the only serious art available to young men and women who were inclined to address themselves to solemn questions about the meaning of life (or "the meaning of it all"). The contemporaneous evolution of liberal capitalism itself encouraged modernism in its quest for moral and spiritual hegemony. It did this in three ways.

First, the increasing affluence that capitalism provided to so many individuals made it possible for them (or, more often, for their children) to relax their energetic pursuit of money, and of the goods that money can buy, in favor of an attention to those nonmaterial goods that used to be called "the higher things in life." The antibourgeois arts in the twentieth century soon came to be quite generously financed by restless, uneasy, and vaguely discontented bourgeois money.

Second, that spirit of worldly rationalism so characteristic of a commercial society and its business civilization (and so well described by Max Weber and Joseph Schumpeter) had the effect of delegitimizing all merely traditional beliefs, tasks, and attitudes. The "new," constructed by design or out of the passion of a moment, came to seem inherently superior to the old and established, this latter having emerged "blindly" out of the interaction of generations. This mode of thinking vindicated the socialist ideal of a planned society. But it also vindicated an anarchic, antinomian, "expressionist" impulse in matters cultural and spiritual.

Third, the tremendous expansion—especially after World War II—of postsecondary education provided a powerful institutional milieu for modernist tastes and attitudes among the mass of both teachers and students. Lionel Trilling, in *Beyond Culture*, poignantly describes the spiritual vitality with which this process began in the humanities—the professors were "liberated" to teach the books that most profoundly moved and interested them—and the vulgarized version of modernism that soon became the mass counterculture among their students who, as consumers, converted it into a pseudobohemian lifestyle.

Simultaneously, and more obviously, in the social sciences, the antibourgeois socialist traditions were absorbed as a matter of course, with "the study of society" coming quickly and surely to mean the management of social change by an elite who understood the verities of social structure and social trends. Economics, as the science of making the best choices in a hard world of inevitable scarcity, resisted for a long while; but the Keynesian revolution—with its promise of permanent prosperity through government management of fiscal and monetary policy—eventually brought much of the economics profession in line with the other social sciences.

So utopian rationalism and utopian romanticism have, between them, established their hegemony as adversary cultures over the modern consciousness and the modern sensibility.

But, inevitably, such victories are accompanied by failure and disillusionment. As socialist reality disappoints, socialist thought fragments into heterogeneous conflicting sects, all of them trying to keep the utopian spark alive while devising explanations for the squalid nature of socialist reality. One is reminded of the experience of Christianity in the first and second centuries, but with this crucial difference: Christianity, as a religion of transcendence, of *otherworldly* hope, of faith not belief, was not really utopian, and the Church Fathers were able to transform the Christian rebellion against the ancient world into a new, vital Christian orthodoxy, teaching its adherents how to live virtuously, that is, how to seek human fulfillment in this world even while waiting for their eventual migration into a better one. Socialism, lacking this transcendent dimension, is purely and simply trapped in this world, whose realities are for it nothing more than an endless series of frustrations. It is no accident, as the Marxists would say, that there is no credible doctrine of "socialist virtue"—a doctrine informing individuals how actually to live "in authenticity" as distinct from empty rhetoric about "autonomous self-fulfillment"—in any nation (and there are so many!) now calling itself socialist. It is paradoxically true that otherwordly religions are more capable of providing authoritative guidance for life in this world than are secular religions.

The utopian romanticism that is the impulse behind modernism in the arts is in a not dissimilar situation. It differs in that it seeks transcendence—all of twentieth-century art is such a quest—but it seeks such transcendence within the secular self. This endeavor can generate that peculiar spiritual intensity that characterizes the antibourgeois culture of our bourgeois era, but in the end it is mired in self-contradiction.

The deeper one explores into the self, without any transcendental frame of reference, the clearer it becomes that nothing is there. One can then, of course, try to construct a metaphysics of nothingness as an absolute truth of the human condition. But this, too, is self-contradictory: If nothingness is the ultimate reality, those somethings called books, or poems, or paintings, or music are mere evasions of truth rather than expressions of it. Suicide is the only appropriate response to this vision of reality (as Dostoevski saw long ago) and in the twentieth century it has in fact become the fate of many of our artists: self-sacrificial martyrs to a hopeless metaphysical enterprise. Those who stop short of this ultimate gesture experience that *tedium vitae*, already mentioned, which has made the "boringness" of human life a recurrent theme, since Baudelaire at least, among our artists.

This modern association of culture and culture heroes with self-annihilation and ennui has no parallel in human history. We are so familiar with it that most of us think of it as natural. It is, in truth, unnatural and cannot endure. Philosophy may, with some justice, be regarded as a preparation for dying, as Plato said—but he assumed that there would never be more than a handful of philosophers at any time. The arts, in contrast, have always been life-affirming, even when dealing with the theme of death. It is only when the arts usurp the role of religion, but without the transcendence that assures us of the meaning of apparent meaninglessness, that we reach our present absurd (and *absurdiste*) condition.

Moreover, though utopian rationalism and utopian romanticism are both hostile to bourgeois society, they turn out to be, in the longer run, equally hostile to one another.

In all socialist nations, of whatever kind, modernism in the arts is repressed—for, as we have seen, this modernism breeds a spirit of nihilism and antinomianism that is subversive of *any* established order. But this repression is never entirely effective, because the pseudo-orthodoxies of socialism can offer no satisfying spiritual alternatives. It turns out that a reading of Franz Kafka can alienate from socialist reality just as easily as from bourgeois reality, and there is no socialist Richardson or Fielding or Jane Austen or Dickens to provide an original equipoise. Who are the "classic" socialist authors or artists worthy of the name? There are none. And so young people in socialist lands naturally turn either to the high modernist culture of the twentieth century or to its debased, popularized version in the counterculture. Picasso and Kafka, blue jeans and rock and roll may yet turn out to be the major internal enemies of socialist bureaucracies, uniting intellectuals and the young in an incorrigible hostility to the status quo. Not only do socialism and modernism end up in blind alleys—their blind alleys are pointed in radically different directions.

Meanwhile, liberal capitalism survives and staggers on. It survives because the market economics of capitalism does work—does promote economic growth and permit the individual to better his condition while enjoying an unprecedented degree of individual freedom. But there is something joyless, even somnambulistic, about this survival.

For it was the Judeo-Christian tradition which, as it were, acted as the Old Testament to the new evangel of liberal, individualistic capitalism—which supplied it with a moral code for the individual to live by, and which also enabled the free individual to find a transcendental meaning in life, to cope joyfully or sadly with all the *rites de passage* that define the human condition. Just as a victorious Christianity needed the Old Testament in its canon because the Ten Commandments were there—along with the assurance that God created the world *"and it was good,"* and along, too, with its corollary that it made sense to be fruitful and multiply on this earth—so liberal capitalism needed the Judeo-Christian tradition to inform it authoritatively about the use and abuse of the individual's newly won freedom. But the adversary culture, in both its utopian-rationalist and utopian-romantic aspects, turns this Judeo-Christian tradition into a mere anachronism. And the churches, now themselves a species of voluntary private enterprise, bereft of all public support and sanction, are increasingly ineffectual in coping with its antagonists.

Is it possible to restore the spiritual base of bourgeois society to something approaching a healthy condition?

One is tempted to answer no, it is not possible to turn back the clock of history. But this answer itself derives from the romantic-rationalist conception of history, as elaborated by Saint-Simon and Hegel and Marx. In fact, human history, read in a certain way, can be seen as full of critical moments when human beings deliberately turned the clock back. The Reformation, properly understood, was just such a moment, and so was the codification of the Talmud in postexile Judaism. What we call the "new" in intellectual and spiritual history is often nothing more than a novel way of turning the clock back. The history of science and technology is a cumulative history, in which new ways of seeing and doing effectively displace old ones. But the histories of religion and culture are not at all cumulative in this way, which is why one cannot study religion and culture without studying their histories, while scientists need not study the history of science to understand what they are up to.

So the possibility is open to us—but, for better or worse, it is not the only possibility. All we can say with some certainty, at this time, is that the future of liberal capitalism may be more significantly shaped by the ideas now germinating in the mind of some young, unknown philosopher or theologian than by any vagaries in annual GNP statistics. Those statistics are not unimportant, but to think they are all-important is to indulge in the silly kind of capitalist idolatry that is subversive of capitalism itself. It is the ethos of capitalism that is in gross disrepair, not the economics of capitalism—which is, indeed, its saving grace. But salvation through this grace alone will not suffice.

From

The View from Sunset Boulevard

(1979)

Ben Stein

A sharp observer of the Hollywood scene, Stein revealed his early understanding of its prevailing mindset, and one that was increasingly influencing the thoughts and dreams of the American public. Stein not only explicated the Hollywood version of social justice and its ties to the world of fantasy; the "alternative reality" of television and the drift in the nation's views about the good life, he asserted, originated in affluent quarters of southern California and the happy world of entertainment.

The image of America on television is far more than a political picture alone. Television tells of life in far greater scope and particularity than simply by its attitudes toward rich or poor or criminals or military men. There is, on prime-time television, a united picture of life in these United States that is an alternate reality.

For hours each day, people can leave the lives they are compelled to lead, lives whose limitations and frustrations hardly need to be detailed, and enter a different world that is more pleasant and less difficult in almost every way—life on television. Most TV shows are set in the present or in a time within the memory of the viewers, [not] an exotic or extraordinary locale like a space station. All of the characters are supposed to be types we are familiar with. While that familiarity may be more imaginary than real, we do see a world on television with which it is not difficult to feel a distant kinship. More than that, we see a world that is extremely appealing in a whole variety of ways. Again these ways have to do largely with simplification. Life on television is in many ways a schematic of real life.

The whole alternate reality that television creates is not a coincidence or a result of random chance. It is the product of the thinking of TV producers and writers about life. We can see reflected on our video screens the attitudes of TV creators. More than that, we can sense the experience and "feel" of a city replicated on television. For what we see on prime-time television is nothing less than the apotheosizing of Los Angeles, and the spreading of the Los Angeles experience across the TV screens of America.

It is important to realize first that television is indeed creating a unified experience, a consistent alternative world. There is no contrast on television such as there is between a Dostoevsky and a Gogol, between an Osborne and a Stoppard, between a Mailer and a Didion, or between a Chandler and a Dunne. There is no major difference in texture or attitude between a "Baretta" and a "Happy Days," which is to say, between a show about a street cop in a dangerous and violent city in 1978 and a show about an utterly happy family in a small Wisconsin town in 1956. Both shows have the same optimistic, cheerful attitude about life, the same utterly unshakable premise that everything will come out right in the end, the same absence of anxiety or worry about daily life or death, the same feeling of life's infinite potential. With the exception of "Mary Hartman, Mary Hartman," there is no major show that says anything the slightest bit pessimistic about the potential for happiness of daily life. ("Mary Hartman" was not on during prime time in most locales.) No show challenges the assumption that the unexamined life is the only life worth living.

No show displays a kind of life that is anything but immaculately clean and neat, in which people are anything but well-groomed and hygienic and their motivations anything but straightforward. Certainly, this has partly to do with the exigencies of a mass culture. Traditionally, the dramas of folk culture are not as complicated as those of high culture. Yet that does not account for everything. In movies (the mass culture of another era) there was dirt and tragedy and complexity, even in films with enormous appeal to mass audiences. The dirt of Tara, the sweat and grime of Scarlett O'Hara's brow, the tawdriness of John Garfield's apartment in *Body and Soul,* the grim grayness and ambiguity of fifty detective stories of the 1940s *film noir* genre are only a tiny fraction of the available evidence on that score.

Even in the early days of television, before it moved so completely to Los Angeles, there was complexity and sadness. When reruns of "Your Show of Shows" appear, their sad endings are almost shocking. The truly frightening and earthy quality of some early "Playhouse 90" and "Kraft

Theatre" shows is amazing when compared with the cheerfulness and antisepsis of the present day's fare on television.

Today's television is purer, in terms of backdrop and story endings, than the lines of a Mercedes convertible. Every day's shows bring fresh examples. Recently I saw an episode of "Charlie's Angels" about massage parlors that were really whorehouses. The three beautiful "angels" of the show were compelled to pretend they worked at massage parlors in seamy areas. (On this particular show, the girls are almost always compelled to act as prostitutes or prisoners or lesbians or nymphomaniacs.) Anyone who has ever passed by a massage parlor knows that they are invariably dirty, shabby places, with pitiful and degraded denizens. On "Charlie's Angels," the Paradise Massage Parlor compared favorably in terms of cleanliness with the surgical theater at Massachusetts General Hospital. The girls were immaculate and well groomed, soft of speech and clear of eye and skin.

On "The Waltons," we are supposed to believe that we are in a Depression-era farming town in backwoods Virginia. Anyone who has been to a backwoods farming town in the South knows that whatever else may be said about them, they are invariably dirty and bedraggled. On "The Waltons," even the barnyard is immaculate. Marie Antoinette could not have asked for more agreeable playfarm quarters. The grittiest TV show is generally believed to be "Baretta." Yet even there, the supposedly shabby boardinghouses are neat, bright, and cheery. Even the junkies wear fresh clothing and sport recent haircuts.

Why is television so clean? Why, when a recent show dramatized living conditions on New York's Lower East Side during the early twentieth century, did every apartment look like something that a DuPont great-grandson had recently redecorated? The answer is simple. TV writers and producers replicate the world in which they live in their art, and the world they live in is the super-clean, super-bright world of Los Angeles, where even the slums are spotless and have palm trees in front. The world on television is the world south of the Tehachapi and north of Frontera.

Until I moved to Los Angeles, I had no idea where the images of television came from. Where on earth, I wondered, were pastel drug stores, low stucco apartments with balconies overlooking artificial waterfalls in the poor neighborhoods, and bars with almost pitch-black interiors, opening onto glaringly bright sidewalks, utterly without litter or refuse? Drive along any boulevard in Los Angeles. There is block after block of pastel drug stores and apartment houses with balconies and artificial waterfalls. Close by are the bars with pitch-black interiors.

When I lived in Washington and in New York, I wondered where in America were all cars bright and shiny, unspattered by mud, with their original colors gleaming in the sun. Where did people have new cars even if they were secretaries or rookie policemen? In Los Angeles, where everyone spends a few hours a day in a car, everyone has a shiny new auto, even if it is a financial sacrifice. In Los Angeles, where the sun shines every day and rain never falls, cars never get muddy. Where are policemen handsome, thin, neatly dressed and polite? They certainly were not in New York or Washington or New Haven or Santa Cruz or anywhere else except Los Angeles. In Los Angeles, the policemen look like male models, except that they do not look effeminate. They are the models for the ruggedly modish cops on a dozen TV shows.

Artists re-create their experiences, and the Los Angeles experience is one of cleanliness, brightness, shininess, and handsomeness. The artists of television do not live in drafty garrets. An artist for television simply never can experience the grittiness of daily life that might be experienced in any other city. Among the TV writers and producers I interviewed, whenever people spoke of Los Angeles they spoke of a "fantasy land," "plastic paradise," "wonderland," "sterile concrete," "lotus land," and similar hackneyed phrases that are nevertheless accurate. The writers and producers see and experience a life of cleanness and emphasis on good appearance that would be unbelievable to anyone who did not live in Los Angeles. That has become their image of life, so that when a world is recreated on television, the Los Angeles world, the one in the creators' minds, is the one that comes out. However much the writers and producers may mock and decry the sterility and cleanliness of Los Angeles, it is Los Angeles they are broadcasting around the world as the model environment. The faces, clothes, haircuts, and cars of people on television are the faces, clothes, haircuts, and cars of people walking down Rodeo Drive in Beverly Hills.

All of this has nothing to do with politics of left, right, or center. It does have to do with the control that the Los Angeles TV community has over television's content. It illustrates powerfully the influence that the experiences in the producers' and writers' minds has over what goes out over the airwaves. Television is not creating a world that reflects a composite of the American experience. Nor is the TV world the result of random chance. Television is what comes out of the Los Angeles TV community's heads, and since Los Angeles is what goes into their heads, Los Angeles is what comes out.

But this applies only to the question of appearance and graphics. There is also a moral and philosophical world on television, and that, too, has to come from somewhere.

Beyond the physical and visual cleanliness on television is an attitude appealing far beyond most of what real life has to offer. On television, everything ends happily, which might be a way of summarizing the TV climate. There is far more, however. Every problem that comes up on television is cured before the show is over. No one suffers from existential terrors. They are not even hinted at.

On a smaller scale, people on television are not small-minded, nasty folks. If they are murderers, at least they are polite. No waitresses neglect to take a diner's order. No busboys spill Coca-Cola on anyone's lap. No one cuts a driver off and makes him slam on the brakes. Clerks in stores are polite and helpful. No one gets caught in traffic jams. There are no blackouts. No shopping-bag ladies, reeking of urine, stalk a traveler in a crowded subway. No snarling teenagers threaten and mock on a deserted sidewalk. Instead, people move along rapidly on highways and byways. Impediments are cleared out of the way, both visually and psychologically. At the end of 60 minutes, at the most, everything has come up roses, even if there were a few minor thorns along the way.

On television, people get things done. No one spends all day in a windowless office going over musty volumes of figures and regulations, seeking to comply with guidelines and plans laid out by persons long since dead. No one on television spends all day in bed, too lethargic or depressed to get up. On television, in fact, there is no such thing as depression. That most widespread of modern psychic ailments simply does not exist in the alternate world of television. Everyone, good or bad, is charged with energy. If someone wants to do something, he or she simply goes out and does it. There are no mental blocks working to derail the TV hero or villain.

Further, people on television think big. They are no longer concerned with telling Ricky Ricardo how much they spent on a hat. Instead, they think about making a million by selling heroin, or about ridding Los Angeles of the most vicious killer of the decade. In a comedy, a poor family thinks of getting rich. A middle-class family thinks of getting into the upper class. A black family thinks of overcoming racism. Nothing trivial occurs as a main theme any longer.

"Out there," for the folks on television, is a big world, full of possibilities. Here, a sharp distinction needs to be made between social activism and personal ambition. The people on television are never interested in social movements. They may want to be more well off themselves, but they are never interested in a political try at massive and immediate redistribution of wealth. Similarly, Edith Bunker may make a stab at social accommodation by accepting the fact that a relative is a lesbian, but she will never march for gay rights. J.J. on "Good Times" will do his best to make a killing in faulty underwear, but he will not demonstrate against double taxation of corporate dividends. Tony Baretta will extend himself to catch a murderer, but he will not agitate for a return of the death penalty. Charlie's Angels will coo with sympathy over the plight of a hooker, but they will never carry placards asking for repeal of laws against prostitution.

People on television want money and happiness for themselves. They want to be great sleuths or great criminals. But they are never interested in social movements. They have big plans and hopes for themselves, but not for society. This entire psychic galaxy is, as far as I can tell, a reflection of the psychic makeup of the Hollywood TV producer and writer. Before I came to the world of TV production I never would have imagined that a group of people as psychologically successful and liberated as TV writers and producers existed. It is their mental world that is up there on the TV screen.

In the world of television are people who are financially successful, creative, living in comfortable surroundings, and generally quite happy. Around a successful TV production company (and the unsuccessful ones quickly vanish) there is an air of confidence and self-satisfaction that is rarely encountered anywhere else. Those people are highly unusual folk, operating in a highly unusual milieu, and it shows. In the eighth decade of American life in the twentieth century, the working situation of Americans has become steadily more bureaucratized. Almost everyone coming out of school goes to work for a large enterprise of some kind, finding a spot on a bureaucratic ladder. The worker must flatter everyone over him and worry about everyone under him. His real rewards come not from producing anything, but from pleasing those above him on the ladder.

Workers derive their security and status from the bureaucratic structure in which they find themselves. They are cogs in a vast machinery. There is little or no creativity in their daily lives. Advancement comes with infuriating slowness. To reach a position of financial independence or modest wealth is almost impossible. Getting that extra few thousand a year in wages becomes the key goal, and few see further than that.

On the other hand, the bureaucratic structure provides a protection against having to actually produce anything. Simply serving one's time at the office is all that is required to get by. Eventually, however, that too takes its toll. The realization that one is doing nothing but serving out a life sentence results in devastating blows to one's self-esteem. The whole process of the engorgement of institutions and the swallowing up of the individual into large enterprises leads, in my experience, to a smallness of mind. Bitterness and pettiness are generated by the unmixed frustration that is each day's portion.

Imagine, on the other hand, the world of Hollywood. It is a throwback to the world of individual entrepreneurs. Each writer sinks or swims on the basis of his product. Those people do not have to wait in a bureaucratic holding pattern all of their lives. If their product is good, they become successful and important immediately. They are not judged by how well they can accommodate themselves to a paranoid boss's suspicions. Rather, they move along or fall out depending on what they get done. They are immediately able to make themselves independent by having a skill that is in great demand and correspondingly highly paid. They float from contract to contract. Each time they begin a project, they have the opportunity to become millionaires, *and many of them do.*

The economics of TV production are such that successful writers can demand and get a proprietary interest in the shows they write. If the show is successful, the rewards become staggering. Each successful TV writer becomes an entrepreneur on some scale. The money comes pouring in. A story about Bob Dylan comes to mind. When Dylan started out, he wrote about depressed, crazy people suffering daily crises. After a few years, when his income had risen to eight figures left of the decimal point, he started to write only about happy, cheerful subjects. When asked about the change, he is reported to have said, "It's hard to be a bitter millionaire."

So it is with the people on television. They have many firm and negative opinions about various groups within the society, but they are basically fairly satisfied with life. There may be, and probably are, starving would-be TV writers in North Hollywood and Studio City who are filled with rage and anger. But the ones who have made it, the ones who are working regularly for many thousands a week, are quite content for the most part.

TV writers are not like novel or play writers. They are simply not allowed to become depressed and unproductive. They must get out a show every week. No sulking or brooding is permitted. To get out a new teleplay each week is not the pastime of blocked people. Those who sulk all day because they get a rude remark from a waiter are not successful TV writers and producers. Those who cannot drag themselves out of the house because of existential dread do not get to see their names in the credits. Life's annoyances and pitfalls are not permitted to throw the train of creation off the tracks.

Imagine, if you will, a Texas wheeler-dealer who is also able to write situation comedies and adventure shows, and there you have a good idea of the personality type of the successful TV writer and producer. He is a person who gets things done and who feels good about it. After spending years in bureaucracies of various kinds, I found it staggering to see how much each individual writer and producer got done each day. In Norman Lear's TAT Communications, there is a full-time staff of fewer than fifty to get out hundreds of millions of dollars worth of TV product. If the government had a department of TV comedy, there would be at least 75,000 employees—and they would do nothing. Naturally, each of those few people who is producing so much feels good about it and about himself. The exact opposite of small-mindedness is generated.

No one is completely or even mostly happy, but the Hollywood TV writers and producers that I met went a long way along that line. They were, and are, people who take risks and live successfully. Their horizons are broad. The small annoyances of life do not faze them unduly. They see life not as a prison sentence but as a garden of rich potentialities.

TV writers and producers are not starving in garrets, cutting off their ears to send to prostitutes. They are generally far more prosperous than the bankers they hate, far more energetic and entrepreneurial than the businessmen they hate, and infinitely more effective than the bureaucrats they tolerate. They lead fulfilled, productive lives, by most standards. They live those lives in an attractive, uncluttered world of immaculate sidewalks and gleaming new cars, pastel storefronts, and artificial waterfalls. They have been a party to striving and success in their own lives, and they have not missed the lesson of the possibilities of life. And it is this way of life that has been translated into the flickering colorful images on hundreds of millions of TV screens.

To set forth a way of life on television is not necessarily political in terms of left, right, or center. Still, it has some policy content. To replicate one's life and tell the world that it is the model of how life should be lived is a normative statement with some degree of power and forcefulness. The people who have created that model world on television are telling the rest of us that we should try to conform to that model—implicit though the demand may be.

The Fashionable Mind
(1978/1981)

Kennedy Fraser

Before becoming the title essay of a book, this selection appeared in the *New Yorker* in 1978, when the respected fashion writer noted the transformation of all things, people, and ideas into trends, media events, and styles. Fraser took a dim view of fashion's accelerating power, persuasiveness, and force in cultural life. Fashionable ideas and gestures, she argued, were seeping "into the realm of those profundities, verities, and values which used to be called moral and spiritual."

Many societies have been openly dominated by fashionable people, but our society is quietly permitting itself to be dominated and transformed by fashionable minds. The word "fashion" (with "fashionable") isn't heard much anymore, and even its successors "trend" and "style" have come to seem a little tasteless and passé. But fashion is everywhere around us just the same. It's there wherever political strategies are planned, movies made, books published, art exhibits mounted, critical columns turned out, dances danced, editorial policies formulated, academic theses germinated: wherever people think, speak, or create our shared forms of self-expression. Fashion usually is neither named nor noted but is simply the lens through which our society perceives itself and the mold to which it increasingly shapes itself. This hidden, powerful, mental sort of fashion is thus worth taking stock of. In spite of its great parade of intellect, its support in influential places, and its mellifluous accompaniment of self-promoting public relations, the new variety of fashion pretty much shares the creed and the limitations of the frivolous, pirouetting old variety of fashion—that of dress. The shared creed is materialistic, and holds that appearances are of greater significance than substance. Among the shared limitations are fickleness, a preoccupation with descrying the will of the majority in order to manipulate it or pander to it, and a concern with the accumulation or protection of power and profit. Although all fashion looks mobile and rebellious at times, its roots are surprisingly constant: to think or act for reasons of fashion in any given field is to support that field's established centers of power. The character and the ancestry of mental fashion become more difficult to detect as it increases its power and its pretensions by annexing "better," previously impregnable departments of society, and converting "more serious," formerly independent minds. In this [conversion] fashion succeeds in fobbing off on more and more people its own distorted imitation of life.

Mental fashion, like any other kind of fashion, is by nature restless—bent on promoting, and profiting by, constant novelty. It is always on the move. It is no longer content merely with slick, razzle-dazzle opinion-making and smart, comet's-tail trend-spotting—the social and external side of mental activity. Such preoccupations were sufficient for fashionable minds in a nation concerned with foreign affairs and public scandals but were not wholly satisfactory later, when the individual citizen withdrew into himself to search for fulfillment through jogging or *cuisine minceur*. So mental fashion turned inward with him, and started to seep down into the realm of those profundities, verities, and values which used to be called moral and spiritual. It is scarcely an improvement that the fashionable mind is beginning to weary of the appearance of cultivating maturity and introspection. Having witnessed fashion's corruption of our definition of the world, we must now sit by as fashion subverts our definition of the self. In advertising, we can see fashionable intellectual hubris at its crudest and its most absurd. Copywriters pepper their prose with references to "individuality," "taste," and "quality," all of which abstractions are taken to be suddenly and deliciously "in." Even if one dismisses the intellectual pretensions of advertising style as harmless shadowboxing, one must feel depressed to see how fashionable minds in more significant fields blur the distinctions between real and spurious quality, between actual life and make-believe. The newly profound faddishness may be daily observed in the work of commentators, critics, editors, artists, television producers, and the like, who presumably transmit its influence to the general public. The sort of people who ought to be professionally protecting real quality and fostering genuine individuality—not just the image of these, or the toy-town versions that advertising fools about with—seem ever more inclined to present thoughts, facts, and values, and human beings, too, simply as fashionable commodities, much like the season's new hats of old. Everything is to be dealt in, acquired, used, promoted, and, in time, inevitably cast off. Sometimes, as if by chance, merchants and promoters of mental fashion throw their weight behind what really seem to be works of quality and originality, and, consequently, of uncertain popularity. But these are presented with such great self-laudatory cymbal clashings and heavy underscorings that the original spark of worth and talent ends up looking feeble and somehow disappointing.

&

Our society is neither so naive nor so cynical as to hand itself over to fashion without in some way believing that fashion is a worthy guide. We have long had an interest in pretending that fashion is something more dignified and substantial than it really is. The new status of fashion became obvious some years back, at the time it changed its name to "style" or "trend." There came to be widespread recognition that fashions of any kind were not merely esoteric and self-contained trinkets but a part of life. They were seen at first as visible, bobbing markers of the otherwise hidden course of one of the great currents of the times, and later as instruments to aid in the interpretation of those currents. From this function as instrument, fashion grew until it came close to being equated with intelligence. In the amount of respect we accord various intellectual attributes, a nose for trend now rivals the power to analyze the present and has surpassed the ability to store the past in memory. Perhaps the fashionable influence in thought has gained power less by its own intrinsic vitality than by the default of competitive influences. Maybe technology and its accompanying calculators, computers, and scientific polls caused the solid, reasoning, "masculine" side of our mind to atrophy, tipping the scale further toward the licensed gadfly that is the intuitive, "feminine" side of our mind—the origin of fashion.

However it develops, the excessive use of fashion as a framework for perception will ultimately warp that perception and, with it, any reasonable picture of the world. The greatest drawback of an overfashionable perception is that fashion is concerned, virtually by definition, with surfaces, images, appearances. This drawback is painfully plain when the fashionable mind is supposedly employed to get at the heart of things, or when the conclusions it reaches may have a lasting effect, as in the reporting or interpretation of national events or the definition of "good" and "bad" art. Fashion is well equipped to pass on to us how things look or seem, and is often good at making assessments peripheral to appearances, such as how much money they are worth, but it is not equipped to tell us what things really are. When the mind surrenders itself to fashion, the first casualty is objective judgment—which is, to all intents, the mind itself. Fashionable perception is incapable of discerning any fixed truth about an object or event, and so leaves the object or event at the mercy of the observer and of the time and circumstance in which it is observed.

A fashionable mind is often distracted from thorough concentration on its object by the question of timing, and will wander into self-congratulation on the observer's impeccably fashionable chronological instinct and into overweening claims to have known and appreciated fashions long before they became widely fashionable. These intrusive assertions of pre-fashionable familiarity with a subject—hyperfashionableness, in other words—crop up frequently these days. Fashionable observation is very far from being self-sufficient, and is highly self-conscious about the company it keeps. It is inclined to rove jumpily around the edges of its object, like the eyes of an ambitious guest roving beyond a conversation partner at a cocktail party full of powerful people, and is distracted by its attempts to encompass the comings and goings of others. To the absolutely fashionable mind, an opinion, a taste, or an enthusiasm is of significance only for a particular, restricted moment—a moment when it is held in common by some right-seeming group of fellow-souls, just before it is adopted by large groups of followers.

Fashion as it exists now, whether in literature or in kitchen equipment, in neckties or in ideas, is intimately connected with money and power. This basis is by no means always apparent, and our careless inherited assumption that fashion is spontaneous, amusing, innocent, and amateurish is likely to keep us from examining or questioning the ways in which it has evolved. The part that commerce plays in fashion is something we are often led to overlook, for the fashionable mind is well practiced in masking a general allegiance to commerce and the status quo behind what seems to an outsider to be an appealingly individualistic enthusiasm for some particular novelty. Fashion is a skillful master of enthusiasm, and of a Pavlovian discernment of certain correspondences—between a current best-seller and a potential successor, for instance—but is an inadequate touchstone in the search for honest, disinterested distinctions. These are born of an isolated, dogged, unfashionable side of the mind—a sort of gawky mental provincialism.

It is important to remain aware of the flaws of the fashionable perception, because that flawed perception is capable of influencing and changing the world it perceives. Fashionable minds and their backers do not just absorb the world passively but, if it is necessary in order to create the trends they seek to promote, actively distort it. Fashions, quite simply, do not exist until a fashionable mind is turned on them. Only in that fashion is free to conjure up the previously nonexistent and is unfettered by the need for consistent loyalty to any client does it distinguish itself from the fancier echelons of the public relations business. In these, as with fashion, underlying commercial and corporate purposes are often suavely concealed beneath a sincere, personal veneer. Fashion and public relations share a charter to turn life to their own advantage, to make malleable and commercially useful the naked human perception. Both interests consider life too small, dull, and colorless to get itself sufficiently noticed without the lobbying efforts of professionals. The mind attuned to trend setting and trend spotting has no regard for the objective, independent pulse of life but, rather, will recklessly declare that trends exist, will invent catchwords and categories for those trends, and will proceed to stuff poor, unsuspecting life and muddled old culture down into profitable slots.

In order to make a real mark, of course, the manipulative, subjective, trend-bent perception loosed on the world must be a corporate subjectivity, and not merely an isolated, personal one. The reason that some phenomenon or other is declared to exist as a trend is that powerful interests have invested in that existence. (The "media event," which is no event at all until the network camera crews tramp in to make it so, is one example of the attempt to shape the world to subjective corporate fiat.) The fashionable outlook never permits itself to wander far from the path that will bring in big-business profits, and is also susceptible to the temptations of personal financial gain. For fashion of all kinds is fundamentally materialistic and utilitarian. Its tendency is to view perception and reflection as commodities, ideas as merchandise, and words as promotional tools.

In spite of its allegiance to the material and its leanings toward the superficial, among other barriers to wisdom, fashion is now setting out boldly to colonize the world's mysterious islands of individuality and the hitherto unexplored territory of the inner life. Thus, trends that look like trends—broad, uniform, and public, that is—are now less fashionable than trends that can pass for the spontaneous impulses of the private mind. Fashion now pivots on a show of the personal and the sensitive, on feelings, values, an air of education, a sense of fine distinctions, and a great play of self-confidence and independence—on what is packaged commercially, in short, as the Quality Life. The increasingly estimable-looking camouflage that fashion is taking on makes the process of detecting its presence and influence infinitely more complex, and makes anyone seem churlish who takes issue with it once it is detected. Is one entitled to complain about the end of quality just because it arrives still trailing a few wisps of the promotional straw it was packaged in? The fact is, though, that the dilemma of withholding admiration from excellence simply because it has been given the backing of fashion rarely comes up. Fashion tends to diminish all that it touches, and what might fool the cursory glance as being genuine and good often turns out on closer inspection to be a mirage of authenticity and a mutated, pastiche version of the good. The paradigm of the fashionizing process is the New York commonplace of a fashionable young man taking over from an unfashionable old man the ownership of a real nineteenth-century saloon, tearing out its insides, and replacing them with a stylized imitation of the insides of a nineteenth-century saloon. Because common sense has been drugged by fashion, albeit the "good" fashion for the solidity and workmanship that originally endeared the premises to the new owner, no normal instinct survives to question the destruction of the irreplaceable, or the validity of the fake that pretends to improve on it. The most tasteful kind of fashion almost always proves the most destructive, because it sets its sights on the worthiest targets.

The dimension in which fashion operates is an amalgam of the mental and the material—a miasmic half-world where ideas have functions and prices, while objects are hung about with thoughts and dreams. The acts of buying and selling have in recent years become more and more densely shrouded in a fuzz of references to individuality and thinking, probably in deference to the college-educated, reputedly self-aware and independent-minded survivors of the tumultuous nineteen-sixties who are now peaceably earning and spending money. These form the natural market for products wrapped up in a fashion whose object is the self—for a materialism that is twined appealingly around unmaterialistic, or even anti-materialistic, thoughts and values. Advertisers, who once sold cars and shampoos by playing on mindless romantic dreams of moonlit tides and slow-motion flowing manes, now play crisply on their audience's complacency about its enlightened consumerism. The habit of cigarette smoking is twisted to become a demonstration of maturity and ratiocination. Clothes that will make people into comfortable carbon copies of their peers are described as inimitably suited to the unique personal style of each of the thousands who buy them. And it is scarcely necessary for advertisers to spell out the notion that a certain codified, ritualized pattern of furnishing a house with homespun textures and materials indicates the vitality and honesty of the inhabitant's mind.

The blurring of the distinction between people and products has led to an assumption that is often voiced these days—that clothing, furniture, and possessions of all kinds are, or ought to be, a form of self-expression. If the premise had remained on an amateurish, human scale, as a declaration of the right to privately enjoy and freely control the props and costumes of one's own little stage without regard to the dictates of social circumstance, it might have had some value. But when fashion took up the originally sound impulse, it perverted that impulse, as is its way. Commercial interests gleefully exploited the notion of self-expression through spending, foreseeing that the path to self-knowledge—the necessary prerequisite of self-expression—must mean false starts and wrong investments by customers, which would prove profitable to business. Still, the invariably disappointing faith that people are what they own and will be better fulfilled if they own better things spread steadily. It is not difficult to resist conversion to this faith when the stereotyped and materialized presentation of a "distinctive" self is made in a clumsily worded advertisement for mass-produced perfume or some part of the denim uniform. It is more tempting to accept this false self when it is encountered further up the scale of worldliness, where materialism looks more incorporeal and fashions look a lot like ideas. A definition of the self as being fixed by a carapace of possessions sits more cozily if those possessions are thoroughly imbued with intelligence and taste.

Americans, acting under the combined influence of rampant acquisitiveness and psychoanalytical self-absorption, seem particularly inclined to mesh possessions with their sense of self-esteem, and to view them as social signposts and emotional milestones. One may see in this country all stages of evolution of the identification of the individual with his goods—from the simplest level of the immigrant who thinks he must be someone because he can now afford a secondhand Buick, through the second-generation status seeker who concludes that he must be someone impressive because he can afford what his friends will recognize as being from Vuitton or Gucci, to the fashionable pinnacle where the most confident and established citizen *knows* that he is someone because he has the good taste and education to possess a particularly fine example of a Coromandel screen together with the self-assurance to take it for granted. If more and more people aspire to belong to this last category, the basic misapprehension remains the same at every level of acquisition. Certainly, though, materialism is upwardly mobile now, causing fashion to try to look as permanent, respectable, and lifelike as possible while status moves on to reside less in the act of buying than in the fact of long-term possession. And today it is not enough even to possess things; you have to be seen to be the sort of person who appreciates their finer points. Shabby chic has been more highly valued than mere chic for some time, but the most fashionable things of all today are those that look not like fashions but like aspects of a completely independent mind.

It is fashionable to give the appearance of being unique—that is, to demonstrate the uniqueness of one's acquisitiveness—by being a connoisseur of some sort and possessing á "collection" of objects. Truly fashionable collections tend to fall into a curiously restricted number of categories; antique corkscrews, miniature shoes, old baskets, and Oriental lacquered boxes are among the current favorites. (The shift away from diamonds, Georgian silver, and other objects of intrinsic monetary value to objects admired for their warmth, their quaintness, their good design, or some other subjectively defined virtue is part of the present fashion for humanized materialism.) Occasionally, to save their clients time, interior decorators assemble collections for them. As it is with such instant collections that supposedly "accessorize" a fashionable individuality, so it is with the individuality itself. The intention is deceitful—designed to trick outsiders into being impressed. The slow, genuine, stop-and-start process of accumulation is circumvented, and the end result is a stereotype. If inanimate objects are left to stand in their world, and are not invited out to mingle with our sense of self, they will quietly console and delight us. But to bind possessions up closely with the mind is less than fair to both. And the more fashionable it becomes to protect a self-conscious individuality, the more surely fashion will erode real individuality. A fashionable individuality has a way of turning out, on further scrutiny, to look less like an individuality than like a fashion.

The fashion for a schematic individuality that begins and ends with the image of one's material circumstances is the domestic aspect of what becomes on the grander and glossier public plane the cult of "celebrity." The promotion of a certain controlled and stylized public personality and the acceptance of this surface as a definition of worth increasingly form the vital motive power of our culture. The cult has spread outward from the performing arts—where a visible face and even an openly displayed private life are part of the job—into fields where personality used to be considered background and best left unemphasized or unseen behind the finished product, such as writing books or communicating the facts of the news. Celebrity, the public side of "individuality," is ostensibly human but really a part of fashion, and, like other aspects of fashion, it operates in a dimension that runs parallel to life and often apes it very closely but is not the same as life itself. Like other aspects of fashion, celebrity specializes in blithe manipulativeness and outrageous volte-face, and operates according to completely self-contained, self-perpetuating criteria. Underlying facts and underpinning fixities, often unattractive or tedious, belong to the real world but not to that of celebrity, where all is bright, swift, and palatable. It is of no significance, for example, whether a man actually has the genius, or even the readership, to lay claim to the title of "distinguished author" as long as he understands the knack of projecting himself in that role within the hermetic confines of the celebrity world, where humanity is less significant than its image. The variety of individuality which is handed down by the mechanism of celebrity proves as disconnected from real individuality as does the hypothetical mass-market self whipped up by advertising or the assembly-line uniqueness summed up by a fashionable collection. It is clear that celebrities do not exist as ordinary people do, by virtue of drawing breath on earth (regardless of who may observe them doing so), but are manufactured and promoted like commodities and fashions.

Fashions in famous people, like every other kind of fashion, have begun to look more educated and discriminating, and to succeed in tricking a wider audience into believing that the world of celebrity is just as admirable and just as real as life itself. The supposedly private, un-celebrity face of the famous has never been spread out before the public with as much intimacy as it is now. The spotlight of publicity swings quite as often, these days, to "serious" people as to the posturings of spangled starlets. And a special subdivision of celebrity, dubbed "eccentricity," has been cooked up by some of the more broadminded celebrity-makers to encompass people like Sarah Caldwell and Woody Allen, who fail to pass the stringent test of physical uniformity which continues to be generally demanded. This category of self-sufficient or unconventional-looking characters represents people-fashion's nod to the "high-class" end of fashion, where reside "quality" and "style."

Sometimes the cloak of celebrity falls over genuine talent and real originality, and sometimes a lack of these is concealed behind a cunning imitation of them. Ideally, talent survives perfectly, in total mastery of itself. But the danger of life's swathing itself in an accessible, simplified, public-relations version of itself is that original talent settles down to fit the comfortable shape of its public image or withers away unnoticed behind it. The public, meanwhile, distracted by a host of shadows and substitutes, is deprived of art. Literature, for instance, has been irrevocably diminished in past decades. More than by the ascendancy of image over print, the damage has been done by the transformation of culture into a fashion-based industry. In fact, by now the association of literature with celebrity faddishness is so far advanced that the general assumption is not merely that literary creators are significant primarily as celebrities and talk-show guests but also that their literary creation should itself look familiar with and know how to harness the money-spinning power of fashion and celebrities.

The criteria of fad and of the celebrity cult do more than mold our opinion of this season's literature; they also determine how much attention and value our society will accord the literary figures of the past. The hagiological-scatological web of biographies and commentaries-on-commentaries and movies-of-the-book which our culture has woven around the Bloomsbury group, F. Scott Fitzgerald, and Ernest Hemingway, among others, is inspired less by any particular respect for the brilliance of the artists' *work* (although the unexamined presence of that brilliance behind the visible and entertaining mound of gossipy secondary information soothes the cultural conscience of the audience for literary best-sellers) than by the seductiveness of the luxurious conditions and the aura of celebrity surrounding the artists in their *lives.* The various literary cults of today illustrate characteristics common to all fashion, and show how, if fashion has a chilling effect on contemporary talent, its power to diminish is all the more discouraging when it is turned on the talents of the past. In addition, literary-historical fashion-mongering, with its concentration on particular "in-groups," shows how all fashion is naturally drawn to discern or create patterns of social or personal power, and how the dimension of fashion tends to seek its frame of reference within itself. It continues to promote, even generations later, those who always made that dimension their home. More often than not, it emerges that the key figures of popular literary history were celebrities and self-publicists in their own day.

The new, thoughtful-looking, lifelike breed of fashion has been fostered by a generation (linked in common cultural impulses, if not necessarily in age) whose perceptions are attuned to and often blunted by the transient images of television and the movies but who also have college educations that have left a taste for the sensation of intellectual activity and a nostalgia for the literary enthusiasms of studenthood. The verbal appetite of this group is powerful enough to send advertising copywriters scratching out their polysyllables and newspaper editors scrambling to fill up their Op-Ed pages with a show of "provocative" thought, but is not discriminating enough to care whether words are being employed in the service of fashion or to advance our understanding of life. This group, in its instinctive use of material possessions as the prism through which it views itself and the world, is middle-class. Here is the natural market for surfaces, fashions, and the patina of culture. In literature, this market picks out work furnished with appealing objects it can fantasize about possessing, "atmospheres" to which it can surrender itself and in which it can happily bathe. Just as this market is willing to accept the décor of its living room as an expression of its inner self, it is inclined to accept the decorative parts of art as art's essence.

The machinery of fashion-making which has been developed to feed an essentially materialistic audience the appearance of opinion, perception, and talent it has learned to demand is profoundly destructive of just such intangibles. Fashion takes up with originality and talent because it knows that these often prove profitable, and also out of its characteristic compulsion to replenish itself by ceaselessly devouring the new. But as soon as fashion adopts its latest find, this is transformed into fashion's creature, existing by the grace of fashionable attention, and drained of the qualities that proved so fatally attractive in the first place. If, as an ambitious fashion increasingly demands, those initially attractive qualities were real independence and integrity, the tragedy of their fall is the greater. Fashion hurts most what it professes to admire most, and does most damage to the best; the fate of mediocrity has never mattered much. Fashion exerts a harmful pressure on the intellect, which either cravenly caves in and accepts the soothing notion that "quality living" means a discerning collection of gouaches and a rather nice taste in wines or chooses to resist the tide of fashion and attempt the perpetual effort to separate truths and values from both parasitic public relations gimmickry and the scent of power. This resistant mind often wears itself out or falls into a habit of stylish ironical dispute and self-conscious enthusiasms felt *in spite of* their being fashionable or *because* they are currently unfashionable. It is evident how this sort of attitude (which brought us kitsch) can very easily flip over into being the trendiest mind of all.

The fashionizing of intellect hurts the society in more ways than by depriving it of the unfashionized intellect's clarifying and constructive influence: the society actually learns to pattern itself on fashion. It has come to be acceptable that the Western democracies should give supreme political power not to the candidates with the most honesty, ability, or character but to those with the most skill at manipulating images and convincing voters that an imitation world—based on power, and self-contained, self-interested, and self-deceiving—is the same world as the voters' own. The rules of politics are rules of fashion. Political minds, like fashionable minds, rarely look hard at themselves or at the real world.

Instead, isolated by vanity and celebrity, they search for the latest fashion in issues and slogans, hoping to latch onto it in time to turn it to their own advantage. Like fashion, politics is learning to *look* less superficial: the "in" thing that all politicians yearn for is no longer the image of "charisma" or "pragmatism" but the image of "leadership" and "integrity."

The arts are in danger of being submerged by fashion, and are increasingly subject to critical definition—their cue for self-confidence—based on frivolously determined opinions of whether this branch or that is "in" or "out." Fashionable critics endow with the magical "vitality" now representational art, now the avant-garde theatre, now dance; and then, sooner or later, withdraw their accolade with a yawn and leave talent, which had its head turned by the praise and money that gushed over it in good times, bewildered and excluded in unmerited bad times. The greatest disservice that fashion does is carelessly to turn life's most precious and fragile assets into marketable products of transient worth. If a great, dark locust cloud of fashion settles upon our world, upon our dream of quality, upon our humble individualities, we must fear that its passing will leave behind a ravaged field of empty gestures. While the rush is on, fashion is good for business, but it is hardly beneficial to society, talent, or the mind. And in the long run fashion may prove very bad for life.

PART II

Cultural Politics

The Appearance of AIDS
(1981/1982)

Three news articles in the *New York Times*, appearing between July 1981 and August 1982, chronicled the emerging horror of a new cancer and lethal disease, at first unnamed, that would kill nearly 80,000 people—mainly homosexual men—before 1990. By 1997, another 150,000 people in the United States had died of AIDS, and outbreaks of other fatal viral afflictions had raised profound questions about public health policy.

Rare Cancer Seen in 41 Homosexuals

Lawrence K. Altman (July 3, 1981)

Doctors in New York and California have diagnosed among homosexual men 41 cases of a rare and often rapidly fatal form of cancer. Eight of the victims died less than 24 months after the diagnosis was made.

The cause of the outbreak is unknown, and there is as yet no evidence of contagion. But the doctors who have made the diagnoses, mostly in New York City and the San Francisco Bay area, are alerting other physicians who treat large numbers of homosexual men to the problem in an effort to help identify more cases and to reduce the delay in offering chemotherapy treatment.

The sudden appearance of the cancer, called Kaposi's sarcoma, has prompted a medical investigation that experts say could have as much scientific as public health importance because of what it may teach about determining the causes of more common types of cancer.

Doctors have been taught in the past that the cancer usually appeared first in spots on the legs and that the disease took a slow course of up to 10 years. But these recent cases have shown that it appears in one or more violet-colored spots anywhere on the body. The spots generally do not itch or cause other symptoms, often can be mistaken for bruises, sometimes appear as lumps and can turn brown after a period of time.

The cancer often causes swollen lymph glands, and then kills by spreading throughout the body.

Doctors investigating the outbreak believe that many cases have gone undetected because of the rarity of the condition and the difficulty even dermatologists may have in diagnosing it.

In a letter alerting other physicians to the problem, Dr. Alvin E. Friedman-Kien of New York University Medical Center, one of the investigators, described the appearance of the outbreak as "rather devastating." Dr. Friedman-Kien said in an interview yesterday that he knew of 41 cases collated in the last five weeks, with the cases themselves dating to the past 30 months. The Federal Centers for Disease Control in Atlanta is expected to publish the first description of the outbreak in its weekly report today, according to a spokesman, Dr. James Curran. The report notes 26 of the cases—20 in New York and six in California.

There is no national registry of cancer victims, but the nationwide incidence of Kaposi's sarcoma in the past had been estimated by the Centers for Disease Control to be less than six-one-hundredths of a case per 100,000 people annually, or about two cases in every three million people. However, the disease accounts for up to 9 percent of all cancers in a belt across equatorial Africa, where it commonly affects children and young adults.

In the United States, it has primarily affected men older than 50 years. But in the recent cases, doctors at nine medical centers in New York and seven hospitals in California have been diagnosing the condition among younger men, all of whom said in the course of standard diagnostic interviews that they were homosexual. Although the ages of the patients have ranged from 26 to 51 years, many have been under 40, with the mean at 39.

Nine of the 41 cases known to Dr. Friedman-Kien were diagnosed in California, and several of those victims reported that they had been in New York in the period preceding the diagnosis. Dr. Friedman-Kien said that his colleagues were checking on reports of two victims diagnosed in Copenhagen, one of whom had visited New York.

No one medical investigator has yet interviewed all the victims, Dr. Curran said. According to Dr. Friedman-Kien, the reporting doctors said that most cases had involved homosexual men who have had multiple and frequent sexual encounters with different partners, as many as 10 sexual encounters each night up to four times a week.

Many of the patients have also been treated for viral infections such as herpes, cytomegalovirus and hepatitis B as well as parasitic infections such as amebiasis and giardiasis. Many patients also reported that they had used drugs such as amyl nitrite and LSD to heighten sexual pleasure.

Cancer is not believed to be contagious, but conditions that might precipitate it, such as particular viruses or environmental factors, might account for an outbreak among a single group. The medical investigators say some indirect evidence actually points away from contagion as a cause. None of the patients knew each other, although the theoretical possibility that some may have had sexual contact with a person with Kaposi's sarcoma at some point in the past could not be excluded, Dr. Friedman-Kien said. Dr. Curran said there was no apparent danger to nonhomosexuals from contagion. "The best evidence against contagion," he said, "is that no cases have been reported to date outside the homosexual community or in women."

Dr. Friedman-Kien said he had tested nine of the victims and found severe defects in their immunological systems. The patients had serious malfunctions of two types of cells called T and B cell lymphocytes, which have important roles in fighting infections and cancer. But Dr. Friedman-Kien emphasized that the researchers did not know whether the immunological defects were the underlying problem or had developed secondarily in the infections or drug use.

The research team is testing various hypotheses, one of which is a possible link between past infection with cytomegalovirus and development of Kaposi's sarcoma.

New Homosexual Disorder Worries Health Officials

Lawrence K. Altman (May 11, 1982)

A serious disorder of the immune system that has been known to doctors for less than a year—a disorder that appears to affect primarily male homosexuals—has now afflicted at least 335 people, of whom it has killed 136, officials of the Centers for Disease Control in Atlanta said yesterday. Federal health officials are concerned that tens of thousands more homosexual men may be silently affected and therefore vulnerable to potentially grave ailments.

Moreover, this immune system breakdown, which has been implicated in a rare type of cancer, called Kaposi's sarcoma, and seems to invite in its wake a wide variety of serious infections and other disorders, has developed among some heterosexual women and bisexual and heterosexual men.

At a recent Congressional hearing, Dr. Bruce A. Chabner of the National Cancer Institute said that the growing problem was now "of concern to all Americans."

The cause of the disorder is unknown. Researchers call it A.I.D., for acquired immuno-deficiency disease, or GRID, for gay-related immunodeficiency. It has been reported in 20 states and seven countries. But the overwhelming majority of cases have been in New York City (158), elsewhere in New York State (10), New Jersey (14) and California (71).

Thirteen of those affected have been heterosexual women. Some male victims are believed to have been heterosexual, and to have been chiefly users of heroin and other drugs by injection into their veins. But most cases have occurred among homosexual men, in particular those who have had numerous sexual partners, often anonymous partners whose identity remain unknown.

According to both the Centers for Disease Control and the National Cancer Institute in Bethesda, Md., GRID has reached epidemic proportions and the current totals probably represent "just the tip of the iceberg." Preliminary results of immunological tests have led some Federal health officials to fear that tens of thousands of homosexual men may have the acquired immune dysfunction and be at risk for developing complications such as Kaposi's cancer, infections and other disorders at some future date.

GRID is "a matter of urgent public heath and scientific importance," Dr. James W. Curran, a Federal epidemiologist who coordinates the Kaposi's sarcoma and opportunistic infections, told the Congressional hearing. Opportunistic infections are those that rarely cause illness except in those whose immunological resistance has been lowered by drugs or disease.

More than human suffering is involved. Hospital costs have reached more than $64,000 per patient, and Dr. Curran said that if such costs are typical, "the first 300 cases account for an estimated $18 million in hospital expenses alone."

Experts currently think of GRID as a sort of immunological time bomb. Once it develops, it may stay silent for an unknown period, and then, at a later date, go on to produce Kaposi's sarcoma, an opportunistic infection, a so-called auto-immune disorder, or any combination of these.

Further, no one is certain that the immune disorder can be reversed. Many patients have survived a bout of pneumonia or other illness, only to succumb to another or to go on to develop Kaposi's sarcoma or some other fatal cancer.

GRID resembles the failures of the immunological system that complicate the treatment of many chronic disorders with steroid and other drugs that suppress the immune system. The same problem occurs among recipients of transplanted kidneys and other organs who take the immunosuppressive drugs to help prevent rejection of the organ. With immunity suppressed, the body becomes vulnerable to a variety of problems, chiefly infections by organisms that otherwise rarely cause disease.

GRID, however, is the first naturally occurring outbreak of immune suppression to affect a community of free-living people, in contrast, for example, to an epidemic in a hospital. The degree of immunological suppression is extraordinary, far greater than usually observed in patients treated with immunosuppressive drugs, according to articles in medical journals and interviews with experts.

Those experts are now reporting finding a wider range of disorders than were associated with GRID when it first came to public attention last summer. These include eye damage, lupus, I.T.P. (idiopathic thrombocytopenic purpura), certain types of anemia, and other cancers, including Burkitt's lymphoma and cancers of the tongue and anus. Doctors are also seeing many cases of generalized lymph gland swelling throughout the body, together with weight loss, fever and thrush, a fungal infection often found in the mouth and throat.

So far, epidemiologists have found no evidence that the condition is spread from person to person like influenza or measles. Therefore, they say, the general public need not fear an epidemic. Rather, Dr. Arthur S. Levine of the National Cancer Institute said, development of the syndrome seems to result from an accumulation of risk factors. Most experts say that if there is an infectious cause, it is not a single organism, but an organism acting together with another factor or factors, perhaps a drug.

Epidemiologists from the Centers for Disease Control have done studies among homosexual men with and without the immune disorder but matched in age, background and other characteristics. After testing for more than 130 potential risk factors, they found that the median number of lifetime male sexual partners for affected homosexual men was 1,160 compared to 524 for male homosexual men who did not have the syndrome. The study also found more use of sexual stimulants and illicit drugs among the GRID patients.

As further evidence against simple contagious spread, epidemiologists note that the syndrome has not spread to other family members, hospital workers, or researchers on the disease.

Kaposi's sarcoma was first described in 1872 in Rumania. Until recently, it was rare in the United States, occurring chiefly in older people, usually of Italian or Jewish ancestry, and among patients receiving immunosuppressive therapy. It affected men much more commonly than women by about 15 to one. It usually developed slowly.

In recent decades, however, Kaposi's sarcoma has been found common in Africa, mainly among young people. In equatorial Africa, it accounts for 9 percent of all cancers, and in some areas it is 100 times more prevalent than in the United States. The cancer has not been linked to homosexuals in Africa, and the reasons for its high frequency there are unknown.

In its new form in this country, the course of Kaposi's sarcoma generally has been rapid and fatal. Only about 15 percent of patients treated with a combination of anticancer drugs experience any remission, as compared to the 90 percent complete response in Africa, according to Dr. Levine.

However, it is not just the cancer that is killing GRID patients. Many such patients develop infections with an often fatal parasitic illness called Pneumocystis carinii. Hitherto, that disease has been seen mainly as a complication of treatment of patients with leukemia and other cancers because their immune systems were depressed by chemotherapy.

Others succumb to cytomegalovirus infection or to a fungal infection called toxoplasmosis. By using sophisticated molecular biology tests in which the genetic messages of the various strains can be compared, scientists have found no evidence that the epidemic is due to a deadly new mutant strain.

But the list of infections diagnosed among GRID patients is long, and some of the organisms are so unusual that even the most experienced infectious disease experts have not treated a case in the past. The newest is cryptosporidiosis, a parasitic infection much more familiar to veterinarians than to physicians because it infects deer and other mammals.

Given the fact that homosexuality is not new, the most puzzling question is why the outbreak is occurring now, and not sometime in the past. Scientific investigations are wide ranging, although most are focused on viruses, other organisms, drugs, or a combination of such factors.

Because homosexuals affected by GRID have reported using nitrite drugs more frequently than homosexuals who have not, some studies have focused on this class of drugs, which have come into widespread street use since the 1960s. But although the epidemiological studies have not "totally exonerated nitrites, the scientific evidence to implicate them is quite shaky," according to Dr. Curran.

Some experts theorize that the immunological disorder may be triggered by the introduction of sperm or seminal fluid into the blood through sexual contact, though infection and drug reaction are still also candidates.

In studies on mice at the National Cancer Institute, Dr. Ursula Hurtenbach and Dr. Gene M. Shearer have reported that a single injection of mouse sperm into the veins of male mice produced a profound and long-lasting suppression of certain immune functions. Dr. Lawrence D. Mass, a New York City physician, said that "gay people whose life style consists of anonymous sexual encounters are going to have to do some serious rethinking."

The urgent need to discover the cause of the immune system disorder and to prevent the problems it creates has been underscored by Dr. Linda Laubenstein of New York University Medical Center. Dr. Laubenstein, who said she has treated 62 such patients in the last year and who is a leading investigator of the syndrome, summarized it by saying: "This problem certainly is not going away."

※

A Disease's Spread Provokes Anxiety

Robin Herman (August 8, 1982)

The persistence of a serious disease whose victims are primarily homosexual men has touched off anxiety among homosexuals in New York City, where nearly half of the nation's cases have been reported.

Doctors treating homosexuals say they are being flooded with telephone calls from old and new patients with minor complaints. Clinics offering testing for the disease are oversubscribed. And homosexual men speak of great confusion over how to adjust their health habits to avoid the disease, which remains largely mysterious in its symptoms and causes.

The disease—called acquired immune deficiency syndrome, or A.I.D.S.—produces a suppression of the body's natural defenses and sets the stage for the intrusion of several deadly afflictions, including a rare form of cancer called Kaposi's sarcoma and a rare pneumonia. The Centers for Disease Control in Atlanta have recorded 505 cases of the syndrome coupled with the cancer, pneumonia or other opportunistic infections since the national facility began gathering data on cases in June of last year. Of those people, 202 have died, or 40 percent. The cases include 243 residents of New York City.

Reports of the disease have not abated. About two new cases a day are recorded at the disease control center. Officials there attribute the increase both to improved reporting and to a real rise in cases. The disease has already killed more people than reported cases of toxic shock syndrome and the original outbreak of Legionnaire's disease, and it has engendered as much fear.

Dr. David J. Sencer, New York City's Health Commissioner, has termed the immune deficiency syndrome "a major health problem." He emphasized that groups other than homosexual men were involved. Groups afflicted with the syndrome include more than 60 heterosexual men and women who were drug abusers and used intravenous needles: 30 male and female immigrants from Haiti, all heterosexual, and some hemophiliacs who use blood products to combat their illness.

Doctors theorize that the disease is an infectious agent transmitted in a complex way through sexual contact or through the blood. Yet in many cases one person in a longtime sexual relationship will get the syndrome, while the partner will not.

The disease has been recorded in 27 states; New York State's 259 cases is the largest concentration.

The Centers for Disease Control, several of New York City's medical centers and the city's Health Department have been working intensely to find the syndrome's cause. Meanwhile, informational groups have sprung up among homosexuals, such as the Gay Men's Health Crisis group, which has published an exhaustive pamphlet on the syndrome and runs a 24-hour hot line. The National Gay Task Force is coordinating a conference on the disease, and publications for homosexuals, including *The Advocate, Christopher Street* and *New York Native*, have been printing extensive articles about it.

"It's basically frightening because no one knows what's causing it," said John Kolman, a 28-year-old law student who went to the St. Mark's Clinic in Greenwich Village last week complaining of persistent swollen glands, thought to be one early symptom of the disease. "Every week a new theory comes out about how you're going to spread it."

Physicians say they are seeing panic-stricken patients who display skin lesions that turn out to be bug bites, poison ivy, black and blue marks or freckles of no medical consequence. One major symptom of Kaposi's sarcoma is purplish or discolored nodules or lumps on top of or beneath the skin.

"There's tremendous anxiety and it translates into panic behavior," said Dr. Roger W. Enlow, a clinical researcher at the Hospital for Joint Diseases, Beth Israel Medical Center, who helps run the all-volunteer St. Mark's Clinic.

Dr. Sencer, the Health Commissioner, said: "It's unfortunate we don't have anything positive to recommend to people at the present time. We just don't know." But he said the limiting of sexual partners was "probably good general advice" because of the number of other sexually transmissible diseases, including venereal diseases such as herpes, parasitic diseases and hepatitis.

Leaders of homosexual groups, including the National Gay Task Force, and several doctors emphasized that the immune deficiency syndrome does not result from being homosexual but rather seems to have settled on this particular group among others.

They said that no homosexual women were known to have the syndrome and that homosexual men have as many different life styles as heterosexual men. Only a segment of them, they said, are the "sexually active" men whom doctors identify as being most at risk of getting the syndrome because of their exposure to more partners.

Dr. James W. Curran, head of the A.I.D.S. project at the Centers for Disease Control, said the concern among homosexuals about the disease was "not ill-founded" because of its severity and the uncertainty about it. "The other concern," he added, "is there are many other groups that seem to be affected with similar illnesses, and the homosexual community does not want to be blamed for this problem."

From

Hunger of Memory

(1982)

Richard Rodriguez

In his autobiography about growing up a Mexican American in midcentury
California, Rodriguez considered the personal cost of social assimilation. In this
passage Rodriguez described his uneasy move forward in academic life during
the seventies, increasingly complicated by the imperatives of affirmative action
and group identity. He did not choose to ride the wave of ethnic consciousness
or to play the role of aggrieved *Chicano.* As a result, Rodriguez faced a unique
kind of isolation.

Officially the academy never lost its enthusiasm for affirmative
action during the years I was a student. But in the early 1970s I
remember hearing professors quietly admit their alarm over various aspects of what was then called the Third World Student Movement.

Faculty members were understandably troubled, though most
seemed unwilling to make their concern public. As more and more nonwhite students arrived on campus, less well prepared, many of them chose
to believe that they were, in some cultural sense, minorities. They imagined themselves belonging to two very different societies. What campus
officials had implied about them—through the policy of affirmative
action—the students came to believe, seizing upon the idea of belonging at
once to academia and to the society of the disadvantaged. Modern-day
scholar-workers, indulging in clownish display, adopted ghetto accents and
assumed costumes of the rural poor. The students insisted they still were
tied to the culture of their past. Nothing in their lives had changed with
their matriculation. They would be able to "go home again." They were certain, as well, that their enrollment implied a general social advance for
many others of their race off campus. (The scholar remained united with
his people.)

For some students perhaps these ideas provided a way of accepting benefits suddenly theirs, accruing simply to race. For others these ideas may have served as a way of accommodating themselves to the life of a campus so culturally foreign. Especially in the early years of the Movement, one often heard nonwhite students complain of feeling lost on the campus. There were demands for separate dormitory facilities, clubhouses, separate cafeteria tables, even for soul-food menus. And in the classroom: "We can't relate to any of this."

Nonwhite activists began to complain that college and university courses took little account of the lives of nonwhite Americans. Their complaint was well founded. And it implied a startling critique of the academy's tendency toward parochialism. Ultimately, it led to the establishment of ethnic studies departments where courses were offered in such fields as nineteenth-century black history and Hispanic-American folk art. The activists made a peculiar claim for these classes. They insisted that the courses would alleviate the cultural anxiety of nonwhite students by permitting them to stay in touch with their home culture.

The perspective gained in the classroom or the library does indeed permit an academic to draw nearer to and understand better the culture of the alien poor. But the academic is brought closer to lower-class culture because of his very distance from it. Leisured, and skilled at abstracting from immediate experience, the scholar is able to see how aspects of individual experience constitute a culture. By contrast, the poor have neither the inclination nor the skill to imagine their lives so abstractly. They remain strangers to the way of life the academic constructs so well on paper.

Ethnic studies departments were founded on romantic hopes. And with the new departments were often instituted "community action" programs. Students were given course credit for work done in working-class neighborhoods. Too often, however, activists encouraged students to believe that they were in league with the poor when, in actuality, any academic who works with the socially disadvantaged is able to be of benefit to them only because he is culturally different from them.

When, for example, Mexican-American students began to proclaim themselves Chicanos, they taught many persons in the barrios of southwestern America to imagine themselves in a new context. *Chicano*, the Spanish word, was a term lower-class Mexican-Americans had long used to name themselves. It was a private word, slangish, even affectionately vulgar, and, when spoken by a stranger, insulting, because it glibly assumed familiarity. Many Mexican-Americans were consequently shocked when they heard the student activist proclaim himself and his listeners

Chicanos. What initially they did not understand was that the English word—which meant literally the same thing (Mexican-American)—was a public word, animated by pride and political purpose, "¡*somos* Chicanos!" the student activist proclaimed, his voice enlarged through a microphone. He thereby taught his listeners to imagine their union with many others like themselves. But the student easily coined the new word because of his very distance from *Chicano* culture.

Let the reader beware at this point: I am not the best person to evaluate the Third World Student Movement. My relationship to many of the self-proclaimed Chicano students was not an easy one. I felt threatened by them. I was made nervous by their insistence that they still were allied to their parents' culture. Walking on campus one day with my mother and father, I relished the surprised look on their faces when they saw some Hispanic students wearing serapes pass by. I needed to laugh at the clownish display. I needed to tell myself that the new minority students were foolish to think themselves unchanged by their schooling. (I needed to justify my own change.)

I never worked in the barrio. I gave myself all the reasons people ever give to explain why they do not work among the disadvantaged. I envied those minority students who graduated to work among lower-class Hispanics at barrio clinics or legal aid centers. I envied them their fluent Spanish. (I had taken Spanish in high school with *gringos*.) But it annoyed me to hear students on campus loudly talking in Spanish or thickening their surnames with rich baroque accents because I distrusted the implied assertion that their tongue proved their bond to the past, to the poor. I spoke in English. I was invited to Chicano student meetings and social events sponsored by *La Raza*. But I never went. I kept my distance. I was a scholarship boy who belonged to an earlier time. I had come to the campus singly; they had come in a group. (It was in the plural that they often referred to themselves—as minority students.) I had been submissive, willing to mimic my teachers, willing to re-form myself in order to become "educated." They were proud, claiming that they didn't need to change by becoming students. I had long before accepted the fact that education exacted a great price for its equally great benefits. They denied that price—any loss.

I was glad to get away from those students when I was awarded a Fulbright Fellowship to study in London. I found myself in the British Museum, at first content, reading English Renaissance literature. But then came the crisis: the domed silence; the dusty pages of books all around me; the days accumulating in lists of obsequious footnotes; the wandering doubts about the value of scholarship. My year in Britain came to an end and I rushed to "come home." Then quickly discovered that I could not. Could not cast off the culture I had assumed. Living with my parents for the summer, I remained an academic—a kind of anthropologist in the family kitchen, searching for evidence of our "cultural ties" as we ate dinner together.

In late summer, I decided to finish my dissertation and to accept a one-year teaching assignment at Berkeley. (It was, after all, where I belonged.)

What I learned from my year at the British Museum and from my summer at home, other academics have learned; others have known the impossibility of going home, going back. Going back to Berkeley, however, I returned to a campus where I was still officially designated a minority—still considered by university officials to be in touch with my native culture. And there were minority students to face.

In my department that year there were five black graduate students. We were the only nonwhite students in a department of nearly three hundred. Initially, I was shy of the black students—afraid of what they'd discover about me. But in seminars they would come and sit by me. They trusted the alliance of color. In soft voices—not wanting to be overheard by the white students around us—they spoke to me. And I felt rewarded by their confidences.

But then one afternoon a group of eight or ten Hispanic students came to my office. They wanted me to teach a "minority literature" course at some barrio community center on Saturday mornings. They were certain that this new literature had an important role to play in helping to shape the consciousness of a people lacking adequate literary representation. I listened warily, found myself moved by their radiant youth. When I began to respond I felt aged by caution and skepticism: . . . that I really didn't agree with them. I didn't think that there *was* such a thing as minority literature. Any novel or play about the lower class will necessarily be alien to the culture it portrays. I rambled: . . . the relationship of the novel to the rise of the middle class in eighteenth-century Europe. Then, changing the subject to Alex Haley's *Roots*: That book tells us more about his difference from his illiterate, tribal ancestors than it does about his link to them. More quickly: The child who learns to read about his nonliterate ancestors necessarily separates himself from their way of life. I saw one of my listeners yawn. Another sort of smiled. My voice climbed to hold their attention. I wanted approval; I was afraid of their scorn. But scorn came inevitably. Someone got up while someone else thanked me for my "valuable time." The others filed out of the room; their voices turned loud when they got out in the hall. Receded. Left me alone at my desk.

After that I was regarded as comic. I became a "coconut"—someone brown on the outside, white on the inside. I was the bleached academic—more white than the *anglo* professors. In my classes several students glared at me, clearly seeing in me the person they feared ever becoming. Who was I, after all, but some comic Queequeg, holding close to my breast a reliquary containing the white powder of a dead European civilization? One woman took to calling me, with exaggerated precision, *Miss-ter Road-ree-gas,* her voice hissing scorn. (The students sitting around her seemed unaware of her message.)

Still, during those months, Berkeley faculty members continued to assure me that—they were certain—I would be able to work as a special counselor to minority students. The truth was that I was a successful teacher of white middle-class students. They were the ones who lined up outside my door during office hours, the ones who called me at night. Still, I continued to receive invitations to conferences to discuss the problems of the disadvantaged. Envelopes found their way to my apartment addressed to *Señor* Ricardo Rodriguez. I heard myself introduced at conferences as a "Chicano intellectual." (And I stood up.)

From
Crime and American Culture
(1983)

James Q. Wilson

Savage behavior and rapidly rising violent crime frightened a large share of the American public by the early 1980s. Wilson, a prominent sociologist, compared philosophies and views of human nature underlying policy disputes over what to do about it. Wilson concluded that rising personal freedom and the loss of informal social controls in contemporary society comprised a crisis of law—and possibly constituted a threat to the liberal ideal itself.

The two opposing theories of human nature that underlie American attitudes toward crime also underlie our political arrangements. Our Constitution was written with an eye to the view of man found in Locke and Hobbes. We are all familiar with those phrases of Publius (chiefly, of James Madison) found in the *Federalist* that explained how our political arrangements were intended to use the calculating and self-seeking nature of man to protect liberty. "Ambition must be made to counteract ambition," Madison wrote, because men are not angels. Factions are inevitable, because the "latent causes of faction are . . . sown in the nature of man." To control the effects of factions and of human ambition, the Founders not only separated the powers of government but gave "to those who administer each department the necessary constitutional means and personal motives to resist encroachments of the others." It was, Madison said, a "policy of supplying, by opposite and rival interests, the defect [i.e., the lack] of better motives." Madison's view of human nature was not wholly Hobbesian; it was, as the late Martin Diamond put it, not a pessimistic view so much as a sober one. "As there is a certain degree of depravity in mankind which requires a certain degree of circumspection and distrust," Madison wrote, "so there are other qualities in human nature which justify a certain portion of esteem and confidence." But—

and this is the crucial point—it was not to be the business of the federal government to create or sustain these "other qualities"; rather, the new government "presupposes the existence" of them.

George Will, in his recent Godkin Lectures at Harvard, has argued that, from a conservative point of view, this presupposition that man is good enough to make free government work is an error. The government, in his phrase, is "ill-founded." No free government can exist unless it exercises some responsibility for the cultivation of virtue among its citizens. If it merely presupposes the existence of these virtues and confines itself to managing arrangements designed to harness self-interest to serve public purposes, it will in time discover that the government, and the society, are no longer capable of serving anything *but* self-interest. Will's view was anticipated by critics of Madison at the time.

The Antifederalists, as we know, chiefly opposed the new Constitution because it claimed to do what they believed was impossible—reconcile the national government of a large republic with the protection of liberty. It was in the small community that men could truly be free. The late Herbert Storing summarized the Antifederalist commitment to the small republic as involving three arguments: Only a small republic could enjoy voluntary obedience to the laws, secure the genuine accountability of the government to the people, and "form the kind of citizens who will maintain republican government." The critics of the new Constitution were not in any obvious sense the descendants of either Jonathan Edwards or Rousseau; like the authors of the Constitution, they chiefly valued liberty. The central difference between the two groups appears to have been a dispute over the means to achieve this goal. The Antifederalists believed that liberty would only be secure if society deliberately promoted civic virtue and the subordination of individual interests to the commonwealth, and this promotion could only occur safely in small republics.

A small republic—or a small community—could only promote civic virtue if its population was relatively homogenous, culturally, ethnically, and economically. The Swiss cantons were an oft-cited model. The new national government—with its capital city, its standing army, its openness to intercourse with foreign nations and foreign habits, and its inclination to aristocratic manners and European luxury—would be the antithesis of civic virtue. In particular, the Antifederalists noted the non-religious, perhaps even anti-religious character of the new Constitution. They were quite aware that many of the emerging national leaders (Madison, Jefferson, Franklin) were children of the Enlightenment who believed, at best, in a vague deism that looked for guidance to the orderly patterns of nature, rather than to the strict commands of God. Madison and Jefferson went much further than almost any other national figures in attempting to separate church and state. In the former's *Memorial and Remonstrance* and the latter's *Notes on the State of Virginia*, they argued not only against coercion of religious beliefs, but also against any state support of churches—against, that is, making religion an "engine of Civil policy." Though the Supreme Court has largely adopted the Madisonian view of church-state relations, that is probably not what most persons at the time believed (and certainly not what the authors of the First Amendment thought they were enacting). The Antifederalists, to be sure, favored freedom of conscience, but expected that government would foster religion, support it, and make passing a religious test a qualification for office. Religion *ought* to be an "engine of Civil policy," though in a nation as diverse as America it could only be so at the local level.

My argument thus far, stripped of important qualifications, is that we grafted a Lockean (and in part, Hobbesian) national government onto a communal life that was explained and defended in the language of Rousseau, and we did so over the objections of many who thought the engrafted national limb would destroy the sturdy communal trunk. The graft was successful in large measure because the defenders of small communal republics could think of no practical alternative (given the need for national defense and orderly commerce), and because the defenders of the Constitution assumed that the center of our collective lives would remain in communities which would nurture the civic virtues on which the national order depended.

Their assumption was not an unreasonable one. The national government, after all, had limited powers and modest responsibilities; the governance of the nation would remain chiefly the duty of towns, cities, and states. If governance required the formation of character by education, religion, or the force of communal opinion, then all this would be done (to the extent it could be done) by the many small republics of which the new nation would be composed.

The events of the Jacksonian era were to reveal the error of that assumption. The small republics became teeming cities in which young men freed of adult supervision became rowdy libertines. Andrew Jackson himself was worried about the moral health of the nation over which he was elected to preside. As Marvin Meyers has argued, his appeal to "the people" was not merely an appeal against the "money power" of the banks and corporations; it was more profoundly an appeal for the restoration of civic virtue that he thought was exemplified in the industrious and economical lives of planters, farmers, and laborers. That virtue consisted of self-reliance and simplicity. The country, he felt, was in a moral crisis.

The response to that crisis, as we have seen, was also cast in moral and communal terms. If the cities and the factories were a new challenge, redoubled efforts would be made to meet that challenge. For the better part of a century, the struggle was waged. It had its ups and downs. Wars and panics interrupted and even, for a while, reversed it; it was aided to a degree by a slow rise in the average age of the population. But not until this century was the effort *formally abandoned*.

ঌ

Today, and for the last few decades, enlightened people scoff at moral uplift, reject temperance as an effort of bluenoses, and are skeptical (with good reason) about the prospects of using prisons (or much of anything else) for rehabilitating offenders. Having replaced the Victorian commitment to controlling impulses with the modern commitment to individual choice, both liberal and conservative students of crime have turned their attention to finding better ways of manipulating the incentives facing individuals who might choose crime. The chief difference of opinion among these thinkers is whether it is better to manipulate the costs of crime (by stressing the deterrent or incapacitative effects of criminal sanctions) or the benefits of non-crime (by stressing the need for better employment and income-maintenance opportunities).

Advocates of manipulating costs are usually regarded as "tough-minded" while advocates of manipulating benefits are often thought to be "tender-minded"; in fact, there is no important philosophical difference between them (though they imagine there is). Both assume that the would-be offender is reasonably rational and generally self-interested, and that he chooses between crime and lawfulness on the basis of the opportunities each offers to satisfy his needs. Indeed, if the model of human nature each school embraces is correct, then it follows that a sound public policy would try to alter *both* costs and benefits. Of course, the tough-minded may believe that it is the attractiveness of crime that leads people to prefer it even to available jobs, whereas the tender-minded may think that it is the unavailability of jobs that "forces" people into crime regardless of its costs. These differences have important political implications but only modest scientific or philosophical ones. The tough-minded stress getting tough and the tender-minded stress doing good, but all they are arguing about is the relative efficiency of sanctions and their alternatives (which is only a matter of more or less); they embrace the same theory of human nature.

The older debate about crime involved very different assumptions about human nature. Both liberals and conservatives (those terms, of course, were not in use at the time) agreed that crime was the result of failure in the moral development of men, in particular the failure of some men to learn how to control their impulses. "Conservatives" thought that human nature was fundamentally evil and that the family and church must work hard to overcome, by rigorous discipline, these base impulses; "liberals" thought human nature was at worst neutral and perhaps good and the task of the family and church was to guide those benign impulses into a "Christian character."

The current ascendancy of the rational-choice view of human nature—the view first sketched by Hobbes and then elaborated by Bentham—is in part the result of the disappointment of those who sought dependable evidence that criminals could be rehabilitated by plan, in large numbers, and at reasonable cost. But science alone rarely shapes our conceptions of human psychology; there were cultural and political reasons as well for the declining acceptability of the communal approach to crime. That view seemed, to many of its adherents, to require an intrusion into personal lives that was quite out of keeping with personal liberation and radical individualism.

The demise of Victorian morality, the inability of the state to recreate that morality, and the growth in personal freedom and social prosperity, have combined to produce an individualistic ethos that both encourages crime and shapes the kind of policies we are prepared to use to combat it. A liberal, commercial society committed to personal self-expression thus discovers that it must rely more, not less, on the criminal justice system and on efforts to manage the labor market. Since 1960 we have invested heavily in trying to improve the criminal justice system and solve the problem of young adult unemployment. Partisans of one strategy or another argue about which tactic has received or should receive the greater emphasis, but in the long view this is little more than a policy quibble.

The factors that most directly influence crime—family structure, moral development, the level of personal freedom are the very things that we cannot easily change or, for persuasive reasons, do not wish to change. The factors that we can change (though perhaps not as much as we wish) are the factors that have only a marginal influence on crime—laws, police and prosecutorial strategies, and government-created job programs. It is possible that very large changes in these formal institutions would make a larger difference, but we are reluctant to risk having a more oppressive police or a more meddlesome state. Besides, we are constrained by a sense of justice: When many are unemployed, it seems unfair to give criminals or would-be criminals priority access to jobs.

Societies that are not free need not rely heavily on the police apparatus to control crime, for, if they manage their unfreedom skillfully, they can use schools, neighborhoods, communes, political parties, and mutual spying to control behavior. Societies that are free need to rely more heavily on the police apparatus and economic management because they have foresworn the use of other methods. Law becomes more important as informal social control becomes less important.

The people are impatient with so bleak a choice, and have, by their actions, indicated their continuing attachment to a more communal form of crime control. Hundreds, probably thousands, of neighborhood organizations and civic enterprises have arisen spontaneously out of a desire to reduce crime by direct popular action. It is a measure of our times that these efforts are often resisted by the police as an intrusion into their official domain, and criticized by the intelligentsia as giving expression to the vigilante spirit. In truth, this recourse to informal, communal action is nothing more than a reaffirmed allegiance to a communal theory of social control, and a repetition of a manner of exercising that control noted by Tocqueville when he visited this country (at a time when crime was beginning to become a problem). He wrote:

> In America the means that the authorities have at their disposal for the discovery of crimes and the arrest of criminals are few. A state police does not exist, and passports are unknown. The criminal police of the United States cannot be compared with that of France; the magistrates and public agents are not numerous; they do not always initiate the measures for arresting the guilty; and the examinations of prisoners are rapid and oral. Yet I believe that in no country does crime more rarely elude punishment. The reason is that everyone conceives himself to be interested in furnishing evidence of the crime and in seizing the delinquent. During my stay in the United States I witnessed the spontaneous formation of committees in a country for the pursuit and prosecution of a man who had committed a great crime. In Europe a criminal is an unhappy man who is struggling for his life, against the agents of power, while the people are merely a spectator of the conflict; in America he is looked upon as an enemy of the human race, and the whole of mankind is against him.

Today, the dominant ethos does not easily support such methods or such views. We have become a nation that takes democracy to mean maximum self-expression (though it never meant that originally), and to be suspicious of any effort to state or enforce a common morality. Democracy has become an end, though it originally was embraced as a means to other ends—a way (to quote the Constitution) of forming a more perfect union, establishing justice, insuring domestic tranquility, providing for the common defense, promoting the general welfare, and securing the blessings of liberty. In the hands of reasonable, decent people, a devotion to "self-actualization" is at best artistic or inspiring, and at worst banal or trivial. In the hands of persons of weak character, a taste for risk, and an impatience for gratification, that ethos is a license to steal and mug.

We have made our society and we must live with it. If the philosophy of Hobbes and Bentham governs our explanations of history and our definitions of policy, so be it; no one, least of all fundamentalist ministers, is going to change that. And so we must labor as patiently as we can to make a liberal society work, and to make the best and sanest use of our laws to control behavior without feeling embarrassed that by invoking the law, we are denying our liberal creed. Far from it—we are reaffirming it.

The New Porn Wars
(1984)

Jean Bethke Elshtain

In-your-face pornography that left nothing to the imagination presented profound challenges to decency and to the First Amendment. The progress of
smut from "shameful twilight zones" into everyday life was one more signal of
an increasingly lewd culture and liberalism's inability to deal with social licentiousness. As Elshtain understood, the eruption of porn was not only a
"women's issue." It was a disturbing expression of radical individualism and a
test of faith for civil libertarians.

Pornography has always been with us, but now it seems to be coming
at us. Once the secret vice of upper-class males, porn is now the
public vice of anyone who chooses to share in it. It is a growth
industry ($7 billion a year by most estimates), and clever entrepreneurs
have fulfilled the classic dream of capitalist society by going from the
humblest beginnings to the pinnacle of success—like the fellow who
began to manufacture dildos in his basement fifteen years ago and now
runs a flourishing million-dollar sexual paraphernalia empire. Sexually
explicit books, magazines, and movies have been joined by pornographic
videocassettes, and millions of customers are taking advantage of "aural
sex" phone services. So much for the satiation hypothesis, the once widely
held view that people would grow rapidly "filled" once they had sampled
all the available pornographic consumables, and porn would recede into
some unspecified but limited "proper place." Pornography has been
democratized.

The progress of pornography from shameful twilight zones in major
cities to grocery-store counters in small towns is a story of the spread of
an aesthetics of mechanistic and often cruel sexuality of profit and of vast
social change—some would say disintegration. Its proliferation tells us
how ineffective are the old unwritten rules of internalized constraint:
taboos, shame, scandal. In tossing off those restraints in the name of free-

dom—in ways that were genuinely liberating for many—we seem to have opened the way to a new coarseness and brutalization in our representations of human sexuality. "The Porn Plague," a *Time* magazine story called it in 1976, the metaphor suggesting that pornography had become a natural force akin to an epidemic disease, and that we were unable to inoculate ourselves against it.

Not so, said the mayor of Indianapolis, William Hudnut II. On May 11 Hudnut signed into law an ordinance approved by a vote of 24 to 5 in the city council that made pornography a violation of women's civil rights. "Pornography is central in creating and maintaining sex as a basis for discrimination," the ordinance declares. Other cities, according to a story by E. R. Shipp in *The New York Times*—including Detroit; Wichita, Kansas; and Madison, Wisconsin—are interested in the law.

≫

This new strategy for attacking pornography originated in Minneapolis last December. In the course of debating an ordinary antipornography zoning ordinance, the Minneapolis City Council was persuaded by Catherine MacKinnon, a law professor at the University of Minnesota, and Andrea Dworkin, a radical feminist writer, to consider a more sweeping approach. MacKinnon and Dworkin defined pornography, simply and unequivocally, as a form of violence against women. Reiterating the slogan of the feminist antipornography movement, "pornography is the theory and rape is the practice," they proposed an amendment to the city's civil rights ordinance that would classify pornography as "a form of discrimination on the basis of sex"—hence a violation of the civil rights of women and a denial of equal protection under the law. Their proposal defined pornography as "the sexually explicit subordination of women, graphically depicted, whether in pictures or words," including the portrayal of women "as sexual objects, things, or commodities; . . . who experience pleasure in being raped, or . . . as whores by nature: or . . . in scenarios of degradation, injury, abasement, torture, shown as filthy or inferior, bleeding, bruised, or hurt in a context that makes these conditions sexual."

The council heard dozens of witnesses, many of them women who claimed they had endured sexual violence inspired by pornography. Several legal experts also testified that the proposed ordinance could not survive a court challenge. On December 30 the ordinance passed by a vote of 7 to 6, but Mayor Don Fraser, noting opposition to the measure by the Minnesota Newspaper Association, the Association of American Publishers, and the American Booksellers Association, decided the free speech concerns outweighed all others and he vetoed the bill. Fraser's veto, however, caught Hudnut's attention, and he got in touch with supporters of the Minneapolis ordinance. They helped the Indianapolis District Attorney's office draft the measure that eventually passed.

What has sprung up in these Midwestern cities is a new war on pornography. The *dramatis personae* are familiar enough: angry feminist antipornographers and equally alarmed civil libertarians. But in the background also lurk conservative and religious antipornographers on one side, and pornographers themselves on the other. Troubled liberals and (some) radicals look on, unable to join either the antipornography or the libertarian camp.

The political anomalies of the pornography debate are confounding. It may be true, as a columnist for *The Wall Street Journal* said, that had the Moral Majority written the Minneapolis ordinance, it would "have been laughed out of this liberal town." But it's equally true that Mayor Hudnut, a Republican, and the Indianapolis City Council, controlled by Republicans, lined up behind a proposal conceived by radical feminists. Pornography makes for strange bedfellows.

One thing is clear from the Minneapolis ordinance and its spin-offs: a large segment of the public is demanding new ways to control the pervasiveness and brutality of pornography. The Minneapolis prototype appeals to diverse members of the antiporn constituency, both feminists and conservative "law and order" types. Why?

The Minneapolis statute extended the notion of harm to encompass any situation in which a "woman . . . could claim she had been injured, or coerced." The injury could have—and most often would have—been psychological, a blow to the woman's sense of well-being and mental health. Coercion could have been construed so broadly as to incorporate a woman's claim that the sight of a book cover she deemed pornographic inhibited her from shopping freely in a supermarket where the book is sold. The ordinance combined this dramatic extension of the notion of harm with the proclamation that pornography constitutes a form of sex discrimination. Dworkin, a writer who proclaims that "men love death . . . men especially love murder," argued in an interview that when she goes into a store and sees material she finds subjectively offensive (not necessarily "hard core"), "My rights as a citizen are violated because of those magazines that show me as an abject degraded victim. [They] in fact subordinate me when I am in the supermarket. They change my civil status and make it different from yours because you're a man and I'm a woman." As the injured party, the woman could bring suit under civil law against "a particular person, place, distributor, exhibitor." To the problem of pornography, the ordinance offered a simple answer: sue.

Proponents of the Minneapolis statue insisted that pornography by definition sets up a clash between First Amendment guarantees on the one hand and the equal protection of the law—the Fourteenth Amendment—on the other. In this clash, Dworkin shows scant regard for First Amendment concerns: "I find the civil liberties stance to be bourgeois hypocrisy a lot of the time. We're talking about the oppression of a class of people." The only question raised in the minds of the feminist antipornographers by the First Amendment was: How can we get around it?

Predictably, civil libertarians in both Minnesota and Indiana made an absolute defense of the First Amendment. In Indianapolis, the Indiana Civil Liberties Union, several bookstores, and a cable TV station challenged the law in federal court less than an hour after Mayor Hudnut signed the bill. The battle lines, of course, had been drawn long before. In 1980, Aryeh Neier, executive director of the American Civil Liberties Union, writing in *The Nation,* termed the women's campaign against pornography a feature of "the new censorship," citing the denunciation of First Amendment defenders by Dworkin, Susan Brownmiller, and others. "Let us make certain the new censors are labeled for what they are." Neier concluded, "That is the best way of impairing their ability to attract adherents to their cause."

The Minnesota Civil Liberties Union opposed the MacKinnon-Dworkin proposal, vowing to fight it all the way to the Supreme Court if necessary. So did the liberal *Minneapolis Tribune* (in the name of "free expression, constitutionalism, and common sense") and *The Washington Post,* which termed the ordinance "absolutely batty." By promulgating a definition of pornography so broad it might indict a John Updike novel along with a snuff film, feminist protesters confirmed the civil libertarians' worst fears. To First Amendment absolutists, this latest antiporn crusade reinforces a world view that no doubt comes to them too easily: the belief that *any* attempt to curb or regulate the new, more pervasive, and more violent pornography invites censorship and threatens liberty.

The civil libertarians, of course, say they are defending the principle of people to publish whatever they want. But in saying that the government must never, or only rarely and cautiously, step into the breach, they find themselves tacitly allied with pornographers. Given the pervasiveness and the brutality of pornography, and its growing preference for children as its subjects, the absolutist stand may be increasingly difficult to uphold as cities like Minneapolis and Indianapolis begin to confront the issue.

Similarly, feminist antipornographers now find themselves in a tacit but uncomfortable alliance with right-wing and religious crusaders who also denounce pornography as our worst modern vice. Syndicated columnist Joseph Sobran has railed against films and magazines that degrade women and objectify their bodies (*Dressed to Kill* and *Playboy* were his examples), and thus provide a rationale for "the nut who hates women." His position on the relationship between images, action, and attitudes is identical to that of Women Against Pornography, the feminist antipornography organization which has an office in New York's Times Square. A WAP leader claims that "pornography is a powerful agent of socialization that degrades women and conveys the notion that women are appropriate and deserving targets for sexual violence." "The essence of pornography is the defamation of womanhood," reads a WAP flyer. Sobran and such conservative groups as Morality in Media, Inc., and Citizens for Decency through Law would agree wholeheartedly, even down to the faintly archaic usage of "womanhood defamed."

Feminist antipornographers vehemently deny any mutual interest with conservative campaigners. In their view, the Moral Majority and other conservative groups have the heaviest interest of all in maintaining male dominance. MacKinnon, for example, says that "right-wing men have too much staked on their dominance" to be allies in the struggle against porn. But if, as feminists claim, the explicit intent of pornography is to keep women in a subordinate position by humiliating and degrading them, it is hard to figure out why "right-wing men" wouldn't implicitly or explicitly favor pornography, seeing it as a weapon in their own self-interest. Despite disavowals from both sides, the right-wing and radical feminist efforts do converge. The rationale may differ, but the ends sought—the elimination of pornography as defined by each group—are identical.

This confusion begins in the ambiguities of our most fundamental political principles. Liberalism, as such, is indifferent to the ways of life any individual chooses to pursue—unless his actions harm anyone else. Holding as self-evident a view of the person as a bearer of inalienable rights who must be free to determine his own ends, liberal society promulgates and protests "negative freedom." The citizen is free *from* a public morality he may not share, and free as well from the intrusions of his neighbors into his "private" affairs. Our political morality, in other words, is agnostic about alternative conceptions of the "good life."

Jefferson's pronouncement that it mattered not to him whether his neighbor believed in twenty gods or no god—it neither picked his pocket nor broke his leg—captures the reigning ethos. If I am threatened, I may call upon civil society to guarantee my protection, just as I may, if necessary, challenge that society if it threatens the rights its procedures are duty-bound to protect. This bracing ideal requires that politics touch nothing but external behavior: my actions can be regulated or punished only if it can be demonstrated that they impinge directly on you.

Our political morality, then, sets the context for debates over pornography. The political language of liberalism presumes a sharp cleavage between public and private. In John Stuart Mill's "On Liberty," this distinction was couched as a cleavage between "self-regarding" and "other-regarding" actions. Mill declared the sphere of untrammeled human liberty to include "conduct which affects only" the individual—including conscience, thought and feeling, opinion and sentiment, tastes and pursuits, expressing and publishing opinions, and uniting "for any purpose not involving harm to others." Celebrating individual choice and rights, classical liberalism grants no similar status to principles of belonging or obligation. Aspects of our moral experience located in ties of friendship, family, and community life are theoretically untouched by liberalism's regulative principles.

In practice, though, the distance between the public citizen and the private person has not been as great. American communities throughout the nineteenth and early twentieth century were held together less by liberal constitutionalism than by churches, ethnic ties, fraternal organizations, and especially Protestant morality. In communities that shared a common set of moral beliefs, from the Puritan colonies to small towns in the Midwest, extreme measures such as public censure and ostracism were available. But the general moral consensus was secure enough to make such measures superfluous. This strong sense of community gradually broke down under the forces of relentless social change and industrialization—the growth of cities, the invention of the car, the disruptions of wars, the spread of the media, and the sprouting of suburbs. Moral consensus—hence outrage at deviation—no longer serves to compel in matters of sexuality and aggressiveness.

In the absence of shared communal norms, protesters and reformers are compelled to make their case in the language of individual rights, in terms of "freedom from." This may account for the rhetorical overinflation that characterizes public debate when questions of moral concern such as abortion are addressed. One extraordinary example of this phenomenon can be found in sexual liberationist tracts that proclaim sexual gratification a *political* right. Thus the authors of a manifesto written in 1976, calling for an unrepressed society, describe masturbation as a "right," declaring that once the right was either seized or granted, the individual could go on to develop new and better "masturbatory techniques" as his or her way of making a "political contribution."

Clearly the idea of "rights" cannot bear all the weight being placed upon it. But without reference to rights, how can someone press the case for cultural change in a liberal society? We are officially indifferent to people's inner worlds, and to the moral visions that animate them and hold them together (or drive them apart). But the feminist antipornographers do have a telling point: Is the private "moral vision" found in violent pornography entirely private? Reformers who answer "no" must in a liberal society prove damages in order to get government to take punitive action. Thus, as traditional social constraints on "private morality" collapse, reformers worried about the effect of morality on public life are increasingly tempted to ignore the distinction between public and private worlds.

The Minneapolis ordinance had as one of its specific concerns "private porn"—pornographic material viewed in people's homes. The framers of the ordinance see this "saturation" of popular culture by the porn industry as a way to make (in Catherine MacKinnon's words) "more abusive treatment of women acceptable." By first defining pornography as harmful by definition, and going on to extend the reach of civil rights violations and discrimination, they clearly hope to make a dent in the 1969 Supreme Court case of *Stanley* v. *Georgia,* which permitted the use of "obscene" materials in the privacy of one's own home. Similarly, conservative antipornographers are trying to outlaw "aural" phone services and X-rated cable "adult" stations. Erasing the distinction between public and private seems the only way to "get at" the pervasiveness of the pornography problem as antipornographers define it.

But for the feminist antipornographers, this solution only illustrates their deeper dilemmas. The inflated rhetoric and the claims of unrelenting victimization, together with their proposed remedy—which features individual, aggrieved women going to court—shows how difficult it is even for radicals to escape from the proceduralism and excessive litigiousness of American society. And paradoxically, the world views of the antipornography feminists and the pornographers wind up mirroring one another. Thus Dworkin sees in pornography a precise portrait of ordinary sexual relations between men and women: "It is what women are in theory and practice." In an anthology entitled *Take Back the Night: Women on Pornography,* she describes pornography as "genocide," "Dachau in the bedroom," a "holocaust." For Dworkin and many other antipornography polemicists—as for pornographers—the phallus stands for the male as a whole; by definition it is an instrument of domination and control.

(Dworkin has written that it is acceptable for women to have sex with men as long as the man's penis isn't erect.)

The view of woman as the inevitable slave of man presented by anti-pornography rhetoricians is precisely the view of women the pornographic imagination demands and feeds on. Both portray sexual relations as atoms bumping up against one another. Both see male-female relations only as sadistic encounters. Both extend the image of dominance and subordination from porn theater to the average heterosexual bedroom. The runaway rhetoric of cruelty insists that the violence is everywhere and that pornography merely tells us the bitter truth of it.

Both pornographers and feminists present us with a world of pervasive control, evil designs, and daily degradation—and this fantasy exerts a morbid fascination. But if pornography mirrors anything, it is the loss of control in a world in which human beings in general and males in particular (for they are under a heavier burden of "performance" and stalwart individualism) see themselves as objects of social forces over which they have no control. Pornography is a crazily delineated mass fantasy. It offers for voyeuristic consumption a vision that attracts precisely because it signifies to "public man" what he is not, either in public or in private; a person who has unlimited power to bend others to his will.

Rather than being a window through which to view "normal" heterosexual intimacy, pornography offers us a magnifying glass that enlarges actual features of our broader social landscape: mechanistic work without joy or real accomplishment, anonymous personal relations, bureaucratic controls, rapid changes in sexual and social standards, and a background of historic desexualization (or hypersexualization) of the female. The pornographer both uses and helps to deepen these forces of anomie and confusion.

The sexual exploitation of children in modern pornography confirms this picture. (It is worth nothing that the language of the Minneapolis and Indianapolis ordinances blacked out this central concern and ignored, as well, the matter of gay porn, probably because it is an exclusively male concern.) Child pornography first appeared regularly in the 1960s, not coincidentally, at the same time the current pornography explosion began. Today, "kiddie porn" is a regular item in hard-core porn shops. As of 1978, there were twenty-five magazines devoted exclusively to portraying children as young as three engaged in every possible form of heterosexual and homosexual activity, including rape, sodomy, and "discipline." Here is a nightmarish fantasy world in which the consumer of pornography enjoys a rare illusion of personal power, engages in the pretense of elusive familial tenderness while venting a deep rage, and escapes the perils of adult intimacy in an era of changing sex roles.

Confronted with this spectacle, civil libertarians avert their eyes. We have reached a point at which the "rights" of children to have sex with anyone they like, if they can only first be freed from their "brutal, authoritarian family prisons and rulers," is promoted by one celebrant of the "freedom" of pedophilia as just another extension of the American dream. The civil libertarian can only challenge this view with the language of "consent"—children are not old enough to choose to be sodomized or otherwise gratified. But this is a thin barrier, especially in the case of adolescents under the age of consent; and it is enforceable only after its violation. Civil libertarians cannot get beyond a picture of isolated individuals, bound up in their rights and their "freedom from," going through the world *en garde* against possible constraints from concerned and potentially "repressive" communities.

The conservative alternative as presented by George Will, in contrast to liberalism's official agnosticism on porn, is attractive in its acknowledgment that the "inner life" matters, and that the character of citizens has something to do with our quality of life. In a column on the Minneapolis law, he astutely identified the feminist anti-pornographers' need for a rhetoric of cruelty, and for proof that one specific pornographic picture directly causes an act of violence—as if human beings were so many pots put on to boil at so many degrees pornographic Fahrenheit. "The logic" of liberal society's jurisprudence, he noted, "requires such unreasonableness before reasonable action can be taken." When he condemned "libertarian laws that express the doctrine that law should be indifferent to the evolution of the nation's character," he hit the central difficulty of expressing "collective concerns" in our hegemonic liberal language.

But he leaped from this point to attack the Minneapolis protesters for rattling "on and on about individual rights and equality." He apparently forgot that his ideal traditional communities restricted many women and denied them full civil identity. Women (and blacks, and others) have relied on their rights as individuals to make real gains. He also added a heavy dose of conventional moralism on sexual behavior in general, as if *any* deviation from the standard "Thou shalt nots" puts us on a slippery slope to sleaze and sadism. Will's "high" standards may, in practice, function rather like the old double standard. For what counted as deviant in traditional communities was all too frequently a woman's desire to break out of an oppressive double standard of sexual morality.

Will argued for stripping away individualism without regard for how precarious and newly won are rights for many. An emphasis on rights is a central feature of our political society—and ought to be. Rather than abandon our emphasis on rights, we need to challenge the over-inflation of rights and the unwarranted extension of them to all spheres of life. The civil libertarian alternative has no way to speak about communal concerns; Will's conservative option threatens to make those concerns suffocating.

It seems we cannot address the porn problem in the language of community or the language of absolute (or nearly so) freedom of expression and freedom from constraint. Yet it is too simple to uneasily and ineffectually straddle the fence between "rights" and "community." So what is to be done? We might begin by drawing on the conservatives' insistence that the character of human beings matters, and that this character is related to quality of life. The brutalizing potential of manufactured mass pornographic fantasy should not be dismissed out of hand. At the same time, we should affirm that the emancipation of women cannot be repealed in the service of controlling porn. Nor should it be necessary for communities to prove some causal link between porn and rape before taking action to prevent an aesthetic of cruelty from taking over Main Street. And finally, the importance of erotic intimacy between men and women must be accepted. Feminist antipornographers cannot brush aside the difference between "normal" heterosexuality and pornographic cruelties. Nor can antisexual moralists airbrush all traces of sexuality from society.

There are legal and political tools to put this theory into practice. In the 1973 Supreme Court decision in *Miller* v. *California,* the Court developed a three-part test for obscenity: (1.) whether an average person, applying "contemporary community standards," would find the work in question prurient; (2.) whether the work is a "patently offensive" depiction of sexual conduct specifically proscribed by state law; and (3.) whether the work taken as a whole "lacks serious literary, artistic, political, or scientific value." The *Miller* case is cumbersome because it requires a judicial determination of local standards of obscenity.

To the central protagonists in today's porn wars, *Miller,* or any local option, invites either proclamations of fear that it goes too far or murmuring of contempt that it does not go far enough. To conservative and feminist antipornographers, *Miller* offers no total solution. To civil libertarians, *Miller* is a potentially dangerous strategy that gives communities too much power over nonprotected, hence bannable, material. Thus, the current debate, including the Indianapolis law, denigrates plausible alternatives *(Miller* being one among several) and demoralizes citizens unhappy with the current moribund options.

Zoning statutes are also available, reducing the amount of pornography and restricting areas in which it can be displayed. In *Paris Adult Theatre* v. *Slaton* in 1973, the Supreme Court mentioned "the interest of the public in the quality of life and the total community environment" in articulating certain state interests in restricting pornography and obscenity. And in *Young* v. *American Mini Theatres* in 1976, the Court explicitly approved a zoning statute restricting the location of adult motion picture theaters showing "sexually explicit" not necessarily obscene—films. In Massachusetts alone, over a dozen towns and cities have successfully discouraged pornographers from setting up shop by restricting them to certain areas. The city solicitor of Lowell, Gerald Moore, told the *Boston Globe* in March that "zoning is one of the few rays of hope in an era when moral outrage is not enough." Despite these zoning victories, local anti-smut conservatives decry zoning as no "cure-all," and civil libertarians say that overly restrictive zoning would not survive a serious legal challenge. Clearly the stage is set for further battles.

This kind of repudiation of local initiatives causes much of the current political discontent about liberalism. Such radical critics as Sheldon Wolin, John Schaar, and Harry Boyte have pointed out often and eloquently that the eclipse (in Boyte's words) of "localist, voluntary, and historically grounded institutions has all too often been seen as unimportant or even beneficent" by reformers committed to grand, overarching visions or to unpopular strategies. "Liberals," Hannah Arendt wrote in an essay in *Dissent,* "fail to understand that the nature of power is such that the power potential of the Union as a whole will suffer if the regional foundations on which this power rests are undermined. . . . If the various sources from which it springs are dried up, the whole structure becomes impotent." The *Miller* test, and the *Young* decision, though perhaps vague, are also pluralistic, recognizing no single, uniform standard. They can serve in democratic efforts to control pornography, bolstering the kind of local activism that Arendt saw as essential to the future of democracy.

Communities should have the power to regulate and to curb open and visible assaults on human dignity, but they should not seek, as some groups avowedly do, to eradicate or condemn either sexual fantasies or erotic representations as such. This invariably must be a process of open political give-and-take, with all points of view represented in the community taking part in the debate. To the extent that pornography is symptomatic of, and helps to further, social disintegration, in which the least powerful (especially children) suffer the most, it becomes an appropriate target for action, regulation, and reproof. But with this proviso: the knowledge that we cannot return to a past in which Americans harmoniously shared one set of moral values. Communities must put pornography "in its place" rather than seeking to eradicate it altogether. Here the language and reality of First Amendment freedom ought to chasten overly zealous efforts to create or demand community consensus.

If we moved in this direction, we might break free from the unacceptable alternatives our civil society seems to throw up fairly consistently: freedom versus community and virtue versus vice. We could break free from the extremists on both sides of the present porn wars. And we might just arrive at some future point when the remorseless fantasies of pornographers no longer carry the force they do today because they would have ceased to speak to our isolation, our resentment, our fear.

Now What?

(1984)

This post-election editorial in the *New Republic*, a standard of liberal thought for six decades, asked the Democratic party to reconsider its program and ideas, calling on it to transcend "the mere sum of these perfectly legitimate but still comparatively narrow group interests" and to abandon the iron premises about social justice that had surfaced in the sixties and that by 1984 had become liberal dogma. The party did not heed the advice.

The Democratic Party has been dealt another shattering defeat, making this the fourth Presidential loss out of the last five elections and the third out of five by landslide proportions. President Reagan carried every state except Minnesota and the District of Columbia, giving him the second biggest electoral-vote victory since the days of George Washington. His 59-41 popular-vote victory was the fifth largest in modern U.S. history. Democrats did pick up two seats in the Senate and lost "only" fourteen to seventeen seats in the House, not enough to give the President automatic control of Congress. The long-awaited realignment of American politics again seems not to have taken place, and there is every reason for Democrats to aspire to take back the Senate in 1986 and the White House in 1988. But the fact has got to be faced: at the Presidential level, the Democrats have taken a historic drubbing.

The party has three fundamental choices. It can simply write this off as a "personal victory" for Ronald Reagan and claim that no Democrat could have done much better against a popular President running on a platform of peace, patriotism, and prosperity. It can pile the blame on Walter Mondale, much as it did on George McGovern and Jimmy Carter, and once again revise its nominating procedures to produce a different kind of nominee four years from now. Or it can look into itself for the reasons for its successive defeats, and resolve to reconsider the way in which it addresses America's problems.

We think that the first two alternatives constitute paths to disaster. There's no question that Ronald Reagan is well-liked, that he has a recovery going, that he hasn't started a war, and that he has improved America's morale. We doubt that any Democrat who ran for President this year could have beaten him. It does not follow from this, however, that if the Democratic Party just waits around for the holes in Mr. Reagan's record to open up for the whole nation to see, Democrats will be triumphantly returned to power. Reaganomics surely is a fraud whose inner contradictions will make themselves manifest, probably in painful ways. A complicated international crisis—in the Philippines, say, or in Chile or Nicaragua—could gravely test Mr. Reagan's limited foreign policy sophistication. And if he supports the agenda of the social issue fanatics in his political family, he may alienate some of the young people who flocked to his cause.

Yet the Democratic Party once before bet its future on antipathy toward Reaganism, and lost. After the debacle of 1980, the party resolved to rethink and retool. Walter Mondale even said he was taking a year off to talk to people around the country and redesign his program. Two or three new Democratic think tanks were created for the purpose of developing new approaches to governmental problems. But the 1982 recession took the heat off, and the party went back to the crusty old formula of baiting Republicans on the issues of unemployment and Social Security. It should have been clear from the election results in 1982 that the formula would not work, especially if prosperity showed signs of returning. The Democrats gained twenty-six House seats when they probably should have gained forty. They picked up no Senate seats at all. And why? Mostly, we think, because the party had no economic alternative to offer except a massive public employment program which the electorate did not find credible.

After 1982, most of those who had dedicated themselves to developing new ideas began working up position papers for the Mondale campaign instead, and the Mondale campaign became enmeshed with special interest. Senator Gary Hart and some of the so-called neoliberals talked about the need for "new ideas," but the truth is that except for Mr. Hart's own military reform proposals and the Bradley-Gephardt tax reform plan, precious few were ever put into concrete form. It could be that the second Reagan term will be so burdened with failure that Democrats will need only maintain a sturdy opposition stance, hold to their traditional principles and programs, and welcome the electorate home in 1986 and 1988. We doubt it. We think the party needs different candidates and different approaches.

This does not mean, however, that Democrats should begin their rethinking process with a ritual scapegoating of Walter Mondale. It's conceivable that another candidate would have lost less badly to Mr. Reagan than Mr. Mondale did, but there's no way to be sure. Some polls may emerge suggesting that Gary Hart would have been a stronger candidate, but we think they should be viewed with suspicion; Mr. Hart has always fared better as a ghostly figure on a pollster's list than he has in the flesh. Mr. Mondale certainly was not an ideal candidate, representing as he did an old-fashioned interest group liberalism that is no longer in fashion. He was not charismatic or particularly eloquent.

And yet, the party would be making a grave mistake to blame its loss exclusively on him. In the first place, Mr. Mondale waged a tough, solid general election campaign based on the fundamental Democratic principles—justice, community, democracy—that the party must maintain regardless of the new ways it finds to express them. Mr. Mondale is a decent man who stayed true to himself and his beliefs. By the end of the campaign, he had learned how to expound a forward-looking vision of hope and opportunity instead of relying solely on a sense of righteous indignation. He also had the imagination to give the nation its first woman Vice Presidential candidate. Mr. Mondale's pledge to raise taxes was a political gamble that he lost, but it still represented an act of courage and an expression of trust in the people's desire to be informed ahead of time about what their Presidents intend to do in office.

Although Mr. Mondale does not deserve to be reviled by his party, it's clear that the Mondale method of campaigning and governing will not attract the support of an electoral majority. And this method—including reliance on and protection of special interest groups—is deeply ingrained in the mentality of the national Democratic Party. When Mr. Mondale won the Democratic nomination this year, he was no interloper; rather, he represented the essence of what the Democratic Party has come to stand for. As speech after speech (and speaker after speaker) at the national convention demonstrated this summer, the Democratic Party thinks it cannot stand for equal rights for blacks unless it meets the specific demands of black leaders—this year, the Congressional Black Caucus and next year, perhaps, the Reverend Jesse Jackson. To be for women's equality means it must dance to the tune played by the National Organization for Women. Being for the interests of working people requires obeying the A.F.L.-C.I.O., being for education means following the N.E.A., being against discrimination against gays means adopting the affirmative action agenda of the National Gay Rights Task Force, etc., etc.

Somehow, the Democratic Party must find a way to represent a national interest that transcends the mere sum of these perfectly legitimate but still comparatively narrow group interests. And it must divorce the goal of representing the aspirations of minorities, working people, women, and other groups from the tendency to obey every demand of interest group spokesmen. To be for workers, for example, ought not mean favoring protectionist trade restrictions, but rather working for freer trade in the world. To be for Hispanics may or may not mean opposing the Simpson-Mazzoli immigration bill; it ought not mean *automatically* opposing it. To be for education means favoring higher pay *and* competency requirements for teachers.

Of all the groups whose special interests may be at variance with those of the party as a whole, blacks may present the most difficult problem. Blacks make up the largest single bloc in the Democratic Party, more than one-quarter of the party's total national vote this year. Politically and morally, blacks have a strong claim on the party, yet a polarizing process is clearly under way in this country which could put the Democratic Party into perpetual minority status if it responds too automatically to black leadership. Over the four Presidential elections prior to 1984, Democrats averaged only 38 percent of the white vote. On Tuesday, Mondale-Ferraro got 36 percent. The Democratic Party must never sacrifice its principles for votes. It cannot stop favoring equal opportunity in order to win elections but neither should it adopt a radical economic and foreign policy agenda because leading black Democrats may demand it. If Jesse Jackson does emerge as the nation's foremost black political spokesman, and if he continues to pursue his advocacy of deeply cutting defense to finance social programs and of aligning with Third World governments and movements that oppose democratic values, then there will be a crisis of direction in the Democratic Party. Black mayors and other black elected officials have no inherent stake in Mr. Jackson's ideological agenda; on the contrary, it tends to work against their interests, and we hope they will move to assert their political leadership of the black community. If they don't the chances will increase that the Democratic Party will become a kind of American counterpart of the British Labor party.

It will probably be argued by some that the way back to power for the Democratic Party should begin with the repudiation and jettisoning of various powerful interest groups such as NOW and the A.F.L.-C.I.O. and possibly the public humiliation of the so-called Washington insiders who purportedly led the party to defeat. The future, it will be said, belongs to the young and the fresh, and finding the future requires eliminating the past. One major policy focus of the emerging forces of youth in the party will be the Fairness Commission called for at the Democratic Convention to rewrite delegate selection rules yet again and make the Presidential nominating process still more "open." The youth guard especially wants to cut back on the number of so-called "superdelegates"—the members of Congress, governors, mayors, and party officials who made up 14 percent of 1984 convention delegates and voted overwhelmingly for Mr. Mondale.

There is some merit in the charge that these delegates, who were supposed to stay uncommitted and save the party from nominating a sure loser, instead threw their support early to Mr. Mondale and stuck with him even when his loss seemed certain. On the other hand, super-delegates do provide the party with a keel, preventing it from being blown by the whims of primary voters. And if it's youth and new ideas that procedural reformers are after, they should realize that a generational transition already has taken place in Congress and in the nation's statehouses.

Instead of purging anybody, the party needs to retain what it has in terms of talent and variety, while loosening the grip of special interest spokesmen. If any one group ought to be elevated in influence, it is the party's governors who have shown a remarkable ability to win elections while national and Congressional candidates have been losing. Prior to last Tuesday's voting, Democrats controlled thirty-five of the nation's governorships. After the deluge, they will still control thirty-three. We are not saying that the party necessarily should look to a governor as its Presidential nominee in 1988; as Jimmy Carter demonstrated, one doesn't automatically acquire national governing skills in a statehouse. We are saying that the governors have been dealing creatively with some of the nation's most difficult domestic problems and balancing budgets at the same time. States such as Arizona, Massachusetts, Virginia, Texas, Arkansas, and North Carolina have dramatically upgraded education and used universities as the magnet for high-tech industrial development. As Arizona Governor Bruce Babbitt observes, the governors tend to be free-market internationalists rather than protectionists and isolationists, because they are eager to have their state economies grow rather than stagnate.

Growth and change have always been major goals of the Democratic Party, but in recent years protection of the status quo has become an increasingly dominant preoccupation. Instead of inventing ways to create new jobs, the party has been trying to maintain existing jobs in out-of-date industries. It has been fighting to keep old bureaucracies alive, and it has been using quotas to dictate equality of results rather than deregulating and encouraging minorities to use the market to advance economically. It has been defending middle-class entitlement programs such as Social Security without heed to the changes that everyone agrees privately are going to have to be made. In the damning phrase of the Republican political analyst Kevin Phillips, the Democratic Party has become dedicated to "reactionary liberalism." It's little wonder that the party did so poorly among young voters. A 73-year-old man told them that the best days of America were yet to come, and the once-dynamic Democratic Party seemed to say it wasn't so. The Democrats need to find leaders who believe it is so—and can make it so in reality, not just in television ads.

The new patriotism that Ronald Reagan invoked is also something that a renewed Democratic Party would take pride in and would advance, rather than disparage and drown with guilt. The Democrats waved American flags at their convention in San Francisco, but their platform and their primary candidates said again and again that America is wrong in defending its interests abroad. Walter Mondale, to his credit, adopted a strong centrist foreign policy position in the general election campaign, saying he would have invaded Grenada as President Reagan did and might quarantine Nicaragua. But one can't blame the electorate for wondering which was the real Mondale—February's more-freezy-than-thou primary candidate advocate or the "commander in chief" of the October debates. All year long, the Democratic Party needs to talk and vote in Congress as Mr. Mondale campaigned at the end.

One of the early fights to come will be over the Democratic Party chairmanship. The field again is filled with party mechanics, fund-raisers, and former state chairs. What the party needs instead is a spokesperson who is interested in what the party stands for, who knows a good idea when he or she hears one, and who can encourage development of new approaches to the nation's problems. The job of rebuilding the Democratic Party is so large that it requires somebody of Presidential caliber to take it on.

Good Vibrations
(1987)

David Brooks

Brooks's report provided a withering account of the resurgent peace movement, which attracted antiwar activists, environmentalists, and others certain
that Republican foreign policy was leading the nation toward nuclear doom. No
matter the gravity of arms control and international diplomacy; the movement
was tediously—sometimes risibly—edged with New Age vapors and one-world
mumbo-jumbo. Still, "globalists" and other peace leaders took themselves and
their cause very, very seriously, and so did many opinion leaders.

Oh God. He's dead. . . . I was at the Jung Foundation's symposium
on U.S.-Soviet relations, checking out the latest in peace movement fads. The elderly gent across the aisle seemed to be paying
attention to the speaker (Robert Kaiser, a former Moscow correspondent
for the *Washington Post,* who was denouncing Reagan) when suddenly the
man's notebook slipped from his hand, his head fell back, and his mouth
gaped toward the ceiling.

The assembled peaceniks seemed oblivious to the old man's fate,
absorbed as they were with the imminent nuclear holocaust. I was more
concerned about imminent rigor mortis. "Is there a doctor in the house?" I
was about to cry to a roomful of psychoanalysts. Suddenly the old guy
twitched and moved his hand. Soon his chest began to rise and fall with
calm, rhythmic breathing. Relieved, I refocused my attention on the
insanity-of-the-nuclear-arms-race, but questions kept obtruding: Is it true
old Jungians never die, they just nod off at symposia?

If Kaiser puts him to sleep, wait until tomorrow when the real
Jungians take the lectern. Jungians are not your ordinary peaceniks. For
one thing, they are richer. But more importantly, Jungians are savvy
enough to know that war is "archetypal energy." Different groups just
don't get along, or, as one of them declares, "In psychoevolutionary terms,
pseudospeciation leads to nonpathological paranoia."

Jungians want us to channel our feelings of hostility so they won't explode in the form of large mushroom clouds. To give us an idea of how it might be done, Jerome Bernstein, a distinguished Jungian analyst from Washington, proposed that the U.S. and the Soviets engage in ritual warfare similar to that practiced by aborigines in New Guinea. Bernstein says that after a few hours of war-game fun in Germany, we and the Soviets would feel a lot closer. Apparently the Libyans were engaging in just this sort of ritual when they fired missiles at some of our fighters a few years back. They missed on purpose, says Bernstein, but unfortunately we broke the ritual by bombing their launching sites and killing some of their men. That just goes to show you how insensitive the U.S. Government is to international realities.

I left the conference pretty sure that Jungians do not represent the future of the peace movement. They employ Helen Caldicott's rhetorical tool—if you don't support unilateral disarmament you are insane—which is a plus for them, but they haven't yet entirely discarded reason.

The peace movement, as I have learned over the past few months, isn't standing still. The old peace movement tried to persuade Americans to disarm, but it found itself at a disadvantage, since its leaders didn't know what they were talking about. The new peace movement goes beyond dumbness, posing new and exciting challenges for its members.

Peace is a state of mind, the new activists admonish us. Don't think, *be.* Don't argue for peace, *be* peace. "For we cannot save our skins without saving our souls," writes M. Scott Peck, author of *The Different Drum,* which at this writing is number seven on the *New York Times* bestseller list. "When I am asked, 'Dr. Peck, what is human nature?'" he says, "my first answer is likely to be, 'Human nature is going to the bathroom in your pants.'" What Dr. Peck means by that elegant formulation is that people are too clever by half. If they would just go back within themselves and liberate their impulses, they wouldn't waste their time building bombs. That focus on inwardness, the new activists say, is what separates them from the naïve idealists of the 1960s. "Through the civil-rights movement and the Vietnam War, I began to understand that the whole system was at fault," writes Shelley Douglass, co-founder of the Ground Zero Center for Nonviolent Action. "Through the women's movement and the nuclear-disarmament movement I have come to see that the deepest roots of evil are in me."

The *Peace Resource Book* lists 5,700 peace groups. As far as I can tell about a third of these groups have sizable chunks of psychopeace babble at their core; a third are traditional leftist; and the middle third have elements of both. Interhelp is a good example of the hard-core mushy type. It conducts sessions to help people cleanse themselves of the bad consciousness that causes nuclear weapons. "I saw another reason for the vacuum in my mind," writes Chellis Glendinning, psychologist and co-founder of Interhelp. "I realized that I know how to awaken. I open my eyes. I allow myself to feel. By naming and grieving what is passing, I clear my psyche of the old and dysfunctional modes of perception."

It worked for her, and through her it works for others. At one Interhelp session, Miss Glendinning writes,

> 150 people were pounding their fists together, sobbing and holding one another. Whereas before we had stood in denial or felt alone and guarded, now we felt angry, scared, and sad. And as we realized how connected we are by the awful fate that hangs over us, a . . . circle spontaneously formed: one of kinship and commitment unlike any other we had known before. The ritual completed itself when a woman placed her nine-month-old child in the center of the circle and everyone held hands and sang songs of commitment and hope.

The baby is not the only one sweating it out at these sessions. As peace literature makes clear, psychic transformation is often very stressful, filled with terrifying mystical experiences. At one peace rally, a college professor described her brush with nuclear annihilation. Walking across campus one day, she suddenly felt that the buildings were crumbling around her. Her eyes closed and she could not work up the courage to open them, convinced that when she did all would be rubble. Some describe fits of nausea that last for days as they contemplate the existence of nuclear weapons. For others, the horror of nuclear weapons hits them as they are driving through the countryside; they can no longer look at streams and hills without seeing a nuclear exchange.

Miss Glendinning is most candid about her own mystical experience:

> I descended into what felt like a deeper realm of consciousness. I saw my own body as the earth. I saw the IUD as one of many assaults on the planet made by our society. I recalled a magazine article I had read about H-bomb testing in the ocean off San Diego in the 1950s. Suddenly, the article's illustrations flashed before my eyes: the bomber ship, the officers, the water erupting like a bubble in a cauldron. I cried aloud: "They're bombing the ocean!" . . . My chest began a rhythm of heaving and then shaking in tiny vibrations, heaving, then shaking.
>
> My mind's eye zoomed back until it encompassed a wide view of the entire West Coast. I saw brown gasses hovering over

the land "oh no!" I shrieked, seeing the smog as if for the first time. "There's poison in the air! It's all over the earth!" I was sweating and arching my torso, tense with pain I had carried for a long time. . . .

For a moment I felt calm. Out of the silence a new vision appeared, first distant and hazy, then close up and stark. I saw Indians descending, methodically and with dignity into the earth, and bringing up uranium. "Do you see that?" I wondered aloud. "Why, they're sending Indians down to get their bombs." I saw the people growing tired and sickly, I saw them dying, and the greatest wave of pain yet coursed through my muscles "JESUS CHRIST! They're sending the Indians down to do their Goddamn dirty work!" Now I was sobbing and writhing in the sheets and sweating. "They're sending the Indians! They're sending the Indians!"

And then it stopped, as instantly as it had begun. . . . I had seen the IUD, the bombing of the ocean, pollution, and the uranium mining in very clear terms. In my work I continually meet other people my age who have experienced, if not as dramatic, at least similar visions.

❧

I happen to be relatively close to Miss Glendinning in age, and I am a person who reads a lot of newspapers and magazines. Yet these sorts of experiences never happen to me. It makes one feel a little superficial.

Recently, I called up Miss Glendinning and asked her how come I never writhe with psychic visions of bomb-toting Indians. I was somewhat relieved to learn that it's not my fault; it's my parents' fault: "You develop your sense of the future around the time of puberty, so what is happening in the world at the time of puberty is going to impact your sense of continuity," Miss Glendinning said. "I am part of the post-Cuban Missile Crisis generation because I came to puberty after that crisis and before the next great historical divide, Three Mile Island." Therefore, I "came into puberty in the time of the Aquarian age while [my] parents were totally numbed out." Historical forces created a certain numbness in me. It is the post-TMI generation, she says, that really feels the tenuousness of our planet. The rest of us are nuclearists, which is the New Age term for someone who is not open to the reality of the imminent nuclear holocaust.

Consequently, I have never experienced earthgrief, a term used by Betty Bumpers, wife of Senator Dale Bumpers, to describe the sadness we should feel about the coming destruction of our planet. Nuclearists like me do not love the earth, the new peace activists say, hence we do not mind raping it. "The phallic nature of our missiles is inescapable," says Marshall Halladay, who went to jail for hitting a missile silo lid with a hammer. "The insertion of a sixty-foot nuclear missile into a buried silo is a graphic image of rape. We are sowing a different crop now, and none can imagine the harvest."

I think that Mr. Halladay has hit on something there, emphasizing the sexual basis of the new peace movement, and if I had been there to watch Miss Glendinning as she had her mystical experience about the bombing of the oceans, I might be able to pin it down a little more precisely.

New Age peace activism finds a lot of ways to help its disciples sublimate their energy. At sessions sponsored by Interhelp or other like-minded groups, workshop leaders guide numb nuclearists through three stages: imaging, scenario writing, and action planning. They discuss actions that will lead to the attainment of the new future. Miss Glendinning has charted her course: "use of solar panels on our homes, honoring the lunar cycles, restructuring our workplaces to meet people's needs—these are heroic because they speak to the questions of meaning, power, and continuity in the context of the defining reality of our times: the potential for planetary extinction."

Others spend their time planning Transarmaments, a new system of defense that will replace our current military system. In *Making the Abolition of War a Realistic Goal*, Gene Sharp describes this post-nuclear defense system. Were the Soviets to occupy our nation, teachers would refuse to teach propaganda. Journalists would continue to write what they pleased. Others might leave trees on the highways to make life difficult for the occupying army. This would so inconvenience the Soviets that, after a while, they would go home. Recently major conferences have been held in Finland, Sweden, Belgium, Norway, and the U.S. to develop the idea. The *New Creation News* recently editorialized, "It is possible as well that the unseen psychological force capability of nonviolent resistance has the potential, once harnessed, to create a weapons system of extraordinary magnitude. Nonviolent resistance may be a way to wage war without violence."

But the proponents of Transarmament have not found total acceptance in the new peace offensive. Advocating civil disobedience, after all, runs counter to the great insight of the Eighties: that social evils are within us. James Douglas, author of *The Nonviolent Cross* and *Resistance and Contemplation*, points out that, an ego-empowering act of civil disobedience will in the end empower both the self and the nuclear state, which while tactically at odds are spiritually in agreement. . . . Civil disobedience, like war, can be used to mask the emptiness of false self."

To really prevent nuclear war we must give up a number of childish myths: the myth that people and nations should be strong; the myth that people and nations should strive toward accomplishment; the myth that power is a good thing. "We are desperately in need of a new ethic of 'soft individualism,'" M. Scott Peck argues, "an understanding of individualism which teaches that we cannot be truly ourselves until we are able to share freely the things we most have in common: our weakness, our incompleteness, our imperfection, our inadequacy, our sins, our lack of wholeness and self-sufficiency." For Peck and many of his activist colleagues, the model organization, which they have imitated in constructing their movement, is Alcoholics Anonymous.

Humiliation is realism for the peace activists; powerlessness, ineptitude, and failure make up the glue that can hold community together. "Community requires the ability to expose our wounds and weakness to our fellow creatures," writes Peck. "It also requires the capacity to be affected by the wounds of others, to be wounded by their wounds." Everybody becomes equal because everybody is weak and powerless.

How long will it take to create a world of universal weakness? Peck is no idealist. He knows that you can't erase international achievement overnight. "When I give disarmament workshops and the participants become all enthused, some of their faces fall when I tell them I expect it will take us a dozen years to achieve disarmament. They thought it might take six months. That is because they are romantics."

The first step, of course, is unilateral disarmament. "What a dramatic gesture of vulnerability and peacemaking that would be!" Peck enthuses. But for others, dismantling American defenses is not enough. Keith Miller, who also tours the nation addressing peace groups, thinks the Soviets deserve an apology: "We should tell them that we have not behaved as Christians toward them. We have not loved them with our whole hearts. We have not wished the best for them. We have not rejoiced in their success."

Thousands of peaceniks do travel to the Soviet Union to make their apologies. They speak of a "special electricity," and "elusive otherness," and an "intimate strangeness" they feel when showing their weakness to the Soviets. The meetings involve plenty of crying. Peace activists don't believe they have really lived peace until they have shed a bucketful of tears on Soviet soil.

The highlight of the Women's Journey for Peace visit to the Soviet Union last year came when the visitors cried over their Soviet hosts at the airport. Another group, led by Molly Young Brown, a peace psychologist, cried at a Soviet school and also at the (ever-popular) airport. Members of the International Physicians for the Prevention of Nuclear War cried as they tried to climb a Soviet mountain. And Betsy Bridwell of the Sunbow Quilt Project, which brings peacequilts to the USSR, cried when she gave a quilt to a district Party leader on a collective near the Black Sea. She also cried when she gave one to a Moscow physical therapist. It was a moment of weakness she will never forget. The Seattle Peace Chorus cried while singing folk songs at a hotel in Tashkent, and they cried again going through customs leaving Leningrad, and finally when they said goodbye to their guides. "I think I've had a taste of the importance of being vulnerable and the reward of finding that, by being so, I don't need to protect myself from enemies. Somehow the 'enemy' is no longer there," reported chorus-member Rebecca Johnson.

All this mystical sobbing upsets those who have remained faithful to the tough ideals of the Sixties peace movement. But the traditional throw-blood-on-the-General activists recognize that psychopeaceniks are valuable, if slightly nauseating, allies. "They can reach the straight family type who may be working in the military industry, who has two station wagons, two TV's, and a dog and a cat," Randy Schutt, a researcher at the Pacific Studies Center, told a reporter recently. Thanks to psychopeace babble, pacifism has become suburban chic.

The Beyond War Foundation is one of the most dynamic of the new middle-class organizations. In just five years, Beyond War has grown to ten thousand active members with an annual "peacechest" of $3 million and four hundred permanent employees. It advertises for new members in *The New Yorker.*

In an article in *Mother Jones* (adapted from one she wrote for the *San José Mercury-News*), Susan Faludi reported the following exchange at a Beyond War training session:

> A new recruit wants to know how Walt would resolve another kind of conflict: "Say a guy breaks in here and holds a gun to your daughter's head?"
>
> Walt says: "Before, I would have bashed him in the head with a baseball bat I used to keep under the bed. Now I might try to reason with him. Or maybe go ahead and hit him with the bat, but just on the shoulder."
>
> Nancy says, "I would throw a lampshade."

"What if it killed him?" the new recruit wants to know.

Nancy says patiently, "As long as you didn't mean to. It's the intent that matters."

In fact, Walt and Nancy are not being totally consistent with their New Age beliefs. To remain true to psychopeace movement ideals, if an intruder broke into their home and held a gun to their daughter's head, they would have to grab a baseball bat and start beating *themselves* over the head. After all, it was the hostility within their psyches that created the psychic environment that caused the intruder's disturbed behavior.

࿐

But consistency is not the psychopeace movement's M.O. The movement is more seductive, broadcasting a mood of warmth, openness, and tranquillity.

The psychopeace activists have co-opted a rhetoric that is extremely powerful these days. They emphasize symbolic gestures of compassion and outward displays of sentimental self-awareness. They advocate an easygoing kind of egotism, a good-natured self-obsession. They never discuss and do not seem aware of people who have ambitions that are not restricted to self-fulfillment, and who are willing to kill to achieve such visions as global equality or cultural hegemony. Politics exists for the psychopeaceniks to ensure survival of the self, and they harbor the strange and historically unwarranted assumption that somebody who feels good about himself would never harm another person. They find happiness in basic emotions that all people can share without effort. Ambition, trying to distinguish oneself from the crowd, is for them a sin. But the great sin is reason, because commitment to rationality inevitably propels a person from contemplation of self to contemplation of society. It kills solipsism, and once people have broader visions, they might come into conflict with their neighbors. And conflict is to be avoided at all costs.

Inner peace at any price—that's the new movement's motto. And if it proves necessary to undergo a spiritual lobotomy in order to obtain release from the anxiety of the nuclear age, the psychopeace activists don't blink. How sad that so many appear willing to sacrifice their humanity to save their skins.

THE EIGHTIES

The Culture of Apathy
(1988)

This *New Republic* editorial, written four years after "Now What?" (see page 82), expressed alarm over "sensate" American culture and its impact on domestic politics. Its indictment of the doctrine of endless personal rights and liberal complicity in "cultural degradation" suggests the escalating cultural politics of the late Eighties—and the moment when many liberals—not least Tipper Gore—began to fear for the future of a nation in which "nothing is true and everything is permitted."

This is a time of crisis in the history of our culture, and liberals are alert to—even frantic about—some of its dimensions. They grasp the prospect of decline that lurks in the erosion of the values and reality of equality in America. They understand, even if Reaganites do not, that a large and ignored underclass weakens a nation. But a fog bank of insouciance envelops the liberal mind when other cultural aspects of our crisis, at least as palpable and almost as quantifiable, are placed on the social agenda.

What leaves them especially cold to the question of cultural decline is the way it challenges their own attachment to the endlessness of personal freedoms. It is not hard to understand why. Contemporary liberalism is so intellectually and psychologically invested in the doctrine of ever-expanding rights—the rights of privacy, the rights of children, the rights of criminals, the rights of pornographers, the rights of everyone to everything—that any suggestion of the baleful consequences of that doctrine appears to them as a threat to the liberal ideal itself. The Moral Majoritarians in our midst intend precisely that threat. It need not, of course, come to that. But this will depend on whether liberals are brave enough to stop averting their eyes from a spectacle for which their ideology has no ready remedy.

The facts are clear. Licentiousness about drugs and sex have put our children at risk, and the most vulnerable of our children, minority and poor children, at greatest risk. The AIDS pandemic may be the most painful and most vivid symptom of that risk, but it is not the only symptom. Lives are ruined by the ethos of "anything goes" just as surely as they are lost. In this insidious culture of lassitude, no one is safe, and no place. The city is the most insecure, and the greater the city the least secure of all. The great historic cities, whatever their well-known tolerance for what we used to call "decadence," were centers of civilization—in the last two centuries especially, enhancing and enriching the lives of ordinary men and women. Our cities have not transformed themselves overnight into Sodom and Gomorrah, but they have fast become centers of barbarism. By barbarism we do not mean just crime, though growing violent and pointless crime has been an accurate index of the failures of urban schools to teach civilization, which is to say to socialize and to civilize.

By barbarism we mean the exacerbated cultural degradation of man and environment. One of the causes is the frustration of grinding poverty, particularly in the wake of both insincere promises and oafish efforts to end it. Since, however, this barbarism afflicts more than the lives of the poor, poverty cannot be its only cause. In any case, the poor can do without the callous form of ideological charity that would lift from their children the sentence of a wanton life only on the condition of their own entrance into the middle class. It was never the case in the past and it surely isn't the case now. What has degraded so many of the young poor and the young black has also degraded many other young people who are neither poor nor black nor without horizons. This is the sense, actively encouraged by our popular culture and propagated by the incessant images of our mass media, that nothing is true and everything is permitted.

"Nice girls do it," in the words of a hit song on black radio. Indeed, they do, as the grim statistics of female-headed poor families unmistakably demonstrate. And so will their daughters, unless and until the culture pervasively states a different message. In the meantime, this anthem or similar anthems are on radio stations across the country. And on everyone's television there is a Walpurgisnacht of value-neutral brutality. By the time your average child is 16, he will have been witness to some 16,000 murders on the tube. It may be difficult to certify cause and effect. But only the willfully blind will argue that there is no cumulative correlation between what we see and what we are. What we are calling for, then, is not a return to Victorian standards of hypocrisy, or censorship, or even repression. Merely the hard-earned recognition that throughout society there is a need for standards of restraint, of measure, even of shame. The ridicule of the emotion of shame in recent times—its association with immaturity, guilt, insecurity, and all the other catchwords of psychoanalysis—has, for all its self-serving appeal, masked an essential truth.

Where there is little sense of shame there can, in fact, be little sense of dignity.

The idea of proportion and propriety that once bounded private and public life will not be restored either by legislation or by exhortation. And we certainly do not propose a restoration of the bland irrelevance of the "Leave It to Beaver" culture to the minds and lives of Americans. Still, there is something we do need to recover from the world we have lost, even if we do not want to return to its narrow confines. For now, it would be a big step forward if we were to become aware of the costs, real and emotional, of living without and beyond boundaries. And for that we need at least to talk.

But the issue of cultural degeneration has become taboo among liberals, provoking *bien pensant* rancor almost as nothing else does. Simply for raising the issue Tipper Gore has not been safe from ridicule. Mention her name in some circles on both coasts, and you are greeted with a curious mixture of boredom and alarm. A few minutes into the conversation, someone will knowingly whisper "censorship," the falsehood disguised as argument. It is hard to avoid the impression, moreover, that her detractors, even when they are men of advanced opinions, are patronizing her because she is a woman. It is why they call her "Tipper" and her effort a "crusade." Campaigns launched by women often attract that derisive label. Aren't women and crusades both, after all, emotional? When 50 years ago Eleanor Roosevelt began to agitate in Washington for racial equality, a cause then widely thought to be favored also primarily by cranks, savvy commentators made it clear that even liberal women should stick to their pastel and mauve responsibilities. The secretary of war, Henry L. Stimson, attacked her "intrusive and impulsive folly." As with the slanders against Tipper Gore, the most brazen fear-mongering was believed by otherwise skeptical people. Many were convinced that Mrs. Roosevelt was actually intent on fomenting insurrection among Negro domestics, at least for starters. And her husband's well-wishers worried that, by her independence, she was somehow undermining FDR's aura of command. In this regard we have not changed all that much. Only a few weeks ago, a valued *New Republic* writer of very advanced opinions on just about everything (and hell, why not?) warned that Mrs. Gore was "unmanning" her husband.

Mrs. Gore co-founded the Parents' Music Resource Center, which, through old-fashioned First Amendment pressure from a concerned public, persuaded the umbrella organization of the recording industry to affix "parental advisory" labels to albums with "explicit lyrics." In the end, this is no big deal. It may even be somewhat counterproductive, enticing young people to really foul lyrics they might otherwise have ignored. But no one at PMRC, least of all Mrs. Gore, believes that labeling a dozen or so record sleeves each year will retard the wantonness of American life. Everybody is aware, moreover, that, where there are no proper parents or where the culture has already so sabotaged parental authority, "parental advisory" labels are hardly effective antidotes to violence and pornography. But this is only a reflection of how deep the problem is—and a measure of how urgent is the national conversation to which Tipper Gore has summoned us.

In these pages Mrs. Gore was recently stigmatized as a prude because out of "all the thousands of causes in the world, she has chosen this one." Well, it is not her only cause. She is the founding chair of Families for the Homeless, a national mobilization aimed at retrieving children (and their parents) from another manifestation of America's stoneheartedness. But what is so wrong with also making as one's cause the protection of children from the numbing norms in our culture of random drugs, random sex, and random violence? Is it only conservatives who are to worry about whether wholesomeness will survive the 20th century?

With the triumph of sensate values, wrote the visionary sociologist Pitirim Sorokin, our society will become a "dumping place" for children. The callousness about the homeless should be seen as at once an expression of this reality and an ominous auguring. But so also should be the callousness that relentlessly inflicts on our children so nasty a culture with so debased a vision of human flourishing. How strange it is that modern interventionist liberals would leave the determination of all this to a rapacious market. No one is calling here for government intercession or any form of censorship. But it is time for more public scrutiny and for more public debate. And if Mrs. Gore is still willing to endure the taunts of fashionable opinion and argue the subtle truth that it really is wise restraints that make us genuinely free, then we will be very much in her debt.

THE EIGHTIES

New Yorkers Growing Angry Over Aggressive Panhandlers
(1988)

Fox Butterfield

Appearing on the front page of the *New York Times* in the heat of the summer, this article reflected growing exasperation with the proliferation of the "homeless." Three years into the "crack" plague, vagrants and beggars seemed to lurk at every bus corner. They were invading downtown streets all over the country. Many people who once thought the "homeless" deserved unrestricted compassion as "social victims" were changing their minds. As it became evident that many "homeless" were drug addicts, criminals, and psychotics, their public image grew tarnished.

It was the fouth time that morning that Kenneth N. Levy had been approached by a panhandler. He gave one dollar to the first beggar, a man with no eyeballs who was going through the subway car with a paper coffee cup. Then he handed another dollar to a man with no legs who propelled himself on a skateboard, and an equal donation to a gray-haired woman in her 70s who reminded him of his grandmother. When still another beggar accosted him, loudly demanding money, Mr. Levy, a hair stylist, snapped. "What do I look like, a bank?" he shouted.

Recounting that incident, he added: "I was raised never to pass a beggar by, but there are too many of them and I'm sick of it. I feel like this is becoming beggar city." Mr. Levy's reaction reflects a growing concern and anger among many New Yorkers as the number of panhandlers appears to have multiplied over the last year and their methods have become increasingly aggressive, even intimidating.

Some psychologists, social-service workers and city officials fear that the rise in begging is further hardening New Yorkers against their fellow citizens and eroding the quality of life. "People are learning to tolerate the intolerable, and the quality of life inevitably deteriorates," said Dr. Marsha Martin, an assistant professor at the Hunter College School of Social Work, who is a specialist on homeless women.

There are no accurate statistics on the number of beggars in New York. But the chairman of the Metropolitan Transportation Authority, Robert R. Kiley, said it took a survey last spring and found that two-thirds of New Yorkers believed there had been a big rise in panhandling in the last few years. "It's having quite a dramatic impact on people and they feel it intrudes on them personally," said Mr. Kiley, who finds himself accosted by a swarm of beggars every morning when he boards the subway at 86th Street and Lexington Avenue on his way to work.

Another sign of the increase in beggars is the growing number of places they now appear and the proliferation of services they presume to offer. Men insistent on wiping a rag across motorists' windshields congregate at stoplights all across the city, and panhandlers station themselves outside off-hours bank cash machines, opening the door for customers. At the Food Emporium at Broadway and 68th Street, one enterprising beggar stands in front of an automatic door opened by an electronic beam pretending to be of help.

Arline L. Bronzaft, a professor of psychology at Lehman College, worries that begging contributes to the phenomenon she calls overload. "One reason why New Yorkers are considered so impolite is that there is so much bombardment of the stimuli, with all the noise, crowding and rushing," she said. "So people tune out. Everyone has this invisible space around them and they don't want people to cross it," she continued. "With panhandlers, they are starting to break through, so people try very hard to tune them out by not seeing them and not giving money. It makes the city a less comfortable place to live in, and eventually there will be an outcry."

Many people who have been solicited say they are concerned over what begging says about the condition of America. "If you understood why we tolerate all this panhandling, you'd know why Sparta defeated Athens," said an Upper East Side psychoanalyst who did not want his name used. "It's guilt, or weakness," he said. He said he became angry recently when he was coming out of a doughnut shop at 86th Street and Lexington Avenue and a beggar demanded, "Give me half of your doughnut." "It provides a new target for my homicidal fantasies," the psychoanalyst said.

"The beggars are expressing hostility, not just asking for money. They want to force you to feel guilty."

The recent increase in panhandling raises a number of questions that are not being extensively studied or publicly debated, specialists say. Among them are these:

- Why are there suddenly so many beggars? Are they part of the broad homeless problem, caused by the deinstitutionalization of the mentally ill, the shortage of affordable housing and the breakup of the family? Or are panhandlers a special group, made up largely of drug addicts, alcoholics and opportunists?

- Is it better to give some spare change to beggars or does this simply create more panhandlers and keep them from turning to city and private social-service agencies where they would get better care?

- Do women give more money than men?

- Is the prevalence of beggars having specific effects, such as deterring people from riding the subway, shunning movie theaters where long lines make easy targets for hustlers, or leading people to give less to charity?

Kim Hopper, a medical anthropologist who has written a history of street begging, said that over the centuries periodic waves of begging have led to major crackdowns or extensive new programs to cope with the problem. Government-organized poor relief, he said, came about in Bruges, Belgium, in 1520 after crowds of ragged beggars, many with oozing sores and stumps for legs, gathered outside the churches, blocking the entry of the devout.

In the United States, during the Depression, with millions of unemployed people wandering from city to city, often on freight trains, President Franklin D. Roosevelt set up a series of 350 camps around the country known as the Federal Transient Program. The camps helped house, feed and clothe these people, said Elizabeth Wickenden, who as a 25-year-old in 1934 became the program's acting director. Ms. Wickenden, who lives on the Upper East Side, said that before the camps were established, "there were panhandlers everywhere in New York."

But in those days the panhandlers were more polite and less aggressive than the current wave, she said, making a pretense of selling apples on street corners or appearing at people's backdoors. "They didn't have any choice," she said. "There wasn't any other care for them at the time."

Mr. Hopper, who works with the Coalition for the Homeless, said, "I suppose there will be modern versions of the camps pretty soon as people get more angry about panhandling." One difference now, he said, is that in 1972 the Supreme Court effectively struck down anti-vagrancy laws as unconstitutional, making legal measures against begging difficult.

Last October, Seattle became the first city in the country to try a legal remedy since the Court's decision, banning what was called "aggressive panhandling" and making it a misdemeanor punishable by a fine of up to $500 and 90 days in jail.

In the M.T.A. survey, of 1,200 New Yorkers, the authority found that while a majority of New Yorkers wanted the panhandlers removed from the subways and 80 percent considered them annoying, 60 percent reported giving to them—11 percent every day.

Diane Sonde, the director of Project Reach Out, a group that works with the mentally ill homeless on the West Side, said she believed that most panhandlers "are related to drug abusers, not the mentally ill." She added, "The mentally ill are too ashamed by their conditions or too frightened to beg." Other experts say there is too little data to draw conclusions on where the beggars come from.

Whatever the case, Ms. Sonde says people are confused about how to deal with them. "We get calls all the time from people who say, 'What should I do?'" Ms. Sonde said, "A lot of mothers are calling because they don't know what to tell their children, especially when they see mothers begging with children." When people are in doubt about whether to believe a beggar's story, she said, she advises them to offer to buy the person food, or in winter, a blanket, rather than giving cash.

But some experts and city officials say giving to beggars only adds to the problem. Last month, Mayor Koch, in response to a question at a business group's lunch about what to do when confronted by a panhandler, said "If you feel guilty, see a priest."

"Just say no" is the best policy, the Mayor recommended.

Dr. Martin, who serves as a consultant to the M.T.A. on the homeless and panhandlers, said, "New Yorkers are 50 percent of the problem with begging." The tiny handouts of coins that people give are too little to really help, but just enough to keep people from going to a shelter, soup kitchen or city agency, Dr. Martin believes.

E. A. Hass, an author of children's books, makes a habit of carrying change to give to panhandlers and always makes sure to take out in a container any food she and her friends leave uneaten in restaurants so that she can distribute it to beggars she sees on her way home. But Ms. Hass, too, is troubled by the rise in aggressive panhandlers. "They undermine chances of people helping the truly homeless and make people resent them," she said.

Dr. Valerie Lewis Wiener, a social psychologist who has studied the differences between men and women in giving to others, believes that women are more likely to give to panhandlers than men. The reason, Dr. Wiener said, is that they are less concerned with getting something in exchange and instead are more concerned with their relationship with the other person.

A panhandler outside the subway station at Broadway and 72nd Street who identified himself only as John, agreed with that assessment. "Women are more nicer—ladies they do give more," he said, standing on crutches.

Dr. Martin Hoffman, chairman of the psychology department at New York University, who studies people's responses to others in distress, said: "With beggars, my observation is that the vast majority of New Yorkers have become habituated to them, have made them just another part of the scenery, so they no longer look to them or give them money. But even if you are habituated, it has some psychological cost. I don't think people feel nothing. A tiny little low-scale war is going on inside. Sometimes it comes out as anger."

On the No. 1 train on the West Side, a tall, shabbily dressed man in his early 30s was asking subway riders for attention. "I was just released from a state maximum-security facility," he intoned above the roar of the train. "They taught me it is better to ask for help than to rob. So I'm asking for your help. Don't make me go back." Just as he finished, with the passengers doing their best to avoid his eyes, another man entered from the other end of the car. "Attention, attention," he said. "I was just released from a state maximum-security facility. . . ."

THE EIGHTIES

Being Black and Feeling Blue

(1989)

Shelby Steele

Racial feelings intensified during the eighties. An agonized white majority tried to repent for its past racism. Good will mixed with doubts about public policies and the underclass. With candor and insight, Steele tried to analyze ambivalent black feeling in light of new opportunities. The gulf between black America and white America—and other minorities—was growing. An increasing number of black Americans rejected "white culture" and blamed any underclass, lagging school achievement, or crime on "institutional racism."

In the early seventies when I was in graduate school, I went out for a beer late one afternoon with another black graduate student whom I'd only known casually before. This student was older than I—a stint in the army had interrupted his education—and he had the reputation of being bright and savvy, of having applied street smarts to the business of getting through graduate school. I suppose I was hoping for what would be called today a little mentoring. But it is probably not wise to drink with someone when you are enamored of his reputation, and it was not long before we stumbled into a moment that seemed to transform him before my very eyes. I asked him what he planned to do when he finished his Ph.D., fully expecting to hear of high aspirations matched with shrewd perceptions on how to reach them. But, before he could think, he said with a kind of exhausted sincerity, "Man, I just want to hold on, get a job that doesn't work me too hard, and do a lot of fishing." Was he joking, I asked. "Hell no," he said with exaggerated umbrage. "I'm not into it like the white boys. I don't need what they need."

I will call this man Henry and report that, until five or six years ago when I lost track of him, he was doing exactly as he said he would do.

With much guile and little ambition he had moved through a succession of low-level administrative and teaching jobs, mainly in black studies programs. Of course, it is no crime to just "hold on," and it is hardly a practice limited to blacks. Still, in Henry's case there was truly a troubling discrepancy between his ambition and a fine intelligence recognized by all who knew him. But in an odd way this intelligence was more lateral than vertical, and I would say that it was rechanneled by a certain unseen fear into the business of merely holding on. It would be easy to say that Henry had simply decided on life in a slower lane than he was capable of traveling in, or that he was that rare person who had achieved ambitionless contentment. But, if this was so, Henry would have had wisdom rather than savvy, and he would not have felt the need to carry himself with more self-importance than his station justified. I don't think Henry was uninterested in ambition; I think he was afraid of it.

It is certainly true that there is a little of Henry in most people. My own compulsion to understand him informs me that I must have seen many elements of myself in him. And though I'm sure he stands for a universal human blockage, I also believe that there is something in the condition of being black in America that makes the kind of hesitancy he represents one of black America's most serious and debilitating problems. As Henry reached the very brink of expanded opportunity, with Ph.D. in hand, he diminished his ambition almost as though his degree delivered him to a kind of semi-retirement, but I do think that, as a group, we have hesitated on the brink of new opportunities that we made enormous sacrifices to win for ourselves. The evidence of this lies in one of the most tragic social ironies of late twentieth-century American life—as black Americans have gained in equality and opportunity, we have also declined in relation to whites, so that by many socio-economic and other measures we are further behind whites today than before the great victories of the civil rights movement. By one report, even the black middle class, which had made great gains in the seventies, began to lose ground to its white counterpart in the eighties. Most distressing of all, the black underclass continues to expand rather than shrink.

Of course, I don't suggest that Henry's peculiar inertia singularly explains social phenomena so complex and tragic. I do believe, however, that blacks in general are susceptible to the same web of attitudes and fears that kept Henry beneath his potential, and that our ineffectiveness in taking better advantage of our greater equality and opportunity has much to do with this. I think there is a specific form of racial anxiety that all blacks are vulnerable to that can, in situations where we must engage the mainstream society, increase our self-doubt and undermine our confidence so that we often back away from the challenges that, if taken, would advance us. I believe this hidden racial anxiety may well now be the strongest barrier to our full participation in the American mainstream—that it is as strong or stronger even than the discrimination we still face. To examine this racial anxiety, allow me first to look at how the Henry was born in me.

Until the sixth grade, I attended a segregated school in a small working-class black suburb of Chicago. The school was a dumping ground for teachers with too little competence or mental stability to teach in the white school in our district. In 1956 when I entered the sixth grade, I encountered a new addition to the menagerie of misfits that was our faculty—an ex-Marine whose cruelty was suggested during our first lunch hour when he bit the cap off his Coke bottle and spit it into the wastebasket. Looking back I can see that there was no interesting depth to the cruelty he began to show us almost immediately—no consumptive hatred, no intelligent malevolence. Although we were all black and he was white, I don't think he was even particularly racist. He had obviously needed us to like him though he had no faith that we would. He ran the class like a gang leader, picking favorites one day and banishing them the next. And then there was a permanent pool of outsiders, myself among them, who were made to carry the specific sins that he must have feared most in himself.

The sin I was made to carry was the sin of stupidity. I misread a sentence on the first day of school, and my fate was sealed. He made my stupidity a part of the classroom lore, and very quickly I in fact became stupid. I all but lost the ability to read and found the simplest math beyond me. His punishments for my errors rose in meanness until one day he ordered me to pick up all of the broken glass on the playground with my bare hands. Of course, this would have to be the age of the pop bottle, and there were sections of this playground that glared like a mirror in sunlight. After half an hour's labor I sat down on strike, more out of despair than rebellion.

Again cruelty was no more than a vibration in this man, and so without even a show of anger he commandeered a bicycle, handed it to an eighth grader—one of his lieutenants—and told the boy to run me around the school grounds "until he passes out." The boy was also given a baseball bat to "use on him when he slows down." I ran two laps, about a mile, and then pretended to pass out. The eighth grader knew I was playing possum but could not bring himself to hit me and finally rode off. I exited the school yard through an adjoining cornfield and never returned.

I mention this experience as an example of how one's innate capacity for insecurity is expanded and deepened, of how a disbelieving part of the self is brought to life and forever joined to the believing self. As children we are all wounded in some way and to some degree by the wild world we encounter. From these wounds a disbelieving *anti-self* is born, an internal antagonist and saboteur that embraces the world's negative view of us, that believes our wounds are justified by our own unworthiness, and that entrenches itself as a lifelong voice of doubt. This anti-self is a hidden but aggressive force that scours the world for fresh evidence of our unworthiness. When the believing self announces its aspirations, the anti-self always argues against them, but never on their merits (this is a healthy function of the believing self). It argues instead against our worthiness to pursue these aspirations and, by its lights, we are never worthy of even our smallest dreams. The mission of the anti-self is to deflate the believing self and, thus, draw it down into inertia, passivity, and faithlessness.

The anti-self is the unseen agent of low self-esteem; it is a catalytic energy that tries to induce low self-esteem in the believing self as though it were the complete truth of the personality. The anti-self can only be contained by the strength of the believing self, and this is where one's early environment becomes crucial. If the childhood environment is stable and positive, if the family is whole and provides love, the schools good, the community safe, then the believing self will be reinforced and made strong. If the family is shattered, the schools indifferent, the neighborhood a mine field of dangers, the anti-self will find evidence everywhere with which to deflate the believing self.

This does not mean that a bad childhood cannot be overcome. But it does mean—as I have experienced and observed it—that one's *capacity* for self-doubt and self-belief are roughly the same from childhood on, so that years later when the believing self may have strengthened enough to control the anti-self, one will still have the same capacity for doubt whether or not one has the actual doubt. I think it is this struggle between our capacities for doubt and belief that gives our personalities one of their peculiar tensions and, in this way, marks our character.

My own anti-self was given new scope and power by this teacher's persecution of me, and it was so successful in deflating my believing self that I secretly vowed never to tell my parents what was happening to me. The anti-self had all but sold my believing self on the idea that I was stupid, and I did not want to feel that shame before my parents. It was my brother who finally told them, and his disclosure led to a boycott that closed the school and eventually won the dismissal of my teacher and several others. But my anti-self transformed even this act of rescue into a cause of shame—if there wasn't something wrong with me, why did I have to be rescued? The anti-self follows only the logic of self-condemnation.

But there was another dimension to this experience that my anti-self was only too happy to seize upon. It was my race that landed me in this segregated school and, as many adults made clear to me, my persecution followed a timeless pattern of racial persecution. The implications of this were rich food for the anti-self—my race was so despised that it had to be segregated; as a black my education was so unimportant that even unbalanced teachers without college degrees were adequate; and ignorance and cruelty that would be intolerable in a classroom of whites was perfectly all right in a classroom of blacks. "The anti-self saw no injustice in any of this, but instead took it all as confirmation of a racial inferiority that it could now add to the well of personal doubt I already had. When the adults thought they were consoling me—"Don't worry. They treat all blacks this way"—they were also deepening the wound and expanding my capacity for doubt.

And this is the point. The condition of being black in America means that one will likely endure more wounds to one's self-esteem than others and that the capacity for self-doubt born of these wounds will be compounded and expanded by the black race's reputation of inferiority. The anti-self will most likely have more ammunition with which to deflate the believing self and its aspirations. And the universal human struggle to have belief win out over doubt will be more difficult.

And, more than difficult, it is also made inescapable by the fact of skin color, which, in America, works as a visual invocation of the problem. Black skin has more dehumanizing stereotypes associated with it than any other skin color in America, if not the world. When a black presents himself in an integrated situation, he knows that his skin alone may bring these stereotypes to life in the minds of those he meets and that he, as an individual, may be diminished by his race before he has a chance to reveal a single aspect of his personality. By the symbology of color that operates in our culture, black skin accuses him of inferiority. Under the weight of this accusation, a black will almost certainly doubt himself on some level and to some degree. The ever-vigilant anti-self will grab this racial doubt and mix it into the pool of personal doubt, so that when a black walks into an integrated situation—a largely white college campus, an employment office, a business lunch—he will be vulnerable to the entire realm of his self-doubt before a single word is spoken.

This constitutes an intense and lifelong racial vulnerability and anxiety for blacks. Even though a white American may have been wounded more than a given black, and therefore have a larger realm of inner doubt, his white skin with its connotations of privilege and superiority will actually help protect him from that doubt and from the undermining power of his anti-self, at least in relations with blacks. In fact, the larger the realm of doubt, the more he may be tempted to rely on his white skin for protection from it. Certainly in every self-avowed white racist, whether businessman or member of the Klan, there is a huge realm of self-contempt and doubt that hides behind the mythology of white skin. The mere need to pursue self-esteem through skin color suggests there is no faith that it can be pursued any other way. But if skin color offers whites a certain false esteem and impunity, it offers blacks vulnerability.

This vulnerability begins for blacks with the recognition that we belong quite simply to the most despised race in the human community of races. To be a member of such a group in a society where all others gain an impunity by merely standing in relation to us is to live with a relentless openness to diminishment and shame. By the devious logic of the anti-self, one cannot be open to such diminishment without in fact being inferior and therefore deserving of diminishment. For the anti-self, the charge verifies the crime, so that racial vulnerability itself is evidence of inferiority. In this sense, the anti-self is an internalized racist, our own subconscious bigot, that conspires with society to diminish us.

So when blacks enter the mainstream, they are not only vulnerable to society's racism but also to the racist within. This internal racist is not restricted by law, morality, or social decorum. It cares nothing about civil rights and equal opportunity. It is the self-doubt born of the original wound of racial oppression, and its mission is to establish the justice of that wound and shackle us with doubt.

Of course, the common response to racial vulnerability, as to most vulnerabilities, is denial—the mind's mechanism for ridding itself of intolerable possibilities. For blacks to acknowledge a vulnerability to inferiority anxiety, in the midst of a society that has endlessly accused us of being inferior, feels nothing less than intolerable—as if we were agreeing with the indictment against us. But denial is not the same as eradication, since it only gives unconscious life to what is intolerable to our consciousness. Denial reassigns rather than vanquishes the terror of racial vulnerability. This reassignment only makes the terror stronger by making it unknown. When we deny we always create a dangerous area of self-ignorance, an entire territory of the self that we cannot afford to know. Without realizing it, we begin to circumscribe our lives by avoiding those people and situations that might breach our denial and force us to see consciously what we fear. Though the denial of racial vulnerability is a human enough response, I think it also makes our public discourse on race circumspect and unproductive, since we cannot talk meaningfully about problems we are afraid to name.

Denial is a refusal of painful self-knowledge. When someone or something threatens to breach this refusal, we receive an unconscious shock of the very vulnerability we have denied—a shock that often makes us retreat and more often makes us intensify our denial. When blacks move into integrated situations or face challenges that are new for blacks, the myth of black inferiority is always present as a *condition* of the situation, and as such it always threatens to breach our denial of racial vulnerability. It threatens to make us realize consciously what is intolerable to us—that we have some anxiety about inferiority. We feel this threat unconsciously as a shock of racial doubt delivered by the racist anti-self (always the inner voice of the myth of black inferiority). Consciously, we will feel this shock as a sharp discomfort or a desire to retreat from the situation. Almost always we will want to intensify our denial.

I will call this shock "integration shock" since it occurs most powerfully when blacks leave their familiar world and enter into the mainstream. Integration shock and denial are mutual intensifiers. The stab of racial doubt that integration shock delivers is a pressure to intensify denial, and a more rigid denial means the next stab of doubt will be more threatening and therefore more intense. The symbiosis of these two forces is, I believe, one of the reasons black Americans have become preoccupied with racial pride, almost to the point of obsession over the past twenty-five or so years. With more exposure to the mainstream we have endured more integration shock, more jolts of inferiority anxiety. And I think we have often responded with rather hyperbolic claims of black pride by which we deny that anxiety. In this sense, our self-consciousness around pride, our need to make a point of it, is, to a degree, a form of denial. Pride becomes denial when it ceases to reflect self-esteem quietly and begins to compensate loudly for unacknowledged inner doubt. Here it also becomes dangerous since it prevents us from confronting and overcoming that doubt.

I think the most recent example of black pride-as-denial is the campaign (which seems to have been launched by a committee) to add yet another name to the litany of names that blacks have given themselves over the past century. Now we are to be African-Americans instead of, or in conjunction with, being black Americans. This self-conscious reaching for pride through nomenclature suggests nothing so much as a despair over the possibility of gaining the less conspicuous pride that follows real advancement. In its invocation of the glories of a remote African past and its wistful suggestion of homeland, this name denies the doubt black

Americans have about their contemporary situation in America. There is
no element of self-confrontation in it, no facing of real racial vulnerabilities, as there was with the name "black." I think "black" easily became the
name of preference in the sixties precisely because it was not a denial but
a confrontation of inferiority anxiety, with the shame associated with the
color black. There was honest self-acceptance in this name, and I think it
diffused much of our vulnerability to the shame of color. Even between
blacks, "black" is hardly the drop-dead fighting word it was when I was a
child. Possibly we are ready now for a new name, but I think "black" has
been our most powerful name yet because it so frankly called out our
shame and doubt and helped us (and others) to accept ourselves. In the
name African-American there is too much false neutralization of doubt,
too much looking away from the caldron of our own experience. It is a
euphemistic name that hides us even from ourselves.

I think blacks have been more preoccupied with pride over the past
twenty-five years because we have been more exposed to integration
shock since the 1964 Civil Rights Bill made equal opportunity the law of
the land (if not quite the full reality of the land). Ironically, it was the
inequality of opportunity and all the other repressions of legal segregation
that buffered us from our racial vulnerability. In a segregated society we
did not have the same accountability to the charge of racial inferiority
since we were given little opportunity to disprove the charge. It was the
opening up of opportunity—anti-discrimination laws, the social programs
of the Great Society, equal opportunity guidelines and mandates, fair
housing laws, Affirmative Action, and so on—that made us individually
and collectively more accountable to the myth of black inferiority and
therefore more racially vulnerable.

This vulnerability has increased in the same proportion that our
freedom and opportunity have increased. The exhilaration of new freedom is always followed by a shock of accountability. Whatever unresolved
doubt follows the oppressed into greater freedom will be inflamed since
freedom always carries a burden of proof, always throws us back on ourselves. And freedom, even imperfect freedom, makes blacks a brutal
proposition: if you're not inferior, prove it. This is the proposition that
shocks us and makes us vulnerable to our underworld of doubt. The whis-
pers of the racist and anti-self are far louder in the harsh accountability of
freedom than in subjugation where the oppressor is so entirely to blame.

The bitter irony of all this is that our doubt and the hesitancy it
breeds now help limit our progress in America almost as systematically as
segregation once did. Integration shock gives the old boundaries of legal
segregation a regenerative power. To avoid the shocks of doubt that come

from entering the mainstream, or plunging more deeply into it, we often pull back at precisely those junctures where segregation once pushed us back. In this way we duplicate the conditions of our oppression and re-enact our role as victims even in the midst of far greater freedom and far less victimization. Certainly there is still racial discrimination in America, but I believe that the unconscious replaying of our oppression is now the greatest barrier to our full equality.

๖๕

The way in which integration shock regenerates the old boundaries of segregation for blacks is most evident in three tendencies—the tendency to minimalize or avoid real opportunities, to withhold effort in areas where few blacks have achieved, and to self-segregate in integrated situations.

If anything, it is the presence of new opportunities in society that triggers integration shock. If opportunity is a chance to succeed, it is also a chance to fail. The vulnerability of blacks to hidden inferiority anxiety makes failure a much more forbidding prospect. If a black pursues an opportunity in the mainstream—opens a business, goes up for a challenging job or difficult promotion—and fails, that failure can be used by the anti-self to confirm both personal and racial inferiority. The diminishment and shame will tap an impersonal as well as personal source of doubt. When a white fails, he alone fails. His doubt is strictly personal, which gives him more control over the failure. He can discover *his* mistakes, learn the reasons *he* made them, and try again. But the black, laboring under the myth of inferiority, will have this impersonal, culturally determined doubt to contend with. This form of doubt robs him of a degree of control over his failure since he alone cannot eradicate the cultural myth that stings him. There will be a degree of impenetrability to his failure that will constitute an added weight of doubt.

The effect of this is to make mainstream opportunity more intimidating and risky for blacks. This is made worse in that blacks, owing to past and present deprivations, may come to the mainstream in the first place with a lower stock of self-esteem. High risk and low self-esteem are hardly the best combination with which to tackle the challenges of a highly advanced society in which others have been blessed by history with very clear advantages. Under these circumstances opportunity can seem more like a chance to fail than a chance to succeed. All this makes for a kind of opportunity aversion that I think was behind the hesitancy I saw in Henry, in myself, and in other blacks of all class backgrounds. It is also, I believe, one of the reasons for the sharp decline in the number of black students entering college, even as many colleges launch recruiting drives to attract more black students.

This aversion to opportunity generates a way of seeing that minimalizes opportunity to the point where it can be ignored. In black communities the most obvious entrepreneurial opportunities are routinely ignored. It is often outsiders or the latest wave of immigrants who own the shops, restaurants, cleaners, gas stations, and even the homes and apartments. Education is a troubled area in black communities for numerous reasons, but certainly one of them is that many black children are not truly imbued with the idea that learning is virtually the same as opportunity. Schools—even bad schools—were the opportunity that so many immigrant groups used to learn the workings and the spirit of American society. In the very worst inner city schools there are accredited teachers who teach the basics, but too often to students who shun those among them who do well, who see studying as a sucker's game and school itself as a waste of time. One sees in many of these children almost a determination not to learn, a suppression of the natural impulse to understand, that cannot be entirely explained by the determinism of poverty. Out of school, in the neighborhood, these same children learn everything. I think it is the meeting with the mainstream that school symbolizes that clicks them off. In the cultural ethos from which they come, it is always these meetings that trigger the aversion to opportunity behind which lies inferiority anxiety. Their parents and their culture send them a double message: go to school but don't really apply yourself. The risk is too high.

This same pattern of avoidance, this unconscious circumvention of possibility, is also evident in our commitment to effort—the catalyst of opportunity. Difficult, sustained effort—in school or career or family life—will be riddled with setbacks, losses, and frustrations. Racial vulnerability erodes effort for blacks by exaggerating the importance of these setbacks, by recasting them as confirmation of racial inferiority rather than the normal pitfalls of sustained effort. The racist anti-self greets these normal difficulties with an I-told-you-so attitude, and the believing self, unwilling to risk seeing that the anti-self is right, may grow timid and pull back from the effort. As with opportunity, racial vulnerability makes hard effort in the mainstream a high-risk activity for blacks.

But this is not the case in those areas where blacks have traditionally excelled. In sports and music, for example, the threat of integration shock is effectively removed. Because so many blacks have succeeded in these areas, a black can enter them without being racially vulnerable. Failure carries no implication of racial inferiority, so the activity itself is far less risky than those in which blacks have no record of special achievement. Certainly in sports and music one sees blacks sustain the most creative and disciplined effort, and they seize opportunities where one would have thought there were none. But all of this changes the instant racial vulnerability becomes a factor. Across the country thousands of young black males take every opportunity and make every effort to reach the elite ranks of the NBA or the NFL. But in the classroom, where racial vulnerability is a hidden terror, they and many of their classmates put forth the meagerest effort and show a virtual indifference to the genuine opportunity that education is.

But the most visible circumvention that results from integration shock is the tendency toward self-segregation that, if anything, seems to have increased over the last twenty years. Along with opportunity and effort, it is also white people themselves who are often avoided. I hear young black professionals say they do not socialize with whites after work unless at some "command performance" that comes with the territory of their career. On largely white university campuses where integration shock is particularly intense, black students often try to enforce a kind of neo-separatism that includes black "theme" dorms, black student unions, Afro-houses, black cultural centers, black student lounges, and so on. There is a geo-politics involved in this activity, where race is tied to territory in a way that mimics the "whites only"/"coloreds only" designations of the past. Only now these race spaces are staked out in the name of pride.

I think this impulse to self-segregate, to avoid whites, has to do with the way white people are received by the black anti-self. Even if the believing self wants to see racial difference as essentially meaningless, the anti-self, that hidden perpetrator of racist doubt, sees white people as better than black people. Its mission is to confirm black inferiority, and so it looks closely at whites, watches the way they walk, talk, and negotiate the world, and then grants these styles of being and acting superiority. Somewhere inside every black is a certain awe at the power and achievement of the white race. In every barbershop gripe session where whites are put through the grinder of black anger, there will be a kind of backhanded respect—"Well, he might be evil, but that white boy is smart." True or not, the anti-self organizes its campaign against the believing self's faith in black equality around this supposition. And so, for blacks (as is true for whites in another way), white people in the generic sense have no neutrality. In themselves they are stimulants to the black anti-self, deliverers of doubt. Their color slips around the deepest need of blacks to believe in their immutable equality and communes directly with their self-suspicion.

So it is not surprising to hear black students on largely white campuses say that they are simply more comfortable with other blacks. Nor is it surprising to see them caught up in absurd contradictions—demanding separate facilities for themselves even as they protest apartheid in South Africa. Racial vulnerability is a species of fear, and, as such, it is the progenitor of countless ironies. More freedom makes us more vulnerable so that in the midst of freedom we feel the impulse to carve out segregated comfort zones that protect us more from our own doubt than from whites. We balk before opportunity and pull back from effort just as these things would bear fruit. We reconstitute the boundaries of segregation just as they become illegal. By averting opportunity and curbing effort for fear of awakening a sense of inferiority, we make inevitable the very failure that shows us inferior.

One of the worst aspects of oppression is that it never ends when the oppressor begins to repent. There is a legacy of doubt in the oppressed that follows long after the cleanest repentance by the oppressor, just as guilt trails the oppressor and makes his redemption incomplete. These themes of doubt and guilt fill in like fresh replacements and work to duplicate the oppression. I think black Americans are today more oppressed by doubt than by racism and that the second phase of our struggle for freedom must be a confrontation with that doubt. Unexamined, this doubt leads us back into the tunnel of our oppression where we re-enact our victimization just as society struggles to end its victimization of us. We are not a people formed in freedom. Freedom is always a call to possibility that demands an overcoming of doubt. We are still new to freedom, new to its challenges, new even to the notion that self-doubt can be the slyest enemy of freedom. For us freedom has so long meant the absence of oppression that we have not yet realized that it also means the conquering of doubt.

Of course, this does not mean that doubt should become a lake we swim in, but it does mean that we should begin our campaign against doubt by acknowledging it, by outlining the contours of the black anti-self so that we can know and accept exactly what it is that we are afraid of. This is knowledge that can be worked with, knowledge that can point with great precision to the actions through which we can best mitigate doubt and advance ourselves. This is the sort of knowledge that gives the believing self a degree of immunity to the anti-self and that enables it to pile up little victories that, in sum, grant it even more immunity.

Certainly inferiority has long been the main theme of the black anti-self, its most lethal weapon against our capacity for self-belief. And so, in a general way, the acceptance of this piece of knowledge implies a mission: to show ourselves and (only indirectly) the larger society that we are not inferior on any dimension. That this should already be assumed goes without saying. But what "should be" falls within the province of the believing self where it has no solidity until the doubt of the anti-self is called out and shown false by demonstrable action in the real world. This is the proof that grants the "should" its rightful solidity, that transforms it from a well-intentioned claim into a certainty.

The temptation is to avoid so severe a challenge, to maintain a black identity, painted in the colors of pride and culture, that provides us with a way of seeing ourselves apart from this challenge. It is easier to be "African-American" than to organize oneself on one's own terms and around one's own aspiration and then, through sustained effort and difficult achievement, put one's insidious anti-self quietly to rest. No black identity, however beautifully conjured, will spare blacks this challenge that, despite its fairness or unfairness, is simply in the nature of things. But then I have faith that in time we will meet this challenge since this, too, is in the nature of things.

PART III

Boomers on the Make

The Mass Market
Is Splitting Apart
(1983)

Bruce Steinberg

Steinberg's early report noted a new middle-class economic stratification, soon
to change the face of the nation. Income patterns and salary schedules were
just then propelling individuals toward upscale and downscale, high end and
low. The yuppie had arrived with "discretionary income," seeking visible proofs
of success in a material world and exhibiting an acquisitive desire to "have it
all." Still, the majority of citizens seemed just to be hanging in there, shopping
at K mart, not Neiman-Marcus.

Most businessmen don't realize it yet, but the middle class—the
principal market for much of what they make—is gradually
being pulled apart. Economic forces are propelling one family
after another toward the high or low end of the income spectrum. For
many marketers, particularly those positioned to sell to the well-to-do,
this presages good times. For others used to selling millions of units of
their products to middle-income folks, the prospects are altogether darker.

By almost all measures, the degree of income inequality between
rich and poor American families has been increasing. The richest one-
fifth of families received nearly 43% of the country's total money income
last year, their largest share in over three decades. That's more than nine
times as much as the poorest fifth took in—vs. 7½ times as much a decade
ago. More critically, the broad middle class, defined as families with
incomes between $15,000 and $35,000 per year (in constant 1982 dollars),
fell from 51% of total families in 1973 to 44% last year. The extremes on
either end, those making less than $15,000 or more than $35,000, grew as
a percentage of all families. This trend seems to have escaped the attention of many American companies, even though it has far-reaching conse-

quences for them as employers and as purveyors of goods. If they're smart, chichi retailers and manufacturers of newfangled electronic wonders should be able to capitalize on the shift. Automakers, home appliance companies, and furniture manufacturers face tough challenges.

As used here, family income is measured before taxes—after tax figures would show the same trend, according to the experts. The income includes earnings of all family members: husbands, wives, and, when they work, children or other relatives. It also encompasses other forms of income besides wages—interest and dividends, as well as transfer payments. This leaves out such benefits as food stamps and Medicaid received by the poor, company-paid health and life insurance received by the middle class, and stock options, expense accounts, and nonrealized capital gains on homes and financial assets, which accrue mainly to the well-off. While it's hard to put a price on these noncash benefits, on balance they probably don't have much effect on the distribution of rewards. Being able to dine out at company expense or borrow against the steadily increasing value of his home may make as big a difference to an executive's income as food stamps do to a poor person's.

What caused this polarization in incomes? The recent slump didn't help matters—with unemployment high, it's hardly surprising that the number of families with low income climbed. But the decline of the middle really began during the long expansion of the late Seventies, when families began to find the economic ground under them shifting.

The key to what's going on lies in the explosive growth of the service economy, which has brought on massive upheaval in employment patterns. During the last decade, manufacturing's share of total employment plummeted. While blue-collar ranks were decimated, the number of professional and technical employees rose. At the same time, nearly nine out of ten new jobs were created in the service and trade sectors of the economy. In fact, over half of them were in just four industries, the new tetrarchs—the four leaders—of the labor market: health, business services, finance, and eating and drinking places. Since the start of the current recovery, with industrial production rising 16%, the entire manufacturing sector—made up of 20 industries by the Department of Labor's classification—added some 800,000 jobs, while the business-services industry alone added over 400,000.

This would be no problem if the rapidly growing industries rewarded their employees as richly as does manufacturing, but they don't. As Barry Bluestone, director of the Social Welfare Research Institute at Boston College, points out, "It takes two department store jobs or three restaurant jobs to equal the earnings of just one average manufacturing job." Retail trade is simply low paying. Service industries, by contrast, display a two-humped distribution in salaries: they employ a larger percentage of their work force at both ends of the earnings spectrum than do manufacturing industries. In a bank, for example, at one end there'll be lots of tellers and guards, at the other end a fair number of loan officers.

In addition, the gap between managerial and nonmanagerial salaries is much wider in services than in manufacturing. In 1980, the last year for which these calculations can be made, production workers in manufacturing earned an average of $15,000 per year vs. $23,000 for managers and professionals. In the service sector, nonsupervisory employees made an average of just $9,900 per year, while their supervisors averaged nearly $30,000 per year. In the health-services industry, the nation's largest employer, doctors, dentists, and health administrators averaged over $43,000 per year, while nonsupervisory workers—orderlies, nurse's aides, most nurses, and health technicians—averaged a meager $9,700.

Inequality of income for full-time male employees increased sharply in all industries between 1977 and 1982, according to Census Bureau calculations. The trend was most pronounced in those industries that were rapidly adding jobs—namely services, finance, and retail trade. Even within manufacturing, the relatively fast-growing industries show the greatest signs of polarization: managers and professionals in the computer industry make more than the manufacturing average, while production workers make somewhat less.

Projections by the Bureau of Labor Statistics indicate that the jobs likely to increase most will continue to be those at opposite ends of the earnings spectrum. Strong growth is expected in the number of professional and technical workers—most are high paid, with some notable exceptions like nurses. Even stronger growth should occur at the low end, among such service workers as janitors, fast-food workers, and hospital orderlies.

These employment trends flow from what's happening to American industries. The BLS expects a modest increase, at best, in manufacturing employment in the Eighties, in line with the overall growth of the economy. Manufacturing is far more sensitive to the overall health of the economy than the service sector, which seems to grow even when times are bad. But while employment growth in manufacturing will be subdued, the tetrarch industries will supply nearly half of all new jobs. The eating and drinking industry, by itself, should *add* nearly three times as many jobs as will *exist* in the computer industry by 1990.

A close look at the business-services industry suggests how the creation of new jobs will, if anything, increase income polarization in service industries generally. Business services are a potpourri of seemingly disparate activities united by a common thread: they perform all sorts of functions that are cheaper for business to contract out than to staff internally. Some of these jobs are high paid, high skilled, and in some cases, even high tech: in data processing and computing, research and development, management consulting, and public relations. Others are low skilled, low paid, and certainly low tech: janitorial services, security, and temporary office help. Business services should show enormous growth, employing many of the 700,000 new secretaries, 500,000 janitors, and 130,000 computer operators that BLS expects will be needed in the Eighties.

Technological change should create substantial economic wealth, but as it pushes productivity up it reduces the need for hands. Nobel Prize-winning economist Wassily Leontief tells the tale of telephone operators: "As automatic switching equipment was adopted, their productivity became so high that their jobs were practically eliminated." This is an extreme example, but while communications looks as if it will be a major growth industry of the Eighties, it is expected to account for only 1% of new jobs because of its very rapid productivity growth. By comparison, in the low-tech, low-paying, but fast-growth eating-and-drinking-place industry, even *fast* food is labor-intensive. A typical Burger King employs nearly 60 people.

International competition is keeping a lid on wages in manufacturing by forcing companies to hold down labor costs or move to the low-wage areas of the world. As Philip E. Benton, Jr., vice president for sales operations at Ford, notes: "Offshore sourcing will definitely increase, whether it be components or cars." What's true for the auto industry is true for much of manufacturing—an increasing share of assembly operations will be performed overseas, though the managerial and technical functions will stay at home. That's fine for those in management positions, not good for blue collar workers.

Plant closings eliminated about four million manufacturing jobs, in the five years through 1982, according to Candee Harris, an economist at the Brookings Institution. Most of the displaced apparently found new employment fairly rapidly, Harris points out, many in other manufacturing jobs. But they lost whatever seniority rights they had at their old jobs, and most took cuts in pay. Consider a laid-off steelworker who had been earning $13.50 an hour. If he took a job in the electronics components industry, he would make $7.50 an hour. Barry Bluestone refers to this process as "skidding."

The discipline that international competition imposes on manufacturing, causing it to raise productivity, isn't there for most trade and service industries: Burger King and Pinkerton's don't have to worry about the Japanese breathing down their necks. However, with productivity low in many of these industries—and hardly growing in most of them—wages must also be kept low. Low wages further obviate the need to introduce labor-saving technology. Hence the prospect for many new jobs.

A big question hangs over one major vocational group: clerical workers. At the moment, it's the single largest occupation, and heavily female. But according to a new study carried out by Leontief and Faye Duchin of the Institute for Economic Analysis at New York University, office automation will eliminate many clerical jobs in this decade. Theirs is a more pessimistic projection than that of the BLS. Such a trend would augur dismally for women's earnings.

It wouldn't be too good for family finances either: the growing number of two-earner households has till now slowed the trend toward greater polarization of family incomes. For one thing, regardless of whether their husband's earnings are high or low, working wives contribute about the same amount to the family kitty. For another, participation of wives in the labor force declines once their husbands earn more than $20,000 a year and drops sharply once male earnings exceed $35,000 a year. As a result, family earnings have displayed less of a shift toward inequality than male earnings.

But this moderating influence on overall income inequality might well reverse itself over the remainder of this decade. For one thing, two-thirds of wives whose husbands work now also work, and it's doubtful that the proportion can increase much more. "The great movement of wives into the labor force has run its course," as Fabian Linden, executive director of the Conference Board's Consumer Research Center, puts it. So the growing polarization of individual incomes can no longer be offset by adding an extra worker to a family's efforts.

The jobs women are increasingly taking, moreover, may actually heighten income disparities. The tendency for women not to work when their husbands' incomes are high may be changing. Even now women are still largely concentrated in the female ghettos of clerical and sales work and the low-paying professions of nursing and teaching. Only in recent years have large numbers of women trained to become attorneys, doctors, and MBA-equipped managers—and these women are mostly in the early phases of their professional lives. As Tony Adams, director of market research at Campbell Soup, notes: "We found growth in female careerism—as opposed to the 'working woman.'" This should narrow the gap between male and female earnings. But given the factors behind spouse selection—love usually strikes people with similar education and backgrounds—it can only exaggerate the polarization of family incomes.

These trends will be amplified if automation displaces many women from clerical jobs. Some might be retrained for managerial or technical positions. Many more will probably end up flipping hamburgers. Kyle T. Craig, executive vice president at Burger King, says: "We already have more middle-aged women working for us than we used to and we think that this will continue." Because the husbands of these women are the likely candidates for downward mobility, it's easy to foresee a situation in which once middle-class blue-collar families keep running but slip behind, while increasing numbers of professional workers bring home two fat paychecks.

Executives in many industries resist the idea that the middle class is being pulled apart. Many say things like: "I just don't believe it." But the consequences are too critical to ignore.

Astute companies are seeking to take advantage of the trends. Paul W. Van Orden, executive vice president of General Electric's consumer-products sector, observes, "We do see more of a bimodal distribution. It gives GE an increasing opportunity at the upper end of the scale." Mary Joan Glynn, vice president of marketing at Bloomingdale's, comments: "In the Seventies it became apparent that the profitable markets would be at the top and the bottom of the scale, because of restrictions on the middle of the market." Lane Cardwell, vice president for strategic planning at one of Pillsbury's restaurant groups, says flatly: "It's a trend that's been in place for years—it's irreversible, it's good for us."

Indeed. The so-called upscale market is growing rapidly—by 1990, according to projections by the Conference Board, about one-third of personal income will be received by households with incomes of $50,000 or more (in constant 1982 dollars) compared with about a quarter now. In the words of Conference Board economist Linden, "The class market will become a mass market."

This pronouncement of good news finesses the rather serious question of what kind of mass market can exist without support from a broadly based middle class. A mass market is generally based on long production runs of standardized products. But those households with incomes in excess of $50,000 will constitute less than 15% of the total number of households. As Philip Benton of Ford puts it, "That kind of trend [toward polarization] would be devastating to any durable goods marketing strategy." Which may be why auto industry executives so resist the implications of the changes taking place, even though upheavals in their own industry helped initiate the erosion of the blue-collar middle class.

The coming of the flexible factory, by virtue of its automation capable of mounting short production runs more economically, may help, but it won't solve the problem. Companies will gain the ability to produce a wider variety of products, but they'll still have to sell millions of units to be profitable.

For industries where product innovation is rapid and markets haven't been saturated—personal computers, say—polarization of income is, if anything, helpful. Having a large group of people who can afford to experiment with new gadgets is a prerequisite for the rapid dissemination of such high-tech products into the home. This allows Randall L. Tobias, president of AT&T Consumer Products, to speak glowingly of the Touch-a-Matic 1600 telephone, priced at around $150, with a date and time display and 15 buttons that can be programmed for frequent calling. It doesn't take much imagination to envision well-to-do households possessing phone-computer centers, while those in more straitened circumstances make do with a $10 special: the voice quality may be lousy but at least you're still hooked into the network.

Companies like General Electric face different challenges. Home appliances are mature products, with most demand coming from the need to replace existing units. GE is fighting this reality by extending its top-of-the-line offerings in product categories from dishwashers to drip coffee makers, often by upgrading the devices with electronics. With delayed starting mechanisms you'll be able to leave your house and have your appliances function while you're away, making the local burglars think that someone is still at home. In a few years, most of GE's top-of-the-line models will be able to be started from a remote site, allowing you to set supper cooking with a phone call.

Still, all the electronics in the world won't change the basic appeal of a refrigerator or a stove. According to Van Orden, with traditional mass-market items facing slower growth in sales, "Growth has to come from increased market share." If GE's consumer strategy succeeds, it will do so at the expense of less innovative manufacturers. You can probably expect more shakeouts in hardgoods industries.

With the affluent spending nearly $2 of every $5 in their food budgets away from home, the restaurant industry can only profit from polarization. Pillsbury's two restaurant groups—Burger King and S&A (named for the Steak & Ale chain the group runs)—are positioned to serve low-income and high-income markets, respectively. For S&A the current emphasis is on expanding Bennigan's, a trendy hangout aimed straight at baby-boomers with money in their pockets. In the evening, Bennigan's becomes a rendezvous for young urban professionals.

The S&A group is also launching a chain of upscale fast-food establishments called J.J. Muggs—a "gourmet hamburger house," in the company's description, where you can get table service and still be out in 20 minutes. Burger King isn't worried about fraternal competition. According to Kyle Craig: "Burger King is an attractive alternative to lower-income segments, as well as to the high-income segments who want a change of pace or convenience."

Retailers, who are as close to the customer as anyone, can fine-tune their appeal even more carefully than manufacturers. Neiman-Marcus and K mart are good examples. The Neiman-Marcus customer has a median income of between $50,000 and $65,000 a year. "Some people think we're positioned for an elitist customer base, and to some extent that's true," says Ferdinand Hauslein, Jr., vice president for marketing. "But we offer merchandise at all price levels—we have shirts as low as $30 or $35. We want to attract the young attorney, for example, and have him trade up as his income and expectations go up."

For most customers at K mart, by contrast, a $30 shirt sounds like a cruel joke. "The typical customer has more demands on income than income," according to Michael G. Wellman, director of planning and research. "We're hot on do-it-yourself. American consumers still want their own home, but it's not like it used to be. Now you stay put and improve your lifestyle through home improvement." If this rationale for working on the old homestead holds true, then put your money into companies that make hammers, saws, and wrenches: a lot more Americans are going to be staying put in the years to come.

The industry growth dynamic that has made for cleavage in the middle-income consumer market reinforces itself. Those industries whose sales benefit most from polarization are precisely those whose employment patterns helped produce it in the first place. At the same time, the industries that spawned the middle class stand to lose that market bit by bit, with every worker laid off, every job lost to foreign competition.

From

Beyond Our Means

(1987)

Alfred L. Malabre, Jr.

While the eighties cornucopia was enriching a new class of citizens, many others were living on plastic. Public deficits were soaring. The *Wall Street Journal* economist Alfred L. Malabre, Jr., considered this shaky scaffolding in his book, subtitled "How America's Long Years of Debt, Deficits and Reckless Borrowing Now Threaten to Overwhelm Us." Malabre combined data and psychological observation to draw astringent conclusions about the nation's prosperity. With the stock market crash of October 1987 and the economic disorders of the late eighties, Malabre's warnings seemed borne out.

To start, a few statistics. Nine of every ten U.S. teenagers have their own camera. Seven of every ten own a stereo. One in three has a television set. One in five has a personal phone. One in six has an automobile. One in eight has a computer.

It may be comforting to suppose that the awesomely high living standard of most Americans—exemplified by this teenage affluence—is founded on unmatched know-how and industriousness. That, indeed, is the popular conception: a can-do nation, innovative and hard-working and therefore quite properly blessed with material benefits unrivaled in the world's less productive economies. The truth is something else. The profusion of goods and services that most Americans enjoy in this century's closing years reflects a very different sort of tendency: to live beyond our means. Primarily this, and not some rare ability to deliver, underlies the seemingly boundless increase in American prosperity through much of the post-World War II era.

Debt is at the root of this tendency to live beyond our means. Massively, debt permeates our economy at all levels—personal, corporate, and governmental. The magnitudes are awesome. In all, as a nation, we are

more than $7 trillion in debt—it's impossible to say the precise amount—
and the total keeps soaring. It has nearly quadrupled since the mid-1970s. It
now approximates $35,000 for each man, woman, and child in the nation. It
comes to more than double the nation's yearly output of goods and services.
The bulk of it—nearly half—is owed by businesses. The rest is owed, in
nearly equal shares, by governmental units—mainly federal, but state and
local as well—and by individuals. The federal portion alone recently swept
past $2 trillion. Interest payments on this federal borrowing now exceed a
tenth of all national income, twice the rate of a decade earlier.

And while the pyramid of debt keeps mounting, the underlying collateral for the debt has begun to erode. Consumer borrowing is largely
secured by housing, but the value of the nation's housing stock no longer
rises apace; of late, home values in many areas have in fact been sinking.
Plant and equipment, brick and mortar, underlie much of the debt that
corporations owe, but at many corporations—a case in point is the steel
business—such assets grow increasingly obsolete. As the recent proliferation of so-called junk bonds suggests, the quality of much corporate debt
keeps deteriorating. Meanwhile, governmental debt rests largely on the
tax base, yet the tax bite has narrowed in the wake of tax cutting and considerable corporate and individual tax breaks. From California to
Massachusetts, voters have forced new limits on local tax authorities. The
nation's vast infrastructure of roads, bridges, and other public facilities
has been built largely through governmental borrowing. The burden of
this debt keeps growing, but the infrastructure itself—witness the spread
of potholes on many major roads—keeps deteriorating.

Our willingness, even determination, to live beyond our means—to
go far more deeply into debt than our resources safely will allow—has led
to other ominous patterns. As we have overborrowed, we have overspent.
In late 1986, the share of after-tax income that Americans saved—including most money set aside for retirement—sank briefly below 2 percent.
This was a postwar low, lower than the comparable reading for any other
major industrial country and less than half the rate at which we saved
only a decade ago.

We have tended as well to overpay ourselves. We complain—rarely
blaming ourselves—that we are unable to compete with goods and services offered by our foreign competitors. Our balance of trade—our sales
abroad minus what we purchase from foreigners—has swung in less than
a decade from a multibillion-dollar surplus to a deficit far exceeding $100
billion a year.

This extravagance—our willingness to overpay ourselves with over-
valued dollars and then to borrow and shop abroad, where things are

cheaper—has led us finally to the unenviable status of debtor nation. In 1985, for the first time since early in the century, the U.S. owed more to the rest of the world than the rest of the world owed it. By late 1986, foreigners had over $1 trillion invested in the U.S., some $170 billion more than the total of U.S. investments abroad. The shortfall is expected to near $300 billion by 1988. As recently as 1982, American holdings abroad exceeded foreigners' assets in the U.S. by nearly $200 billion.

This new debtor status is precisely what has long prevailed—the condition has begun to assume a permanent look—in such financially troubled lands as Brazil, Mexico, and Argentina. Indebtedness has imposed no immediate adverse impact on the American economy. Indeed, foreigners' desire to hold American assets has helped the U.S. economy in a number of ways, from financing federal borrowing to suppressing U.S. inflation by tending to bolster the U.S. dollar. But if the trend persists, if America sinks deeper and deeper into debtor-nation status, painful bills will begin coming due. Americans will be compelled to give up more and more of their income simply to pay interest to overseas creditors. To service its global obligations, the U.S. will be forced to run larger and larger trade surpluses—there are none now—on goods and services, something that cannot be achieved without a severe further decline in the dollar's international value. We'll be forced, in other words, to sell our goods more cheaply, which means among other things paying ourselves less. Ultimately, the generous living standards that so many Americans have enjoyed for so many years are bound to erode.

. . . [W]e have persistently, stubbornly lived far beyond our means— to a point where now, sadly, it is beyond our means to put things right readily. At long last we are facing an impasse, one of our own making. . . . Economic Cassandras have been issuing warnings for years. I know. As a financial writer, I've been bombarded with the gloomy press releases of such noted pessimists as Eliot Janeway and Howard Ruff for more years than I have gray hairs. But the dire consequences never seem to come to pass. Instead, employment and incomes rise, the two-car garage proliferates, roaming midwestern schoolteachers tour Paris and Rome, gourmet sections spring up and then swiftly expand in massive supermarkets as Americans consume seven hundred thousand pounds of caviar yearly, four times the late-1970s intake.

Notwithstanding all this, the scary scenarios keep arriving in the morning mail. A notable sample is contained in a 1985 issue of *International Moneyline,* an economic newsletter published by Julian M. Snyder. The issue outlines Snyder's "Armageddon" for the economy, an eventuality that he clearly regards as inescapable "sooner or later." The five-phase script begins with "stepped up money creation" in the face of "deflationary pressure and debt problems" and progresses through assorted economic difficulties until, with phase five, a depression settles in.

I continue, as I have done for more than a quarter century, to lob such hair-raising (and often headline-seeking) missives into a generous deskside wastebasket. But now I do so more gingerly and not without a quick glance and perhaps even a scribbled note or two for future reference—just in case. For as the nation's debt load—private as well as public—continues to pile up, as savings and investment keep lagging, as pay continues to outstrip comparable levels abroad while productivity remains lackluster, the dark pessimism of the apocalyptic forecasters grows less improbable.

Throughout our history we have shown an enviable disdain for limits, reflected in our national compulsion to consume and grow. We are not people accustomed to constraints—even as it becomes increasingly clear that we can no longer afford our aspirations. Meanwhile, the Reagan administration provides an extreme, even grotesque, illustration of our collective abandon in its reluctance to seek appreciably higher taxes or to rein in spending.

⊀↷

The sources of today's predicament extend far back—beyond the last recession, beyond the long years of stagflation that marked much of the 1970s and late 1960s, even beyond the early post-World War II expansion, with its minimal inflation and unemployment levels. They reach all the way back to the grim, drab years of economic depression that preceded the Second World War, when unemployment wasn't 10 percent of the labor force or even 15 percent or 20 percent—but 25 percent. The combined losses of American corporations in some Great Depression years worked out to huge (for those times) numbers—$1.3 billion in 1932 and $1.2 billion in 1933.

Franklin Delano Roosevelt's New Deal was remedial and timely. The establishment of such agencies as the Federal Deposit Insurance Corporation (designed to safeguard savings with freshly printed dollar bills if need be) was and continues to be appropriate. But many of today's problems stem from the fact that Americans now feel entitled to the handout programs these Depression-inspired measures have become.

A statistic: Even after six years of Reagan, nearly one of every two Americans depends entirely or in large part on some variety of governmental "transfer" payment—money gathered largely through taxation and then transferred to individuals supposedly on the basis of need, but in reality, more often than not largely unrelated to need. In the past decade and a half, the number of Americans living largely or entirely off a governmental check for which they perform no labor has risen some 25 percent, to roughly 100 million. That constitutes nearly one government-dependent individual for each working citizen. In the early 1970s this ratio was one in three, one dependent for every three workers. The number of government-dependent Americans approximates 150 million nowadays if one also includes people at work whose employment depends on a government contract—such as a worker building submarines for the Electric Boat division of General Dynamics in Groton, Conn., for instance, or an economist at the University of Chicago who serves on the side as consultant to the Commerce Department. The federal government now pays over $4,000 to each American each year on the average, up from $1,705 in 1976 and only $685 in 1966. The current total exceeds $7,000 if state and local government payments are added.

Thirty-eight million Americans receive Social Security payments, over 30 million get Medicare, some 23 million receive Medicaid, over 20 million collect food stamps, children from nearly 6 million households get school lunches, and 2.8 million households receive public-housing benefits. To this long list should be added more than 4 million recipients of Supplemental Security Income and some 11 million recipients of so-called Aid to Families with Dependent Children. To be sure, there is overlapping in these statistics, and they do reflect many instances of bona fide need. But they also reflect countless instances of "welfare" for the well off.

A twenty-year perspective, spanning the Johnson, Nixon, Ford, Carter, and early Reagan presidencies, shows the rise of transfer-payment entitlements in unmistakable terms. Over the twenty years, entitlement payments rose from 24 percent of federal spending to 41 percent. Some of this remarkable increase represents a noble determination to help the nation's needy with funds collected from relatively productive individuals. But the bulk of these huge payments clearly has been delivered to Americans who are relatively well off. A 1986 study by the Heritage Foundation shows that one of every four recipients of low-cost Federal Housing Administration loans earns over $40,000 annually.

When welfare is called habit-forming, as it often is, the standard implication is that it's habit-forming for the indigent. But postwar experience in America shows that it's habit-forming for nearly everyone who receives it. In 1985, federal outlays for social programs reached an estimated $459 billion, a record, up from $307 billion in 1980, $166 billion in 1975, $73 billion in 1970, and $36 billion in 1965. Less than $100 billion of the latest total, however, represents money aimed mainly at helping the poor through such programs as Medicaid, public assistance, and food stamps. The bulk of the total, some $370 billion, comprises governmental nonpoverty payments for Social Security, Medicare, and federal employees' retirement. Through the past couple of decades, it should be added, by far the greatest spending growth has occurred within these nonpoverty categories. Just since 1980, such outlays have swelled about $130 billion, while antipoverty spending has risen only some $20 billion.

The corporate scene is similar. In 1984 alone, the government paid $14 billion in direct support for programs designed to assist American businesses in such diverse areas as energy and aeronautical research, farm-price maintenance, shipbuilding, and mineral exploration. In addition, corporations benefited to the tune of some $68 billion through tax breaks ranging from investment-tax credits to the exclusion of interest payments on so-called industrial development bonds issued through state and local governments.

In a recent four-year period, General Dynamics earned nearly $2 billion but, by taking advantage of various corporate tax breaks, paid no federal income taxes. Other business giants that paid not a nickel in federal income taxes in the same period include DuPont, which had profits of nearly $4 billion, General Mills, which earned over $1 billion, and W. R. Grace & Co., with a net of $483 million. In all, forty major companies paid no federal taxes in the four years and many claimed tax *refunds* from the government totaling hundreds of millions.

The largest income-transfer program is Social Security, which distributed approximately $185 billion in 1985, some $70 billion more than five years earlier. And projections show that the yearly totals will reach about a quarter of a trillion dollars by the end of this decade, a trend that results from a declining ratio of tax-paying workers to check-collecting retirees, along with the cost-of-living adjustments in monthly payments that have perennially overcompensated for inflation.

The popular conception, or misconception, is that the nation's elderly as a rule suffer much deprivation. Yet the over-sixty-five-year-old population enjoys a per capita yearly income that's actually higher—by $335 in 1985—than that of the citizenry as a whole. And if benefits are taken into account, the percentage of elderly poor—at 3.3 percent—is far lower than among the nation generally. Moreover, a survey of new Social Security recipients by the General Accounting Office in Washington shows that 91.3 percent have such additional sources of income as public and private pension programs (68 percent), earned income (49 percent), and income from stocks, bonds, and other such assets (67 percent).

It is nonsense to assert that Social Security payments are merely sums that have been paid into the program by the recipients. Consider, for instance, a worker who began paying into the system in 1937, when it was launched, and worked until 1982. If he had paid the maximum in Social Security taxes each of the forty-five working years, his payments would have totaled $12,828. His benefits would have begun at $734 a month. If he were married, his wife would collect half of his benefit, or an additional $367 monthly, bringing their total first-year benefit to $13,217, or more than he had paid in the forty-five years of employment.

At age sixty-five, moreover, he had a life expectancy of 14.2 more years and his wife had a life expectancy of 18.5 more years. This means that if Social Security benefits were to keep increasing at the same rate at which they rose in the fourteen years prior to his retirement, the combined benefits for the retiree and his wife would come to $2,632 a month at the time of his death. Then his widow would become eligible to collect an indexed pension of $1,316 monthly. Thus, the couple's lifetime Social Security benefits, based on average life expectancies, would amount to some $375,000—all from a contribution of $12,828.

The Commerce Department reckons that an over-sixty-five couple needs appreciably less in income to live at a given standard than a similar couple younger than sixty-five. After taking into account the tax status of Social Security income and special tax benefits for the elderly, Commerce officials estimate that an individual with a preretirement income of $10,000 annually would require only about $8,180 in income after retiring to maintain the same living standard. A person earning $25,000 before retirement would need only about $18,000.

In our concern for the elderly, we have equated them with the poor. However, it's clear that as a group they are relatively well off—better off, in fact, than most younger citizens. In the late 1960s, about one quarter of aged Americans lived below the poverty level—twice the poverty rate for the U.S. population as a whole. Now, the poverty rate for elderly Americans is down to about 23 percent, which is actually two percentage points lower than the overall poverty rate. Meanwhile, about 10 percent of Social Security spending goes to households with independent incomes of more than $30,000. We have created a system of transfer payments that shifts funds not from the rich to the poor, but mainly from the young to the old.

Recipients of military pensions are among the wealthiest 20 percent of all U.S. households. And some 60 percent of all military retirement benefits—an estimated $18.3 billion was paid out in 1986—goes to such households. The median age of a new military pensioner is only forty-one; two thirds of all military retirees still work and only 15 percent are over sixty-five. Under generous rules, individuals can retire after twenty years of service and receive 50 percent of their base pay. Such pensions now account for some 8 percent of all military expenditures, up from less than 2 percent in the early 1960s.

In 1985, according to the Department of Education, over 13,000 students in families earning more than $100,000 yearly were receiving low-interest government loans for college. (A Harris poll shows that 77 percent of Americans feel that too many well-to-do youths receive such loans.) Among 106 New York City area residents sued by the government in 1985 for defaulting on such loans after college, five were budding investment bankers, five were doctors, two were dentists, and others included college professors, accountants, computer programmers, and even three policemen. I am reminded of a young friend of mine, an upstanding youth from a family whose yearly income approached $200,000 a year. While at Yale in the late 1970s, when the loan program was even more generous than in later years and there were no income limits on applicants, my friend borrowed some $7,000. His Yale education fully paid for by his parents, he then turned around and invested the loan money in a certificate of deposit yielding some 14 percent, or roughly double the amount he would owe in interest on the government-subsidized loan. His attitude was that if the government was silly enough to allow him to pick up some $500 a year quite legally and quite without effort, why not do it? He told me at the time, I should add, that his maneuver was by no means unique on campus. He said that most of his Yale pals, similarly well heeled, were doing the same thing.

The picture is much the same on the farm. A 1986 study by the General Accounting Office (GAO) in Washington shows that two thirds of direct federal farm subsidies go to farmers who are relatively well off, with little debt and few financial worries. The reason, according to the GAO, is that the subsidies are based largely on production and so wind up mostly in the hands of the bigger, richer farm operators.

In 1984, for instance, the government paid out $3.3 billion in direct farm subsidies, and $2.1 billion of this went to farmers with debt-to-assets ratios of less than 40 percent, a relatively sound level. These farmers, in fact, are defined by the Department of Agriculture as having "few financial problems and very strong net worth." Another $753 million of the $3.3 billion went to farmers with debt-to-assets ratios between 40 percent and 69 percent, and a mere $400 million went to farmers with debt ratios of 70 percent or more. This latter level is deemed dangerously high by the department's analysts.

The rise of transfer payments since the early years of the Great Depression has been remarkable. In 1929 and again in 1930, transfer payments totaled $1.5 billion. As the slump worsened, the sums transferred yearly moved slowly up into the $2 billion-plus area. But as the Depression dragged on, the yearly transfers showed only modest gains. In some years, in fact, the totals dropped—as in 1932, to $2.2 billion from $2.7 billion in 1931, and as in 1937, to $2.4 billion from $3.5 billion in 1936. As late as 1940, the total transferred was $3.1 billion, only slightly higher than the $2.7 billion paid out in 1931, before the New Deal programs were even in place. At $3.5 billion in 1936, transfer payments actually fell through the second half of the depressed 1930s.

All through this period, of course, new income-transfer arrangements were being established under Roosevelt's leadership. For example, a single day during the so-called Hundred Days of the new president's first term—May 12, 1933—witnessed three pieces of legislation that would eventually boost transfer payments mightily. These were the Federal Emergency Relief Act, which funneled some $5 billion in direct relief money to states, cities, towns and counties; the Agricultural Adjustment Act, which provided several hundred million dollars to farmers for not planting crops and channeled large amounts of food free to relief families; and the Emergency Farm Mortgage Act, which halted foreclosures and provided federal refunding of mortgages.

After the war, transfer payments soared. An economist visiting from Mars, if asked to inspect the record of transfer payments for a clue to when times were really bad in America, would surely conclude that by comparison with the 1930s, the postwar decades were years of deep depression, for after the relatively flat showing of the 1930s, transfer payments began to escalate steeply. From $1.5 billion in 1930, $3.1 billion in 1940, and $3.6 billion in 1944, the last full year of the war, the yearly totals moved sharply higher. They rose to $6.2 billion in 1945 and $11.3 billion in 1946. By 1950, the total was up to $15.1 billion; by 1960, to $28.5 billion; by 1970, to $79.9 billion; and by the start of the present decade, to $297.6 billion. For all the Reagan team's rhetoric about spending restraint, the $500-billion mark is fast approaching. For perspective, it's noteworthy that transfer payments have climbed roughly three hundredfold since the Depression, while the consumer price index has risen only about sevenfold.

In 1930, transfer payments comprised 1.9 percent of all personal income. By 1940, the rate reached 4 percent. By 1950, it was 6.6 percent;

by 1960, 7.1 percent; by 1970, 10 percent; by 1980, 13.7 percent. Recently, the rate has approximated 15 percent.

The message is plain enough. Programs instituted decades ago to keep the economy together in a very bad time have become a permanent and increasingly influential feature of the prosperous postwar era. To be sure, the transfer-payment numbers encompass a very wide assortment of programs—from sundry Social Security benefits to pensions for the military to all manner of welfare. Nonetheless, a huge slice of the swiftly mounting sums transferred each postwar year reflects long-ago legislation aimed initially, and quite properly, at fighting the Great Depression. Now, as we have seen, the bulk of the money winds up not with the needy but within the prosperous American mainstream.

&

Since the late 1970s, I have periodically consulted several economists to ascertain whether they felt that another Great Depression might be just over the horizon. These include several Nobel laureates, former Federal Reserve Board chairmen and the like, such people as Paul Samuelson, Milton Friedman, Arthur Burns, and John Kenneth Galbraith. By and large, they have consistently discounted the likelihood of another Great Depression. And time and again, a major factor in this optimism has been transfer payments, the conviction that the huge rise in such income through the postwar years precludes the sort of collapse that occurred in the 1930s. The various economists maintain steadfastly that the rise in transfers, especially to jobless individuals during recessionary stages of the business cycle, has meant that the demand for goods and services will not again shrink—as happened in the Great Depression—no matter how much unemployment spreads.

There's no doubt that the rising flow of income transfers by and large from producers to nonproducers, has fed the postwar prosperity and limited the severity of the various postwar recessions. It has served as a built-in stabilizer—to borrow the economic jargon—against any self-feeding cyclical contraction of economic activity. It has, without a doubt, kept the money flowing in times of spreading joblessness, when otherwise there would surely have been a nasty shortage of demand. Always, in contrast to the Depression years, Americans collectively have had the income, be it earned or transferred, to maintain demand for goods and services until a recovery comes around once again.

But with the rise in transfers has come the rise in federal debt. Moreover, this income-stabilizing process has produced a change in attitudes. We now expect that Uncle Sam will somehow always provide our financial support.

Those of us whose memories stretch back beyond the relatively prosperous postwar era to the Great Depression may sense additional changes. No one in the couple of decades that spanned the Depression, World War II, and the early postwar era applied the term *workaholic* to a man like my father, a busy family doctor. The connotation nowadays is slightly unpleasant, suggesting excessive, perhaps even pointless, labor, as if one were addicted to a potentially destructive substance. But in my father's time his daily routine, which stretched from 7 A.M. to late evening and included many house calls between long office hours and hospital duty, was simply the typical schedule of a hard-working man. There was nothing distasteful about it.

Another sign of change comes to mind. I have lived in Manhattan most of my life and for nearly three decades have motored on Friday afternoons to a summer cottage some eighty-five miles to the east in a tiny Long Island village called Quogue. When this Friday routine began, in the early 1960s, I found that by escaping my office no later than 4:30 P.M. I was able to exit the city slightly ahead of a rush-hour-plus end-of-the-week exodus, a maneuver that chopped perhaps a half hour from the eastward drive. By the early 1970s, however, I discovered that to maintain my slight lead on the rush-hour surge, I had to slip out of the office by no later than 4 P.M. and in recent years, the getaway hour has moved even earlier: Now I have to be on the road by 3 P.M. or be prepared for stop-go, stop-go. Meanwhile, I've found that the trip east, in sharp contrast to a couple of decades ago, has become relatively traffic free at what was once the rush hour, 5 to 6 P.M. By that late in the day, the bulk of Friday's eastbound early-leavers have already flown the office coop.

The Money Society
(1987)

Myron Magnet

Leveraged buyouts, junk bonds, and venture capital flushed vast amounts of cash into the accounts of a fortunate few. But real estate, investment, and rising salaries in technical and professional work rewarded many more. Five years into the economic boom, the fever of acquisition and fast profit was out of control, particularly among the young, educated, and urban. In this well-observed essay, Magnet captured the frenzy at the top and its impact on culture. A few weeks after this article was written, the stock market plunged, bubbles started to burst, and the party began to wind down.

Money, money, money is the incantation of today. Bewitched by an epidemic of money enchantment, Americans in the Eighties wriggle in a St. Vitus's dance of materialism unseen since the Gilded Age or the Roaring Twenties. Under the blazing sun of money, all other values shine palely. And the M&A decade acclaims but one breed of hero: He's the honcho with the condo and the limo and the Miró and lots and lots of dough.

The evidence is everywhere you turn. Open the scarlet covers of the Saks Fifth Avenue Christmas catalogue, for starters, and look at what Santa offers today's young family, from Dad's $1,650 ostrich-skin briefcase and Mom's $39,500 fur coat to Junior's $4,000, 15-mph miniature Mercedes, driven by a 5-year-old Donald Trump look-alike in pleated evening shirt, studs, and red suspenders. Take a stroll along Manhattan's Madison Avenue and gape at the Arabian Nights' bazaar of shop windows, where money translates life's commonest objects into rarities rich and strange. Behold embroidery encrusted sheets fine enough for the princess and the pea, or ladies' shoes as fanciful and elaborate as any that artisans painstakingly toiled over when Marie Antoinette graced the throne, or sumptuous lace underwear that makes the inconspicuous yet another arena for conspicuous consumption and adds the charm of wealth to the ordinariness of seduction. Visit Bijan, the temple of excess on Rodeo Drive and Fifth Avenue, and pick up five matched crocodile suitcases for $75,000—yes, thousand—perhaps to be filled with business shirts at $550 and $650 apiece.

Statistics tell the same glitzy story as the evidence of your senses. Luxury car imports more than doubled between 1982 and 1986, while the average age of the growing hordes of first-time fur coat owners has fallen from a matronly 50 to a yuppier 26 in ten years. An overwhelming 93% of recently surveyed teenage girls deemed shopping their favorite past-time, way ahead of sixth-rated dating. Back in 1967, around 40% of U.S. college freshmen told pollsters that it was important to them to be well off financially, as against around 80% who listed developing a meaningful philosophy of life as an important objective. But by 1986 the numbers had reversed, with almost 80% aspiring plutocrats as against 40% philosophers. The number and wealth of the rich have swollen accordingly, with U.S. millionaires proliferating sixfold over the last 20 years to around 1.3 million souls today. The richest 1% of Americans, who owned 31.8% of the national wealth in 1963, had upped their share to an even heftier 34.4% of it two decades later.

But you needn't be rich to catch the money fever—as witness those 26 million middle-class Americans, mostly earning under $40,000 a year, who treat themselves to such badges of affluence as $380 Burberry raincoats and $200 Mont Blanc pens, in the process raising consumer debt to its highest level ever. Their children have the bug too: In many high schools, they roll up to the senior prom in limousines, rented at $250 for the night. So many high schoolers work such long hours at after-school jobs that teachers have been going easier on homework assignments. "Saving for college?" you ask approvingly. Nope. Most of these earnings go for stereos, cars, trendy clothes, and the other material trappings of modern kid life.

As the stock market roared upward in the 1920s, securities and investing turned from being topics not discussed before ladies to the centerpieces of the politest dinner table conversation. Today we obsessively talk about money almost nonstop: how much they paid for their house, their boat, their painting; how big the deal was; how much this one makes—and that one and that one. We read about it too, not just in Judith Krantz sex-and-shopping novels but in magazines that author Tom Wolfe lumps together as *plutography*, the graphic depiction of the acts of the rich. Peep into their windows in *Architectural Digest*, admire their indulgences in *Town & Country* or *Connoisseur*, eavesdrop on their gossip in *Vanity Fair*. Or tune in to the same fare on TV, from the wildly successful

Lifestyles of the Rich and Famous to the goings-on of their fictional counter-parts on *Dallas* or *Dynasty* and its clones. Says veteran Washington hostess Oatsie Charles: "It's hard for the young to realize how much things have changed. I don't remember in my lifetime being so conscious of money."

And what people won't do for it. Forget about televangelists Jim and Tammy Bakker and their squandered millions: Magnified by TV, they've only expanded on an old American tradition, rather than inventing something new. But John Walker Jr., the spy, seems entirely an emanation of our own age. Previous spies—the Rosenbergs, say—turned traitors out of conviction, however contemptibly deluded. Walker, by contrast, corrupted his family and betrayed his country for nothing but money. And what about wellborn Sydney Biddle Barrows, the Mayflower Madam? Add to vice a dash of marketing flair and managerial skill, and—poof—you're an entrepreneurial culture hero like Steven Jobs, welcome at the dinner tables of the fashionable and selling as many entrepreneur's-true-confessions books as a more upstanding competitor like T. Boone Pickens.

All this, however, isn't a call to repent for the end is nigh. Modern materialism doesn't mean that America is hopelessly mired in corruption, despite some luminous instances of it, including those on Wall Street. A portion of the money furor has a healthy impulse at its base, and most of it grows naturally out of big changes in American life. Some of the excesses of the money craze will moderate as the circumstances causing them shift. Others are deeply rooted in the basic facts of modern life—and it's there that you'll have to look if you seek to change them.

In an earlier age, a whole generation had its attitudes, its very feelings, formed by the Depression. Though a much less spectacular or painful event, the inflation of the Seventies similarly sank into the marrow of many Americans. Saving and shunning debt was for saps, the lesson seemed to be; buy, buy, buy, before the money visibly crumbling to dust in your hand vanishes completely. Harvard Business School Professor Samuel Hayes III describes what happened to one of his elderly relatives: "He was the epitome of the Protestant ethic. He had inherited money, he had saved, he was very frugal, had a very modest house, had part of his investment money in bonds and short-term securities, had always maintained liquidity. And he came out of the Seventies looking like a fool. The people who had frittered away their money, as he would say, on elaborate homes and material possessions were laughing all the way to the bank."

Not just economic values but also moral ones got turned upside down by the inflation, in other words, and in the process the moral and the economic orders seemed to pull apart. Like a host of lucky Pierres unaccountably embraced by the Fates, people who had bought houses simply for shelter suddenly found themselves much richer than their neighbors who hadn't. That, along with the fortunes made by more calculating speculators, led many to feel that, as in a lottery, one's economic fate bore little relation to one's hard work or self-denial or contribution to human well-being. Compounding the sense of the injustice of the economic order was the spectacle of a Sheik Yamani lecturing the West on discipline and restraint, while his countrymen, inflation's accessories and No. 1 beneficiaries, gorged on every luxury that only the West and Japan had the skill and industry to produce.

Europeans might have turned resentful. Americans had a different, purely American, response. Says James Kouzes, director of Santa Clara University's Executive Development Center: "When other people are achieving certain things, you feel, 'How come not me? I'm entitled.' Some of the feeling of entitlement comes from the feeling that we all ought to be treated fairly." The practical expression of that sense of entitlement turned out to be a sharper money hunger and materialism.

Don't forget that inflation made these impulses eminently realistic. You had to wonder whether you would have the things you had always expected to be able to earn—a home, college for your kids, a non-poor-house retirement. Kouzes, for instance, says he couldn't afford to buy from his mother the suburban Washington house he grew up in—a house his father had afforded on a mid-level civil servant's income. "So," says he, "it's real hard not to focus on making a lot more than I'm now making."

✣

What inflation started in the Seventies, the corporate restructuring of the Eighties completed. However necessary for improving U.S. competitiveness in a newly global marketplace, the plant closings and headquarters shutdowns, the give-backs and two-tier wage scales imposed on production workers, the purges of middle managers that followed bust-ups, mergers, and slim-downs—all these stunned not only victims but also survivors, suffusing them with insecurity. Every man for himself was the implicit message; if you don't look out for No. 1, you can bet no one else will. Certainly not the top guys in your company: Spurred by their own fear of takeover, they often seem too busy protecting their own interests to attend to yours or the corporation's.

Young people, in particular, took this lesson to heart. Roderick Gilkey, a psychologist who teaches management at the Emory Business School in Atlanta, says that students who are children of purged managers have been especially anxious to go out and make as much money as they can, to ensure a cushion for the hard times they see as inevitable. But even in students personally unaffected by the restructuring he sees a "desperate, worried flight to get on the train before it leaves—a sort of window-of-opportunity mentality that you've got to grab it while you can."

Part of what makes the materialism of the Eighties different from that of the Fifties is this edge of anxiety. Says Senior Vice President Ann Clurman of the Yankelovich Clancy Shulman market research firm: "The 1950s sense was, 'If I play by all the rules, I'll make it up the economic ladder rung by rung.' Now it's more like, 'I'm not sure I'm going to win even if I play by all the rules.' "

Meanwhile, watching the investment bankers who preside over the restructuring wallow so conspicuously in money, observers feel the same sense of unfairness and entitlement they felt when speculators made fortunes from the inflation of the Seventies. Whether they think, wrongly, that the restructuring is nothing but unproductive paper shuffling or, more accurately, that the Glass-Steagall Act gives investment bankers a windfall that a free market would withhold, they perceive the fees as undeserved—whereas they don't begrudge Steven Jobs his fortune, earned by producing something of tangible value. Under the slightly Frankensteinian toupee of junk bond alchemist Michael Milken, they know, bubbles a redoubtable brain; but is it an organ worth the half billion dollars it has earned? They doubt it. And discovering that insider trading has helped make some of the Wall Street money only fans their sense of inequity and entitlement.

The corporate restructuring isn't just an economic change. It is also a social change, transforming the relationships between individuals and their employers. Altered sometimes unrecognizably, cut loose from their traditions, no longer able to offer long-term career commitment, old companies can inspire neither attachment nor loyalty in employees. "What we're living in now is an age of Hessians," says University of Rhode Island historian Maury Klein, biographer of robber baron Jay Gould. A realignment like this cuts people adrift from the traditional moorings by which they identify themselves, as do other of our era's social and cultural changes, from family breakdown to the newfangled relations between the sexes to the continuing attenuation of community ties.

What has this to do with the money craze? Everything. Says historian Klein, "Money tends to be more or less important in an age, depending on the degree of turbulence and social change that is taking place." Like the rapidly urbanizing and industrializing era of the robber barons, Klein says, ours is "an age where traditional self-identities are under great attack and great strain just from the pace of change. In that situation, money becomes a way of defining who you are by what you have."

That way of defining a self is rampant in the money society. Classic cases seem shoulder to pin-striped shoulder on Wall Street, where it's worth looking for the full-blown symptoms of a malady widespread in the society as a whole. "Wall Streeters heavily look on their self-worth by their W-2," says the vice president in charge of compensation at a major Wall Street firm. And they look at others that way, too. "I think people are being measured again by money rather than by how good a journalist or social activist or lawyer they are," says an investment banker at a prestigious New York firm. Explains one representative Wall Streeter, a managing director in the corporate finance wing of a major commercial bank: "What differentiates you and says you're successful is the house in the Hamptons and the Ferrari in the driveway."

As a result, this banker is continually comparing himself with others to make sure he's okay. He schmoozes about compensation to try to determine if he makes more or less than the person he's talking to. But such conversations can be inconclusive, so when he visits friends or business acquaintances he's continually sizing up the towels, the cars, the silver, with practically an auctioneer's eye to see what he's worth by comparison. Told by his wife that friends were drinking out of Baccarat glasses, more expensive than his Waterford ones, he demanded to know why she hadn't bought Baccarat, too.

"It frightens me to be sensitive to the idea that my neighbor just got a big-screen TV that's three inches bigger than mine," says the banker. "But that's something I look at. Or I know the guy got $100,000 more in his compensation package last year than I did. Why should that bother me? Can I spend it? Do I need it? Do I want it? Only because I want to make more than him. I think the stress and internal turmoil that creates in most of us is unhealthy."

For this is an endless and unwinnable competition, even on purely economic terms. Says Harvard professor of political economy Robert Reich: "When everybody is buying into the same status objects, such as the house in the Hamptons or the co-op on the East Side, they balloon in price, so it costs more and more to achieve relative status. It becomes a fruitless exercise after a while. That is part of the cycle of disillusionment that sets in." Out of this phenomenon came a recent, and notorious, *New York Times* story about investment bankers feeling poor on $600,000 a year—a story that investment bankers, without irony, earnestly assure you is true.

More important, this is an unwinnable game psychologically. Like an addiction, it requires higher and higher doses for the same thrill. Psychoanalysts find that many money addicts are children of parents too preoccupied, overworked, or withdrawn to respond with the appropriate oohs and ahs to baby's smiles and antics. The children consequently never stop looking for the withheld applause and pleased response, and money helps them get it—even takes the place of it, as a sign of the employer's pleasure and approval. But, says Dr. Arnold Goldberg, a Chicago psychoanalyst, "The ante always goes up because the need is never satisfied. The kid wants a human response; money is a nonhuman response." Some of these people, rich and successful, end up in Goldberg's office complaining that their life has no purpose. Worse, those cashoholics who fail to get their needed infusion of money, according to Dr. Jay Rohrlich, a psychiatrist with offices in the heart of Wall Street, become agitated, anxious, combative, and depressed, like addicts deprived of their fix.

Trouble is, money is only money. "There's a kind of bewilderment over what sources can be drawn upon to provide money with a sense of distinction, purpose, or value," says Hilton Kramer, editor of *The New Criterion,* a cultural review. The very rich have a smorgasbord of strategies. There's the high society route. Says Lazard Frères partner Felix Rohatyn: "Today you can essentially buy social status immediately, with all the trimmings." That's because in the Eighties the old rich increasingly seem to take their cue from the new rich, rather than vice versa. Presumably that's because they like the glamour and glitz. "Social status today involves an enormous amount of publicity and a certain level of stardom," says Rohatyn. "We've become Beverly Hills."

Or you can try to cloak yourself in the authority and solidity of the old regime. Here on the cover of the home entertaining section of the *New York Times Magazine* is dress designer Carolyn Roehm, wife of investment banker Henry Kravis of Kohlberg Kravis Roberts, the leveraged buyout kings. In sweeping floor-length gown, she's just getting ready for a dinner party for 18 in an opulent dining room so perfect in every detail of its superb antique furniture and breathtaking 18th- and 19th-century paintings that it looks like a stage set or a model room in a museum. Add to this that she's displaying it all on a magazine cover and vaporing inside about how "in college, when traditions went asunder, we all dined in blue jeans on the floor," and you can't help thinking that while some girls play house, this lady is playing castle. On a more demotic level, the Gatsby-like clothes and advertisements of designer Ralph Lauren, along with his baronial New York store in a mansion refurbished to look as if the original

tycoon still lives there, have the same intent of using the outward trappings of a vanished order to appropriate its rootedness and dignity.

Finally, there's the way of art. "In this whole materialist explosion,
an interest in art represents an interest in spirit," says Hilton Kramer. So
urgent is this spiritual interest that the prices of paintings have rocketed
in the last five years, with a Jasper Johns recently selling for $3.6 million.
Some dignitaries of the money society buy pictures because of the status
art confers; others really get to care about it.

What then is one to make of that patron of the arts Saul Steinberg,
chairman of Reliance Group Holdings, sometime greenmailer, and recently
host to a gathering of such writers as Norman Mailer and Allen Ginsberg?
What does he think when he walks in his door after a hard day at the office
and sees, first thing, his Francis Bacon triptych? On one side, a naked man
throws up into a sink; on the other, a naked man strains on a toilet; in the
middle, grotesque and half hidden, a third naked figure casts a batwinged,
demonic, and loathsome shadow ominously across the floor. Who knows
what these images might say to Steinberg of life in high finance?

৵৬

All this is what is really meant by the word "lifestyle"—more superficial style than rooted, meaningful life. And the point of these examples is
not that the money society has triumphantly driven out all the solid,
estimable values, like the shaggy barbarians at the gates of Rome. Rather,
the money society has expanded to fill the vacuum left after the institutions that embodied and nourished those values—community, religion,
school, university, and especially family—sagged or collapsed or sometimes even self-destructed.

Now we live in a world where all values are relative, equal, and
therefore without authority, truly matters of mere style. Says Dee Hock,
former chief of the Visa bank-card operation: "It's not that people value
money more but that they value everything else so much less—not that
they are more greedy but that they have no other values to keep greed in
check. They don't know what else to value." Or as University of
Pennsylvania sociologist E. Digby Baltzell puts it: "When there are no values, money counts."

Editorialists who recently have been haranguing the young to give
up all this soulless materialism and return to the commitment of the
Sixties have got it exactly wrong. That "commitment," with its heavy
charge of destructive anger and protest, ultimately helped bleed the value

out of existing institutions, giving them their present zombielike character. Many who chose the materialist life were consciously rejecting the Sixties and their legacy of destructiveness and nihilism. They were trying to choose the solid bourgeois existence of home and hearth and work that the Sixties had jeered down as worthless. But after the mutilation of so many of the values that in the past had given that life its meaningfulness and security, many who opted for it discovered that little more than an empty shell was left for them. That this life should end up being only one more "lifestyle" is really what the problem of the money society is all about.

THE EIGHTIES

From
Money and Class in America
(1988)

Lewis H. Lapham

Taking a caustic view of corporate America's elites, Lapham wrote a quirky, often brilliant book that dissected the eighties plutocracy and its "equestrian classes." Lapham's view of the rich was devastating and all too accurate. Working from the premise that "obsession with money dulls the capacity for feeling and thought," Lapham concluded that the nation's captains of finance and industry were "coined souls."

E very few days one or another of the country's eminent prophets wonders what has gone wrong with the once prosperous American enterprise. Why has the nation's productivity declined? Why is the debt so heavy and the balance of international trade so skewed in favor of Germany or Japan? What has become of the moral commonwealth, and why are so many politicians under indictment or in jail?

Perhaps I have been corrupted by my upbringing in the precincts of wealth, or possibly I have lived too long in the city of New York, but I suspect that the answers have to do with the ascribing of authority to something as abstract and as inherently meaningless as money. The crippling effects of the general stupefaction account for phenomena as diverse as the passion for mergers and acquisitions, for the trade deficit and the absence of vigorous political debate among either Democrats or Republicans, for the emptiness of spirit that stares out of the face of national television. The ratings accorded to *Dynasty* define the ethos of an age that thinks it possible to buy the future as if it were an oyster or a dress.

That the obsession with money dulls the capacity for feeling and thought I think can be accepted as an axiom requiring no further argument. The paralysis can be seen in statistical tables as well as in the expressions of art and politics. The economy weakens, and so do the indices of perception. Immobilized by fears of various denominations, too many people begin to look like animals standing perfectly still in attitudes of trembling defense. This oddly somnambulist attitude of mind leads not to safety, not to the "steady state" so lovingly promoted in the early 1970s as the rich man's dream of Heaven, but, by the degrees made apparent during the late 1970s and early 1980s, into decadence, subtraction and debt.

From the beginning of the American argument the equestrian classes have done their best to prevent the introduction of new ideas and new products as well as to forestall any seditious shifts in the balance of capital. During the years of the Reagan ascendancy the defense of the status quo (defined as property or as received wisdom) had become a radical cause. Given the cost of bringing to market a newly designed car, weapons system or situation comedy, the ladies and gentlemen charged with making the necessary commitments find it hard to take chances with anything that isn't as safe as it is banal. The money looms so large (roughly $400 billion, for instance, in the nation's pension funds) that the people responsible for its deployment become easily frightened and prefer to leave the decisions to a computer program. Of the trades taking place on the New York Stock Exchange, 80 percent involve institutions—banks, mutual and pension funds, insurance companies. The individual investor has all but disappeared from the market, and the notion of the exchange as a reflection of "the people's capitalism" (a slogan popular in the early 1960s) has been reduced to absurdity.

The tax "reforms" passed by the Congress in the autumn of 1986 amidst almost universal applause clearly favor the safest and most sterile investments (i.e., municipal bonds) and work to the advantage of the least creative of the country's professions (i.e., lawyers, accountants, retailers, broadcasters, suppliers of franchised hamburgers). Labor allies itself with management in the effort to make time stand still, and their agents jointly lobby the Congress for protective tariffs against the foreign manufactures with which they no longer can compete. The frenzied speculation in the stock market adds nothing to the sum of the nation's well-being or common store of value. A few people become very, very rich, usually at the cost of destroying one or more companies that prior to their dismemberment had been providing employment, tax revenues and the hope of innovation. People who can think of nothing else to do resort to the law courts as a means of transferring wealth from one account to another. Again, their efforts add nothing to the commonwealth. The shuffling of paper (a macroeconomic variation on the game of three-card monte) consumes more and more of the nation's energy and intellect. The litigiousness of the society aids and abets the shriveling of the national enterprise. People wonder, with T. S. Eliot's Prufrock, whether they dare to eat a peach or move across the street. Relatively few people under the age of thirty-five can afford to buy a house—or even entertain the hope of ever buying a house. Business can do nothing without consulting the lawyers. Newspaper editors worried about libel suits speak of a "chilling effect" and interpret the First Amendment as a license temporarily on loan from a sullen prince. Too many people, often against their will and better judgment, feel they have little choice except to join the legion of speculators. Their houses turn into real-estate deals, and their assets ebb and flow like the tide, in and out of the stock market, the money funds, the gambling casinos.

To the extent that the desire for profit exceeds the desire for life, the translations of human beings into body counts or paying customers supersedes their uses as people. They become monuments, or toys, or statistics, or objects that can be sold at auction in celebrity raffles. As a result of his dying even a man of modest means becomes an estate, and his friends and heirs need concern themselves no longer with the waywardness of a living mind. Flesh has been transformed into property, which, in a commercial society, is akin to salvation. The rich achieve in life the apotheosis that lesser men achieve only in death. They become their own masterpieces, rare jewels for which the world offers more or less satisfactory settings, precious ornaments infinitely more beautiful than anything else in their art collections. At an expensive dinner party in Dallas I once sat next to a woman wearing a dress made of such heavy metallic fabric that she couldn't bend from the waist and could barely lift her arms. Taking into account her immaculate silence it occurred to me that she might as well have sent the dress on a hanger.

At Yale University in the autumn of 1984 a drama student satisfied the requirement for his senior theater project by declaring himself a work of art. He walked around the campus for several weeks in the company of a friend whom he had appointed as his curator. He construed his mere presence (walking to class, shaving, doing his laundry, etc.) as an exhibition. Precisely the same aesthetic governs the lives of people stunted by their faith in money. Remarking on the impoverishment of coined souls, Henry Fairlie, the British journalist, once said: "The rich—in their own eyes, one fears, as well as ours—are toys. The longer one gazes at them, the less enviable they seem. They only go through the motions of being themselves. They run down if they're not wound up during the day."

The translation of human beings into objects of art entails certain disadvantages. Most of these were revealed to the Lydian King Midas, who, being owed a wish by a satyr, asked that everything he touched be turned to gold. The wish was granted, and Midas, who was a fool as well as a poor judge of music, discovered that his meat and drink were made of gold. He would have starved to death had not the gods taken pity on his paralysis and released him from the prison of his golden wish.

The heirs to his stupidity lack his connections on Olympus. The substitution of money for all other value becomes so complete as to change them, if not into gold, at least into stone. To describe the rich as people is often to make a mistake with the language. Rich nouns or pronouns, perhaps, but not people. The rich tend to identify themselves with a sum of money, and by so doing they relinquish most of their claims to their own humanity. Their money becomes a synthetic fabrication of heart and mind, an artificial circulatory system. This is why it is so difficult to borrow from the rich, why they forget to pay their bills. To ask them for money is to ask them, literally, for blood. Having lost the capacity to distinguish between money as necessity and money as luxury and power, they imagine that the loss of the third car or the second sailboat will cause them to vanish. When preoccupied with the existential question of their net worth, the expression in their eyes narrows into a lizard's stare.

It is an expression I have seen often enough in the eyes of stockbrokers, gamblers and petty thieves. Maxime Du Camp noticed it in Gustave Flaubert's eyes when the novelist abandoned himself to the dreams of luxury. Assuming an income of 1 million francs a year, Flaubert liked to imagine himself possessed of coach horses that would be the envy of England, of servants who eased his feet into diamond-studded shoes, of a dining room decorated with espaliers of flowering jasmine and the fluttering of bright finches.

"When these dreams took possession of him," Du Camp noted in his diary, "he became almost rigid and reminded one of an opium eater in a state of trance. He seemed to have his head in the clouds, to be living in a dream of gold. This habit was one reason why he found steady work difficult."

The transformation of men into stone can take place within the instant of a single misplaced phrase. The abrupt change of manner often has been remarked upon by people who raise funds for charitable causes. For weeks or months they stalk their quarries of wealth, but if they make a careless movement (i.e., if they mention a specific sum at anything other than the precise moment) the prospective patron takes alarm and lumbers off into the library like a startled wildebeest. Whenever possible, of course, the rich prefer to endow monuments and tombs, and I never can pass by the Metropolitan Museum of Art in New York without thinking of it not as a gallery of living portraits but as a cemetery of tax-deductible wealth.

The coldness and indifference of the rich follow from their inability to take seriously other people's desires, and they constantly ask themselves the peevish questions, "Who *are* all those other people out there, and what in Heaven's name do they *want?*" The self becomes so inextricably identified with money that the rich man imagines that only his attachment to it gives it meaning, substance and virtue. Money has no discernible reality in the hands of lesser mortals because lesser mortals have no use for it. When seized by occasional bouts of romantic sympathy for the poor, the rich construe the lower classes as a kind of clay in which to mold the images of reform. They get easily annoyed if the little marionettes begin to speak and think and move of their own volition. Nelson Rockefeller's son, Rodman, struck precisely the right tone when, during the moral excitements of the 1960s, he decided to sponsor the cause of human rights. He made arrangements for a grand fete at his family estate in Pocantico Hills, offering to raise several million dollars for the NAACP if Martin Luther King, Jr., would issue a statement endorsing Rodman's father's candidacy for governor of New York. King refused to do so, and Rodman canceled the fete. His aides pointed out that King's political endorsement hadn't been previously discussed, that the invitations already had been sent, and that it would be exceedingly embarrassing, not to say humiliating, to rescind one's humanitarian concern on such short notice.

"I don't care," Rodman said. "It's my house and my money, and I can do what I want."

In order to preserve the condition of soul appropriate to an object, the rich man learns to alienate himself from anything so subversive as thought, passion, intellect or imagination. He can buy a place in the midst of events (a box at the tennis matches, say, or an ambassador's post in London), but if he knows what's good for him and heeds the advice of the family lawyers, he will avoid the stronger and more dangerous sentiments. Among all the emotions, the rich have the least talent for love. It is possible to love one's dog, dress or duck-shooting hat, but a human being presents a more difficult problem. The rich might wish to experience feelings of affection, but it is almost impossible to chip away at the enamel of their narcissism. They take up all the space in all the mirrors in the house. Their children, who represent the most present and therefore the most annoying claim on their attention, usually receive the brunt of their irritation.

Writing in *Ms.* magazine in the spring of 1986, Sallie Bingham, the estranged heiress to the Louisville newspaper fortune, noted the consequences of what could be called "the Midas effect": "Rich families shed, in each generation, their most passionate and outspoken members. In the shedding the family loses the possibility of renewal, of change. Safety is gained, but a safety that is rigid and judgmental."

What can be said of the rich family also can be said of the rich nation.

Of all the stories I have heard on this point, the saddest was one told to me by an acquaintance named Mills, who reached the age of thirty-five before he found the courage to ask his father why his father had never loved him. Mills had been born to the privileges of wealth, but he had chosen to make his career as a professor of political theories of which his father disapproved. Mills put the question at a time when his father was senior partner in a New York investment bank, a director of corporations and a faithful servant of the plutocracy. He had deeded his fortune to the Smithsonian Institution—on the ground that an institution would be more respectful of it than his errant son and unkempt grandchildren—and his answer to his son's question was as quick and instinctive as the movement of an alarmed wolf. Mills told me the story several years later, but he could remember the expression on his father's face as vividly as if the conversation had taken place that same afternoon.

"That's not true," his father had said. "I've always been utterly honest with you. I've always tried to deal with you exactly as I would deal with the Justice Department or the IRS."

Subject to the prejudices of his class, Mills's father over the years had been known to compare both the Justice Department and the IRS to marauding bands of the envious poor.

"I know that," Mills said, "but I am your eldest son, and I thought . . ."

He never succeeded in saying what it was that he thought. Nor could he remember what he might have said. Before he could get to the end of his sentence, his father said:

"That's your mistake."

Mills never again mentioned the subject of his inheritance except in the presence of his own and his father's lawyer.

A comparable style of feeling animates the current generation of heroes in the movies and MTV rock videos, most of whom bear an unhappy resemblance to weapons designed by Northrop or General Dynamics. Hard and androgynous figures, almost metallic in their dress and expression, they take pride in their indifference to the pain of human feeling. Just as a marble cenotaph is safer than a living heir, so a hero carved in stone seems to offer a surer defense against the world's uncertainty than a man or woman made of moral clay. Researchers into the questions of human sexuality at UCLA report clinical evidence of ISD (inhibited sexual desire) among 20 percent of the population, and the users of cocaine uniformly describe their changing into "hard," "enameled," "artificial" surfaces, as if they had become "indestructible," "perfect," "the giant of your dreams," "bulletproof."

In the cultural arenas the stupefaction induced by the excessive faith in money results in an audible silence. The large publishing houses and Hollywood studios suffer the same inhibitions as General Motors and the Pentagon. The scripts must pass the judgment of committees, and the committees, mindful of the enormous expense necessary to the manufacture and sale of the product, seldom gamble on anything that hasn't been done before. The immense sums of money press down, like the weight of gravity, on the buoyancy of imaginative thought.

The debate that takes place in the nominally enlightened journals of opinion betrays an equivalent lack of courage. The conversation minces along like a dog on a leash, the arc of acceptable thought as narrow as the perimeters established by American troops in the wilderness of Vietnam. The writer who insults the wisdom in office risks losing his or her hope of patronage. The professors and sober-minded journalists who comprise the American intelligentsia yield to nobody, not even to George Steinbrenner, in the keenness of their desire for money and preferment. Their writing reflects the calculation of their advantage rather than their talent for expression. In the midst of the intellectual enthusiasms of the 1960s, I remember engaging in a heated argument with a Texas oil entrepreneur who held the New York literary crowd in open contempt. "How much do you think it would cost," he said, "to change them all into obedient hounds? Fifty thousand dollars a year? One hundred thousand a year? Seventy-five thousand dollars a year and guaranteed invitations to the White House?" At the time I thought the gentleman both a Philistine and a fool. Not many years later, having seen an impressive number of *soi-disant* liberals transform themselves into rabid conservatives for the sake of tenure, a foundation grant or their names in the literary press, I still thought the gentleman a Philistine, but not a stupid or unobservant Philistine.

Having been obliged to edit the kind of prose that A. Bartlett Giamatti once described as "the higher institutional," I suspect that its weakness and deadly earnestness reflects a fear of giving offense. Who can afford to say the wrong thing? Who knows what will happen next, or who will be appointed to what office, or what critic will be given one's book to review for *The New York Times*? Given the possible financial consequences, only very young writers or very old and famous writers can afford the risks of wit or plain speaking. Writers who still have reputations to protect have become successful by virtue of having become commodities, and they dare not take chances with the product. If William F. Buckley, Jr., allowed himself to endorse a liberal opinion, his readers might become restive and confused. They wouldn't be getting what they thought they had paid for, and they could complain that the label on the box of Buckley's conservatism falsely represented the merchandise within.

Remarking on the intellectual despotism characteristic of American discourse, Tocqueville said: "I know no country in which, speaking generally, there is less independence of mind and true freedom of expression than in America." Fortunately for the Reagan administration, Tocqueville's dictum is as appropriate to the 1980s as it was to the 1840s. The citizenry uncomplainingly submits to examinations of its blood, its urine and its speech. At the end of 1983 the General Accounting Office estimated that 225,000 current and former government employees with access to classified information had consented to the principle of censorship. The clerks in question signed an agreement stating that they would submit any text they might write (even unto the days of their death) to government review.

When highly placed government officials resign their office for reasons of principle or conscience, they go as quietly as thieves. By definition members of the equestrian class, usually lawyers or Wall Street bond salesmen, they preserve their silence out of respect for the protocols of wealth. If they were discovered to be "unsound" (i.e., the sort of people who make scenes and say what they think) their peers might pronounce them, by mutual silent consent, ineligible for other places and titles within the honeycombs of privilege. An impressive number of functionaries quit the Johnson administration in disagreement with the President's self-defeating policies in Vietnam (among them Cyrus Vance, McGeorge Bundy, Bill Moyers and Robert McNamara), but none of them raised even a whisper of a public objection. The criminal syndicates refer to the practice as the code of *omerta*.

The fear of change is as traditional among the vicars of the American media as it is among the captains of American industry. Nothing so terrifies most reporters and editors as the arrival of a new idea. Hoping to extend indefinitely the perpetual present in which images pass for reality, the media deal in the semblance, not the substance, of change. Wars might come and go, but the seven o'clock news lives forever. When, in the winter of 1986–87, Premier Mikhail Gorbachev advocated radical changes in Soviet society and foreign policy, the American media insisted that he was lying, that his much-advertised *glasnost* was nothing more than a charade.

The Washington columnists held as tightly to their inventories of stereo-typed truth as a child to its nurse. To entertain, even briefly, the thought of genuine change was a possibility too painful to bear.

The performances in the national political theater might degenerate into farce or opéra bouffe, but only a licensed satirist can afford to say so. Being dependent upon the gossip and good will of his patrons in office, no ambitious journalist dares risk giving offense to anybody important enough to provide him with a steady supply of news. Henry Kissinger played on this weakness of the press with consummate skill, and over din-ner one night in a New York restaurant I remember both Tom Wicker and Edwin Newman explaining that while they were in service as White House correspondents it never occurred to them to ask a President a rude question. Katharine Graham, the publisher of *The Washington Post,* contin-ued to write coquettish little notes to President Nixon even while her paper was demanding his impeachment. In the few weeks before Nixon left the White House, Mrs. Graham was still assuring him that they were the best of friends and would have dinner together once the unpleasant-ness had been put safely out of mind.

At miscellaneous intervals over the last several years I have had occasion to make a fair number of speeches in various parts of the coun-try, and I have been struck by the passivity of the audiences. In response to even the most controversial statement hardly anybody wants to ask a question or risk an objection. New York newspaper editors speak of the "fragility of the world" and advise discretion when approaching topics like-ly to alarm the buyers of large advertising space. Comparable feelings of apprehension about the delicate nature of the financial markets seem to have prompted the Securities and Exchange Commission to allow Ivan Boesky to sell his holdings, estimated at $1.5 billion, before announcing his indictment for insider trading. Apparently the SEC thought that too sudden a punishment might let loose a panic and wreck the international banking system. By assigning Boesky the equivalent of a nuclear capabili-ty, the SEC raised an embezzler to the power of a sovereign government.

The balance of the current political argument favors the weight of objects, not the force of ideas, and the wisdom in office (both in govern-ment and the media) interprets the word "conservative" to mean the safe-keeping of property as opposed to the preservation of a habit of mind or a process of becoming. The Department of Health and Human Services needs fifty-five employees to respond to a letter from the secretary. Arms manufacturers applying for Pentagon contracts report having to fill out forms that sometimes number as many as 23,000 pages of small type. The Congress, intent upon buying allies, insists that those countries receiving

American aid payments vote with the United States at the United Nations. The American armed services worry more about budgets than about military tactics. Only one soldier in every four can boast of a "combat specialty"; everybody else belongs to a headquarters' staff and ascribes to the belief that the orderly arrangement of documents takes precedence over the training of troops. When it comes time to appoint a secretary of state nobody can think of more than two or three ornamental gentlemen capable of performing the duties of so august and ceremonial an office. Within the purviews of the sciences the fear of litigation and the emphasis on profit (i.e., on applied rather than basic research) stifles the impulse toward experiment and innovation. The large amount of government money distributed through the institutes and the universities favors orthodox lines of reasoning. The venture capitalist money seeks out, especially in the biotechnologies, miraculous cures and transformations that can be sold at miraculous prices. The inertia of money and the presence of lawyers combine to yield a state of intellectual paralysis. Offering advice conforming to the wisdom of the age, a Washington attorney in the autumn of 1985 told his client, a research group supposedly on the frontier of the future, "Don't innovate; don't experiment; don't be venturesome; don't go out on a limb."

He might also have said, "don't think." Certainly this was the rigid and somnambulist posture of the statesmen responsible for the American debacle in Vietnam. In *The March of Folly,* Barbara Tuchman attributes the stupidity of our military expedition in Southeast Asia to the nonpartisan states of "self-hypnosis" that afflicted three successive presidents and their circles of sleep-walking advisers. Against all sense, and despite the contradictions apparent in the facts, the American high command, both civilian and military, insisted on its cherished dream of power. Our reasons for fighting the war changed with the circumstances: first we were defending all of Asia against Communist subversion ("the domino theory"), then we were proving the credibility of American power (for fear that other nations on other continents might smile behind their hands), and lastly, after 50,000 Americans had been killed, to prove a point of honor. Tuchman cites the dictum of George Kennan, who said of the men in Washington (most notably Dean Rusk, Walt Rostow and Maxwell Taylor), "they were like men in a dream" incapable of "any realistic assessment of the effects of their own acts." Elsewhere in her book, Tuchman compares the stewards of the American empire during the Vietnam War with the eighteenth-century British aristocrats who presided over the loss of the American Colonies. Both companies of fatuous gentlemen were distinguished by their ignorance and pride. Like the modern Americans, the

British ministers and peers thought themselves invulnerable to the arrows of fortune. Being accustomed to the illusion of omnipotence (i.e., to the obedience of their domestic servants) they lacked a sense of political realism. Describing their qualities in a letter to Charles Fox, Edmund Burke attributed their foolishness to "plentiful fortunes, assured rank and quiet homes."

The states of somnambulism characteristic of large business corporations can be fairly well inferred from the number of companies lost over the past several years in the maelstrom of takeovers and leveraged buyouts. When denounced as upstarts, the acquisitors—gentlemen on the order of T. Boone Pickens, the Belzberg brothers and the once fortunate Ivan Boesky—invariably say that the companies were too indolently managed, that the assets were dribbling through the fingers of corporate hirelings too soft and too frightened to command the respect of their accountants. The more sardonic of the speculators, notably Pickens, present themselves as blessings in disguise, agents of a divine financial ecology sent to thin the herds and winnow the wheat from the chaff. The argument is exaggerated, but it is true that the corporate executive, unlike the small businessman or free-booting entrepreneur, isn't paid to take chances.

Anybody who says this in public, of course, is likely to be thought un-American. In November 1986, Richard Darman, then deputy secretary of the Treasury, told an audience at the Japan Society in New York that the conventional American business establishment was "bloated, risk-averse, inefficient and unimaginative." Executives paid $1 million a year, he said, devote less time to research and development than "they spend reviewing their golf scores." He observed that most high-ranking members of "the corpocracy" owe their places not to their character or intelligence but to "the strength of their demeanor and a failure to make observable mistakes." As can be well imagined, the publication of Darman's remarks provoked a flurry of outraged denials in the business magazines.

The corpocracy doesn't like to be reminded that an accomplished CEO bears comparison to a butler or gamekeeper—a dull but stouthearted and boyish fellow who can be counted upon to look after the porcelain or the grouse; reliable enough to act as the custodian of a large and valuable property, but not clever enough to steal anything important. In a word, he is precisely the sort of man prepared at Hotchkiss and Yale to fit the norm of mediocrity once defined by Paul D. Cravath, patriarch of the New York law firm of Cravath, Swaine and Moore, in terms of the qualities desirable in apprentice lawyers. "Brilliant intellectual powers are not essential. Too much imagination, too much wit, too great cleverness, too facile fluency, if not leavened by a sound sense of proportion, are quite as likely to impede success as to promote it. The best clients are apt to be afraid of those qualities."

The makers of mythologies about American business often mention "profit maximization" as the raison d'être of the corporate mechanism. Only seldom have I found this to be so. Maximization of profit would imply an operation run according to the arithmetic of performance, which would wreak havoc on everybody's comfortable arrangements. Let the rabbit of free enterprise out of its velveteen bag and too many people would have to be fired, too much idiocy exposed to the light of judgment or ridicule, too much vanity sacrificed to the fires of efficiency. Such a catastrophe obviously would threaten the American way of life, to say nothing of the belief in free markets. As dependent as a child on the institution that suckles him, the devoted corporate manager seeks to build protective layers of bureaucracy, to expand and make stronger the shell of hierarchy, to keep the systems comfortably in place. Once all the institutional needs have been met (i.e., tending the slowly revolving water wheel that yields jobs, money, income, taxes, benefits, insurance, stock options, picnics, limousines, pensions, dividends, etc.) then, if anybody has any surplus time or energy to invest, the institution might direct its attention to the making of a profit. The $190 billion spent on mergers and acquisitions in 1986 often resulted in institutions of elephantine size, but it has yet to be proved that the stately rearrangement of the tables of organization resulted in better products or more intelligent management. Too much money was employed in the service of debt, which, like the money watering the sterile deserts of the weapons industry, heavily depletes the funds available for thought.

Subsequent to the explosion of the *Challenger* in January 1986, the investigation conducted by the Rogers Commission left no doubt in anybody's mind about the state of dreamlike trance prevailing in the upper atmospheres of large American institutions. Always pressed for money, more concerned about the safety of its budget appropriations than the safety of its people, NASA approved the routine falsification of inspection records and systematically ignored unwelcome reports about the trouble with the orbiter's rocket engines. Reduced to a condition of paralysis, the bureaucracy could do nothing but wait for cold weather and what one of its suppressed memoranda anticipated as "a catastrophe of the highest order."

The promoters of the American dream inevitably speak of the "rugged individual" who sets himself against the resident establishment— cultural, political, scientific—and goes off into the appropriate wilderness to unearth beauty, truth or a fortune in California real estate. The hero is largely imaginary, apparently the invention of the literary East in the latter decades of the nineteenth century. Disenchanted with what they knew of the crowded commerce in the seaboard towns, the writers in Boston and New York comforted themselves with tales of the noble frontiersmen still at large on the Great Plains. In the 1920s and 1930s the romance was cut into strips of movie film by a generation of displaced Europeans who confused the history of the United States with their own reasons for leaving Odessa or Berlin. The image of the rugged individualist might sell automobiles and cigarettes, but as an exemplary model of a successful American life it is ruinous. Except in a few well-publicized instances (enough to lend credence to the iconography painted on the walls of the media), the rigorous practice of rugged individualism usually leads to poverty, ostracism and disgrace. The rugged individualist is too often mistaken for the misfit, the maverick, the spoilsport, the sore thumb.

No matter how effusive our rhetoric to the contrary, most Americans cannot bring themselves to trust the unaffiliated individual. We prefer to repose our confidence in institutions: a brand name, a corporation, a bank. It is the figure of Babbitt or Cyrus Vance, not Clint Eastwood, who represents the triumph of the American dream—the man who goes along to get along, who knows the right people and belongs to the right clubs, whose every opinion seconds the nomination of the chairman, who submits easily, and with a winning smile, to what Tocqueville called "the tyranny of the majority."

As often as not, corporate success depends upon the aspirant's willingness, over many years and under a bewildering variety of circumstances, to sacrifice whatever trace elements of personality might get him in trouble with the management or the police. The poor fellow learns to submerge his own being in the corporate being, to subvert his own voice to the institutional voice, to acquire the "plastic capability" that President Nixon so much admired in General Alexander Haig. Only when the candidate has enlisted in the ranks of the Hollow Men does he become eligible for the reward of a tax-deductible personality; only when it is certain that he will have nothing to say does the corporation set him up with a microphone and an audience.

Much the same process takes place within the withered groves of the American academy. The winning of tenure at a prominent university almost always obliges the candidate to give up his own voice and applaud, with possibly a few urbane and scholarly asides, the opinions approved by the head of the department. The resulting stultification, described in some detail in Allan Bloom's *The Closing of the American Mind,* leads to an intellectual orthodoxy as narrow and as humorless as the dogma espoused by the National Association of Manufacturers.

As Americans, we have a genius for organization, and we achieve our most impressive results when working together in groups. This appears to have been true of the national temperament since the first arriviste theologians formed a joint-stock company in Massachusetts Bay for the development of Puritan real estate. The pioneers moving west in the 1840s and 1850s gathered at Independence, Missouri, to join their wagon trains into corporate entities meant to last just long enough for the trek to California. Any man attempting to go it on his own would have been lucky to see Colorado. The hazards of the journey needed at least fifty wagons to set up a coherent defense against the terrain, the Indians and the weather. The same talent for cooperation characterized the building of American barns and the settling of American towns. During the twentieth century the preference for large institutional combination increasingly has come to define American scientific and technological discovery as well as the method of American business and journalism. The distinctively American art forms—musical comedy, jazz, the movies—all rely on the work of collaboration. So also the making of public personalities, which, contrary to the fables about stars born overnight in a shower of klieg light, requires a large supporting cast of technicians, distributors, agents, publicists, and beauticians, all harnessed together in the kind of team effort necessary to the construction of a shopping mall or an F-16. Big-time American journalism is group journalism, and the people who succeed at it learn to speak or write in the institutional voice of *The New Yorker, Newsweek* or *The CBS Evening News.* Dan Rather's voice is the voice of a committee. More than illness or death, the American journalist fears standing alone against the whim of his owners or the prejudices of his audience. Deprive William Safire of the insignia of *The New York Times*, and he would have a hard time selling his truths to a weekly broadside in suburban Duluth.

When the chairman of a large corporation retires or finds it expedient to quit the premises in the custody of the police, the event almost never affects the price of the company's stock. The investors know that the institution, not the individual, tends the engines of commerce. Nor is it ever just one publishing house or automobile company that stumbles into financial ruin; it is all the publishing houses and all the automobile companies. If the practice of free enterprise coincided with the theory, it would be reasonable to expect that an exceptionally gifted organization (more attuned to social change, more subtle in its technology, more aggressive in its marketing strategy) would defy the prevailing trends and so accumulate earnings worthy of the sainted J. P. Morgan. But except on the margins of the major industries, or among companies small enough to retain the character of free-booting partnerships, the miracle almost never occurs. The oligopolies behave in the manner of stately sheep, all tending in the same direction, all comforting themselves with the same bleating explanations borrowed from the same newsletters and trade association speeches.

Whether lawyer, politician or executive, the American who knows what's good for his career seeks an institutional rather than an individual identity. He becomes the man from NBC or IBM. The institutional imprint furnishes him with pension, meaning, proofs of existence. A man without a company name is a man without a country. Strip him of his corporate rank and titles, and not only does he sink into obscurity, but also he is likely to vanish from the sight of the insurance companies—which means that his life, invisible and uninsured, is no longer worth the price of salvation.

In the faces of innumerable company functionaries (within the ateliers of the media as well as in the honeycombs of the large corporations), I have seen precisely the same hunted look that I noticed in George Amory's eyes that winter afternoon at the Plaza Hotel. What would happen to them if they were to be abandoned by the organization that furnishes them with titles, degree, comfort and permission to exist? Where would they go, and who would hire them? Who would notice them? In what voices would they speak?

The loss of an institutional identity gives rise to the spectacle of the retired corporate hierarch revolving like a dead moon in the orbit of his extinct influence. If he retires on Monday, his telephones fall silent on Tuesday; on Wednesday his portrait disappears from the brightly lit galleries of the business press, and by Friday nobody is much interested in his observations about NATO or the rate of inflation. The effect is even worse in Washington. Government functionaries deprived of their function have nothing else on which to base their claims to self, which is why American officials so seldom resign on matters of principle.

Money always implies the promise of magic, but the effect is much magnified when, as now, people have lost faith in everything else. During the 1960s and early 1970s the political and cultural argument in the United States still reflected at least a residual belief in competing systems of value, in the possibilities loosely associated with the talk of disarmament, social justice, environmentalism and human rights. By the time President Reagan arrived in the White House the aspirations of the prior decades were seen as so much dreaming nonsense.

To the extent that we forget how to love or respect one another—preferring to regard each other as commodities or targets of opportunity—we settle for the emblems of status. Retreating into the states of somnambulism, we abandon our hopes for what Schopenhauer meant by happiness *in concreto* and set our whole hearts on happiness *in abstracto*—that is, on money. The belief in what isn't there, in a fiction instead of a fact, accords with the transcendential bias of the American mind and our long-established preference for the impalpable, the unseen and the abstract.

THE EIGHTIES

The Last Days
of Drexel Burnham
(1990)

Brett Duval Fromson

Drexel Burnham Lambert was the investment banking firm that changed the
rules of corporate finance and mergers and acquisitions in the eighties. Drexel's
legendary inventor of "junk bonds" and other financial vehicles, Michael Milken,
engineered remarkable deals from his Beverly Hills offices, exerting vast influence on other banks and institutions. But after Milken's and his associates'
activities crossed the line from fast-and-loose to illegal, the government
stepped in. Drexel came crashing down in 1990, becoming a symbol of investment banking's excesses and chicanery during the decade.

D
on't weep for Michael Milken. Though he broke down in court
when he had to admit he was a felon, he certainly cut a good deal
for himself. In all likelihood he'll still be plenty rich when he gets
out of prison. Contrast that to the dismal fate of his firm, Drexel Burnham
Lambert—bankrupt within months of settling similar charges for a similar
amount of money. How did so powerful a firm fall so quickly?

At year-end 1988, Drexel Burnham had a brawny $1.4 billion in capi-
tal and 50 percent of junk-bond underwriting. A year later its market
share had dwindled to 38 percent, top executives were scrambling to roll
over $300 million of the firm's own commercial paper, and Drexel was
hemorrhaging—losing $86 million in one month alone.

Did Drexel do itself in? Or was it done in? The truth is that this was a
case of suicide—and murder. So potent had the firm become that employees truly believed they could do whatever they wanted without fear of retribution. That's why they could threaten Fortune 500 corporations with
takeovers and never expect political retaliation. And that's why they could
leverage themselves and their clients to the hilt without preparing for the

day debt would go out of fashion. Says a former officer: "You see, we thought, 'We are invulnerable.'"

Management was as misguided as it was self-confident. In the good times, CEO Frederick Joseph and the board of directors were lax supervisors, allowing the firm to be run like a Middle Eastern souk. Milken sat at the center of his X-shaped desk in Beverly Hills and was accountable to no one. Eager for Drexel to become an investment banking powerhouse, Joseph knew better than to tinker with the marvelous Milken money machine he needed to finance hostile takeovers. That led to abuses in Milken's operation, which created a backlash ending in federal felony charges.

Even after it settled with the government, Drexel had a chance to survive if it could slim down. But Joseph lost control over his top dealmakers, who, to prove that the firm could flourish without Milken, went on a disastrous spree at precisely the wrong time. Because the bright and hardworking staff had been motivated almost solely by making a buck, esprit de corps degenerated rapidly into every man for himself once the money slowed. The firm floated issues for marginal companies and then flogged them furiously to customers. What couldn't be sold—and this became fatal—had to be inventoried.

Although few participants are willing to speak on the record, the picture that emerges of Drexel's final days is of a firm thrashing desperately to avoid the inevitable. That was nowhere more evident than in the last-ditch efforts to raise cash. Although Joseph and his chief financial officer, Richard Wright, had been warned that a liquidity crisis would likely hit the firm, they failed to alert the directors and senior officers until a few days before the end. As the junk-bond market was tanking in the U.S. last fall, Drexel Chairman John Shad, the former chairman of the Securities and Exchange Commission who had railed against junk-bond takeovers, was in the Far East assisting Drexel's effort to raise money for the firm by selling junk that couldn't be sold domestically. Even after the onset of the credit crisis, Wright continued urging Drexel's reluctant salesmen to peddle the firm's own risky commercial paper.

Drexel's final throes obscure another story of how business really works when inexperienced outsiders try to wrest power from those who are used to having it. As Drexel's capital evaporated, its bank lenders quietly abandoned it. By February 1990, when regulators stepped in to stop Joseph from dissipating what capital remained, only the top officials at the Treasury Department and the Federal Reserve could have saved the firm. And they were not about to. Says a former Treasury official: "People down here said, 'Hell, no. There's no reason anybody should do anything. We don't like 'em.'"

⁂

The story of Drexel's demise goes back to 1978, when Milken moved the high-yield bond department from New York to his hometown of Los Angeles. Milken's father was dying of cancer, and Mike's young children had health problems. Milken told his superiors that at least one of his kids was subject to epileptic seizures, and that he and his wife, Lori, wanted to be closer to their families on the West Coast. The move paradoxically brought Milken closer to Fred Joseph, then head of the corporate finance department in New York, which had serious image problems. At the time the only Harvard business school graduates Joseph could recruit were those who had been turned down by other Wall Street firms. But the view of Drexel as an investment banking backwater began to change with Joseph's discovery that Milken's big junk buyers—companies like Rapid-American and Reliance Insurance—were also eager to be big junk issuers. They were the engine that propelled Drexel to fourth place among all underwriters by 1986 and enabled Joseph to hire attractive, personable bankers like Martin Siegel, who had made a name for himself in mergers and acquisitions at Kidder Peabody.

Milken and Joseph were a team from the beginning. Milken may have been the much-pampered genius with gleaming new offices in Beverly Hills, but Joseph was the smooth, articulate voice of the firm and the man who was building the institution around Milken. From their offices on opposite coasts, they spoke to each other five to fifteen times a day. One former Drexelite describes the West Coast office that Milken ran as "structurally antisocial," entrepreneurship bordering on anarchy. Milken's Hobbesian style of management may explain much of the corner-cutting that went on in Beverly Hills and caused so much trouble with the regulators. A former Drexel broker recalls hearing one of Milken's salesmen threaten a client over the phone: "If you don't buy these bonds from me, I'll burn your house down!"

Back in New York it was easy to ignore Milken's managerial weaknesses. Fees were rolling in like the waves at Malibu, and Joseph took his fair share of credit for them at the board meetings. Of every dollar the high-yield department made, close to two-thirds went to the firm, and the rest went to Milken and his group. Drexel's East Coast executives, many of them holdovers from the old Burnham & Co., the retail brokerage firm that had bought Drexel Firestone in 1973, had never seen such money. An executive who joined Drexel in the mid-1970s recalls being shocked that a senior partner's interest in the firm was then worth only about $400,000—a pittance even by the standards of the day. By the mid-1980s, he said, a partner with this much equity was worth about $15 million. Another former officer recalls hearing Robert Linton, then chairman, say that one of his great motivations was watching the book value of his stock go up every month.

When Joseph and Milken committed Drexel to the hostile tender offer financed by junk bonds, they enraged a powerful special-interest group—the CEOs of big corporations and their board members, lawyers, bankers, and political representatives. Drexel also made a dangerous enemy on Wall Street in Salomon Brothers, heretofore the top bond house and every bit as tough and sharp-elbowed as Drexel itself.

As early in 1984, Drexel was trying to monopolize the high-yield business. It refused to allocate any bonds on a deal it underwrote for Golden Nugget, the casino operator, to Salomon Brothers, which had customers for them. According to two eyewitnesses, Salomon's chairman, John Gutfreund, was in such a frenzy over these tactics that he warned Joseph that he was going to get Milken. Gutfreund's precise phrase, though his firm denies it, was "knee his nuts off."

The more genteel but equally direct reaction of big business came in 1985 when Drexel financed T. Boone Pickens's $8.1 billion raid on Unocal Corp., then the twelfth largest U.S. oil producer. Fred Hartley, who was Unocal's forceful CEO, had plenty of Washington connections. His investment banker was Nicholas Brady, then head of Dillon Read, a former U.S. Senator from New Jersey, and a good friend of the Vice President, George Bush. While Hartley worked the press, equating Drexel to a terrorist group, Brady and other Washington insiders got Congress on the warpath. Says a former White House official: "Nick really hung Drexel out to dry. He put the firm in Congress's gunsights."

More specifically, in the sights of then-Congressman (now Senator) Timothy Wirth of Colorado and New York Senator Alfonse D'Amato, who chaired hearings on the dangers of takeovers and junk financing. Fred Joseph was called to testify, as were such Drexel-financed raiders as Carl Icahn and Boone Pickens. Among the chorus of Cassandras prophesying the doom of financial markets if junk-bond takeovers were not curbed was SEC Chairman Shad. Said he: "The more leveraged takeovers and buyouts today, the more bankruptcies tomorrow." Unocal ultimately bought Pickens off, and Congress never acted on the thirty or so bills that came out of the hearings, but Drexel had been warned.

On November 14, 1986, Ivan Boesky, a longtime Milken client, pleaded guilty to SEC charges of insider-trading violations based on allegations made by investment banker Dennis Levine. Burnham & Co. founder I. W. "Tubby" Burnham, chairman emeritus, was the only board member to suggest that Drexel might throttle back on junk bonds. When Milken heard about Burnham's radical idea, he threatened to quit. Fearing they would lose their Midas, board members put Burnham's proposal to a vote and defeated it resoundingly.

Within two months of what became known as Boesky Day, Aetna Life & Casualty Co. notified Joseph that it would not renew Drexel's excess insurance protection, which guarantees replacement of securities in a customer's account above the $500,000 covered by the Securities Investor Protection Corp. According to sources at Drexel, Joseph was told that Aetna's decision not to renew had been made "at a very senior level" and was "not appealable." Drexel had to self-insure, and that cost the firm about $11 million more than it paid Aetna.

Senior Drexel officials were convinced that Aetna's blue-ribbon board of directors was behind the decision not to renew coverage. On the board were David Roderick, former chairman of USX, and Warren Anderson, former chairman of Union Carbide, both of whom had faced Drexel-financed raiders and been forced into painful restructurings. An Aetna spokesman says that the board was not involved in the decision but that, because of the Boesky scandal, it was made at a higher level of the company than normal.

The government began subpoenaing witnesses and preparing indictments against Drexel and Milken based on information it had obtained from Boesky. Throughout 1988 the competitive pressure on all Wall Street firms to do deals, even bad deals, was intense. Says one of Milken's key West Coast lieutenants: "The government investigation spurred us on to prove that we were still the most powerful. That's why the quality of the credits we underwrote began to fall off."

Preoccupied with preparing a legal defense, Milken was giving the firm only 25 percent of his prior time and effort. He recognized that Drexel, like everyone on Wall Street, was doing deals on the dangerous assumption that companies could sell assets tomorrow for more than they were worth today, and therefore could afford staggering levels of debt. But he was as much of a deal junkie as anyone else.

Drexel had been negotiating with the U.S. Attorney's office and the SEC for almost two years, and government lawyers were furious that the firm had not yet done the decent thing—dump Milken and plead guilty. An impatient U.S. Attorney for the Southern District of New York, Rudolph

Giuliani, encouraged his subordinates to threaten Drexel with a RICO (Racketeer Influenced and Corrupt Organizations) indictment if the firm did not settle. RICO frightened Joseph, and with good reason. Under the statute, the government might be able to lodge a claim on Drexel's assets that would be senior to the claims of the firm's banks. Joseph believed that could lead the lenders to pull their lines of credit if Drexel were indicted.

Shortly after Thanksgiving, Joseph told the other members of the "war committee," a small group that had been set up to coordinate Drexel's resistance to the indictment, that he was thinking of settling. He also kept the twenty-two board members informed of his every move. The lone voice in opposition to settling belonged to John Kissick, forty-eight, the strapping head of West Coast corporate finance. Hugely popular within the firm, Kissick argued that admitting to guilt would be a mistake on principle because the firm did not know if it *was* guilty. Kissick had been hired by Fred Joseph in 1975 to run the West Coast corporate finance department, where he worked closely with Milken. He was torn between supporting Joseph—the man who had been his mentor—and Milken, the man who was his friend.

Two of Drexel's other stars faced a similar dilemma. Peter Ackerman, forty-three, was Milken's brilliant and aloof deputy who designed the packages of securities that the issuers offered. Leon Black, thirty-eight, was the head of mergers and acquisitions; he found the targets for Drexel's raiders. Both were busy helping Henry Kravis structure $9 billion in debt securities that Kohlberg Kravis Roberts would use to pay for the monumental RJR Nabisco buyout. Joseph had then pulled out of a meeting to discuss rumors that they might leave if Drexel sold out Milken. According to a senior officer, all Ackerman would say was "Let's see how this plays out." But neither man resigned. Then the Giuliani team infuriated the Drexel board by demanding that the firm's employees waive attorney-client privileges in any future investigations. That meant the employees could be prosecuted later on the basis of information they had given Drexel's lawyers who were preparing the firm's defense. On December 19 the board voted overwhelmingly not to settle.

That night the corporate finance department held its Christmas party in the grand ballroom of the Waldorf-Astoria hotel. Board Chairman Robert Linton appeared onstage to sing, "Rudy the Red-Nosed Reindeer," with lyrics that made it clear Rudy was no reindeer and Drexel was remaining defiant. The crowd of about eight hundred people went wild, screaming and banging the tables. One skeptical senior investment banker recalls going over to Joseph, sticking his finger in Fred's stomach, and saying, "I hope it's not helium in there like the Macy's Thanksgiving Day balloons."

Joseph's reply came two days later. He met with the board in the morning and announced that a settlement had been worked out. Giuliani backed off on the issue of attorney-client privilege, and Drexel agreed to plead guilty to six felony counts that included dealings with Ivan Boesky. The firm would also pay $650 million in penalties and cooperate fully with the government investigations of its employees and customers.

What apparently tipped Joseph toward settling was hearing a taped conversation of accusations against Milken made by a Drexel trader. This was the first time Joseph realized the government had more against Milken than just Boesky's allegations. He was also shown some spread sheets on transactions that, combined with the tape, would lead knowledgeable people to the conclusion that Milken bent the rules too far. Joseph informed the board that Giuliani required an answer by four that afternoon, or he would hold a press conference announcing a RICO indictment.

After two years and hundreds of millions of dollars spent warring with the government, the decision came down to a board vote, and it wasn't even close—sixteen to six in favor of settling. Kissick voted no, as did Joseph in a misguided symbolic protest that infuriated employees, who thought he was being hypocritical. Especially demoralized were the employees on the West Coast, who thought they saw a sellout. Unsubstantiated rumors spread quickly in Beverly Hills that Joseph cut the deal in exchange for personal immunity from prosecution. Aware of the plunge in morale, Joseph moved quickly to hold his top producers in the high-yield department and corporate finance.

The firm seemed to have money to burn—$1.4 billion in capital, $1 billion more than required by regulations—and Joseph started spreading it around. He guaranteed key employees, although not in writing, that their 1989 compensation would equal at least 75 percent of 1988's, which had been huge. But unlike the previous arrangement Drexel had had with the high-yield group when Milken was running it, the new package did not tie compensation to the profitability of the firm.

Joseph, according to a senior manager of the firm, had long thought that Bear Stearns & Co. had made a big mistake to let Henry Kravis get away rather than meet his demands for more money. Joseph was determined to keep Ackerman, Black, and Kissick, even at the risk of paying them so much that he became, in effect, their subordinate. In April 1989 he agreed to give Ackerman at least $100 million as a reward for his performance in 1988 and for helping sell the RJR Nabisco bonds in 1989. In addition, Ackerman and Black were told that the more deals they brought in, the higher their bonuses.

When rumors got out about the special arrangements Ackerman, Black, and a few others had negotiated, morale took another nose dive. A former member of the Drexel board jeers, "The key to success was being a pig." To allow his other investment bankers to vent their anger and envy, Joseph brought in a psychologist named Ned Kennan, who is used by many companies, including KKR. What did employees tell Kennan? According to a former top investment banker, "That everybody hated Peter and Leon."

Milken's departure in 1989 forced Joseph to restructure the firm around Ackerman, Black, and Kissick: Black became one of the new heads of corporate finance, Kissick was given Milken's old job as head of the high-yield department, and Ackerman was named head of a new capital markets group. The settlement also brought John Shad, sixty-six, out of retirement. The SEC insisted that Joseph find a Mr. Clean to install as chairman of the board of the holding company. Howard Baker, former White House chief of staff and Senate majority leader, had turned Drexel down because Joseph would not yield the CEO's title. But Shad, who had been Joseph's former boss in the early 1970s when they were both at E.F. Hutton, consulted with his old friends Nicholas Brady, now Secretary of the Treasury, and Alan Greenspan, chairman of the Federal Reserve, and took the job. Shad's $3.1 million salary went into a trust set up for the Harvard business school, to which he had pledged $20 million for the study of leadership and ethics.

Black, Ackerman, and their colleagues were determined to prove that Drexel could still do deals better than any other firm. In the first half of 1989, its market share actually *increased* to 70 percent, vs. 40 percent for the first half of 1988. But much of that came from the two big bond offerings that Drexel managed for the RJR Nabisco buyout. And now doing deals was putting the investment bankers themselves increasingly at risk. Like everyone else on Wall Street, Drexel had to compete by putting up its own money as a bridge loan. In the past Milken's network of ready buyers made this practice unnecessary. Kissick tried hard to stop questionable deals but lacked the needed clout. As an investment banker, he knew little about selling and trading junk bonds and was still broken up over the firm's shabby treatment of Milken.

Among Drexel's worst-selling underwritings of 1989 were those that Leon Black did to help William Farley, the T-shirt titan, take over textile maker West Point-Pepperell. Farley needed over $1 billion to swing the acquisition, and Kissick questioned whether such a deal could be sold. But Black did not want to see Drexel welsh on its promise to raise the money for Farley, so he and Ackerman bulled it through. Unfortunately for the firm, Kissick's concerns were verified by the market when Drexel failed to sell $250 million of the paper and had to inventory the stuff.

Ackerman also had his fair share of fiascoes. Drexel raised about $140 million to refinance the purchase of one of his clients, Edgcomb Metals, a Tulsa steel wholesaler, by the Blackstone Group, a Wall Street buyout boutique. Six weeks after the deal closed, the company's business deteriorated and over half the bonds were still in Drexel's inventory. A wrinkle in the refinancing suggests that the motivation behind it was not simply helping a client. Ackerman profited personally. He owned part of Edgcomb through a private partnership, and according to an informed Drexel executive received $6 million to $7 million when the company was sold. A Drexel spokesman disputes this figure as being "way off." But a senior West Coast manager says Drexel sometimes did deals in order to "cash out" its officers' positions.

Unsold private placements and bridge loans Drexel made to clients began piling up in the holding company's inventory. Like many brokerage firms, Drexel was set up as a holding company with a broker-dealer subsidiary; while the broker-dealer was regulated by the SEC, the holding company was not unless it held publicly traded securities. The SEC requires that broker-dealers mark their inventories to market, and as the public junk market slid, the broker-dealer inventory showed losses. But Drexel did not have to mark to market the private debt and bridge loans that were in the holding company's hands, and could maintain the fiction that they were worth their paper values. By the third quarter of 1989, Drexel's holding company was stuck with an estimated $1 billion of private junk bonds and bridge loans. These represented capital commitments the firm had made to customers, and Drexel had to borrow the money to carry them and to remain in business. Says an ex-Drexel officer: "Our bridges had turned into piers."

Meanwhile junk-bond offerings that Drexel had already sold were coming apart. Some, like the bonds of Integrated Resources, the issuer most closely associated with Drexel, were old deals. Integrated was a financial services company that sold real estate tax shelters until the 1986 Tax Reform Act eliminated most write-offs for limited partnerships and cut the heart out of its business. By June 1989 it was unable to roll over its commercial paper, but Drexel did not step up to become the buyer of last resort as the market expected. Says a former Drexel salesman: "When we let Integrated go down, the buyers lost all confidence."

But most of the deals that singed customers were of more recent vintage. One that resulted in third-degree burns was Memorex, the maker of magnetic computer tape, for which Ackerman raised $555 million last

July. Two months after the offering, the company reported a 66 percent decline in operating income, and the bonds plunged from par to 50 cents on the dollar. It turned out that foreign investors had the right to sell their Memorex bonds back to Drexel at par. When some did so, the firm booked an estimated $30 million loss. Drexel did not step in to support the market for its other customers, however. The impact of Drexel's refusal to support Integrated and Memorex cannot be overemphasized. The firm had finally killed its famed network of buyers.

That summer Congress passed the savings and loan bailout bill, which required thrifts that owned junk bonds to sell them by 1994. The S&Ls promptly stampeded out of junk, and the secondary market began to slide. Issuers were beginning to default on a weekly basis. Many of the exploding deals were not Drexel's, but the firm suffered the consequences more than anyone else because it depended so heavily on the business. Fees from new underwritings dropped, and trading in the secondary market became markedly less profitable. In August and September the firm began losing money. In October the losses hit $86 million.

By late summer Ackerman, who has a Ph.D. in political science from the Fletcher School of Law and Diplomacy near Boston, was telling Joseph that he wanted to move to London to write a follow-up to his doctoral dissertation on the strategy of nonviolent resistance. To hang on to Ackerman, Joseph created a position for him in London developing overseas business for the firm. This sojourn by one of the biggest producers puzzled many at the firm, but not a friend of Ackerman's, who says, "Peter wanted to get as far away as he could."

As Drexel's situation deteriorated, Joseph became more withdrawn. According to a longtime Drexel executive, "Fred sort of blew his cork and became a different human being the last year." Meanwhile Chairman John Shad and an entourage spent a good part of the fall in the Far East trying to sell junk bonds. Shad says he talked only about general market conditions in high-yield bonds and leveraged buyouts. But Drexel's former Hong Kong managing director Marc Faber says: "I took him to see Jardine Matheson, a conservative, blue-chip company. Shad asked the treasurer, 'Do you have any high-yield bonds in your portfolio?' The treasurer said, 'Of course not.' These were investors in quality. Shad was crazy to try to sell junk to these people."

More ominously, Drexel's lenders were losing their nerve. Hit with bad loans to real estate developers, many began to back away from Drexel. That was a nightmare for Joseph and Richard Wright, the chief financial officer, because without bank loans, Drexel didn't have enough capital to finance its inventory and run its business. The banks were offered the inventory of private placements and bridge loans as collateral for the lines but said it wasn't good enough. Wright's staff began to warn him that the high-yield position had to be reduced and that Drexel was on borrowed time. Wright did not pass the dire message along to the board. Why not? Says one of his former subordinates: "It was difficult to tell whether he didn't believe the warning or whether he felt his timing was wrong."

&

In November, Standard & Poor's lowered its rating on the holding company's commercial paper from A2 to A3. Overnight Drexel was shut out of the commercial paper market, the source of $700 million of financing. Within three weeks, as holders refused to buy Drexel's paper when it came due, it was reduced to only $300 million of borrowings. Desperate, Wright flew to Paris to ask Groupe Bruxelles Lambert, the French and Belgian investors who were Drexel's largest shareholders, for more money. Their reply: *Non, merci.* They wanted to see a return to profitability first. Wright took ill in Paris and was hospitalized, reportedly with an ulcer.

As the new year approached, Joseph and Shad, the head of the compensation committee, made a final decision on the bonus pool. While knowing that the firm might lose money for the year, they set the payout at a healthy $270 million, vs. $506 million in 1988, but decided that 24 percent of that pool would be given in Drexel stock. When the bonuses were announced in December, Leon Black was perturbed at how small his was, a mere $12 million. According to several Drexel officers, Black went home and sulked for a couple of days before Joseph relented and gave him $3 million more. Joseph, as if to compensate the firm for the cash drain, took his $2.5 million bonus entirely in Drexel stock. Meanwhile, Drexel's financial plight was worsening. Throughout the year the firm had borrowed $650 million from its commodities trading unit. The commodities group usually borrowed gold from foreign central banks, then sold the gold and lent the cash to the holding company. But in December, when Drexel was unable to roll over more commercial paper, it could no longer pay back its commodities unit on demand.

The new year began badly. After months of erosion, the junk-bond market collapsed as jittery holders began dumping en masse. In January, Drexel lost $60 million. As more and more banks refused to extend the lines of credit backing up Drexel's commercial paper, the money from the firm's commodities trading unit no longer sufficed to finance the holding company's inventory. Wright, with the approval of Fred Joseph, began to raid the broker-dealer, which still had capital in excess of the regulatory minimum, and Drexel's government-securities dealer. In late January he drained these two units of about $400 million, despite warnings from his staff that the firm would run out of capital within thirty days. He told a member of his group, "Well, maybe the salesmen can sell more commercial paper."

Neither Wright nor Joseph informed the board of directors about Drexel's precarious state. Nor did they report to the New York Stock Exchange or the SEC—which both require that brokers have a certain amount of capital to meet their obligations—that they were taking money out of the broker-dealer. But on February 2, the New York Fed got wind of the transfers and passed the word to the SEC and the exchange regulators, who were aghast. Drexel firmly believed that its longtime nemesis, Salomon Brothers, tipped off the Fed, but Salomon denies the charge. From this point on, the regulators called the shots. On Thursday, February 8, the stock exchange officials, after consultations with SEC Chairman Richard Breeden, telephoned Wright and told him that he could not take more money from the broker-dealer without SEC approval. Wright relayed the bad news to Joseph, who was at his farm in rural New Jersey.

A meeting of the department heads who ran the firm was hastily convened, and Joseph was hooked in by phone. Wright explained that $400 million in unsecured debt was coming due within the next two weeks, with another $330 million scheduled to mature in March. Then the senior officers heard the head of the commodities trading unit explain his Rube Goldberg borrowing arrangement with the foreign central banks. And by the way, he told his dumbfounded peers, he needed his $650 million back, pronto, to repay the loans. According to a department head, recriminations began to fly about who knew what—and when—about the firm's financial condition.

On Friday, February 9, Wright was feeling the pressure. According to former Drexel officers, in the morning he and his treasurer were urging Drexel's commercial paper salesmen to sell more paper, despite widespread fears that the firm was on the edge of bankruptcy. Incredibly enough, the salesmen were able to flog millions of dollars' worth only two days before Drexel went belly-up.

In the afternoon the department heads reconvened to consider the options. About a year too late, Joseph proposed a draconian plan to save the firm: Cut costs, sell inventories of stocks and high-grade bonds, pull out of the commodities and mortgage-backed securities business, and sell off the junk holdings. Everyone was working around the clock that weekend. But when Joseph telephoned Peter Ackerman to tell him of the liquidity crisis, Ackerman resigned from the board on the spot.

Saturday was spent trying to sell operations to free up capital. But says a board member: "You don't get out of business in a day or week. They were either blind and dumb or in some dream world." By Saturday night a frantic search was on for a merger partner. Desperate senior officers began calling their Wall Street competitors, saying in effect, "How about sending in a team to take a look tomorrow?" A few browsed, including Smith Barney and Nomura, but no one bought. On Monday morning rumors of Drexel's imminent bankruptcy were sweeping the world's bourses. Says a former Drexel floor broker: "When I walked out onto the floor of the [New York Stock] exchange, I could sense that something was the matter. Stories were flying that we were already out of business."

They were—almost. Drexel's only hope of salvation was its banks, which had been hounding various members of the firm for days trying to find out whether rumors of bankruptcy were true. Joseph spent the day readying a $1.1 billion bundle of securities that the banks might accept as collateral for a $300 million to $400 million loan. These securities were the same old bridge loans and private placements that Drexel hadn't been able to sell before, plus the right to income from a portfolio of leases. After giving the securities a haircut for their illiquidity, Joseph and the bankruptcy experts he had called in over the weekend put the package's worth at $800 million.

At dusk on Monday, February 12, a bevy of bankers in pinstripes, armed with calculators, marched into a seventh-floor conference room at Drexel Burnham's headquarters. Joseph knew he was not adequately prepared for the meeting and that the bankers would have serious questions about the quality of the merchandise he was offering as collateral. But he thought there was a better than even chance they would lend Drexel the money anyway. After all, he was sure that the regulators were urging the banks to help out. In fact, he figured the federal government, with a wink and a nod, had already lobbied the lenders to make the loan rather than let Drexel fail. Isn't that the way these things are done?

For their part, the bankers were angry that Drexel hadn't come clean earlier. Joseph announced to the not altogether surprised group that Drexel had a liquidity problem and needed to borrow $300 million to $400 million. According to a banker at the meeting, he said the foreign central banks that had been funding Drexel were unwilling to continue that arrangement, but that certainly Drexel's loyal commercial lenders had more courage. Then the bankers received a list of the collateral and recognized it as the same junk they had disdained earlier. They were being asked to take a credit they had already passed on.

Fred Joseph then sealed Drexel's fate. He said in response to a banker's query that the firm had missed a scheduled repayment earlier in the day to holders of some commercial paper. Says a banker who was in the room: "So the situation was already worse than we had thought before the meeting. Drexel was in danger of cross-defaulting on all its loans." The bankers went through the motions of caucusing. After a few minutes they told Joseph that they could not make a decision that night and that they were not inclined to make the loan anyway. Joseph implored them to call their headquarters and seek approval. The bankers dutifully telephoned. The answer? Forget it.

They huddled again. Sentiment had hardened, but Joseph was not going to give up. He pleaded for the home phone numbers of the banks' top officers so that he could make personal appeals. Joseph's calls took them away from their dinner tables and televisions. But to no effect. There had been no regulatory winks and nods. By 12:30 A.M., Joseph let his exhausted troops drift home.

He, however, had one more humiliation to undergo. At 1:30 A.M. he telephoned the SEC's Richard Breeden and Gerald Corrigan of the New York Federal Reserve, who were at their homes, and informed them—as if they did not already know—that the banks had turned Drexel down. Breeden and Corrigan said that they were speaking for their respective bosses, Treasury Secretary Nicholas Brady and Fed Chairman Alan Greenspan. They suggested that Drexel file for Chapter 11 the next day or face government liquidation. It was only then that Joseph realized his firm was history. As he said to a colleague, "God has spoken."

PART IV

Hot and Cool

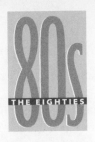

R. I. P.

(1982)

James Wolcott

When it appeared, Jean Stein's *Edie: An American Biography,* was the talk of the town in New York, Boston, and Southern California. The rise and fall of doomed sixties superstar Edie Sedgwick provided a unique glimpse of the siren-like attitude that Sedgwick embodied—with enduring appeal for scenemakers in the early eighties. As Wolcott's acute review of the book indicated, what lay behind the story was the nexus of celebrity, glamour, and art that Andy Warhol had pioneered. Warhol himself continued to draw the beautiful and damned into his circle until his death in 1987 (see p. 203).

For a brief spell in the mid-Sixties, Edie Sedgwick was the debutante princess of piss-elegance, an Andy Warhol "superstar" whose fashion trademark was a snowy white mink draped over a dimestore t-shirt. Edie was always abuzz with debbie enthusiasm—as Warhol himself put it, even when she was asleep, her hands were wide awake. But the all-American Edie was soon eclipsed on the Warhol scene by the icily cosmopolitan Nico, whose moody, ghostly voice adorned the music of the Velvet Underground. Like Nico, Edie had a fondness for soothing candlelight, but where Nico could bathe by candlelight without setting off fire alarms Edie nearly torched herself twice—once in her East Side apartment, the next time in her room at the Chelsea Hotel. She also banged herself up once in a traffic accident, engaged in monkey-wild bouts of indiscriminate sex, and spent a number of stretches in the swankier and, later, rattier loony bins.

But it was drugs that finally cashiered Edie Sedgwick. After years of skin-popping acquaintance with amphetamine, after years of rooting through her pocketbook for loose pills, Edie expired in a barbituated daze in 1971 at the age of twenty-eight, perhaps the most notable name in that string of casualties from the Warhol camp which includes Candy Darling

(cancer), Andrea Feldman (suicide), and Eric Emerson (rumored overdose).

In life, Edie Sedgwick may have been the crowning ornament of the
Warhol entourage, but in death she's being elevated into the company of
Jim Morrison, Brian Jones, and Jimi Hendrix—that pop cavalcade of the
beautiful slain. Not long ago, *Rolling Stone* ran a cover photograph of a
pouty, surly Jim Morrison with the headline, "He's hot, he's sexy, and he's
dead." Edie Sedgwick too is now a hot, sexy slice of necrophilia—an
exploitable piece of nostalgia for those who miss the unruly, dissolute
swagger of the Sixties. *Edie,* by Jean Stein and George Plimpton, is not
only her catapult into the celestial big time but a small, brightly lit shrine.
It may be pop journalism's first compact, disposable death kit.

Excerpted in *Rolling Stone, Edie* is on one level another saga of golden
lives gone astray, a countercultural *Haywire.* Even with all its golden-
doomed allure, however, Edie Sedgwick's life would at first glance seem a
rather slender bough on which to hang a full-scale biography. With her
stalky legs and silver hair and long, swinging earrings, Edie was perhaps
the forerunner of new-wavish pop stars like Patti Smith (who's interviewed in *Edie*) and Blondie's Deborah Harry (who, not incidentally, used
to waitress at Max's, Kansas City, chief hangout for the Warhol scenemakers). But that is at best a trickling influence, and it can hardly be argued
that Edie actually *did* anything beyond dressing up and having a giggle;
Diana Cooper she certainly wasn't. Indeed, she emerges in *Edie* as little
more than a likable, spoiled ditz who allowed herself to be ruled and then
ruined by a barrage of bad chemicals. And despite *Edie*'s subtitle—"An
American Biography"—there's nothing peculiarly American about her
demise: English debs, too, have been known to slump over at parties, their
pretty little arms punctuated by needletracks.

But for all that, *Edie* is fascinating, if only because Jean Stein and
George Plimpton have pulled off something provocative and novel in biography writing. Instead of sifting through details and probing into motives,
Edie's authors offer a smartly edited weave of recollections, with the testi-
monies of Edie's friends and kin presented without comment in small
quick doses, like clips in a documentary. The book is all chatter, the chapters are brief and snappy, the photographs plentiful. Other books have
been programmed for those readers with short attention spans, but except
for the best pages of Mailer's *The Executioner's Song,* none had *Edie*'s ingenious intelligence and eye for the succinct, telling detail. It's a technique
best suited for a marginal figure of glamour like Edie—someone whose
greatest deliberations were over which makeup to apply, which party to
adorn. Were Edie a more driven, ambitious, and rounded-off heroine—an

actress of rich accomplishment—the reader would expect to delve into the wellsprings of her calling. But Edie futilely splashed on the surface, and the disturbed surface is where *Edie* (thick on behavior, thin on psychology) stays. For better or ill, *Edie* is a spring forward to the televisionization of the prose narrative.

The book begins with a powerful haunting image. "Have you ever seen the old graveyard up there in Stockbridge?" asks John P. Marquand, Jr. Sedgwick Pie, he explains, is where the descendants of Judge Sedgwick are buried in concentric circles, with the Judge and his wife Pamela at the commanding center. "The descendants of Judge Sedgwick, from generation unto generation, are all buried with their heads facing out and their feet pointing in toward their ancestor. The legend is that on Judgment Day when they arise and face the Judge, they will have to see no one but Sedgwicks." *Edie* then takes us on a tour through the layered crusts of that pie, from the illustrious members of the line (like Ellery Sedgwick, who served a formidable term as editor of the *Atlantic Monthly*) to the more eccentric (Charles Sedgwick, who used to wander about the farm lecturing to the livestock). As the tour progresses, you have a sense of will and energy being held in clenched fists then squandered, then—by the time we get to Edie herself—flung away with reckless insolence.

Casting the longest and most damaging shadow by far in *Edie* is Edie's father, Francis. Nicknamed "Fuzzy," Francis was anything but an adorable huggy-bear. A novelist of modest distinction (*The Rim*), Fuzzy was a bullying hunk of beefcake who paraded about like a water-dwelling god, plucking the virtues of awed girls. Attending a wedding at the Sedgwick ranch in California in 1954, Susan Wilkins recalls, "It was a stud farm, that house, with this great stallion parading around in as little as he could. We were the mares. But it wasn't sex, it was breeding . . . and there's a difference, of course. The air was filled with an aura of procreation. Not carnal lust, but just breeding in the sense of not only re-creating life but a certain kind of life, a certain elite, a superior race." To those not fitted to sup with the gods, Fuzzy could be belittlingly cruel. Edie's sister Saucie reports, "For me, life at Corral de Quati was one long degradation, in front of anyone—guests, cowboys—my father would say I was fat, or stupid, or a liar."

So the Sedgwick line, once rich in culture, rectitude, and achievement, degenerated into a blight of small tormenting rancors and self-loathing mortification. If Edie can be believed (she was given to lurid exaggeration), her father once tried to seduce her, and she in turn tried to lure her brother Jonathan into the sack years later. She was also an anorectic binger, bolting down food, then shooting off to the bathroom for a heave.

Her brother Minty flipped out and eventually committed suicide, hanging himself with a necktie; another brother, Bobby, died when he cracked his motorcycle into the side of a bus, a daredevil stunt that might be labeled a near-suicide. (Characteristically, he wasn't wearing a crash helmet.) Anorexia, incest, suicide, all of it played out in the grassy splendor of life among the well-bred—small wonder reviewers are going to see F. Scott Fitzgerald's famous green light blinking in the distance, summoning the Sedgwicks to excess and orgy. But it is in its *absence* of lyricism, its fidelity to unfinished, grinding fact, that *Edie* is most convincing. Were the book more artful and polished, it might have succumbed to swoons of lamentation. Like Warhol's films, *Edie* is an emission of tarnished, silver-gray cool.

The book's one interlude of carefree indulgence comes when Edie skips off to Cambridge and becomes the darling of Harvard's homosexual dandies. "Edie loved the very nitroglycerine queens, the really smart ones who knew everything," remembers René Ricard. "She wanted high, very brilliant faggot friends who posed no threat to her body." Perhaps the most plumishly brilliant was the infamous Cloke Dosset, a lecherous athlete who draped his walls in satiny black and gave cocktail parties attended mostly by men who gave women the silent treatment. Says Patricia Sullivan, "Many of them had these wonderful names which Cloke would give them: Columbine Streetwalker, Halloween Pederast, Gardenia Boredom, and Gloriana, which is the name of Spenser's Faerie Queene, and Appassionata von Climax. The girls did not get nicknames."

Clearly, Cloke Dosset's brilliance consisted of prunings from Ronald Firbank, and clearly too these frolics served Edie as a run-through for the Warhol whirlwind, where the girls *did* get nicknames (Ingrid Superstar, International Velvet) and she would find herself cavorting through a shrill, fruity trashing of Catholicism which married Firbank to the fleshier side of gay stud-dom. *Edie* isn't unaware of these connections. Another one of Edie's friends at Cambridge recalls that the hallowed hangout for the nitroglycerine set was the Casablanca bar, located downstairs from the Brattle movie theater. "When one came through the plywood door, it was into her total world, and what heightened the experience was that one often had come down from the Brattle—that factory of illusions." So from there it was but a skipping bounce to Andy Warhol's factory of illusions.

For many readers, the account of Edie's brief sputter of incandescence at the Factory will be the most absorbing section in the book, so spiked is it with gossip, drugginess, and bitching malice. Perhaps I'm turning a trifle jaded, but the anecdotes of amphetamine dementia in *Edie* struck me as tired and familiar stories about "superstars" thwacking each other in the backsides with syringes and tossing screaming tantrums are now as stale as those fabled accounts of F. Scott Fitzgerald and Hemingway in the men's room together, comparing thingies. Too familiar also are the darts aimed at Paul Morrissey for mousing his way into Warhol's confidence and commercializing the Factory's operations. What's new are the details, which are far more blotched and gruesome than even the particulars of skin-puncturing abuse served up by Warhol and Pat Hackett in their sordidly entertaining memoir *POPism* (Harcourt Brace Jovanovich, 1980). Needle after needle is inserted into the asses of speedfreaks until their bottoms are eroded into crusty ridges.

Edie was no stranger to needles—as a child, she received Vitamin B shots in the behind like a sickly animal at the vet's—and she too developed scar tissue. In an excerpt from the tapes for a pseudo-documentary film called *Ciao! Manhattan,* Edie does a riff about the perils of amphetamine.

> You want to hear something I wrote about the horror of speed? Well, maybe you don't, but the nearly incommunicable torments of speed, buzzerama, that acrylic high, horrorous, yodeling, repetitious echoes of an infinity so brutally harrowing that words cannot capture the devastation nor the tone of such a vicious nightmare.

But then Edie does a fast flipflop testifying to the raptures of speed.

> It's hard to choose between the climactic ecstasies of speed and cocaine. They're similar. . . . That fantabulous sexual exhilaration. Which is better, coke or speed? It's hard to choose. The purest speed, the purest coke, and sex is a deadlock.

So surfing on the curve of one hopped-up high after another, Edie became a rattled, radiant wreck. Henry Geldzahler: "She was very nervous, very fragile, very thin, very hysterical. You could hear her screaming even when she wasn't screaming—this sort of supersonic whistling." And, in a puzzling comment, Diana Vreeland notes that when Edie modeled for *Vogue* she had lovely skin-tone, "but then I've never seen anyone on drugs that didn't have wonderful skin." (God, I have.) Curiously, *Edie* skimps most on what matters most in sizing up Edie's true measure of fame and attraction—her antics on film. The one keen paragraph on Edie's film legacy comes from Norman Mailer. "One hundred years from now they will look at *Kitchen* and see that incredibly cramped little set, which was indeed a kitchen. . . . You can see nothing but the kitchen table, the refrigerator, the stove, and the actors. The refrigerator hummed and droned on that sound track. Edie had the sniffles. She had a dreadful cold. She had one of those colds you get spending the long winter in a cold-water flat. The dialogue was dull and bounced off the enamel and plastic surfaces. It was a horror to watch. It captured the essence of every boring, dead day one's ever had in a city, a time when everything is imbued with the odor of damp washcloths and old drains."

Mailer's evocative comments aside, *Edie* shows a lazy hand in trying to nail down what was *special* about the Sedgwick mystique—what made her bob higher in the esteem of the hiply knowing than those in the Warhol stable who gave it a much heartier go. The best pin-down of Edie's appeal I know of appears in Stephen Koch's 1973 study of the splendors and miseries of Warholiana, *Stargazer*. How did Edie Sedgwick carve out a calm nook for herself in all that shriek and squalor?

> . . . [Edie] was unique among the women superstars because she never played the female clown. All the others—Baby Jane Holzer in the grotesquerie of her voguishness; Ingrid Superstar, a perfectly conscious comedienne forever varying on the theme of the dumb blond; Tiger Morse (who appeared more often at Max's Kansas City than in films) camping and squealing like a schoolgirl; Viva, with her interminable frizzy-haired account of schizophrenia, lascivious priests, and a badly damaged ego—all of them were in one way or another involved in a more or less comic display of their fears and weaknesses and overcompensations as women. But Sedgwick always kept her cool. When she spoke, she made sense; her response in a contretemps on screen (and part of the technique was to create those contretemps) was never the customary hysteria but a visibly intelligent effort to cope. . . .

Koch then swerves his attention to Warhol's *Beauty No. 2*, in which Sedgwick perches on the edge of a bed, "ice cubes in her glass tinkling (one associates tinkling with her presence, of ice cubes, jewelry, and her voice and eyes). . . ."

> Lithe and small-breasted, she's wearing a pair of black bikini panties, her long legs alternately girlish and regal. Her movements are nothing but the merest business: sipping her drink, fiddling with her pack of cigarettes, patting the overly friendly dog, until such small stuff at last resolves itself into an attempt at love-making with the silent Gino Peschio (who, shortly after the opening of the first reel, strips to his underwear).

But throughout, there is a continuing and largely inaudible conversation with [Chuck] Wein and [Gerard] Malanga out of frame. The visual field is assailed by their disembodied voices provoking the astonishingly various and precise textures of Sedgwick's responses, the nagging intrusions on her peace that proceed to make her portrait come alive. But those remarks being made at her are also ideal illustrations of a much favored directorial mode in the Factory at that time: Taunt and betrayal. . . . Under the influence of this technique, the conversation in *Beauty No. 2* moves from trivia to desperation. There is even a terrible moment near the end in which Sedgwick . . . speaks more or less inaudibly, but from real fear, of her horror of death. In other places, certain things are said off camera (I have been unable to decipher them) that plainly hurt and offend her (some others provoke the small miracle of her laugh); later, as the lovemaking demanded by the scenario begins, a series of cutting, catty remarks from the kibbitzers at last make her abruptly pull herself up, fold her arms around her knees and stop in unflustered, but visible, fury.

Koch's comments are worth quoting at such length not only because they frame Edie Sedgwick's film manner in sharp focus perspective but because such appreciations appear nowhere in *Edie*, which is rich in idle chat—wow, *fabulous, fantastic*—and slim on critical insight. *Edie*, taut as it is, is composed of rather stringy fibers.

Once Edie splits with the Warhol sect, her life becomes a tailspin of speed binges, casual rutting with dopers and bikers, recuperations in the hospital, sweet enthusiasms, and the futile hopes. She becomes a noisy blur in the book, a crackle of laughter and energy at the edge of the party. When Edie finally does die in bed with her husband, her death stirs in the reader little more than a small, fond sadness—small, because Edie's death seems so tediously inevitable. With bones and mannerisms as birdlike as hers, a ravenous appetite for drugs and kicks could only lead to a racking toll on her stamina, a fluttering collapse. She seems to have been fitted for a life both brief and flaring. Had she lived, she might—might—have become a housewifey recluse (like Patti Smith), but she also might have turned into a bloated caricature of herself, banging her head against the crib in one of John Waters's suburban travesties, the "small miracle of her laugh" coarsened into a fag-hag cackle.

According to *Edie,* when Warhol heard of Edie's death, he greeted the news with shrugging small talk. Death or recovery, it's all the same to the Prince of Ether, he admits with rare candor in *POPism.* After Ondine kicks speed and becomes a calm, normal person, Warhol offers a sigh of regret. "Sure, it was good he was off drugs (I supposed), and I was glad for him (I supposed), but it was so *boring:* there was no getting around that. The brilliance was all gone." To be wired-up is to be dramatic, and Warhol's parenthetical asides indicate that he preferred having those around him laced up with drugs and like cockatoos to their loitering about in the quiet. Edie Sedgwick was wired-up before she met Warhol, and wired-up after she left him, but Warhol created a theater of heightened sensations in which her own brittleness could take on a self-consuming sparkle. Like Fuzzy, Cloke Dosset, and the acid doctors that followed, Warhol was a careless father-figure allowing his daughter to cast about with wolves. Andy Warhol didn't destroy Edie Sedgwick, but he did make destruction seem like a glorious goof, an acrylic high—the ultimate buzzerama. And he left his camp-followers with nothing to cushion their falls.

Of course, Warhol himself is now a dazed whisper of death with a dubious thatch of ash-white hair—"the ghost of a genius," as Taylor Mead describes him in *Edie.* So feyly out of it is Warhol that it's pointless to expect him to express deep feelings of loss or regret over Edie's death: he's lived in the pop of flashbulbs for so long that his emotions are flaked and scattered, bleached out. If anything, he might feel a sliver of perverse pride at having a book like *Edie* dish the dirt on the lurid doings at his dream factory. Warhol was always star-struck, his moviemaking tricked-out Hollywood myths in topsy-turvy drag, and now, with *Edie,* he's inspired a book which rakes through the muck and intrigue of his passive reign like a thinking man's *Hollywood Babylon,* with Edie Sedgwick as the waif tossed upon the smoking slag-heap. Edie Sedgwick's death received a curt paragraph in the postscript to *POPism,* and the value of *Edie* is that it cracks open that paragraph to capture the arc of a life in its dying fall. For all its babble and gossip, for all the time spent with its eye glued to the keyhole, *Edie* is a serious, painstaking enterprise. And it has a disquieting symmetry. If the dead at Stockbridge were to rise from their graves, they would find themselves ringed about Judge Sedgwick but, reading *Edie* you feel that *these* dead—Candy Darling, Eric Emerson, Andrea Feldman, Edie Sedgwick—will find themselves staring at Andy Warhol. Poor wayward Edie; she deserved better fathers, a better fate.

THE EIGHTIES

Limelight
(1983)

When New York City's Limelight nightclub opened in November 1983, the media gave it adoring coverage—but had little clue as to what was really going on. For the press, then discovering celebrity culture, decadence was a kick, not a menace, and provocative style was the measure of all things. "One partygoer caused gasps and giggles by arriving on a cross," gushed the photo caption in *People* magazine. "Inside, he dragged it dutifully across the dance floor." Not far away was Andy Warhol and his latest, a disorderly Cornelia Guest, debutante. Two reports follow.

First-Nighters who weren't able to get in to Andy Warhol's Wednesday night party at Limelight, the controversial church-nunnery-parish-house-rectory-turned-disco, weren't quite so passive. They searched madly for secret entryways and they and their limousines tied up traffic for blocks. This, clearly, was an Event. "There goes our parking space," said a dejected Kevin Walz, the interior designer, who lives in the neighborhood.

Those who did succeed in being seen inside included Matt Dillon, Richard Gere, Cheryl Tiegs, Daryl Hall and John Oates, Francis Ford Coppola, Jacklyn Smith, Eddie Murphy, Cornelia Guest, Peter Frampton, Patti LuPone, and Karen Allen. Next to gawking at the town's newest shrine to dance, the biggest crowd-pleaser seemed to be gaping from a stained-glass window at those who couldn't get in.

New York Times, November 11, 1983

It was billed by Andy Warhol, whose *Interview* magazine was sponsoring the opening, as "the party of the year." But after the Episcopal Bishop of New York, the Rt. Rev. Paul Moore, Jr. huffed, "We are horrified," the question became whether Manhattan's newest disco, Limelight, operating from the former Church of the Holy Communion, might not wind up being the scandal of the year.

No matter that the 137-year-old church had been deconsecrated 11 years ago and until recently had served as a drug rehabilitation center. The disco's kinky kicks obviously come from its ecclesiastical trimmings, including pews, an altar, a gilded church pipe organ that descends from the organ loft and laser beams bouncing off the stained-glass windows.

"Is this consecrated ground?" asked fashion photographer Francesco Scavullo nervously. "Everybody's having a good time, so I'm not putting it down," said supermodel Cheryl Tiegs, there with hubby Peter Beard. "Listen," chimed in Judy Garland's daughter Lorna Luft, "they've been dancing in churches for a long time. Now we've just got a little bass added."

More than just a little bass. Megadecibel rock music boomed through the nave as the throng boogied and scenes from *The Ten Commandments* flashed on a giant video screen, "I think it's a little sacrilegious—and I'm Jewish," said Dr. Stephen Kritsick, co-author of *Creature Comforts: The Adventures of a City Vet*.

Untroubled by clerical overtones was the proprietor of the scene, Peter Gatien, 31, a Canadian self-made millionaire who purchased the former church for $1.6 million, then spent $3.5 million restoring and decorating it. "New York is dying for something new," says Gatien. "Studio 54 is nearly seven years old now." And as his two previous Limelight discos (in Hollywood, Fla. and Atlanta) show, Gatien has a flair for novelty. His Atlanta club made headlines when sharks swam under the glass dance floor and again when Anita Bryant glided atop it with a minister devoted to reforming gays.

"In New York you've really got to knock 'em dead," Gatien says, so he gave his real estate agent one directive: "Find me a church." Though he kept most of the architecture intact ("Eighty percent of the stained glass is original, but it needed repair"), innovations, including a spiral staircase up to the bell tower and three balconies overlooking the nave, were installed. "People watching, in New York more than anywhere else, has got to be the greatest entertainment," Gatien explains. Quake, wind and snow machines, as well as a hologram of a "supernatural figure" are planned. "I want high-energy music," he says. "You want it to be happening when you walk in at 2 o'clock in the morning."

People, November 28, 1983

On First Looking into Emily Post's *Etiquette*

(1984)

P. J. O'Rourke

O'Rourke's memoir expressed more than a little regret for the relaxed rules of the anything-goes eighties. Reflecting on his own juvenile aspirations, as he sought to rise above the rough blue-collar world he knew firsthand, O'Rourke tells how he encountered a more decorous state available to anyone with "instinctive decency, ethical integrity, self-respect, and loyalty." As old courtesies and manners went out of fashion, O'Rourke wondered, what would replace them, if anything, to inspire boys and girls to rise and shine in the future?

I've been paging through the new, totally revised, terribly up-to-date version of Emily Post's *Etiquette* written by Mrs. Post's granddaughter-in-law Elizabeth L. Post. It's a big book, thorough, tidy of organization, and legibly printed. I have no doubt it would be handy if I were planning my wedding or funeral. And I'm sure it contains all manner of sound advice for conducting a new, totally revised, terribly up-to-date life. However, all the people I know have been left out.

Muriel Manners, Mr. and Mrs. Eminent, Sarah Stranger, and Mrs. Kindheart are nowhere to be found. The late Mrs. Post used these friends and acquaintances to illustrate her little dramas of courtesy and faux pas. She sketched her characters with marvelous economy—never a word about their physical appearance, inner conflicts, or personal history. Yet they came alive upon the page. I give this example from my mother's copy of the eighth edition, published in 1945:

NAMES LEGALLY CHANGED

Whatever may have been the reason for changing the name by which one has been known, social and business associates should be notified of the change if embarrassing situations are to be avoided. The quickest and simplest way of telling them is to send out formal announcements.

MR. AND MRS. JOHN ORIGINAL NAME
ANNOUNCE THAT BY PERMISSION OF THE COURT
THEY AND THEIR CHILDREN
HAVE TAKEN THE FAMILY NAME OF
BROWN

What subtlety there is in "embarrassing situations," social "associates," and "Whatever may have been the reason." One knows it didn't turn out well for the sad and rather pushing Name family (pronounced Nam-ay). Their import business was expanded with vain optimism and sank beneath a weight of bank debt. Today, John Original, Jr., is some sort of rapscallion Hollywood person and the Name daughter, on her fourth divorce, drinks before noon.

There are no such adventures in the new edition. The exotic Names have been replaced by the prosaic Milsokovichs, who are changing their handle to Miller, probably to get something that will fit on a Visa card. And that rapier thrust "may have been" is gone from the opening sentence.

In this and every other way Elizabeth L. Post's *Etiquette* is blunt and homely. It contains paragraphs on such subjects as BYOB parties, pregnant brides, illegal drugs, meeting people through personal ads, and unmarried couples who live together. To tell the truth, I already know how unmarried couples live together. I probably need to learn less. Anyway, Emily Post would never have broached the subject. She would have thought it, well, bad manners.

Nor would the elder Mrs. Post have held a respectable lady's past up to ridicule. But the new edition of *Etiquette* is decorated with facsimile quotations from the first edition of 1922.

Dishes are *never* passed from hand to hand at dinner, not even at the smallest and most informal one.

There are many places which are unsuitable for young girls to go whether they are chaperoned or not. No well-brought-up young girl should be allowed to go to supper at a cabaret until she is married. . . .

Do not greet anyone until you are out on the church steps. . . . "Hello" should not be said on this occasion because it is too "familiar" for the solemnity of church surroundings.

Perhaps these weren't inserted for amusement but to show how manners change with time. I found them, though, neither funny nor informative. Instead they filled me with sad longing for the elegance, dignity, and sophistication I knew in my youth.

That is, the elegance, dignity, and sophistication I knew *about*. And the way I knew about it was from Emily Post. I was a bookish child brought up in a house with few books. What reading material we had was stuck on some shelves by the front door. One rainy Saturday when I was about eleven, I was sitting on the linoleum examining the spines of a New Testament, a Fannie Farmer Cookbook, *How to Win Friends and Influence People,* a *Reader's Digest* condensation of *Kitty Foyle,* a paperback *Bridge Over the River Kwai,* which I'd already read, and a family snapshot album. It was then I noticed a large book on the bottom shelf. The binding was a deep, compelling shade of blue embossed with the single foreign-seeming word *Etiquette* in silver cursive letters. I pulled it out and cracked it open. I think the first thing I saw was a black-and-white photograph of delicate rattan chairs arranged around a low table in a little garden. In the background were brick gateposts with a small fountain visible behind them. The caption read, "AT TEA IN A CITY YARD. The inviting charm of a garden setting—even that of a city yard—is all too often overlooked." Undeniably true of the yards in the factory town where I was growing up. I turned the pages.

> If you carry a stick, it should be of plain Malacca. . . . Above all—unless you are a dancer on the stage (like Fred Astaire)— avoid an ebony cane with an ivory top.

> Boston's older ladies and gentlemen always dance at balls, and the fact that older ladies of distinction dance with dignity has an inevitable effect on younger ones, so that dancing at balls has not degenerated into the vulgarities of wiggling contortions.

> Champagne glasses ought to be thin as soap bubbles . . . a thick glass will lower the temperature at which a really fine champagne should be served and spoil its perfection.

I was transported. Here was a world I did not know, had not even hoped, existed. Here was a society where beauty and grace were serious matters. Here were people who made studied efforts not to act like fools. I read on.

> The endeavor of a hostess, when seating her table, is to put together those who are likely to be interested in each other. Professor Bugge might bore *you* to tears, but Mrs. Entomoid

would probably delight in him, just as Mr. Stocksan Bonds and Mrs. Rich would probably have interests in common.

I didn't think I'd be bored to tears by any of them. They all sounded like preferable dinner companions to my two screaming sisters and fat, bullying stepfather. I was only a simple eleven-year-old, but I thought I'd get along all right. After all, Mrs. Post said "Simplicity is not crudeness or anything like it. On the contrary simplicity of speech and manners means language in its purest form, and manners of such perfection that they do not suggest 'manner' at all." Simplicity I had. As for the other guests, I supposed not even Mrs. Rich would tell me to get the hell out of the house or go soak my head. "The code of a thoroughbred," said Mrs. Post, "is the code of instinctive decency, ethical integrity, self-respect, and loyalty."

These people did drink (champagne, at least) but they didn't argue and back over my bicycle in the driveway afterward. And it wasn't just because they were wealthy, for I found my own mother described in *Etiquette.* She was "Mrs. Three-in-one" who had no servants and "must be cook and waitress and apparently unoccupied hostess." Her parties were said to be a delight and invitations to them eagerly sought. Why, my family could live in this world, I thought, if we but willed it. We wouldn't even have to move into the better neighborhood on the other side of Upton Avenue. Mrs. Post said, "A gem of a house may be of no size at all, but its lines are honest and its painting and furnishing in good taste . . . all of which may very well contribute as unmistakenly to the impression of 'quality' as the luxury of a palace." I resolved never to carry an ebony cane with an ivory ball top to my sixth grade class.

The *Etiquette* book had been a wedding present to my mother from exactly the kind of aunt who would give a twenty-eight-year-old woman an etiquette book for a wedding present. I doubt it had been opened before. I appropriated it to my own use and spent hours studying how to address a Duke (call him "Duke," "Your Grace" is for servants and retainers), what color waistcoat to wear with a cutaway (black), and when to use the "cut direct" (never, and I heartily wished the same were true for a punch in the eye in Toledo, Ohio).

But the people were what I liked the best, and they came to populate my fantasies. There was Mrs. Toplofty, very reserved and dignified but awfully decent once you got to know her and she invited you in for Kool-Aid. And Mr. Worldly, who always had something clever to say about the Detroit Tigers. Mr. Clubwin Doe was lots of fun at the YMCA. And the Oncewere family, though they'd fallen on hard times, still had plenty of style at kick-the-can and stoop tag. There were visitors, too, members of

European noble families such as Lord Blank, and the vague and haughty Duke of Overthere (none of *us* ever called him "Your Grace"). We always suspected these fellows of having designs on the "better situated" neighborhood debutantes, especially on the spoiled and willful daughter of Mr. and Mrs. Richan Vulgar. No one would actually "cut" the Vulgars, but we were rather cool to them when they wanted to borrow the leaf rake. Actually, certain members of our own set were a bit "fast" themselves. Mr. and Mrs. Uppal Knight, for instance, gave parties that went on until after 11:00 P.M. And the frankly naughty Cigret Colcreme was "separated" and had men friends who drove convertibles.

And thus it was that while my boyhood chums were pulling wings off flies I was discussing ants and grubs with Professor Bugge and Mrs. Entomoid and handling three forks and four different kinds of stemware.

Of course, in the real world, I have never quite made my way to that perfect land of kindness, taste, and tact. Though I'd like to think, sometimes, I've been on the path. I hope to get there yet. But I wonder if any bored eleven-year-olds, sitting by bookshelf in trailer or tract house, will be inspired to undertake the same journey by the new edition of Emily Post's *Etiquette*. I fear not.

From

Amusing Ourselves to Death

(1985)

Neil Postman

The decline of print media and the rise of television, Postman argued, was the most significant cultural fact of the late twentieth century. As a result, politics, religion, education, and culture had to recast themselves to fit forms suitable to television. TV couldn't stand complexity or nuance, he said. When complex public issues became "show business," Postman warned, cultural debasement—"dumbing down"—was inevitable.

At different times in our history, different cities have been the focal point of a radiating American spirit. In the late eighteenth century, for example, Boston was the center of a political radicalism that ignited a shot heard round the world—a shot that could not have been fired any other place but the suburbs of Boston, At its report, all Americans, including Virginians, became Bostonians at heart. In the mid-nineteenth century, New York became the symbol of the idea of a melting-pot America—or at least a non-English one—as the wretched refuse from all over the world disembarked at Ellis Island and spread over the land their strange languages and even stranger ways. In the early twentieth century, Chicago, the city of big shoulders and heavy winds, came to symbolize the industrial energy and dynamism of America. If there is a statue of a hog butcher somewhere in Chicago, then it stands as a reminder of the time when America was railroads, cattle, steel mills and entrepreneurial adventures. If there is no such statue, there ought to be, just as there is a statue of a Minute Man to recall the Age of Boston, as the Statue of Liberty recalls the Age of New York.

Today, we must look to the city of Las Vegas, Nevada, as a metaphor of our national character and aspiration, its symbol a thirty-foot-high cardboard picture of a slot machine and a chorus girl. For Las Vegas is a city entirely devoted to the idea of entertainment, and as such proclaims the spirit of a culture in which all public discourse increasingly takes the form of entertainment. Our politics, religion, news, athletics, education and commerce have been transformed into congenial adjuncts of show business, largely without protest or even much popular notice. The result is that we are a people on the verge of amusing ourselves to death.

As I write, the President of the United States is a former Hollywood movie actor. One of his principal challengers in 1984 was once a featured player on television's most glamorous show of the 1960s, that is to say, an astronaut. Naturally, a movie has been made about his extraterrestrial adventure. Former nominee George McGovern has hosted the popular television show "Saturday Night Live." So has a candidate of more recent vintage, the Reverend Jesse Jackson.

Meanwhile, former President Richard Nixon, who once claimed he lost an election because he was sabotaged by make-up men, has offered Senator Edward Kennedy advice on how to make a serious run for the presidency: lose twenty pounds. Although the Constitution makes no mention of it, it would appear that fat people are now effectively excluded from running for high political office. Probably bald people as well. Almost certainly those whose looks are not significantly enhanced by the cosmetician's art. Indeed, we may have reached the point where cosmetics has replaced ideology as the field of expertise over which a politician must have competent control.

America's journalists, i.e., television newscasters, have not missed the point. Most spend more time with their hair dryers than with their scripts, with the result that they comprise the most glamorous group of people this side of Las Vegas. Although the Federal Communications Act makes no mention of it, those without camera appeal are excluded from addressing the public about what is called "the news of the day." Those with camera appeal can command salaries exceeding one million dollars a year.

American businessmen discovered, long before the rest of us, that the quality and usefulness of their goods are subordinate to the artifice of their display; that, in fact, half the principles of capitalism as praised by Adam Smith or condemned by Karl Marx are irrelevant. Even the Japanese, who are said to make better cars than the Americans, know that economics is less a science than a performing art, as Toyota's yearly advertising budget confirms.

Not long ago, I saw Billy Graham join with Shecky Green, Red Buttons, Dionne Warwick, Milton Berle and other theologians in a tribute to George Burns, who was celebrating himself for surviving eighty years in show business. The Reverend Graham exchanged one-liners with Burns about making preparations for Eternity. Although the Bible makes no mention of it, the Reverend Graham assured the audience that God loves those who make people laugh. It was an honest mistake. He merely mistook NBC for God.

Dr. Ruth Westheimer is a psychologist who has a popular radio program and a nightclub act in which she informs her audiences about sex in all of its infinite variety and in language once reserved for the bedroom and street corners. She is almost as entertaining as the Reverend Billy Graham, and has been quoted as saying, "I don't start out to be funny. But if it comes out that way, I use it. If they call me an entertainer, I say that's great. When a professor teaches with a sense of humor, people walk away remembering." She did not say what they remember or of what use their remembering is. But she has a point: It's those who possess both a talent and a format to amuse, whether they be preachers, athletes, entrepreneurs, politicians, teachers or journalists. In America, the least amusing people are its professional entertainers.

Culture watchers and worriers . . . know that the examples above are not aberrations but, in fact, clichés. There is no shortage of critics who have observed and recorded the dissolution of public discourse in America and its conversion into the arts of show business. But most of them, I believe, have barely begun to tell the story of the origin and meaning of this descent into a vast triviality. Those who have written vigorously on the matter tell us, for example, that what is happening is the residue of an exhausted capitalism; or, on the contrary, that it is the tasteless fruit of the maturing of capitalism; or that it is the neurotic aftermath of the Age of Freud; or the retribution of our allowing God to perish; or that it all comes from the old stand-bys, greed and ambition.

I have attended carefully to these explanations, and I do not say there is nothing to learn from them. Marxists, Freudians, Lévi-Straussians, even Creation Scientists are not to be taken lightly. And, in any case, I should be very surprised if the story I have to tell is anywhere near the whole truth. We are all, as Huxley says someplace, Great Abbreviators, meaning that none of us has the wit to know the whole truth, the time to tell it if we believed we did, or an audience so gullible as to accept it. But you *will* find an argument here that presumes a clearer grasp of the matter than many that have come before. Its value, such as it is, resides in the directness of its perspective, which has its origins in observations made 2,300 years ago by Plato. It is an argument that fixes its attention on the forms of human conversation, and postulates that how we are obliged to conduct such conversations will have the strongest possible influence on what ideas we can conveniently express. And what ideas are convenient to express inevitably become the important content of a culture.

I use the word "conversation" metaphorically to refer not only to speech but to all techniques and technologies that permit people of a particular culture to exchange messages. In this sense, all culture is a conversation or, more precisely, a corporation of conversations, conducted in a variety of symbolic modes. Our attention here is on how forms of public discourse regulate and even dictate what kind of content can issue from such forms.

To take a simple example of what this means, consider the primitive technology of smoke signals. While I do not know exactly what content was once carried in the smoke signals of American Indians, I can safely guess that it did not include philosophical argument. Puffs of smoke are insufficiently complex to express ideas on the nature of existence, and even if they were not, a Cherokee philosopher would run short of either wood or blankets long before he reached his second axiom. You cannot use smoke to do philosophy. Its form excludes the content.

To take an example closer to home: As I suggested earlier, it is implausible to imagine that anyone like our twenty-seventh President, the multi-chinned, three-hundred-pound William Howard Taft, could be put forward as a presidential candidate in today's world. The shape of a man's body is largely irrelevant to the shape of his ideas when he is addressing a public in writing or on the radio or, for that matter, in smoke signals. But it is quite relevant on television. The grossness of a three-hundred-pound image, even a talking one, would easily overwhelm any logical or spiritual subtleties conveyed by speech. For on television, discourse is conducted largely through visual imagery, which is to say that television gives us a conversation in images, not words. The emergence of the image manager in the political arena and the concomitant decline of the speech writer attest to the fact that television demands a different kind of content from other media. You cannot do political philosophy on television. Its form works against the content.

To give still another example, one of more complexity: The information, the content, or, if you will, the "stuff" that makes up what is called "the news of the day" did not exist—could not exist—in a world that lacked the media to give it expression. I do not mean that things like fires, wars, murders and love affairs did not, ever and always, happen in places all over the world. I mean that lacking a technology to advertise them, people could not attend to them, could not include then in their daily business. Such information simply could not exist as part of the content of culture. This idea—that there is a content called "the news of the day"—was entirely created by the telegraph (and since amplified by newer media), which made it possible to move decontextualized information over vast spaces at incredible speed. The news of the day is a figment of our technological imagination. It is, quite precisely, a media event. We attend to fragments of events from all over the world because we have multiple media whose forms are well suited to fragmented conversation. Cultures without speed-of-light media—let us say, cultures in which smoke signals are the most efficient space-conquering tool available—do not have news of the day. Without a medium to create its form, the news of the day does not exist.

To say it, then, as plainly as I can . . . the most significant American cultural fact of the second half of the twentieth century [is] the decline of the Age of Typography and the ascendancy of the Age of Television. This change-over has dramatically and irreversibly shifted the content and meaning of public discourse, since two media so vastly different cannot accommodate the same ideas. As the influence of print wanes, the content of politics, religion, education, and anything else that comprises public business must change and be recast in terms that are most suitable to television.

Sitcom

(1987)

Eric Bogosian

Bogosian's theater pieces sketched sharp profiles of dislocated American souls, exploring with stinging humor the dark fantasies, meretricious gestures, reckless pursuit of pleasure, and spiritual despair among the morally disengaged. Sid, a cocaine-driven Hollywood idea man, was one of Bogosian's over-the-top characters. But Sid's style and line of thinking bore more than passing resemblance to the perpetual hustle and what passed for the creative spirit in "entertainment."

A *man picks up the phone at a table, answering in a shrill, fast-talking voice.*

Arnie! Arnie! Yeah, yeah, listen. Sid! You got two minutes? Yeah, yeah, listen, I got a great idea for a sitcom . . . sitcom, Arnie, sitcom! Situation comedy, what are you doing up there in your office, take the straw outa ya nose for two minutes and listen to me for a second. Arnie! Arnie! Concentrate! Follow me.

Scenario: New York City! Apartment building in New York. Black guy lives in the apartment. Nice black guy, middle-class black guy, button-down-sweater type of guy, smokes a pipe. Yeah, yeah . . . harmless black guy. Benson! Benson! We got Benson in this apartment . . . Across the hall from him, paraplegic kid in a wheelchair . . . Huh? You don't need a real one, you just get any cute kid and stick him in a wheelchair. What? Fuck the unions! The kid's in a wheelchair here, black guy across the hall. They got a real nice relationship here. Big brother, interracial kind of thing. Yeah. Mushy liberal stuff . . . a show with meaning . . . Yeah, a show with relevance to the social problems of today . . . yeah, yeah, *Mary Tyler Moore, Hill Street, M*A*S*H, Cosby, The Waltons!*

Wait, wait, more! Top floor of the building we got a whorehouse! Hookers going up and down the stairs all time of night and day. Falling over the kid with the wheelchair, sticking lollipops in his mouth, patting his head. Cute stuff like that, sweet stuff, light humor, family humor. . . .

Ground floor of the apartment building: gay health club! Homos working out with weights, building up the pectoral muscles. . . . See what I'm saying? We got the beefcake down here doing sit-ups while the cheese-cake's up here doing push-ups! Something for everybody! Wait, wait, one more apartment, teen-age kid living with his mother, OK, this is the humor of the show. Kid wants to kill everybody in New York City! One week he makes an atom bomb in his bedroom, next week he puts LSD in the city water supply, then he derails a subway car, who knows? Crazy stuff, funny stuff, hilarious stuff! We'll call the show *Upstairs, Downstairs* . . . Huh? Who's PBS? Fuck PBS! . . . Those are little people. They don't count. We'll buy the title off of them. . . . Arnie, what are you busting my balls about this thing for? Yeah? That was two years ago! Yeah, I know what's good for me. What's good for me is what's good for you! Arnie we'll have lunch next week and discuss the project, OK? Huh? Look Arnie, I got a call on the other line, I got to get off . . . Arnie, I'm getting off . . . Arnie? . . . Yes, I love you, but I'm getting off . . . I'm getting, off, Arnie! Arnie . . . Arnie . . . Arnie . . . Good-bye! (*hangs up*)

The Death of
Andy Warhol
(1987)

Hilton Kramer

From the early sixties until his death, Warhol was able to exploit new forces on the art scene, including the growing appeal of outlaw and celebrity culture combined with indifference to standards and seriousness. As a result of his singular influence in linking fashion to art and art to glamour, Warhol was, Kramer concluded, "far more important as a social phenomenon than he ever was or could be as an artist."

The death of Andy Warhol was bound to be a media event, and so it was. For the media, after all, it was like a death in the family. Here was a figure who was famous for being famous, for knowing the famous, and for serving as an avatar of fame, and nothing so pleases the media as an opportunity to celebrate one of their own creations. The front-page obituary in *The New York Times,* the special segment on the MacNeil-Lehrer News Hour, the cover story in *New York* magazine, not to mention the many pictures and news stories in the daily tabloids and on the network news programs—the coverage could hardly have been better (or worse) if Warhol himself had orchestrated it. Which, in a sense, he had. The most distinguishing characteristic of this prodigious outpouring of commentary, homage, and celebrity-worship was the way it confined itself to the terms which Warhol himself had set for the discussion of his life and work. Even writers who, on other occasions, find it appropriate to apply more elevated standards to art (and life) proved ready and eager to suspend them in discussing Warhol and his significance. It was as if no language but Warhol's own—the language of hype—could be expected to have any meaning when it came to explaining just what it was that made him important.

All the same, it is my impression that Warhol's death caused some of these volunteer laureates of hype and celebrity a good deal of uneasiness. Suddenly they were on the spot. They couldn't in good conscience bring themselves to say that Warhol had been a great artist even though they had often written about him as if he were. They couldn't, in many cases, even bring themselves to explain why he should be considered an important artist even though they had long taken it for granted that he was. No one is under oath, of course, in writing obituary notices. Even so, there was a general tendency on this occasion to take refuge in the subject's fame, in his personality, in his business affairs and his entourage, even his wig, and leave the art more or less unexamined. Amid the expected encomiums, there was in fact a discernible hedge and wariness to be observed in the claims advanced for Warhol's artistic achievement. It turned out that almost no one could bring any conviction to the task of specifying what that achievement had consisted of.

The truth is, even among his friends and admirers it was widely recognized—even if seldom admitted—that, although being an artist was essential to his social position, Warhol was far more important as a social phenomenon than he ever was or could be *as* an artist. That was what gave him his special aura, after all—and his influence. *As* an artist he ended his career exactly as he began it—as a gifted *commercial* artist with a flair for the arresting graphic image and skillful layout. He was never much of a painter, and as a sculptor he didn't exist. (As for his movies, it is probably enough to observe that, having served their purpose—which was to propagate the Warhol myth—they had long ago predeceased their creator. Of aesthetic merit they had none whatever.) Warhol's "genius" (if it can be called that) consisted of his shrewdness in parlaying this essentially commercial talent into a career in an art world that no longer had the moral stamina to resist it; a career that would have been unthinkable, for example, ten years earlier.

To an extent that was unrivaled among his contemporaries in the Pop Art movement, if only because they knew so much less than he did about the dynamics of the fashion world, Warhol understood that something momentous had happened to the art scene in the late Fifties—that the relation which had formerly obtained between art and fashion (and hence between art and publicity, and between art and money) had undergone a decisive change. Which is to say that he understood the success of Robert Rauschenberg and Jasper Johns better than they did. (Not that they were slow to catch on—but that is another story.) Their success owed much to the international acclaim which Abstract Expressionism, having passed through its avant-garde phase, was receiving for the first time, and to their putative role as both the heirs and the rebels of that movement. Warhol understood that something else was involved; that with the success of Rauschenberg and Johns, the age of the avant-garde had drawn to a close. Their success had been, initially, an art world success, but it quickly developed into a much larger phenomenon. A boundary separating art and fashion had been breached, and never again would the really big successes of the art world be confined to that world. Henceforth success in that art world would be played on a much larger stage.

Rauschenberg and Johns came out of the school of Marcel Duchamp. They stood in relation to Abstract Expressionism very much as Duchamp had stood to Cubism—as plenipotentiaries to the world of publicity and chic, agents of "advanced" styles that offered just the right dash of scandal (the stuffed goat, the paint-splattered bed, the targets and flags, etc.) to excite a taste that had wearied of the rigors of abstract art. Warhol, on the other hand, belonged to the school of Condé Nast, where such "scandals" are recognized as marketable commodities and routinely processed as the materials of fashion. In moving from a career in fashion illustration to a career in this swiftly expanding art world, Warhol saw that the product needed only the most superficial modification to win attention and garner rewards—rewards far greater than any to be found in the realm of fashion illustration. Art, no matter how debased, still offered a kind of status that was denied to advertising, but otherwise there were now fewer and fewer differences separating the art world from the advertising world. The ethos was getting to be essentially the same. Success was the goal, the media would provide the means of achieving it, and what the media loved more than anything else—certainly more than art—was a product based on their own stock-in-trade. And that, from his "Marilyns" to his "Maos," is what Warhol mainly specialized in giving them. Considering the magnitude of his accomplishment in this respect, it would be churlish to deny that he did indeed have genius of a sort. No ordinary talent could have done it— but the talent, alas, was not primarily an artistic talent.

As everyone knows, the art world never really recovered from this fateful incursion. As a movement Pop Art came and went in a flash, but it was the kind of flash that left everything changed. The art public was now a different public—larger, to be sure, but less serious, less introspective, less willing or able to distinguish between achievement and its trashy simulacrum. Moreover, everything connected with the life of art—everything, anyway, that might have been expected to offer some resistance to this wholesale vulgarization and demoralization—was now cheapened and corrupted. The museums began their rapid descent into show biz and the retail trade. Their exhibitions were now mounted like Broadway shows, complete with set designers and lighting consultants, and their directors pressed into service as hucksters, promoting their wares in radio and television spots and selling their facilities for cocktail parties and other entertainments, while their so-called "education" programs likewise degenerated into sundry forms of entertainment and promotion. The critics were co-opted, the art magazines commercialized, and the academy, which had once taken a certain pride in remaining aloof from the blandishments of the cultural marketplace, now proved eager to join the crowd—for there was no longer any standard in the name of which a sellout could be rejected. When the boundary separating art and fashion was breached, so was the dividing line between high art and popular culture, and upon all those institutions and professions which had been painstakingly created to preserve high art from the corruptions of popular culture the effect was devastating. Some surrendered their standards with greater alacrity than others, but the drift was unmistakable and all in the same direction—and the momentum has only accelerated with the passage of time.

There was no more telling symbol of this surrender of standards than Warhol himself, the cheerful nihilist who became the unlikely culture hero of a new era. Anyone who was around at the time will remember exactly when it was that we were given our first taste of its lethal character. It came, of course, in the early Sixties with the false dawn and specious glamour of the Kennedy administration—the media-fabricated glamour that in retrospect has turned out to be the perfect political analogue for what was occurring on the cultural scene. There is an important book to be written about the cultural fallout of the Kennedy years, and Warhol's would by no means be the only significant career that would require a place in the story. So, among many others, would Norman Mailer's and Arthur Schlesinger, Jr.'s and George Plimpton's, and so too, in their own spheres, would the history of *New York, The New Yorker,* and *The New York Review of Books,* not to mention less exalted branches of the media. Still, in any such study a special place would have to be reserved for the Warhol phenomenon, which gave to the art world—but not to the art world alone—a model that has proved to be so irresistible that it is now a permanent, and permanently disabling, component of cultural life. It was really that ghastly model, rather than the man or his art, that the media celebrated so copiously in their obituary notices of Andy Warhol—a model that continues to exhibit a potency his art could never achieve.

The Literary Brat Pack

(1987)

Bruce Bawer

Bawer's essay about the eighties' new short fiction form and its flashy practitioners stated some original doubts about the changing nature of the literary world,
where hype and vogue seemed to be gaining an upper hand on criticism and
talent. In addition, Bawer considered the language and themes of the hip young
voices, finding much of their *oeuvre* repetitious and more than a little dreary.

Meg Wolitzer. David Leavitt. Peter Cameron. Susan Minot.
Elizabeth Tallent. In the past couple of years these names, and
one or two others, have become extremely familiar to readers of
book sections, high-toned magazines, and articles about The Future Of
American Literature. These are the writers, we are told time and again,
who are revolutionizing American fiction, who have initiated a short-story
renaissance. They publish their stories primarily in *The New Yorker,* are
invited to participate in symposia with their distinguished literary elders,
and are reviewed prominently and respectfully; despite their youth—most
of them are in their twenties and early thirties—universities clamor to
have their services as teachers of creative writing. Honors abound. It was
Leavitt, for instance, whose first book, the 1984 short story collection
Family Dancing, was nominated for the National Book Critics Circle Award
in fiction; it was Leavitt, again, who was asked by the editors of *Esquire* to
follow in the footsteps of F. Scott Fitzgerald and William Styron by writing,
for the magazine's May 1985 issue, the decennial essay on his generation
of Americans. It was Susan Minot whose first book, *Monkeys* (1986), was
the subject of one of the most unequivocally positive reviews to appear on
the front page of the *New York Times Book Review* in recent memory.

And yet, when one turns from the breathless critical encomia to the
works of these young writers, they strike one—to be kind about it—as

decidedly modest accomplishments. So great, in fact, is the disparity between the public image and the performance that one is tempted to refer to this overly hyped circle of writers as the Literary Brat Pack. Like the Hollywood Brat Pack, they have an excessive sense of their own importance in the scheme of things, and—by means of the enthusiastic blurbs and reviews that many of them have given to each other—have helped to distract the attention of their audience from many of their more deserving contemporaries. Like the Hollywood Brat Pack, finally, the members of the Literary Brat Pack have one outstanding skill: they promote themselves extremely well.

Where, one might ask, did all these young writers come from? Many are graduates of that most peculiar of contemporary American cultural institutions, the university writing workshop—a place where literary trends are assiduously followed and where the history of American short fiction tends to be thought of as extending back no further than 1961 or so (the year J. D. Salinger published *Franny and Zooey*). David Leavitt, for instance, wrote his first serious fiction for a Yale writing workshop taught by Gordon Lish.

Lish—who is a senior editor at Alfred A. Knopf, Inc., the publishing house which issued Leavitt's *Family Dancing*—figures in the histories of many of the Brat Packers. Amy Hempel studied under Lish in the Columbia University writing program and dedicated her first book, the Knopf short story collection *Reasons to Live* (1985), to him: "For the teacher, Gordon Lish." Other Brat Packers' connections to Lish go back even further. Meg Wolitzer, whose book *Sleepwalking* (1982) was also published by Knopf, is the daughter of novelist Hilma Wolitzer, who used to write for Lish when he was an editor at *Esquire* and whose 1977 book *In the Flesh* carried the dedication: "Special thanks to Gordon Lish."

In a recent profile for *Spy* magazine, Mimi Kramer referred to Lish as "the Joseph Papp of American fiction." He's an editor who "claims not to believe there's any such thing as genius or talent," a teacher who tells his students that any of them can become the writer of their time. For "greatness," to Lish—and to the countless students who have made his sensibility their own—is less a matter of literary excellence than it is of cheap Hollywood-like celebrity. Lish tells his students that "he wants . . . to be the teacher who produces the greatest number of important writers." And, since Knopf is (as Kramer notes) "the most prestigious publisher of new American fiction," Lish is in a splendid position to create "important writers"—that is, writers who will be reviewed widely and discussed seriously by literary critics.

And make no mistake, Lish is far from shy about publishing the work of his own students and protégés; in fact, perhaps the majority of the modish young fiction writers of our day—many of them ex-students of Lish—had their first books published by Knopf. It is fair to say, then, that the Literary Brat Pack is in large part the product of the Gordon Lish fiction factory, and consequently of the Gordon Lish sensibility—a sensibility that equates greatness with notoriety, that seems to consider talent somewhat less important than P.R.

Speaking of P.R., the principal document in the study of the Literary Brat Pack is an article—"New Voices and Old Values"—which is one of the neatest pieces of literary public relations that I've ever seen. The article appeared on the first page of the May 12, 1985, issue of the *New York Times Book Review*, and its author was David Leavitt, who is presently the most celebrated—and, it must be said, is probably the most talented—of the Brat Pack writers. Leavitt's article trumpeted the arrival on the literary scene of "a new generation of writers who are recording through their fiction the changes in the way young people think about family, marriage, love and loyalty." Leavitt listed the names of these writers, modestly omitting himself from the lineup: Marian Thurm, Elizabeth Tallent, Peter Cameron, Meg Wolitzer, Amy Hempel. These writers, he observed, "have in general limited themselves to the short story, a form they seem to find appropriate to the age of shortened attention spans, fractured marriages and splintering families in which they grew up."

And perhaps, one wonders, appropriate to their own limitations as well? Leavitt's assumptions about the short story form are disturbing, to say the least. I, for one, have always thought of the short story as a form which, far from being designed for readers whose minds wander, is more tightly compressed than a novel and therefore often demands greater powers of concentration on the part of the reader; as a form which, far from being appropriate to an era of fragmenting families, at its best tolerates far less disorder than does the novel. Leavitt's apparent failure to recognize these things—to respect, in short, the exquisite possibilities of the short story form—seems endemic among the Literary Brat pack; reading their work, one continually gets the impression that they are writing short stories not because they find the form challenging but because they find it easy.

But enough. To return to Leavitt: "What they [Thurm, Tallent, *et al.*] share is not only their youth—there are many other notable young writers whose work differs vastly from theirs—but their predilections and obsessions, both in style and content. Stylistically, their work owes a strong debt to older writers such as Raymond Carver, Ann Beattie and Mary Robison, but the concerns of their fiction are as specific to their generation—especially the precariousness of families and the ways young people react to the shattering of the familial or parental edifice."

There's a shorter, blunter way of putting all this, of course. Namely: "All of us Literary Brat Packers write exactly alike." Well, *almost* exactly. Almost everything they do derives directly from Carver, Robison, and—perhaps most of all—Beattie, whose aggressively flat, affectless, detail-happy manner is faithfully represented by this passage from her 1976 novel *Chilly Scenes of Winter*:

> He drives to a store and buys a big package of pork chops and a bag of potatoes and a bunch of broccoli and a six-pack of Coke. He remembers cigarettes for Sam when he is checking out, in case he's well enough to smoke. He buys a *National Enquirer* that features a story about Jackie Onassis's face-lift. James Dean is supposed to be alive and in hiding somewhere, too. Another vegetable. Not dead at all. *East of Eden* is one of his favorite films. He saw it, strangely enough, on television after he and Laura went to a carnival and rode on a Ferris wheel. . . .

And so on. Beattie's prose is plain and unsurprising, often written in the present tense and the first person; her characters, in the main, are dull and passive ciphers. Her fiction is chock-full of the names of TV shows, movies, celebrities, popular songs, and consumer items; it's as thick with irrelevant (or, at best, only tangentially relevant) concrete particulars as it is thin on character development.

If anything, the typical Brat Pack fiction outdoes Beattie in these regards. David Leavitt's hero in "Territory" runs across his mother's daily list of things to do (which Leavitt reproduces *in toto*) and "observes the accretion of names, *the arbitrary specifics that give a sense of his mother's life*." (My emphasis.) Too often, the writers of the Literary Brat Pack seem truly to believe that it is precisely out of such "arbitrary specifics" that convincing, flesh-and-blood fictional characters are made.

Thus, if a character in a Literary Brat Pack story is taking a course, the writer will almost certainly tell us the full name under which it is listed in the college catalog; if there's a song playing down the hall or a book lying on a bedside table, we'll know the title of it; if somebody goes for groceries, we don't have to wonder for a moment whether it's an A&P or a Safeway. (Actually, it's usually 7-Eleven.) The Brat Pack writers are more likely to give a detailed run-down on the contents of a given character's cupboard or clothes closet or television viewing schedule than to provide a coherent and convincing set of clues to the contents of that character's soul. After reading a story by one of the Brat Packers, in fact, it's often difficult to describe any of the characters in such a way as to distinguish them from numerous similar—and equally superficial—characters in other Brat Pack works. Sometimes the only noticeable differences are the external ones—the names they go by, the TV shows they watch. Read enough Brat Pack stories in a row and the young characters begin to run together in your mind—and the same goes for their mothers and their fathers, their apartments and their jobs, their parents' divorces and cancer cases, and (above all) their failed and failing "relationships."

Back in college, I remember, an English professor of mine joked about the hyperrealism of early French realists like Champfleury and the brothers Goncourt, who, he told us, actually reproduced balance sheets in their novels! Had we ever heard of such a thing? The class laughed—but that was ten years ago. Now professors in university creative writing programs tell their students that this is the way to write: load up on concrete details, relevant or not. The more particulars, the better. Who could've imagined?

The Brat Packers are especially big on the details surrounding "relationships": his brand of cologne, her favorite song. They seem to believe that one of the principal purposes of literature is to provide readers with a sort of pop sociology of young romance. Leavitt's "New Voices" piece, accordingly, is full of sentences like this: "No matter how seriously Miss Tallent's people commit themselves to each other, they can never really make the connections that form the foundation of lasting relationships." Commitments, connections, relationships: perhaps these words, better than any others, suggest the attitudes and assumptions that shape the typical Brat Pack novel or story.

What's frustrating about these fictions, of course, is that the set decorations—the bags of groceries, the copies of *GQ* and *People* and *Vogue,* the BMWs and MTV and *Sound of Music* cast albums—tend, time and again, to overwhelm the frail narratives. In one pale, passionless Brat Pack narrative after another, we are presented with young people—or young people and their families—who are in extreme emotional crisis, victims of divorce or cancer or a death in the family or an "inability to communicate," but who as a rule speak to each other only about the most banal domestic matters—about, in other words, the stories' furnishings.

These families are almost always broken (or breaking), almost always upper-middle-class. They have summer places and boathouses and swimming pools; the mothers have time to do volunteer work (usually for liberal causes). The young heroes and heroines—if they're not teenagers or pre-teens who are still living at home—tend to reside in small, seedy sublets in Manhattan, where they either (a) take courses at Columbia, NYU, or the New School or (b) hold down marginal, funky jobs in second-hand clothing stores or travel agencies or publishing firms. Often they own a cat. Judging from their cultural references, they grew up on lots of television and on the scores of *My Fair Lady* and most of Rodgers and Hammerstein.

There are about four basic Brat Pack story themes: the folks' divorce (Thurm's "Starlight," Leavitt's "The Lost Cottage"), the troubled relationship with Mom (Cameron's "Memorial Day," Leavitt's "Territory"), the frustrations of romance (Cameron's "The Last Possible Moment," Thurm's "California," etc.), and dead or dying mothers (Cameron's "Fast Forward," Thurm's "Aftermath," Leavitt's "Counting Months"). Many of these mothers die of cancer, and in fact cancer is a particularly popular topic in Brat Pack fiction: in one story after another, characters talk about their chemotherapy, undergo tests, or mention friends with leukemia.

Some Brat Pack stories are unusually similar to one another. Cameron's "Jump or Dive," about a boy whose uncle lives with his male lover in Arizona, is reminiscent of Leavitt's "Danny in Transit," about a boy whose father lives with his male lover in Greenwich Village. And Cameron's "Excerpts from Swan Lake," in which a nice, sensitive young gay man spends a week at his grandmother's house with his grandmother and his boyfriend, reminds one immediately of Leavitt's "Territory," in which a nice, sensitive young man spends a week at his mother's house with his mother and his boyfriend. Cameron's "Memorial Day," with its strained mother-son relationship, also seems to echo "Territory": the intelligent but tragically distant mother in the former story, who tells her son "You are breaking my heart," is barely distinguishable from the intelligent but tragically distant mother in the latter, who tells her son, "I wanted you to grow up happy. And I'm very tolerant, very understanding. But I can only take so much."

There are numerous other—and more recondite—recurrent motifs. For instance, there are several Brat Pack stories in which children (escaping, presumably, from the lovelessness and anonymity of real life) pretend to be putting on TV shows. In Leavitt's "Danny in Transit," Danny invents "an episode of 'The Perfect Brothers Show,' the variety show on his personal network." In Susan Minot's *Monkeys*, the children imitate acts that they see on the Ted Mack and Ed Sullivan shows. And in Cameron's "Odd Jobs," a man named Keith and his daughter, Violet, play "a game they called Christmas Special. . . . Violet was pretending she was Marie Osmond; Keith was Perry Como—the choice was him or Andy Williams. They had linked arms and were strolling through the snow, in a small circle singing."

And there are T-shirts galore. One of the principal tenets of the Literary Brat Pack's creative philosophy, it sometimes seems, is that all you need to do to define a character is to put him in a T-shirt that has something printed on it:

> He was wearing an old T-shirt that showed an anatomical drawing of a heart, the separate chambers carefully labeled.
>
> Elizabeth Tallent, "Comings and Goings" from *In Constant Flight* (1983)

> Lynn is wearing maternity jeans that she cut down into shorts at the beginning of the summer, and a red T-shirt, size Extra Large, which says "Coke Adds Life" in white letters that have turned pink from the chlorine.
>
> Marian Thurm, "Floating" from *Floating* (1984)

> Lonnie gets up and walks over to me, towel in hand. He has on plaid Bermuda shorts and a Disney World T-shirt.
>
> Peter Cameron, "Memorial Day" from *One Way or Another* (1986)

> The husband wears a fraying T-shirt that says "The Only Safe Fast Breeder Is a Rabbit."
>
> Elizabeth Tallent, "Natural Law"

> Sam drops down on the carpet in the living room. He is large-boned and slightly overweight and is wearing a T-shirt with a subway map of New York City on it. In his lap he holds a dispenser of Windex, a sponge, a rag, and a plastic bottle of ammonia.
>
> Marian Thurm, "Winter"

> Both of the boys are wearing T-shirts which say *Coca-Cola* in Arabic.
>
> David Leavitt, "Danny in Transit" from *Family Dancing* (1984)

> Petrovsky makes his way toward us through the crowd. He is thin, wearing a Star Wars T-shirt and tattered Adidas.
>
> Elizabeth Tallent, "In Constant Flight"

> Ray was Alex's much-younger brother, a commercial artist in his late thirties who dressed in jeans and T-shirts with pictures of rock bands on them, and who, in Grace's mind, was about as grown-up as a college student.
>
> Marian Thurm, "Grace"

In his "New Voices" piece, amazingly enough, Leavitt looks upon the sameness of Brat Pack fiction as a virtue. Summarizing one short story after another, he continually points up the parallels between them, as if numbing monotony itself were some sort of virtue. He observes, for instance, that the parents in these stories are all alike in that "The one thing [they] seem to feel they can count on is disappointment, inevitably and repeatedly, and they hammer their fatalism relentlessly into the heads and hearts of their children." These parents, moreover, are "usually leaving each other and taking up with unsuitable partners." As for the young people in these stories, they're "dreamy, supersensitive youths" who "do not believe their vulnerability, bewilderment and sadness set them apart in any way from the rest of humanity."

But they've got one thing over on their sad, selfish, screwed-up folks. "Where the younger characters differ from their parents," Leavitt writes,

> is in their energetic insistence on rallying in the face of potential disaster. Born in an era of flux and instability, they are blessed with remarkable flexibility. They can weather changes that would floor their elders, while at the same time they cling to the values of family and marriage with a tenacity unknown to their alternately wayward and crippled parents. By necessity and disposition, they are willing to compromise—with their families, with one another and the history into which they were born.

In short, Brat Pack families are all unhappy, and they are all unhappy in precisely the same way. And the young protagonists of Brat Pack stories are all heroic in the same way, too. (The capacity of some of these writers for jejune self-celebration is often breathtaking.) That this sameness—not only of content, as Leavitt cheerfully reminds us, but of style—might be considered by a discriminating reader to be artificial, modish, and representative of a woeful lack of imagination doesn't seem to have occurred to Leavitt.

It's not just Leavitt, though, who's convinced of the Brat Pack's supreme importance: it's the whole lot of them. In an article published last August 31 in the *New York Times,* reporter Colin Campbell retailed some literary anecdotes that he'd picked up in Long Island's exclusive Hamptons district. One of them concerned Leavitt and Wolitzer and a few of their friends (including Gary Glickman, a close friend of Leavitt's whose first novel, *Years From Now,* is to be published this spring by Knopf). The whole gang, according to Campbell, was driving around the Hamptons in a car when Meg Wolitzer asked "what it might mean to the future of American fiction if they crashed." Strong though the temptation may be, I'll refrain from answering that. But I will say that the remark sums up, better than anything else I've read, these kids' single most irritating collective characteristic: namely, their insularity, their smugness, their fatuous certainty that—in a country populated by a quarter of a billion people—they and their tepid, adolescent little fictions represent the future of the national literature.

Time, of course, rolls on. Since the publication of "New Voices," one or two of the Brat Pack writers have published their second books, and the reviews have been mixed, many of them surprisingly cool—cool, at least, compared to the warm praise that greeted their previous books. More and more critics, it would seem, are beginning to look more critically at Brat Pack fiction. Why? Part of the reason almost certainly is that the once-worshipful critics are tiring of the narrowness of the Brat Pack writers' interests, the flatness of their styles, and the monotony of their characters and settings. The similarities that unite the Literary Brat Pack, in short, have perhaps become—or, at least, may well be on their way to becoming—a definite liability.

This may explain why Leavitt, in his introduction to a recent issue of the *Mississippi Review* for which he served as guest editor, made a slick 180-degree turn. The issue, entitled "These Young People Today," consisted mostly of stories by Thurm, Hempel, Cameron, Glickman, and two or three skilled Brat-Pack imitators. "While it's true," Leavitt said in the introduction, "that these stories provide a generational perspective on the world which is unique, and true as well that common concerns and themes link many of them, I'm struck more by the diversity of voices, concerns and locales, as I read them over, than I am by the parallels." Though he assured us, he's generally "given to looking for commonality," it was "the rich difference—not the narrowing sameness—which made me want to read these stories over and over again." And just in case we hadn't already gotten the point, he repeated it once more in his penultimate sentence: "All together," he insisted, these stories "comprise a gathering of stunningly unconnectable voices."

Amazing, isn't it, how a group of strikingly similar voices can, in only a year or so, become "stunningly unconnectable"? But whether this amusing switch marks the beginning of the end of the Literary Brat Pack's heyday, or merely indicates the beginning of another chapter in a saga that has yet to reach its climax, only time can tell.

Forever Young

(1988)

Ronald Steel

Fit and well-tanned trendoes flocked to idylls such as Jackson Hole, Aspen, Santa Fe, and Tahoe in the eighties, searching for purity and authenticity, blissing out, getting in touch with nature. Hollywood arrived and these resorts became even more showy. But keeping up with cool demanded a lot of cash—and God forbid that one might smoke a cigarette or be twenty pounds overweight.

We swooped in low through amazing peaks and dropped down into a lush valley dotted with condos as far as the eye could see. I had a café crème and pain au chocolat at the airport snack bar, and watched the suntans and tennis rackets come and go. Eventually I sauntered over to an exceedingly hip clerk and asked when he thought my bags might be in. "No problem," he reassured me. "On the next plane from Denver. Or maybe the one after. They always come through eventually." No hurry. No problem.

Donning my cool, I hopped into a Mellow Yellow taxi and headed for the village of Aspen, which nestles in a valley cupped between mountains as lushly green as Astroturf. Between the simulated redwood and cedar condos are sprinkled quaint Victorian houses in hues of apricot, fuchsia, and heather, San Francisco style. They and their quarter-acre plots sell for upward of $400,000 each. Only a commodity trader or a cocaine dealer could afford them. Happily Aspen has many such entrepreneurs. Most, however, prefer to live on the slopes of the mountain overlooking the town. There they build multiterraced dwellings with huge sheets of glass wrapped around jutting timbers. From marbled Jacuzzis they watch the last rays of the sun bathe Aspen Mountain in a golden Krugerrand glow and ponder the justice of a system that has brought them such rewards.

Not everyone in Aspen is rich, or even young, though a first-time visitor would be apt to think so. All the men seem to be 32 years old, with sandy moustaches, bulging pectorals, and perpetual tans. All the women are 29, with straight blond hair, fashionably flat chests, and long legs. (For summer tourists subtract ten years.) Naturally none of these people was born here. All come from Cedar Rapids, Bayonne, or Dayton. Most of them work at one thing or another, though the jobs are usually below both their level of education and expectation. They are waitresses and tour guides and carpenters and clerks. They are here not to advance themselves—there is nowhere much to go, except in the real estate business—but simply to prolong the Aspen experience. You can see them jogging along the streets and bicycle trails, even up the mountain roads. They breathe easily, despite the thinness of the air at 8,000 feet. Their smooth complexions are rarely marred by a drop of sweat.

Keeping in shape is a tyranny from which there is no respite. But for the golden young people of Aspen it is the affirmation of the good life. It is also the passport into it, for fatties are not permitted. And a good life it is: congenial folks, amusing restaurants, a constant inflow of new bodies, and hardly a rumble of the troubles that preoccupy the outside world. The very rich fly in and out on their Lear jets to check up on their property and test the slopes or the tennis courts. The locals house-sit for them and provide services that the rich require. This allows the youngish locals to stay on in their Shangri-La. Few of them can afford to live in Aspen itself. The tourists and second-home fatcats have driven property values up so high that those who actually do the work in Aspen have been mostly forced to live in cheaper locales down the road. They drive in every day as commuters to the town that was taken away from them.

They come for the scenery, which is as spectacular as it's supposed to be; for the hassle-free existence, which they can have, within certain sharp limits; for the days that are interchangeable in their bucolic ordinariness, and the nights that offer hope of instant adventure or psychic transformation; for the anticipation of the first run down the slopes on last night's powder snow; for the experience of living on a *Zauberberg* just a little bit outside of time; for the possibility that tomorrow a beautiful (or rich) stranger will walk into their lives and all will be changed magically. The place lends itself to dreams. Not so long ago it was a scruffy mining town that time and venture capitalists had forgotten.

Others had come here once before in search of instant riches, built their palaces, spent their money, and then went off to hitch their broken dreams to other stars. Down the road a piece of Aspen, tucked away in the folds of a valley green in summer but totally snowbound in winter, lie the remnants of a little village called Ashworth. It was once as rich and sinful as Babel, or even Aspen. Chanteuses came to sing from Europe; gamblers and whores would snatch up your money in a glorious flash you'd remember for a lifetime. Now it's a few weathered boards, the wind whistling through the cracks, and a faint echo of coyotes. *Sic transit.* But that isn't the lesson of Aspen either. All dreams speed by too fast, all Xanadus become cracked boards and dust. When was it any different? So why not dance a little faster under the strobe light at the Paragon Café—the one in front of the video camera that captures your image and projects it on a screen above you, so that you can see yourself on MTV? To be the observer of oneself—what could be more tantalizing or forbiddingly satisfying? Who can even bother to notice one's partner at such an epiphanic moment? Come back tomorrow night for more.

Does the image ever fade? Does the time ever come when you say: I don't want to watch myself being watched? I don't care if I get fat? I get tired of being cool? I'm choking on fresh air, whole grain biscuits, and raw milk? I want to ride the subway? The answer is: I don't know. I didn't stay long enough. I walked through fields of asphodels so high up in the peaks called the Maroon Bells that I thought I could hear them ringing. A few hours later I lounged in a hot tub watching a double rainbow that appeared after a spectacular lightning storm that left half the sky purple-black and the other half baby-blue dotted with raspberry-lemon clouds. Why be upwardly mobile? I asked myself. Is there anything up there at the top of the ladder? Why not kiss the A Train and the Sheridan Road Express and the Harbor Freeway goodbye? Why not just take another hike into a wilderness of crater lakes and mountain meadows? Maybe I'd stayed on too long myself. Or not long enough. I ordered another Margarita and decided to think about it tomorrow.

PART V

The House of Intellect

The Fall of the American Adam

(1981)

C. Vann Woodward

One of the nation's preeminent liberal historians, Woodward explored the ideological "inversions" of revisionism, a line of thought with awesome force in
American historiography by the early eighties. The battle over America's character and cultural symbols was already beginning to convulse the history profession, years before the culture wars had a name. The new history sometimes
seemed intent on demolishing the national good in favor of the bad, replacing
old myths of American innocence with new myths of collective guilt.

I am speaking primarily of the present, but of attitudes toward the
American past in the present and of how these attitudes have undergone some significant changes. I am particularly concerned with the
relatively recent inversion of traditional myths and especially the shift
from collective innocence toward collective guilt. For perspective on the
extent of change and its relative recency we do not have to go back very
far. In fact we can rely on the testimony and views of a few worthy historians still much alive in the memories and in the affections of many people,
including the present writer.

It was only a few decades ago that Samuel Eliot Morison could
remark that the prevailing view of Americans toward their national past
was "a friendly, almost affectionate attitude," and proclaim the existence
of a "seller's market in early Americana," benignly and traditionally conceived. More recently the late Arthur M. Schlesinger wrote of how
America had "held up a lamp to Europe and, more recently, to Asia and
Africa." Writing of the American record of leadership in Western civilization during the two world wars and the Cold War, Allan Nevins could say,

"It stands invested with all the radiance of the Periclean era, the Elizabethan era, and the era of Pitt and the long struggle against Napoleon." Toward the close of his book of memoirs, Dexter Perkins wrote in 1969, "I end this chapter with a paean of praise to American democracy" and its citizens. "In their capacity for self-government, for the successful operation of one of the most difficult enterprises in the history of man, they can be proud of their past and hopeful of their future."

Samuel Flagg Bemis was somewhat more restrained about the present century, but for what he called "the great and happy successes" of the nineteenth century words all but failed him: "Oh, wondrous century, so fortuitously fortunate for our nation! Oh, happy, golden, bygone years of safety, in lucky innocence, apart from the world around us!" The Union had to be preserved at a cost, to be sure, but to my old colleague Professor Bemis, "the greatest achievement of American nationality was expansion of the nation across the empty continent to the shores of the 'other ocean.' It established the territorial basis of the United States as a world power and a bastion of freedom today . . . expansively perfected by peaceful diplomacy between 1783 and 1867"—one great succession of peaceful real-estate transactions—save for the Mexican lapse.

I do not cite these professions of faith and pride in the national past to illustrate or characterize the views of the historians. I quote them, of course, out of context. Each of them was capable of more sophisticated views of the past and the present, and we are indebted to all of them for critical assessments and interpretations of the aspects of American history in which they specialized. The more remarkable then, that all of them should have given voice to the myth of innocence of the American past. It would be possible to adduce other voices in support of the myth, but few more faithful to the tradition that extends back to George Bancroft and far beyond to the first chroniclers.

It was the virtues of the past the historians were praising, but the character of the modern period during which they voiced their pride in the past is worth recalling. That was a period of unprecedented American power, wealth, and prestige, a period of Pax Americana in which monopoly or predominant command of the ultimate weapon seemed for a while secure. The United States in the 1950s was at once the policeman of the world and the self-acclaimed model for revolutions of liberation. Influential books of the time bore such titles as *People of Plenty* and *The Affluent Society.* We were the *Redeemer Nation,* a country with a divinely assigned Errand, a World Mission. Americans commonly assumed their country to be the envy of all nations, and called it "the Galahad among nations."

Friendly critics there were, even then, to remind us of the moral risks of combining pretensions of innocency with unprecedented power and wealth. Reinhold Niebuhr warned of "ironic perils which compound the experiences of Babylon and Israel." Others spoke of "The Illusion of American Omnipotence" and of "The Arrogance of Power." They cautioned that the legend of American invincibility did not guarantee that all wars ended in victory, and that great power could not be wielded without incurring guilt. These admonitions may have had some impact on policy. But with a few exceptions the legend of an essentially innocent past held intact. . . . The remarkable thing is the degree to which the myth of Adamic innocency held together until it was in danger of being overwhelmed by a spreading conviction of national guilt.

Collective guilt has not enjoyed the long growing season or the fertile seed bed of tradition from which the myth of national innocence has perennially sprung. It has nevertheless struck roots and flourished of late in a climate that seems specially suited to it. And it has been nourished by a public that evidently feels a need for its fruits. A seller's market for guilt now exists, only whetted, not satiated in the sixties. Though the demand may be inspired by recent events, the bargains in guilt are to be found mainly in the past. Ancestral atrocities and injustices, historic evils and inhumanities, and the brutalities and cruelties of past centuries can be acknowledged without assuming corresponding burdens of expiation. Ancient evils can thus be deplored and lamented, and pretensions of innocence scorned. But the grievances are antique and their perpetrators long gone. The guilt thus acknowledged can hardly be called redhanded.

The appreciating supply of historic guilt for the new market results not so much from revision of history or from new historic evidence as from the transposition of symbols and the inversion of myths. The new image of the past sometimes replaces the ethnocentrism of the mythmakers with that of its victims. Thus "discovery" of the New World becomes "invasion" thereof; "settlement" becomes "conquest," and Europeans the "savages." The "Virgin Land" becomes the "Widowed Land," the "howling wilderness" a desecrated Indian "hunting park." The "Garden of the World" becomes a "Waste Land," ravaged home of exterminated or endangered species. Professor Bemis's "empty continent" teems with outraged and betrayed First Americans. The advancement of the Western frontier is sometimes pictured as a species of genocide, wave on wave of holocausts. One symbol that has been proposed to stand for the West so won is "A Pyramid of Skulls," Tartar model.

One of the ironies of the story is that the major burden of historic guilt was incurred in the age of innocence. Instead of ignoring the crimes, however, Americans of the earlier era often attacked and exposed them—not usually as collective guilt, but as the transgressions of individuals, groups, classes, sections—evils and injustices that threatened innocence and were to be corrected, punished, reformed, abolished. Slavery was the crime of southern slaveholders, injustice to Indians the fault of frontiersmen or their agents and influence. And so, with whatever justice or accuracy, specific evils were assigned to culprits such as Indian-haters, lords of the lash, lords of the loom, political bosses, big business, jingoes, "merchants of death," and "economic royalists." Guilt was something to be redressed, and its exposers looked to the future for expiation. The American jeremiad, as Sacvan Berkovitch tells us, both laments an apostasy and heralds a restoration.

The new guilt is different. It is something congenital, inherent, intrinsic, collective, something possibly inexpiable, and probably ineradicable. The first English settlers, south as well as north, arrived with it in their hearts, and they never should have come in the first place. Invasion was their initial offense. The pattern of collective rapacity and inhuman cruelty to darker peoples that characterized their westward conquests of the Pacific shores and on across the ocean ever westward through Asia is seen as existing from the very outset. From this point of view the line of precedents stretched from the slaughter of braves in the Pequot War of 1637 on for three centuries and more to Lieutenant Calley at My Lai, with little more than changes in the technology of annihilation. Thus interpreted, American history becomes primarily a history of oppression, and the focus is upon the oppressed. The latter vary in color or identity as the center of interest shifts from one of these groups to another. The most conspicuous among them of late have been the Afro-Americans, though popular concern with their grievances has not been unwavering and they have had to share attention from time to time with other groups.

The primary objective in all this would not seem to be so much the exposure of evil or the identification of transgressors as it is an oblique exercise in the analysis of national character. And yet, "national" seems too comprehensive a word to be employed in its customary sense in this connection, for the characterizations are racially assigned or circumscribed, even though directed at the dominant or majority group. A favored characterization, often quoted and sometimes misused, is a famous definition of "the myth of the essential white America" by D. H. Lawrence, published in 1923. "The essential American soul," he writes, "is hard, isolate, stoic, and a killer. It has never yet melted. . . . This is the very intrinsic-most American. He is at the core of all the other flux and fluff"—such as love and democracy and equality.

The exercise of defining national (or racial) character in terms of guilt attributes takes on some peculiar traits in the American instance. It might be called, in a sense, unilateral. In most instances, that is, the guilt is to all appearances unshared, the offenses incurring it unprovoked, unique, and confined to the dominant group. If other nations have perpetrated comparable or worse offenses against *their* native population, black slaves and freedmen, racial minorities, neighboring countries, or remote Asian or African cultures, the opportunities for perspective by comparing the magnitude of the offenses and the number of casualties are passed over. Those American offenses that were confined to intraracial conflict also go largely unremarked. That more American casualties were sustained in one battle of the Civil War than in all previous American wars, or that more Americans lost their lives in that war than in all subsequent wars of the nation goes unnoticed. Similar indifference in the national guilt market greets historic atrocities of one minority race against another, or intraracial mayhem among minorities.

Rejection of collective innocence and embracing of collective guilt have not invariably dispelled national myths that accompanied or sustained the myth of innocence. Inverting myths may be a way of preserving them. The quest for guilt continues to seek new and far-flung frontiers. When things go wrong in the Third World—and sometimes even in the Second—we are now taught to look inward for the cause. This teaching recalls by contrast the recent time when we were taught that America "held up a lamp" of hope to Asia and Africa. What has remained, if somewhat altered in the process, is the illusion of American omnipotence and moral responsibility and the cosmic self-centeredness of the national world view. "America," says a generally friendly Italian critic of ours, "is alone in the world."

Americans evidently have some special problems of a self-destructive nature in dealing with national guilt. If so, it is for no lack of guilt in the national and pre-national experience. The conquest of a continent, the dispossession and subjection of its natives, the exploitation of imported African slaves, the imposition of our will on other races and nations abroad, and the establishment of a brief Pax Americana by the world's most powerful nation are not exploits brought off without the incurring of guilt—impressive amounts of it. No intelligent citizen can have escaped awareness of this at some time. Still draped in legends of national infancy, myths of innocence, success, invincibility, and righteousness, however, we were caught short at the climax of our mythic national pretensions and exposed in deeds and failures that mocked all the old myths. It was then that the obsession with guilt took hold. Other nations with bloodier disgraces on their heads—Germany and her death camps; France and her Vichy, her Vietnam, and her Algeria; Japan and her imperial conquests; not to mention Russia and China with their multimillions of domestic victims—all seemed to manage recovery without excesses of self-detestation or self-revilement.

It is a Freudian truism I will not presume to attest that the problem of guilt is as much within the heart as within the act. Guilt looks inward. Psychoanalysts suggest that when a person inflicts punishment on himself, he should engage in historical recollection or exploration of the past to bring to consciousness and acceptance the cause of the guilt feelings. Presumably the same could be said of societies. We are also told on good authority that no one develops a sense of guilt without a punitive parent image—real or projectively imagined. We are guilty because we have not lived up to high standards represented by our parents. Or so we are told.

The curious thing about American experiments in self-therapy through the discovery and proclaiming of historic guilt is that it is the punitive progenitors themselves, the founding fathers and founding mothers, who have come to be regarded as the guilty parties—or at least the original sinners. As such they make rather poor punitive parent images, and provide their progeny with more escape from guilt than acceptance of it. When it is recent rather than historic transgression, the accusers conceive of it as the guilt of all. It is collective guilt. "When all are guilty," wrote Hannah Arendt, "no one is; confessions of collective guilt," she continues, "are the best possible safeguards against the discovery of culprits, and the very magnitude of the crime the best excuse for doing nothing."

Neither the old myth of innocence nor the self-therapy of historic or collective guilt has proved to be of much help to Americans with their problems. The sudden shift from the one extreme to the other may well portend a reaction in the opposite direction—and there are already some ominous signs of such a reaction. President Reagan and the opinion polls assured us that Americans have made a sudden recovery from their malaise, restored their self-esteem and self-confidence, and face the future and a skeptical world with old-time assurance. An aggressive foreign policy and bold commitments around the world indicate that changes have indeed taken place—whether the result of restored confidence or not. They suggest that the national conscience is preparing to take on new and unpredictable burdens.

If this means a swing back to the old myths, a return to fatuous complacency and self-righteousness, it is not likely to produce an equilibrium of spiritual well-being or a salutary balance in the American conscience. It might even contrive a spurious absolution of the very real guilt that so recently precipitated the obsession and cover with a mantle of counterfeit innocence the perpetrators themselves. That would be an ironic outcome, indeed.

Both the old myth of innocence and the obsession with its opposite would nevertheless seem destined to abide with us. They are deeply embedded in our tradition and in our literature. Perhaps the most profound and, to me, the most moving treatment of them in American letters is that of Robert Penn Warren in *Brother to Dragons.* You may recall that the subject of the dramatic dialogue of this book is the inhuman murder of a slave committed by two of Thomas Jefferson's nephews at their home in Jefferson's golden land of hope, the West. The crime is a matter of historical record. In *Brother to Dragons,* the author has Lucy, the sister of Thomas Jefferson and mother of his criminal nephews, say to Jefferson: "Dear Brother, the burden of innocence is heavier than the burden of guilt." But the poet goes on to make it evident that the latter burden is by no means a light one, for all that.

Our Listless Universities
(1982)

Allan Bloom

Ideas borrowed from Nietzsche, Marx, and the French deconstructionists elbowed their way into university life by the eighties. University of Chicago philosopher Allan Bloom took these trends to task in this little-known 1982 essay, which led directly to his book, *The Closing of the American Mind,* five years later. The book's phenomenal reception permanently altered the debate over the contemporary university and general knowledge. By the end of the decade, depending on where you stood in academic circles, Bloom was a hero or a villain.

I begin with my conclusion: students in our best universities do not believe in anything, and those universities are doing nothing about it, nor can they. An easy-going American kind of nihilism has descended upon us, a nihilism without terror of the abyss. The great questions—God, freedom, and immortality, according to Kant—hardly touch the young. And the universities, which should encourage the quest for clarification of such questions, are the very source of the doctrine which makes that quest appear futile.

The heads of the young are stuffed with a jargon derived from the despair of European thinkers, gaily repackaged for American consumption and presented as the foundation for a pluralistic society. That jargon becomes a substitute for real experiences and instinct; one suspects that modern thought has produced an artificial soul to replace the old one supplied by nature, which was full of dangerous longings, loves, hates, and awes. The new soul's language consists of terms like *value, ideology, self, commitment, identity*—every word derived from recent German philosophy, and each carrying a heavy baggage of dubious theoretical interpretation of which its users are blissfully unaware. They take such language to be as unproblematic and immediate as night and day. It now constitutes our peculiar common sense.

The new language subtly injects into our system the perspective of "do your own thing" as the only plausible way of life. I know that sounds vaguely passé, a remnant leftover from the Sixties. But it is precisely the routinization of the passions of the Sixties that is the core of what is going on now, just as the Sixties were merely a radicalization of earlier tendencies.

The American regime has always attempted to palliate extreme beliefs that lead to civil strife, particularly religious beliefs. The members of sects had to obey the laws and be loyal to the Constitution; if they did so, others had to leave them alone. To make things work, it was thought helpful that men's beliefs be moderated. There was a conscious, if covert, effort to weaken religious fervor by assigning religion to the realm of opinion as opposed to knowledge. But everyone had to have an intense belief in the right of freedom of religion; the existence of that natural right was not to be treated as a matter of opinion.

The insatiable appetite for freedom to live as one pleases thrives on this aspect of modern democratic thought. The expansion of the area exempt from legitimate regulation is effected by contracting the claims to moral and political knowledge. It appears that full freedom can be attained only when there is no such knowledge. The effective way to defang oppressors is to persuade them that they are ignorant of the good. There are no absolutes: freedom is absolute.

A doctrine that gives equal rights to any way of life whatsoever has the double advantage of licensing one's own way of life and of giving one a democratic good conscience. The very lack of morality is a morality and permits what Saul Bellow has called "easy virtue," a mixture of egotism and high-mindedness. Now, in feeling as well as in speech, a large segment of our young are open, open to every "lifestyle." But the fatal consequence of this openness has been the withering capacity of their belief in their own way of life and of their capacity to generate goals. The palliation of beliefs culminates in pallid belief. A soul which esteems indiscriminately must be an artificial soul, and that, to repeat, is what we are coming near to constituting, not by some inevitable historical process but by a conscious educational project. This project masquerades as the essential democratic theory without which we would collapse into tyranny or the war of all prejudices against all. Its premise is that truth itself must be prejudice or at least treated as such.

The tendency toward indiscriminateness—the currently negative connotation of the word *discrimination* tells us much—is apparently perennial in democracy. The need to subordinate the more refined sensibilities to a common denominator and the unwillingness to order the soul's desires according to their rank conduce to easy-goingness. The democratic ethos obscures the reason for the desirability of such self-mastery. This is the moral problem of democracy and why fortuitous external necessities like war or poverty seem to bring out the best in us. Plato describes the natural bent of the democratic man thus:

> He . . . also lives along day by day, gratifying the desire that occurs to him, at one time drinking and listening to the flute, at another downing water and reducing; now practicing gymnastics, and again idling and neglecting everything; and sometimes spending his time as though he were occupied with philosophy. Often he engages in politics and, jumping up, says and does whatever chances to come to him; and if he ever admires any soldiers, he turns in that direction; and if it's moneymakers, in that one. And there is neither order nor necessity in his life, but calling this life sweet, free, and blessed he follows it throughout.

This account is easily recognizable when applied to the middle-class youth who attend America's top colleges and universities. But Plato's description omits a more sinister element in our situation. Plato's young man believes that each of the lives he follows is really good, at least when he follows it. His problem is that he cannot keep his mind made up. Our young person, by contrast, is always plagued by a gnawing doubt as to whether the activity he undertakes is worth anything, whether this end is not just another "value," an illusion that men once believed in but which our "historical consciousness" reveals as only a cultural phenomenon. There are a thousand and one such goals; they are not believed in because they exist, they exist because one believes in them. Since we now know this, we can no longer believe. The veil of illusion has been torn away forever. The trendy language for this alleged experience is *demystification* or *demythologization*. This teaching now has the status of dogma. It leads to a loss of immediacy in all experience and a suspicion that every way of life is a "role." The substitution of the expression "lifestyle," which we can change at will, for the good life, the rational quest for which is the origin of philosophy, tells the story. That is what I mean by nihilism, and this nihilism has resulted from a questionable doctrine that we seem no longer able to question.

All of us who are under sixty know something about this doctrine and its transmission, for since the Thirties it is what the schools have been teaching. For fifty years the only spiritual substance they have been trying to convey is openness, the disdain for the ethnocentric. Of course, they have also been teaching the three Rs, but their moral and intellectual energy has been turned almost exclusively in this direction. Schools once produced citizens, or gentlemen, or believers; now they produce the unprejudiced. A university professor confronting entering freshmen can be almost certain that most of them will know that there are no absolutes and that one cannot say that one culture is superior to another. They can scarcely believe that someone might seriously argue the contrary; the attempt to do so meets either self-satisfied smiles at something so old-fashioned or outbursts of anger at a threat to decent respect for other human beings. In the Thirties this teaching was actually warring against some real prejudices of race, religion, or nation; but what remains now is mostly the means for weakening conviction when convictions have disappeared.

The doctrine of cultural relativism did not emerge from the study of cultures. It was a philosophic doctrine that gave a special interpretation of the meaning of culture and had a special political attractiveness. It could appeal to the taste for diversity as opposed to our principled homogeneity. All kinds of people climbed aboard—disaffected Southern snobs who had never accepted the Declaration and the Constitution anyhow, Stalinists who wanted us to love Soviet tyranny without being too explicit about it, and similar types. No choices would have to be made. We could have the charms of old cultures, of what one now calls roots, along with democratic liberties. All that was required was an education making other ways attractive and disenchanting one's own. It is not so much the knowledge of other cultures that is important, but the consciousness that one loves one's own way because it is one's own, not because it is good. People must understand that they are what they are and what they believe only because of accidents of time and place.

The equality of values seemed to be a decisive step in the march of equality. So sure were our social scientists of the truth and vigor of democracy that they did not even dimly perceive what Weber knew, that his view undermined democracy, which stands or falls with reason. Only democracy traces all its authority to reason; other kinds of regimes can more or less explicitly appeal to other sources. When we talk about the West's lack of conviction or lack of will, we show that we are beginning to recognize what has happened to us. Exhortations to believe, however, are useless. It is only by thinking ideas through again that we can determine whether our reasons can any longer give assent to our principles.

But this serious reconsideration is not taking place in the universities.

৯৬

Today a young person does not generally go off to the university with the expectation of having an intellectual adventure, of discovering strange new worlds, of finding out what the comprehensive truth about man is. This is partly because he thinks he already knows, partly because he thinks such truth unavailable. And the university does not try to persuade him that he is coming to it for the purpose of being liberally educated, at least in any meaningful sense of the term—to study how to be free, to be able to think for himself. The university has no vision, no view of what a human being must know in order to be considered educated. Its general purpose is lost amid the incoherent variety of special purposes that have accreted within it. Such a general purpose may be vague and undemonstrable, but for just this reason it requires the most study. The meaning of life is unclear, but that is why we must spend our lives clarifying it rather than letting the question go. The university's function is to remind students of the importance and urgency of the question and give them the means to pursue it. Universities do have other responsibilities, but this should be their highest priority.

They have, however, been so battered by modern doctrines, social demands, the requirements of the emancipated specialties, that they have tacitly agreed not to open Pandora's box and start a civil war. They provide a general framework that keeps the peace but they lack a goal of their own.

When the arriving student surveys the scene, he sees a bewildering variety of choices. The professional schools beckon him by providing him with an immediate motive: a lucrative and prestigious livelihood guaranteed by simply staying in the university to the conclusion of training. Medicine and law were always such possibilities; with the recent addition of the MBA, the temptation has radically increased. If the student decides to take this route, liberal education is practically over for him.

If he first turns his eye to what was traditionally thought to be the center of the university, he will confront—aside from a few hot programs like black studies, native studies, women's studies, which are largely exercises in consciousness-raising—the natural sciences, the social sciences, and the humanities.

The natural sciences thrive, full of good conscience and good works. But they are ever more specialized and ever more separate from the rest of the university; they have no need of it. They don't object to liberal education, if it doesn't get in the way of their research and training. And they have nothing to say, even about themselves or their role in the whole human picture, let alone about the kinds of questions that agitated Descartes, Newton, and Leibniz. Their results speak for themselves, but they do not say quite enough.

The social sciences are the source of much useful research and information, but they are long past the first effervescence of their Marxist-Freudian-Weberian period. Then they expected to find a new and more scientific way to answer the old questions of philosophy. Such hopes and claims quietly disappeared from the scene during the past 15 years. Their solid reasons for existence are in specialized study of interest rates, Iranian politics, or urban trends. Practically no economist conceives of doing what Adam Smith did, and the few who try produce petty and trivial stuff. The case is pretty much the same for the other social sciences. They are theoretically barren, and the literature read and used by them is mostly ephemera of the last fifty years.

The remainder is to be found in the humanities, the smallest, least funded, most dispirited part of the university. The humanities are the repository of the books that are at the foundation of our religion, our philosophy, our politics, our science, as well as our art. Here, if anywhere, one ought to find the means to doubt what seems most certain. Only here are the questions about knowledge, about the good life, about God and love and death, at home in the university. If, however, one looks at the humanistic side of the campus, one finds a hodgepodge of disciplines, not integrally related with one another and without much sense of common purpose. The books are divided up among language departments, according to the largely accidental fact of the language in which they were written. Such departments have as their primary responsibility the teaching of the language in question (a very depressing responsibility now that languages have fallen into particular disfavor with students).

Humanists in general are the guardians of great books, but rarely take seriously the naive notion that these books might contain the truth which has escaped us. Yet without the belief that from Plato one might learn how to live or that from Shakespeare one might get the deepest insight into the passions and the virtues, no one who is not professionally obligated will take them seriously. Try as they may, the humanities will fail to interest if they do not teach *the truth*, even as natural and social science are supposed to do. To present the great writers and artists as representatives of cultures or examples of the way thought is related to society, or in any of the other modes common today, is to render them uninteresting to the healthy intellect. The comprehensive questions have their natural home in the humanities, but it is there that the historical-cultural doubt about the possibility of answering them is most acute. Professors of humanities more than any others wonder whether they have a truth to tell.

Philosophy should, of course, provide the focus for the most needful study. But it is just one department among many and, in the democracy of the specialties, it no longer has the will to insist that it is the queen of the sciences. Moreover, in most philosophy departments the study of the classic texts is not central. Professors "do" their own philosophy and do not try to pose the questions as they were posed by the old writers. This is especially the case for the dominant school of thought in the United States, the Oxford school.

Of all university members, humanists have the least self-confidence. The students are abandoning them, and they have difficulty speaking to the concerns of the age. They fear they may have to huckster—if they are not already doing so—in order to keep afloat. In their heart of hearts many doubt that they have much to say. After all, most of the writers they promote can be convicted of elitism and sexism, the paramount sins of the day.

There are, to be sure, many dedicated individuals in the humanities who know what needs to be done and can draw students' attention to the impoverished state of their experience and show them that great texts address their concerns. But the endeavor of these professors is a lonely one with little corporate resonance. The students are not reading the same books and addressing the same questions, so that their common social life cannot be affected by a common intellectual life.

It should be added that the humanities are also the center of some of the fastest selling intellectual items of the day—structuralism, deconstructionism, and Marxist humanism. The members of these schools—particularly rampant in comparative literature—do read books and talk big ideas. In that sense they are the closest thing to what the university should be about. The problem with them, and all of them are alike in this respect, is that the books are not taken seriously on their own grounds but are used as vile bodies for the sake of demonstrating theses brought to them by the interpreters. They know what they are looking for before they begin. Their approaches are ultimately derived from Marx or Nietzsche, whose teachings are tacitly taken to be true.

It is small wonder that the student is bewildered about what it means to be educated. The new liberal education requirements some universities are instituting are little more than tours of what is being done in the various workshops. To be sure, they always add on a course requirement, in a non-Western civilization or culture, but that is just another bit of demagogy serving the indoctrination of openness. Serious physicists would never require a course in non-Western physics. Culture and civilization are irrelevant to the truth. One finds it where one can. Only if truth is relative to culture does this make sense. But, once again, this is our dogma, accepted for covert political reasons. This dogma is the greatest enemy of liberal education. It undermines the unity of man, our common humanity in the intellect, which makes the university possible and permits it to treat man as simply without distinction.

❧

Three conclusions have forced themselves on me about students, their characters and ways, conclusions that have to do with their education and their educability. They are not scientific generalizations based on survey research, but they are the result of long observation of, and careful listening to, young people in our better universities by one who is intensely interested in their real openness, their openness to higher learning.

1. *Books.* They are no longer an important part of the lives of students. "Information" is important, but profound and beautiful books are not where they go for it. They have no books that are companions and friends to which they look for counsel, companionship, inspiration, or pleasure. They do not expect to find in them sympathy for, or clarification of, their inmost desires and experiences. The link between the classic books and the young, which persisted for so long and in so many circumstances, and is the only means of connecting the here and the now with the always, this link has been broken. The Bible and Plutarch have ceased to be a part of the soul's furniture, an incalculable loss of fullness and awareness of which the victims are unaware.

The loss of the taste for reading has been blamed on television, the universal villain of social critics. But lack of reverence for antiquity and contempt for tradition are democratic tendencies. It should be the university's business to provide a corrective to these tendencies; however, I believe that the universities are most to blame for them. After all, they taught the schoolteachers. For a very long time now the universities have been preoccupied with abstract modern schools of thought that were understood to have surpassed all earlier thought and rendered it obsolete. And their primary concern has been to indoctrinate social attitudes, to "socialize," rather than to educate. The old books are still around, but one "knows" that they contain mere opinions, no better than any others. The result is true philistinism, a withering of taste and a conformity to what is prevalent in the present. It means the young have no heroes, no objects of aspiration. It is all both relaxing and boring, a soft imprisonment.

2. *Music.* While I am not certain about the effects of television, I am quite certain about those of music. Many students do not watch much television while in college, but they do listen to music. From the time of puberty, and earlier, music has been the food of their souls. This is the

audio generation. And classical music is dead, at least as a common taste. Rock is all there is.

There is now one culture for everyone, in music as in language. It is a music that moves the young powerfully and immediately. Its beat goes to the depth of their souls and inarticulately expresses their inarticulate longings. Those longings are sexual, and the beat appeals almost exclusively to that. It caters to kiddy sexuality, at best to puppy love. The first untutored feelings of adolescents are taken over by this music and given a form and a satisfaction. The words make little difference; they may be explicitly sexual, or sermons in favor of nuclear disarmament, or even religious—the motor of it all is eroticism. The youngsters know this perfectly well, even if their parents do not.

Rock music caused a great evolution in the relations between parents and children. Its success was the result of an amazing cooperation among lust, art, and commercial shrewdness. Without parents realizing it, their children were liberated from them. The children had money to spend. The record companies recognized as much and sold them music appealing to their secret desires. Never before was a form of art (however questionable) directed to so young an audience. This art gave children's feelings public respectability. The education of children had escaped their parents, no matter how hard they tried to prevent it. The most powerful formative influence on children between 12 and 18 is not the school, not the church, not the home, but rock music and all that goes with it. It is not an elevating but a leveling influence. The children have as their heroes banal, drug- and sex-ridden guttersnipes who foment rebellion not only against parents but against all noble sentiments. This is the emotional nourishment they ingest in these precious years. It is the real junk food.

One thing I have no difficulty teaching students today is the passage in the *Republic* where Socrates explains that control over music is control over character and that the rhythm and the melody are more powerful than the words. They do not especially like Socrates's views on music, but they understand perfectly what he is about and the importance of the issue.

3. *Sex.* No change has been so rapid, so great, and so surprising as the change in the last twenty years concerning sex and the relations between the sexes. Young people of college age are very much affected by the sexual passion and preoccupied with love, marriage, and the family (to use an old formula that is now painfully inadequate for what is really meant). It is an age of excitement and uncertainty, and much of the motivation for study and reflection of a broader sort comes from the will to adorn and clarify erotic longings.

It is, however, in this domain that the listless, nihilistic mood has its practical expression and most affects the life of the students. The prevailing atmosphere deprives sex of seriousness as well as of charm. And, what is more, it makes it very difficult to think about sex. In a permissive era, when it is almost respectable to think and even do the deeds of Oedipus, shame and guilt have taken refuge in a new redoubt and made certain things unthinkable. Terror grips man at the thought he might be sexist. For all other tastes there is sympathy and support in universities. Sexism, whatever it may mean, is unpardonable.

The great change in sexual behavior has taken place in two stages. The first is what was called the sexual revolution. This meant simply that pre- and extra-marital sex became much more common, and the various penalties for promiscuity were either much reduced or disappeared. In the middle Sixties I noticed that very nice students who previously would have hidden their affairs abandoned all pretense. They would invite their professors to dine in apartments where they lived together and not hesitate to give expression to physical intimacy in a way that even married couples would rarely do before their peers.

This kind of change, of course, implied a very different way of thinking about things. Desire always existed, but it used to war with conscience, shame, and modesty. These now had to be deprecated as prejudices, as pointing to nothing beyond themselves. Religious and philosophic moral teachings that supported such sentiments became old hat, and a certain materialism which justified bodily satisfaction seemed more plausible.

The world looks very different than it once did to young people entering college. The kinds of questions they ask, and the sensitivities they bring to these fresh circumstances, are vastly altered. The tension of high expectation has been relaxed; there is much they no longer have to find out. A significant minority of students couple off very early and live together throughout college with full awareness that they intend to go their separate ways afterward. They are just taking care of certain needs in a sensible way. There is, for a member of an older generation, an incomprehensible slackness of soul in all this. Certainly the adventurousness of such people, who are half-married but without the moral benefits of responsibility, is lamed. There is nothing wild, Dionysian, searching, in our promiscuity. It has a dull, sterilized, scientific character.

One must add that an increasing number of students come from divorced families and include in their calculation the possibility or the likelihood of divorce in their own future. The possibility of separation is not a neutral fact, allowing people to stay or go; it encourages separation because it establishes a psychology of separateness.

The result is inevitably egotism, not because the individuals are evil or naturally more prone to selfishness than those of another era. If there is no other thing to be attached to, the desires concerning ourselves are ever present. This tendency is particularly pronounced in an age when political ties are weak. People can hardly be blamed for not being attached when there is nothing that calls forth attachment. There can be no doubt that the sexual revolution plays a great role in dissolving the bonds founded on sexual relationships. What is not sufficiently understood is that in modern society there is little else that can be the basis for moral association. There is a repulsive lack of self-knowledge in those who attack the "nuclear family" and are rhapsodic about the "extended family" and real "community." Looseness is thus made into an ethical critique of our society. The "extended family" is no more possible in our time or consonant with our principles than is feudalism, while the "nuclear family" is still a viable alternative, but one that needs support in theory and practice. It provides a natural basis for connectedness. One can give it up, but one has to know the price. There is simply nothing else that is generally operative in society at large.

But even more powerful than all of the above changes are the effects of feminism, which is still early in its career of reform and is the second stage of the great change of which I am speaking. The theme is too vast to treat properly, but one can say that it, much more than the sexual revolution, takes place on the level of thought rather than that of instinct. Consciousness must be altered. Women have been exploited and misused throughout the entire past, and only now can one find out their real potential. We are on the threshold of a whole new world and a whole new understanding. And Right and Left are in large measure united on the issue. There is an almost universal agreement, among those who count for university students, that feminism is simply justified as is.

The degree of common agreement comes home to me when I teach the Socrates fantasy in the *Republic* about the abolition of the difference between the sexes. Twenty years ago it was an occasion of laughter, and my problem was to get students to take it seriously. Today it seems perfectly commonplace, and students take it all too seriously, failing to catch the irony. They do not note the degree to which Socrates acts as though men and women have no bodies and lightly give up all the things that are one's own, particularly those one loves—parents, spouses, children. All of them are connected with the bisexuality of the species. In doing this, Socrates shows the ambiguity of our nature and the degree of tension between our common humanity and our sexual separateness. The balance between the two is always fraught with difficulties. One must decide which has primacy; and this decision must be made in full awareness of the loss entailed by it. Our students no longer understand this.

It is here that a great difference between the situation of women and that of men comes to light. Women today have, to use our new talk, an agenda. They want to have the opportunity to pursue careers, and they want to find ways to reconcile this goal with having families. Also, it is their movement, so they are involved and excited, have much to talk about. The men, on the other hand, are waiting to be told what is on the agenda and ready to conform to its demands. There is little inclination to resist. All the principles have been accepted; it only remains to see how to live by them. Women are to have careers just as do men and, if there is to be marriage, the wife's career is not to be sacrificed to the man's; home and children are a shared responsibility; when and if there are to be children is up to the woman, and the decision to terminate or complete a pregnancy is a woman's right. Above all, women are not to have a "role" imposed on them. They have a right of self-definition. The women were the victims and must be the leaders in their recovery from victimization. The men, as they themselves see it, have to be understanding and flexible. There are no guidelines; each case is individual. One can't know what to expect. Openness, again, is the virtue.

The result is a desexualization of life, all the while that a lot of sexual activity is going on, and a reduction of the differences between the sexes. Anger and spiritedness are definitely out. Men and women in universities frequently share common dwellings and common facilities. Sex is all right, but it creates a problem. There are no forms in which it is to express itself, and it is a reminder of differentiation where there is supposed to be none. It is difficult to shift from the mode of sameness into that of romance. Therefore advances are tentative, nobody is quite sure where they are to begin, and men's fear of stereotyping women is ever-present. It is love that is being sacrificed, for it makes woman into an object to be possessed. Dating is almost a thing of the past. Men and women are together in what is supposed to be an easy camaraderie. If coupling takes place, it must not disturb the smooth surface of common human endeavor. Above all: no courtship or courtliness. Now there is friendship, mutual respect, communication; realism without foolish fabulation or hopes. One wonders what primal feelings and desires are pushed down beneath the pat uniformity of the speech they almost all use, a self-congratulatory speech which affirms that they are the first to have discovered how to relate to other people.

This conviction has as its first consequence that all old books are no longer relevant, because their authors were sexists (if they happened to be

women, they were maimed by living in sexist society). There is little need
of the commissars who are popping up all over the place to make the
point that Eve, Cleopatra, Emma Bovary, and Anna Karenina are parts of
male chauvinist propaganda. The students have gotten the point. These
figures can't move their imaginations because their situations have nothing to do with situations in which students expect to find themselves.
They need no inquisition to root out sexist heresies—although they will
get one. And in the absence (temporary, of course) of a literature produced by feminism to rival the literature of Sophocles, Shakespeare,
Racine, and Stendhal, students are without literary inspiration. Teaching
romantic novels to university students (in spite of the healthy persever-
ance of this genre, as indicated by the success of the Harlequin
romances—I find one free in every box of Hefty garbage bags I buy these
days) is a quasi-impossibility. Students are either not interested or use it
as grist for their ideological mill. Such books do not cause them to wonder
whether they are missing something. All that passion seems pointless.

Notwithstanding all our relativism, there are certain things we know
and which cannot be doubted. These are the tenets of the egalitarian
creed, and today its primary tenet is that the past was sexist. This means
that all the doubts which tradition should inspire in us in order to liberate
us from the prejudices of our time are in principle closed to us. This is the
source of the contentless certainty that is the hallmark of the young. This
is what a teacher faces today. I do not say that the situation is impossible
or worse than it ever was. The human condition is always beset by problems. But these are *our* problems, and we must face them clearly. They
constitute a crisis for humane learning but also reaffirm the need for it.
The bleak picture is often relieved by the rays of natural curiosity about a
better way: it can happen any time a student confronts a great book.

THE EIGHTIES

Cultural Literacy
(1983)

E. D. Hirsch, Jr.

The proposition that a culture needed to have a universal core of knowledge—shared facts, symbols, and information—in order to function and remain coherent was a view Hirsch first asserted in this essay and elaborated on in an influential book of the same name four years later. This view provoked great controversy at a time when other educators were trumpeting the ideas of "diversity" and "inclusion"—and when "monoculturalism" was coming under fierce attack inside and outside the academy.

For the past twelve years I have been pursuing technical research in the teaching of reading and writing. I now wish to emerge from my closet to declare that technical research is not going to remedy the national decline in our literacy that is documented in the decline of verbal SAT scores. We already know enough about methodology to do a good job of teaching reading and writing. Of course we would profit from knowing still more about teaching methods, but better teaching techniques alone would produce only a marginal improvement in the literacy of our students. Raising their reading and writing levels will depend far less on our methods of instruction (there are many acceptable methods) than on the specific contents of our school curricula. Commonsensical as this proposition might seem to the man in the street, it is regarded as heresy by many (I hope by ever fewer) professional educators. The received and dominant view of educational specialists is that the specific materials of reading and writing instruction are interchangeable so long as they are "appropriate," and of "high quality."

But consider this historical fact. The national decline in our literacy has accompanied a decline in our use of common, nationwide materials in the subject most closely connected with literacy, "English." From the 1890s to 1900 we taught in English courses what amounted to a national core curriculum. As Arthur Applebee observes in his excellent book *Tradition and*

Reform in the Teaching of English, the following texts were used in those days in more than 25 percent of our schools: *The Merchant of Venice, Julius Caesar,* "First Bunker Hill Oration," *The Sketch Book, Evangeline,* "The Vision of Sir Launfal," "Snow-Bound," *Macbeth,* "The Lady of the Lake," *Hamlet,* "The Deserted Village," Gray's "Elegy," "Thanatopsis," *As You Like It.* Other widely used books will strike a resonance in those who are over fifty. "The Courtship of Miles Standish," "Il Penseroso," *Paradise Lost,* "L'Allegro," "Lycidas," *Ivanhoe, David Copperfield, Silas Marner,* etc., etc. Then in 1901 the College Entrance Examination Board issued its first "uniform lists" of texts required to be known by students in applying to colleges. This core curriculum, though narrower, became even more widespread than the earlier canon. Lest anyone assume that I shall urge a return to those particular texts, let me at once deny it. By way of introducing my subject, I simply want to claim that the decline in our literacy and the decline in the commonly shared knowledge that we acquire in school are casually related facts. Why this should be so and what we might do about it are my twin subjects.

That a decline in our national level of literacy has occurred few will seriously doubt. The chief and decisive piece of evidence for it is the decline in verbal SAT scores among the white middle class. (This takes into account the still greater lowering of scores caused by an increased proportion of poor and minority students taking the tests.) Now scores on the verbal SAT show a high correlation with reading and writing skills that have been tested independently by other means. So, as a rough index to the literacy levels of our students, the verbal SAT is a reliable guide. That is unsurprising if we accept the point made by John Carroll and others that the verbal SAT is chiefly a vocabulary test, for no one is surprised by a correlation between a rich vocabulary and a high level of literacy. A rich vocabulary is not a purely technical or rote-learnable skill. Knowledge of words is an adjunct to knowledge of cultural realities signified by words, and to whole domains of experience to which words refer. Specific words go with specific knowledge. And when we begin to contemplate how to teach specific knowledge, we are led back inexorably to the contents of the school curriculum, whether or not those contents are linked, as they used to be, to specific texts.

From the start of our national life, the school curriculum has been an especially important formative element of our national culture. In the schools we not only tried to harmonize the various traditions of our parent cultures, we also wanted to strike out on our own within the dominant British heritage. Being rebellious children, we produced our own dictionary and were destined, according to Melville, to produce our own Shakespeare.

In this self-conscious job of culture making, the schools played a necessary role. That was especially true in the teaching of history and English, the two subjects central to culture making. In the nineteenth century we held national conferences on school curricula. We formed the College Board, which created the "uniform lists" already referred to. The dominant symbol for the role of the school was the symbol of the melting pot.

.   But from early times we have also resisted this narrow uniformity in our culture. The symbol of the melting pot was opposed by the symbol of the stew pot, where our national ingredients kept their individual characteristics and contributed to the flavor and vitality of the whole. That is the doctrine of pluralism. It has now become the dominant doctrine in our schools, especially in those subjects, English and history, that are closest to culture making. In math and science, by contrast, there is wide agreement about the contents of a common curriculum. But in English courses, diversity and pluralism now reign without challenge. I am persuaded that if we want to achieve a more literate culture than we now have, we shall need to restore the balance between these two equally American traditions of unity and diversity. We shall need to restore certain common contents to the humanistic side of the school curriculum. But before we can make much headway in that direction, we shall also need to modify the now-dominant educational principle that holds that any suitable materials of instruction can be used to teach the skills of reading and writing. I call this the doctrine of educational formalism.

The current curriculum guide to the study of English in the state of California is a remarkable document. In its several pages of advice to teachers I do not find the title of a single recommended work. Such "curricular guides" are produced on the theory that the actual contents of English courses are simply vehicles for inculcating formal skills, and that contents can be left to local choice. But wouldn't even a dyed-in-the-wool formalist concede that teachers might be saved time if some merely illustrative, non-compulsory titles were listed? Of course; but another doctrine, in alliance with formalism, conspires against even that concession to content—the doctrine of pluralism. An illustrative list put out by the state would imply official sanction of the cultural and ideological values expressed by the works on the list. The California Education Department is not in the business of imposing cultures and ideologies. Its business is to inculcate "skills" and "positive self-concepts," regardless of the students' cultural backgrounds. The contents of English should be left to local communities.

This is an attractive theory to educators in those places where spokesmen for minority cultures are especially vocal in their attack on the melting-pot idea. That concept, they say, is nothing but cultural imperialism (true), which submerges cultural identities (true) and gives minority children a sense of inferiority (often true). In recent years such attitudes have led to attacks on teaching school courses exclusively in standard English; in the bilingual movement (really a monolingual movement) it has led to attacks on an exclusive use of the English language for instruction. This kind of political pressure has encouraged a retreat to the extreme and untenable educational formalism reflected in the California curriculum guide.

What the current controversies have really demonstrated is a truth that is quite contrary to the spirit of neutrality implied by educational formalism. Literacy is not just a formal skill; it is also a political decision. The decision to *want* a literate society is a value-laden one that carries costs as well as advantages. English teachers by profession are committed to the ideology of literacy. They cannot successfully avoid the political implications of that ideology by hiding behind the skirts of methodology and research. Literacy implies specific contents as well as formal skills. Extreme formalism is misleading and evasive. But allow me to illustrate that point with some specific examples.

During most of the time that I was pursuing research in literacy I was, like others in the field, a confirmed formalist. In 1977 I came out with a book on the subject, *The Philosophy of Composition,* that was entirely formalistic in outlook. One of my arguments, for instance, was that the effectiveness of English prose as an instrument of communication gradually increased, after the invention of printing, through a trial and error process that slowly uncovered some of the psycholinguistic principles of efficient communication in prose. I suggested that freshmen could learn in a semester what earlier writers had taken centuries to achieve, if they were directly taught those underlying psycholinguistic principles. (With respect to certain formal structures of clauses, this idea still seems valid.) I predicted further that we could learn how to teach those formal principles still more effectively if we pursued appropriately controlled pedagogical research.

So intent was I upon this idea that I undertook some arduous research into one of the most important aspects of writing pedagogy—evaluation. After all, in order to decide upon the best methods of inculcating the skills of writing, it was essential to evaluate the results of using the different teaching methods. For that we needed non-arbitrary, reliable techniques for evaluating student writing. In my book I had made some suggestions about how we might do this, and those ideas seemed cogent enough to a National Endowment for the Humanities panel to get me a grant to go forward with the research. For about two years I was deeply engaged in this work. It was this detailed engagement with the realities of reading and writing under controlled conditions that caused me finally to abandon my formalistic assumptions. (Later I discovered that experimentation on a much bigger scale had brought Richard C. Anderson, the premier scholar in reading research, to similar conclusions.)

The experiments that changed my mind were, briefly, these: To get a non-arbitrary evaluation of writing, we decided to base our evaluations on actual audience effects. We devised a way of comparing the effects of well-written and badly written versions of the same paper. Our method was to pair off two large groups of readers (about a hundred in each group), each of which, when given the *same* piece of writing, would read it collectively with the same speed and comprehension. In other words, we matched the reading skills of these two large groups. Then, when one group was given a good version and the other given a degraded version, we measured the overall effect of these stylistic differences on speed and accuracy of comprehension. To our delight, we discovered that good style did make an appreciable difference, and that the degree of difference was replicable and predictable. So far so good. But what became very disconcerting about these results was that they came out properly only when the subjects of the papers were highly familiar to our audiences. When, later in the experiments, we introduced unfamiliar materials, the results were not only messy, they were "counterintuitive," the term of art for results that go against one's expectations. (Real scientists generally like to get counterintuitive results, but we were not altogether disinterested onlookers and were dismayed.) For what we discovered was that good writing makes very little difference when the subject is unfamiliar. We English teachers tend to believe that a good style is all the more helpful when the content is difficult, but it turns out that we are wrong. The reasons for this unexpected result are complex, and I will not pause to discuss them at length, since the important issues lie elsewhere.

Briefly, good style contributes little to our reading of unfamiliar material because we must continually backtrack to test out different hypotheses about what is being meant or referred to. Thus, a reader of a text about Grant and Lee who is unsure just who Grant and Lee are would have to get clues from later parts of the text, and then go back to re-read earlier parts in the light of surer conjectures. This trial-and-error backtracking with unfamiliar material is so much more time-consuming than the delays caused by a bad style alone that style begins to lose its importance as a factor in reading unfamiliar material. The contribution of style in such cases can no longer be measured with statistical confidence.

The significance of this result is, first of all, that one cannot, even in principle, base writing evaluations on audience effects—the only non-arbitrary principle that makes any sense. The reading skill of an audience is not a constant against which prose can be reliably measured. Audience reading skills vary unpredictably with the subject matter of the text. Although we were trying to measure our prose samples with the yardstick of paired audiences, the contrary had, in effect, occurred: our carefully contrived prose samples were measuring the background knowledge of our audiences. For instance, if the subject of a text was "Friendship," all audience pairs, everywhere we gave the trials, exhibited the same differentials. Also, for all audiences, if the subject was "Hegel's Metaphysics," the differential between good and bad writing tended to disappear. Also, as long as we used university audiences, a text on Grant and Lee gave the same sort of appropriate results as did a text on friendship. But for one community college audience (in, no less, Richmond, Virginia) "Grant and Lee" turned out to be as unfamiliar as "Hegel's Metaphysics"—a complacency-shattering result.

While the variability of reading skills within the same person was making itself disconcertingly known to me, I learned that similar variability was showing up in formal writing skills—and for the same reasons. Researchers at the City University of New York were finding that when a topic is unfamiliar, writing skill declines in all of its dimensions—including grammar and spelling—not to mention sentence structure, parallelism, unity, focus, and other skills taught in writing courses. One part of the explanation for such results is that we all have limited attention space, and cannot pay much heed to form when we are devoting a lot of our attention to unfamiliar content. But another part of the explanation is more interesting. Part of our skill in reading and in writing is skill not just with linguistic structures but with words. Words are not purely formal counters of language; they represent large underlying domains of content. Part of language skill is content skill. As Apeneck Sweeney profoundly observed: "I gotta use words when I talk to you."

When I therefore assert that reading and writing skills are content-bound, I mean also to make the corollary assertion that important aspects of reading and writing skills are *not* transferable. Of course some skills *are* carried over from task to task; we know that broad strategies of reading and writing can become second nature, and thereby facilitate literary skills at all levels. But the content-indifferent, how-to approach to literacy skills is enormously oversimplified. As my final example of this, I shall mention an ingenious experiment conducted by Richard C. Anderson and his colleagues at the University of Illinois. It, too, was an experiment with paired audiences and paired texts. The texts were two letters, each describing a wedding, each of similar length, word-familiarity, sentence complexity, and number of idea units. Each audience group was similarly paired according to age, educational level, marital status, sex, professional specialty, etc. Structurally speaking, the texts were similar and the audiences were similar. The crucial variables were these: one letter described a wedding in America, the other a wedding in India. One audience was American, the other Indian. Both audiences read both letters. The results were that the reading skills of the two groups—their speed and accuracy of comprehension—were very different in reading the two linguistically similar letters. The Americans read about an American wedding skillfully, accurately, and with good recall. They did poorly with the letter about the Indian wedding. The reverse was the case with the group of Indian readers. Anderson and his colleagues concluded that reading is not just a linguistic skill, but involves translinguistic knowledge beyond the abstract sense of words. They suggested that reading involves both "linguistic-schemata" (systems of expectation) and "content-schemata" as well. In short, the assumptions of educational formalism are incorrect.

Every writer is aware that the subtlety and complexity of what can be conveyed in writing depends on the amount of relevant tacit knowledge that can be assumed in readers. As psycholinguists have shown, the explicitly stated words on the page often represent the smaller part of the literary transaction. Some of this assumed knowledge involves such matters as generic conventions, that is, what to expect in a business letter, a technical report, a detective story, etc. An equally significant part of the assumed knowledge—often a more significant part—concerns tacit knowledge of the experiential realities embraced by the discourse. Not only have I gotta use words to talk to you, I gotta assume you know *something* about what I am saying. If I had to start from scratch, I couldn't start at all.

We adjust for this in the most casual talk. It has been shown that we always explain ourselves more fully to strangers than to intimates. But, when the strangers being addressed are some unknown collectivity to whom we are writing, how much shall we then need to explain? This was one of the most difficult authorial problems that arose with the advent of printing and mass literacy. Later on, in the eighteenth century, Dr. Johnson confidently assumed he could predict the knowledge possessed by a personage whom he called "the common reader." Some such construct is a necessary fiction for every writer in every literate culture and subculture. Even a writer for an astrophysics journal must assume a "common reader" for the subculture being addressed. A newspaper writer must also assume a "common reader" but for a much bigger part of the culture, perhaps for the literate culture as a whole. In our own culture, Jefferson wanted to create a highly informed "common reader," and he must have assumed the real existence of such a personage when he said he would prefer newspapers without government to government without newspapers. But, without appropriate, tacitly shared background knowledge, people cannot understand newspapers. A certain extent of shared, canonical knowledge is inherently necessary to a literate democracy.

For this canonical information I have proposed the term "cultural literacy." It is the translinguistic knowledge on which linguistic literacy depends. You cannot have the one without the other. Teachers of foreign languages are aware of this interdependency between linguistic proficiency and translinguistic, cultural knowledge. To get very far in reading or writing French, a student must come to know facets of French culture quite different from his own. By the same token, American children learning to read and write English get instruction in aspects of their own national culture that are as foreign to them as French. National culture always has this "foreignness" with respect to family culture alone. School materials contain unfamiliar materials that promote the "acculturation" that is a universal part of growing up in any tribe or nation. Acculturation into a national literate culture might be defined as learning what the "common reader" of a newspaper in a literate culture could be expected to know. That would include knowledge of certain values (whether or not one accepted them), and knowledge of such things as (for example) the First Amendment, Grant and Lee, and DNA. In our own culture, what should these contents be? Surely our answer to that should partly define our school curriculum. Acculturation into a literate culture (the minimal aim of schooling; we should aim still higher) could be defined as the gaining of cultural literacy.

Such canonical knowledge could not be fixed once and for all, "Grant and Lee" could not have been part of it in 1840, or "DNA" in 1940. The canon changeth. And in our media-paced era, it might change from month to month—faster at the edges, more slowly at the center, and some of its contents would be connected to events beyond our control. But much of it is within our control and is part of our traditional task of culture making. One reassuring feature of our responsibilities as makers of culture is the implicit and automatic character of most canonical cultural knowledge; we get it through the pores. Another reassuring aspect is its vagueness. How much do I *really* have to know about DNA in order to comprehend a newspaper text directed to the common reader? Not much. Such vagueness in our background knowledge is a feature of cultural literacy that Hilary Putnam has analyzed brilliantly as "the division of linguistic labor." An immensely literate person, Putnam claims that he does not know the difference between a beech tree and an elm. Still, when reading those words he gets along acceptably well because he knows that under the vision of linguistic labor somebody in the culture could supply more precise knowledge if it should be needed. Putnam's observation suggests that the school curriculum can be vague enough to leave plenty of room for local choice regarding what things shall be studied in detail, and what things shall be touched on just far enough to get us by. This vagueness in cultural literacy permits a reasonable compromise between lockstep, Napoleonic prescription of texts on the one side, and extreme laissez-faire pluralism on the other. Between these two extremes we have a national responsibility to take stock of the contents of schooling.

Although I have argued that a literate society depends upon shared information, I have said little about what that information should be. That is chiefly a political question. Estimable cultures exist that are ignorant of Shakespeare and the First Amendment. Indeed, estimable cultures exist that are entirely ignorant of reading and writing. On the other hand, no culture exists that is ignorant of its own traditions. In a literate society, culture and cultural literacy are nearly synonymous terms. American culture, always large and heterogeneous, and increasingly lacking a common acculturative curriculum, is perhaps getting fragmented enough to lose its coherence as a culture. Television is perhaps our only national curriculum, despite the justified complaints against it as a partial cause of the literacy decline. My hunch is that this complaint is overstated. The decline in literacy skills, I have suggested, is mainly a result of cultural fragmentation. Within black culture, for instance, blacks are more literate than whites, a point that was demonstrated by Robert L. Williams, as I learned from a recent article on the SAT by Jay Amberg (*The American Scholar*, Autumn 1982). The big political question that has to be decided first of all is whether we *want* a broadly literate culture that unites our cultural fragments enough to allow us to write to one another and read what our fellow citizens have written. Our traditional, Jeffersonian answer has been yes. But even if that political decision remains the dominant one, as I very much hope, we still face the much more difficult political decision of choosing the contents of cultural literacy.

The answer to this question is not going to be supplied by theoretical speculation and educational research. It will be worked out, if at all, by discussion, argument, and compromise. Professional educators have understandably avoided this political arena. Indeed, educators should *not* be left to decide so momentous an issue as the canonical contents of our culture. Within a democracy, educational technicians do not want and should not be awarded the function that Plato reserved for philosopher kings. But who is making such decisions at a national level? Nobody, I fear, because we are transfixed by the twin doctrines of pluralism and formalism.

Having made this technical point where I have some expertise, I must now leave any pretense of authority, except as a parent and citizen. The question of guidance for our national school curriculum is a political question on which I have only a citizen's opinion. For my own part, I wish we could have a National Board of Education on the pattern of the New York State Board of Regents—our most successful and admirable body for educational leadership. This imposing body of practical idealists is insulated by law from short-term demagogic pressures. It is a pluralistic group, too, with representation for minority as well as majority cultures. Its influence for good may be gauged by comparing the patterns of SAT scores in New York with those in California, two otherwise comparable states. To give just one example of the Regents' leadership in the field of writing, they have instituted a requirement that no New Yorker can receive a high school diploma before passing a statewide writing test that requires three types of prose composition.

Of course I am aware that the New York Regents have powers that no National Board in this country could possibly gain. But what a National Board could hope to achieve would be the respect of the country, a respect that could give it genuine influence over our schools. Such influence, based on leadership rather than compulsion, would be quite consistent with our federalist and pluralist principles. The Board, for instance, could present broad lists of suggested literary works for the different grades, lists broad enough to yield local freedom but also to yield a measure of commonality in our literary heritage. The teachers whom I know, while valuing their independence, are eager for intelligent guidance in such matters.

But I doubt that such a Curriculum Board would ever be established in this country. So strong is our suspicion of anything like a central "ministry of culture," that the Board is probably not a politically feasible idea. But perhaps a consortium of universities, or of national associations, or of foundations could make ongoing recommendations that arise from broadly based discussions of the national curriculum. In any case, we need leadership at the national level, and we need specific guidance.

It would be useful, for instance, to have guidance about the *words* that high school graduates ought to know—a lexicon of cultural literacy. I am thinking of a special sort of lexicon that would include not just ordinary dictionary words, but would also include proper names, important phrases, and conventions. Nobody likes word lists as objects of instruction; for one thing, they don't work. But I am not thinking of such a lexicon as an object of instruction. I am thinking of it rather as a guide to objects of instruction. Take the phrase "First Amendment," for instance. That is a lexical item that can hardly be used without bringing in a lot of associated information. Just what *are* the words and phrases that our school graduates should know? Right now, this seems to be decided by the makers of the SAT, which is, as I have mentioned, chiefly a vocabulary test. The educational technicians who choose the words that appear on the SAT are already the implicit makers of our national curriculum. Is then the Educational Testing Service our hidden National Board of Education? Does it sponsor our hidden national curriculum? If so, the ETS is rather to be praised than blamed. For if we wish to raise our national level of literacy, a hidden national curriculum is far better than no curriculum at all.

Where does this leave us? What issues are raised? If I am right in my interpretation of the evidence—and I have seen no alternative interpretation in the literature—then we can only raise our reading and writing skills significantly by consciously redefining and extending our cultural literacy. And yet our current national effort in the schools is largely run on the premise that the best way to proceed is through a culturally neutral, skills-approach to reading and writing. But if skill in writing and in reading comes about chiefly through what I have termed cultural literacy, then radical consequences follow. These consequences are not merely educational but social and political in their scope—and that scope is vast. I shall not attempt to set out these consequences here, but it will be obvious that acting upon them would involve our dismantling and casting aside the leading educational assumptions of the past half century.

THE EIGHTIES

Radicalism for Yuppies
(1986)

Louis Menand

Menand's discerning review of the Critical Legal Studies movement then afoot in the nation's leading law schools expressed well-placed doubt about a partisan attack on "legal liberalism" and the effort to extend "deconstruction" into new areas of academic life. The attempt to colonize the arm of the university that produced the nation's jurists and power lawyers, Menand noted, had a powerful aroma of radical chic.

D uncan Kennedy—Andover, Harvard, and Yale Law School, now a professor at Harvard Law—advises young lawyers to resist oppression by refusing to laugh at the senior partners' jokes. This professional risk-taking is in order, he explains, because "all over the world, workers and peasants and political activists have risked and lost their lives." The progressive lawyer does not want to risk actually being fired, of course. That would be counterrevolutionary. For contrary to the conventional belief that progressive politics means working on behalf of the underprivileged, the first duty of leftist intellectuals is to "combat . . . their own experience of oppression" wherever it may occur—at the corporate law firm, or the Ivy League faculty meeting, or the upper-middle-class dinner party.

Kennedy's guide to revolutionary etiquette is laid out in a little book called *Legal Education and the Reproduction of Hierarchy* (1983). It belongs to the political program of the academic movement known as Critical Legal Studies. The "Crits," as they're known, eschew the tradition of academic radicals like the British Fabians, who simply ignored the contradictions between their revolutionary beliefs and their bourgeois life-styles. Instead, they have developed a sophisticated (although basically fatuous) justification for their lives as guerrillas with tenure.

Critical Legal Studies has been in the news lately, thanks to accounts of faculty tensions at Harvard Law School. Six senior faculty members are

254

said to be so unhappy about the influence of the Crits that they are actually thinking about moving to other law schools—a shocking development for Harvard. One already has done so. And until last week, no outsider had accepted an offer of tenure from Harvard since 1981. Dean James Vorenberg has had to send a calming letter to the school's alumni, and university president Derek Bok has announced that he will step into the law school's appointment process. On the other hand, even some non-Crits admire the Crits for having injected some excitement into a discipline, and an institution, not known for polemical fireworks in recent years.

What exactly *is* Critical Legal Studies? The movement now has adherents among the tenured faculty at many of the nation's top schools, and its method of scholarship is spreading. The lawyer or judge who picks up a law review these days, in the modest expectation of learning about developments in some point of contract doctrine is likely to be confronted instead by titles like "Deconstructing the Legislative Veto" and "Nihilism and Legal Theory" and "Constitutional Adjudication and the Indeterminate Text."

Critical Legal Studies is an attack on what its practitioners refer to as "liberal legalism." The phrase is meant to denote nearly everything the traditional way of thinking about law in our society takes for granted: in a nutshell, the notion that the law is a body of more or less neutral principles that, when applied to real-life disputes, produce results that are more or less consistent and more or less derived from considerations of justice rather than power. No one, of course, actually believes that the law is a magic wand that, if waved correctly, always produces a just result. But most legal scholars think that something like this is at least the goal of the American legal system. That's why they're devoting their lives to the law. The Crits reject this basic premise.

According to CLS, legal principles are not neutral, but biased in favor of certain economic and social arrangements that are themselves neither inevitable nor just. What's more, the law is not consistent, but radically indeterminate, capable of producing opposite results in similar cases depending on the outcome the judge desires or the system requires. Finally, the law is not apolitical, but in fact the instrument and the enforcer of a specific political ideology—the ideology of liberal capitalism. The idea of "the rule of law" is, according to the CLS view, nothing more (and nothing less) than the glue that holds present arrangements in place.

In broad outline, this bears a strong resemblance to the Legal Realist movement of the 1920s and 1930s, which noted the effect of economic developments such as industrialization on supposedly neutral legal principles.

But the legal realists never challenged the *aspiration* of law to serve justice. To nonlegal scholars, CLS's claim to have demystified the law may seem only a fancy prelude to a familiar exercise in establishment-bashing. But two features of Critical Legal thought distinguish it from the usual leftist program.

The first concerns the choice of political area. The Critical Legal scholar holds a position at an elite law school and writes articles for law reviews on the traditional subject of legal scholarship—appellate court decisions. Community organizing, free legal work for the poor, amicus briefs in Supreme Court cases—all the sorts of things activist lawyers usually engage in—play no role. Some Crits may spend their time and legal talent on these kinds of activities, but the movement's gospel holds that there is no such thing as a progressive legal solution to any actual social problem.

The purpose of Critical Legal scholarship is not to identify injustices in specific areas of the law, or to attack lines of precedent in which democratic principles have been perverted, or to argue for more social science in judicial decision-making. The purpose is to expose the entire system of legal thought as an intellectual prison house. The language of the law, the Critical Legal scholar explains, is so much a part of the way we think that it dictates not only how we judge present arrangements, but our ability to dream up better alternatives. "The vocation of legal thought," as Northeastern's Karl Klare (J.D. Harvard '75) puts it, is "to render radical, nonliberal visions of freedom literally inconceivable."

Thus the second difference between CLS and traditional leftism: CLS has no explicit political agenda. It offers only the fuzziest idea of what the good life might be and how it can be attained. And it operates with no expectation of developing a theory of politics or the state. No target is out of bounds, since whatever exists helps to maintain the ideological hegemony of the powers that be, and is thus deserving of disrespect. On the other hand, CLS's most concrete political advice tends to be the trivial kind Duncan Kennedy dispenses: practice "risk-taking, insubordination, defiance"—when you can get away with it. Only by disrupting the institution from the inside can the idea of a more just world be expected to take shape. And the more prestigious and powerful the institution the better—so feel free to pursue your conventional ambitions at the same time.

Where did this radicalism for yuppies come from? Part of the answer is that the various "post-structuralist" theories that have become standard fare over the past decade in philosophy and literary criticism have finally invaded legal scholarship. The typical critical legal scholar considers himself a "deconstructionist"—he is interested above all in demonstrating the semantic incoherence of legal texts. Stanford professor Mark Kelman (J.D. Harvard '76) calls the method "trashing." The premise is that once the theoretical incoherence of liberal legalism has been exposed, we will be able to reconceive all our political values because we will now understand what is really going on.

"To expose the limitations of doctrine," explains Harvard professor Clare Dalton (LL.M. Harvard '73) in a recent article titled "An Essay in the Deconstruction of Contract Doctrine," ". . . is one of the major goals of this piece. That done, it becomes possible systematically to surface the core issues underlying contractual disputes, by decoding doctrinal formulations." This is a typical bit of CLS prose. Dalton cites Jacques Derrida and his " 'deconstructive' textual strategies" as the source of her method.

What Dalton proposes, however, has nothing to do with the actual theory. Deconstruction is a train most riders choose to get off before the end of the line. Unfortunately, the train itself travels straight into the abyss. The belief that there are things coherent and intelligible enough to be called "core issues" underlying legal texts—and that legal doctrine is a sort of code that, when cracked, reads "politics"—reflects just the sort of "naive" idea of meaning that deconstructionist theory is intended to explode. If a true deconstructionist were presented with the conclusion that legal language masked political ideology, he or she could only reply, "Politics? And what is that?"

Deconstruction is in fact the least practical intellectual strategy for a political movement—even a movement whose politics are as conveniently abstract as those of Critical Legal Studies. The reason is that *nothing* follows from it, and it can therefore be made to serve anybody's end. One reason the Crits like to bandy the term "deconstruction" is that it sounds so threatening. And a number of traditional legal scholars have expressed suitable alarm. Yale Law School professor Owen Fiss condemned CLS not long ago as "the new nihilism," and Duke Law School dean Paul Carrington wrote last year in the *Journal of Legal Education* that if the Crits are serious about what they preach, they have "an ethical duty to depart the law school."

But surely there is less here for mainstream law professors to be worried about than they think. For in spite of its noises about transforming the world, Critical Legal Studies is the most academic of enterprises. Who but an academic would think that an idea is rendered useless once it has been shown to be philosophically incoherent? Everyday political life involves a thousand beliefs whose truthfulness and efficacy are entirely a function of the good faith of the participants—and are nonetheless useful for it. The law school graduate who sets up shop in the real world on

Critical Legal principles will not only find himself unable to practice much law, he will find himself unable—for good or ill—to practice much politics either.

The slogan "Everything is politics" is like the slogan "Everything is art": in order to make the perfectly unexceptionable point that those categories are, in the end, arbitrary, constructed things, the terms are drained of the practical meaning we give them. For just as it is useful to know the difference, however factitious, between a sculpture and a refrigerator, so it is useful to acknowledge a distinction between a policy and a principle. The politicization of everything is, after all, one of the characteristics of totalitarian societies (a problem scarcely touched on, by the way, in the CLS literature I have read).

The Critical Legal scholars are not, of course, totalitarian. Their vision is communitarian: a vision of a world of homogeneous, small-scale groups—"cells," Kennedy calls them—where rules can be the subjects of constant negotiation because everyone can afford to be his or her own lawyer. But it has been a long time since this vision had any realistic force. We feel the need for neutral principles of justice today precisely because we live in a world of sharply competing notions of the good life. Neutral principles, though they may prevent us from getting exactly the society we want, at least protect us from getting only the society somebody else wants. In a society in which every question of human relations was settled solely on the basis of a political power struggle, even the Critical Legal scholar might be glad for some sort of neutral principle—and would scarcely mind its being a fiction.

But Critical Legal Studies is not, in spite of its theoretical fashion, a French import. Its political spirit is easy enough to recognize; it is even a little out of date. It is the spirit of a certain strain of 1960s student radicalism—the kind that believed that college professors wield real class power, and that being able to take a course pass/fail is a victory against oppression. Thus the Crits devote their energies to schemes for professors and janitors to share in communal decision-making at law schools, as a substitute for asking why—given their analysis—law schools (and thus their own comfortable jobs) should exist.

The typical Critical Legal scholar attended an Ivy League (or comparably selective) college in the 1960s or early 1970s, went on to study at an elite law school, perhaps spent a year clerking for a prestigious judge, and then proceeded directly to a position on the faculty of a top-tier law school. It must be difficult indeed, in such a hothouse career, not to think that all the conditions of one's work have real-world import—not to think that one's professional frustrations reflect an oppressive hierarchy, that one's personal satisfactions represent a universal ideal, that every administrative decision at one's institution is a matter of genuine political moment.

But if one is a professor at Harvard or Stanford or Georgetown law school, one enjoys a rather desirable set of occupational conditions to have to worry about. It's nice to have available a style of radical politics that doesn't require giving any of them up.

Debating the Humanities at Yale

(1986)

Roger Kimball

Kimball's report of a Yale University humanities conference provided a detailed account of rising disturbances in academic life in the middle of the eighties. New theories and curricula were sweeping across campuses, gaining *éclat* and camp followers. Postmodernism allowed its academic votaries to feel daring and adventurous, like intellectual Clark Kents. For some, it offered relief from tedious and more rigorous forms of scholarship or had transgressive appeal. Traditionalists who affirmed older tests of content in the humanities were put on the defensive.

Early this April, the Whitney Humanities Center at Yale University sponsored a one-day, public symposium entitled "The Humanities and the Public Interest." The symposium convened at nine o'clock on a Saturday morning and consisted of three sessions. The purpose of the event, in the words of a University press release, was "to re-examine the traditional association between the study of the humanities and the guardianship of humanistic values in the context of contemporary American society." Peter Brooks, director of the Whitney Humanities Center and professor of the humanities at Yale, expanded on this: "The symposium will ask whether the case for the humanities can rest on traditional assumptions," he was quoted in the press release as saying "or whether a new rationale is needed if the humanities are to claim a major place in contemporary modes of thought and analysis."

One might think this a tall order for a single day's discussion. But the Yale community proved itself undaunted by the prospect. Even the symposium's first session, which was devoted to "Technology in the Humanities, the Humanities in Technology," drew an audience of over a hundred people; and the second two sessions—"The Social Mission of the Humanities" in the late morning and "A New Rationale for the Humanities?" after lunch—both filled the house with an audience of some three hundred or more. Each session featured two speakers and two respondents, with a member of the Yale faculty serving as moderator.

The symposium opened with some introductory remarks by Professor Brooks, who noted that the original impetus for the symposium was Secretary of Education William J. Bennett's report on higher education in the humanities, *To Reclaim a Legacy*. Among much else, Bennett had argued that "each college and university should recognize and accept its vital role as a conveyor of the accumulated wisdom of our civilization."

It is of course this final affirmation that has troubled Secretary Bennett's opponents. For one thing, who decides what counts as "the accumulated wisdom of our civilization"? In Matthew Arnold's terms, why should the humanities be concerned primarily with the *best* that has been thought and said? Does that not exclude a large portion of human experience? And does not that mass of experience deserve "equal time" in our institutions of higher education? Here again, who is to say what counts as "best"? Perhaps the Arnoldian injunction has been interpreted too narrowly, too "ideologically," too exclusively? Furthermore, why should the humanities focus so intently upon the past? Why should they not concern themselves as much with the *creation* as with the *preservation* of culture? Such questions are at the heart of Professor Brooks's "profound disagreement" and charge of "intellectual fundamentalism"—a charge that has been loudly echoed in the academy and that was to be advanced with great zeal that Saturday at Yale's Whitney Humanities Center.

The symposium's first session, however, on technology and the humanities was notable mostly for its lack of focus. Alan Trachtenberg, professor of American Studies and chairman of the American Studies Program at Yale, served as moderator. He opened the session by noting that the antagonism between technology and the humanities has become something of a "cliché." The antagonism might be overcome, he suggested, if we were to invert the terms of the discussion and try to show how technology and the humanities are at bottom "interrelated systems" that point to a "common destiny." This sounds lovely, of course—who wouldn't wish to show that the rationalistic imperatives of modern science and technology are somehow compatible with the intrinsically value-laden life of the humanities? Unfortunately, though, Professor Trachtenberg failed to specify what it might mean for technology and the humanities to be "interrelated systems," and in default of such specification his dream of their "common destiny" can be little more than wishful thinking. Clichés rarely provide one with an "interesting" interpretation of phenomena, but it sometimes happens that they express an obvious truth.

The principal speakers in this first session were Elting Morison, professor emeritus at MIT, and Daniel C. Dennett, professor of philosophy at Tufts University. Professor Morison offered us some rather commonplace reflections on the disintegration of the "received scheme of things" in the modern world and on the academy's accompanying shift away from the humanities as traditionally conceived toward more technical subjects. In a formidable phrase that captured the imagination of the other speakers, he called for the establishment of a "laboratory for the study of epistemological disorders" that could bring the humanities and technology together. Professor Dennett read part of a paper on ethics in which he discussed some of the special ethical quandaries with which our modern, technological society confronts us. He was especially concerned with analyzing the increased moral responsibility we feel in the face of our greater knowledge of the world's miseries. Given that knowledge and our immense technical capabilities, he asked, where does our responsibility end? At the same time, he criticized our "misbegotten reliance" on technology and—in the session's second arresting phrase—lobbied for "a moral first-aid kit" that would be more responsive to particular ethical problems.

The respondents added little to the discussion. Jules Chametsky, professor of English and director of the Institute for Advanced Study in the Humanities at the University of Massachusetts, wondered whether Professor Dennett's proposals were capable of addressing "real problems" and made the novel observation that the prospect of a nuclear holocaust weighs heavily on modern consciousness. Professor Chametsky also offered us some wandering reflections on the moral wisdom expressed in Wallace Shawn's play *Aunt Dan and Lemon* and concluded by noting that in "Reagan's America" it is difficult to make the humanities "relevant." The other respondent in the first session was Leo Marx, professor of American cultural history at MIT. Professor Marx began by reminding us how difficult it is to establish compelling criteria for moral action. He liked the notion of a "laboratory for epistemological disorders," he told us, but in general felt that the proposals made that morning were too "sanitized," too abstract and detached from real-life problems. He emphasized the "embedded" quality of moral problems, observing that for moral guidance most people rely not on abstract cogitation but on inherited belief systems. The real function of the humanities, he suggested, was not to provide us with "instrumental values" but to help us distinguish and discriminate among belief systems, to reflect critically on inherited values.

While the question of the relation between technology and the humanities is undoubtedly a pressing one, the contributions that morning rarely proceeded beyond assorted—and often dubious—platitudes, on the one hand, and fairly abstract speculation about ethics, on the other. The discussion became considerably more concrete in the second, and most publicized, session of the symposium, "The Social Mission of the Humanities." This session featured a "dialogue" between Yale President A. Bartlett Giamatti and Norman Podhoretz, the well-known writer and editor of *Commentary* magazine; the respondents were Henry Rosovsky, professor of social science at Harvard, and Cornel West, associate professor of the philosophy of religion at the Yale Divinity School. It was in this session that the real issues facing the humanities in contemporary American society were most clearly set forth.

Mr. Podhoretz spoke first. The humanities, he said, cannot be justified on practical grounds. Because the knowledge and culture they represent are "good in themselves," their ultimate justification is simply their intrinsic value. From this it follows that the humanities cannot directly help us in the formulation of public policy; nor do they yield any particular political position, nor indeed does acquaintance with the humanities necessarily make us morally more upright or more humane—think only of the cultivated Nazi commandants who also savored Mozart. Echoing the sentiments expressed in Secretary Bennett's report, Mr. Podhoretz identified the chief function of the humanities to be the creation of a "common culture." Central to this view of the humanities is the idea of a more or less generally recognized canon of works that define the tradition. Mr. Podhoretz admitted that there will always be disagreement about the composition of the canon at, as it were, its edges, but he claimed that, at least until recently, there has been a widely shared consensus about the core body of works that constitute "the best that has been thought and said."

In one sense, of course, this view of the humanities can be said to be exclusive or "elitist," since it presupposes a rigorously defined notion of what it means to be an educated person. But in another sense, it is deeply democratic, for it locates authority not in any class or race or sex, but in a tradition before which all are equal. Indeed, as Mr. Podhoretz observed, to the extent that the humanities are crucial to the maintenance of civilized life, it is essential that as many people as possible be exposed to the canon: only thus is high culture preserved and transmitted. Furthermore, as the transmitter of the canon, of what Mr. Podhoretz described as our "intellectual patrimony," the humanities have traditionally instilled a sense of the value of the democratic tradition we have inherited. And it is in this respect, he noted, that the humanities *do* have a political dimension, insofar as they rest upon a belief in the value and importance of Western culture and the civilization that gave birth to it.

With the social and political upheaval of the Sixties and early Seventies, Mr. Podhoretz continued, this entire conception of the humanities came under radical assault. Not only the idea of a common culture, founded upon a recognized canon of great works, but the very notion of a politically autonomous realm of culture, was dismissed as naïve, ethnocentric, or somehow repressive. Even the fundamental belief in the value of Western culture and civilization—the value, that is to say, of the whole humanistic enterprise—was undermined. And while it is true that the more extreme manifestations of this revolt have disappeared, Mr. Podhoretz maintained that the radical attitudes espoused in the Sixties and Seventies live on in attenuated form in the academy—even, or rather especially, in the humanistic disciplines, in the values and assumptions that typically inform the teaching and study of the humanities. For the most part, he said, a study of the humanities now tends at best to encourage a feeling of "mild contempt" for culture as traditionally defined and at worst to inspire outright hatred of our civilization and everything it stands for. And because of this sedimented radicalism in the academy, the humanities, however much they may still add to an individual's enlightenment and culture, no longer really contribute to the common good.

It cannot be said that Mr. Podhoretz's diagnosis was sympathetically received. I overheard the idea of a "common culture," for example, variously described as "moribund," "imperialistic," and "fascist." It was considered to be equally "sexist," I gathered, judging from the knowing looks that his use of the phrase "intellectual patrimony" occasioned. President Giamatti began by telling us that he found Mr. Podhoretz's talk "internally contradictory," for is there not a contradiction between asserting the essentially private nature of the humanities and then lamenting that they no longer conduce to the commonweal? In fact, though, President Giamatti's charge depended upon distorting Mr. Podhoretz's description of the humanities. It is one thing to say that the humanities cannot be justified on instrumental grounds, as Mr. Podhoretz did, quite another to say that they are a private affair entirely without social consequence, which no one but President Giamatti thought to propose.

The President of Yale University, himself a scholar of Renaissance literature, also came out strongly against the idea of a canon. Instead, he thought that the humanities should encourage "modes of thinking that would discipline the imagination without pretending to direct it"—the idea being, I suppose, that it doesn't much matter what one learns so long as one learns something. President Giamatti even claimed that this was the "Greek view" of education. Perhaps he meant the view current in contemporary Greece; certainly, the idea that education should seek "to discipline the imagination without pretending to direct it" is completely foreign to the teachings of Plato and Aristotle—think, for example, of the quite definite ideas that Plato had about what should and should not be taught in his discussion of education in the third book of *The Republic.* But leaving the Greek view of education to one side, President Giamatti's reservations about the importance of the canon do help us to understand his central charge against Mr. Podhoretz: that his view of the humanities is "solipsistic" and "spiritually selfish." Basically, President Giamatti presented Mr. Podhoretz as an elitist who wanted to keep culture for himself. But as I understand it, the real difference between them was that Mr. Podhoretz wanted the *humanities* to be as widely available as possible, whereas President Giamatti was happy with what we might call universal schooling—the substance, the content, of what was taught was for him more or less up for grabs.

If nothing else, President Giamatti exemplified the strategy that Henry Rosovky, the session's first respondent, identified as the prime imperative for academic administrators—"Be vague." Professor Rosovsky, himself a social scientist, began his response with some amusing reflections on the difference between the humanities and the social sciences. For example, he found it "very humanistic" that there should be no formal papers at the session; and thinking over the discrepancy in income and prestige between faculty in the social sciences and the humanities, he couldn't but wonder whether the true social mission of the humanities "may in fact be sacrificial." About the humanities themselves, Professor Rosovsky suggested that their hallmark was "an eternal dissatisfaction," that they ought in fact to "engender a kind of dissatisfaction," and hence that they "should not be conservative." Against Mr. Podhoretz's vision of a "common culture," Professor Rosovsky sided with President Giamatti in questioning the desirability of adhering to a canon and in extolling the ideal of a "multi-culture" nourished by disparate sources and traditions.

But the most articulate, as well as the most histrionic, response to Mr. Podhoretz came from the Yale Divinity School Professor Cornel West. Professor West's performance, approximating the fervor of a political rally or revival meeting, clearly won the hearts and minds of the Yale audience. They thrilled to his rhetoric, punctuating his impassioned speech with enthusiastic applause. Professor West warmed up with a few words about "decolonization," "the eclipse of European dominance" in the world, and the disintegration of "white, male, WASP hegemony" in the academy. (I had thought that WASPs were white by definition, but no matter: "white, male, WASP hegemony" has an edifying ring to it.) He pictured the evolution of the humanities in recent years as a reflection of a world-wide struggle for freedom against what it has pleased him to describe elsewhere as "the final fruits of bourgeois humanism: North Atlantic ethnocentrism."

In Professor West's view, the "collapsing consensus" that Mr. Podhoretz spoke of tokened not decline but liberation. The Sixties, far from being a debacle, was a "watershed" for the humanities. For one thing, the "onslaught" of popular culture that began then has helped undermine elitist notions of high culture. Then, too, the attention lavished on the history and literature of blacks, women, peasants, and other groups has revealed the traditional canon to be the biased, ethnocentric construction that it is. Hence the "self-contempt" that Mr. Podhoretz said a study of the humanities tended to instill these days is really "a deeper self-critique" that mirrors important changes in the world ("the eclipse of European dominance," etc.), changes that must be recognized and accommodated "if we are not to blow up the planet."

I hasten to add, though, that in criticizing Mr. Podhoretz, Professor West by no means sought to align himself with President Giamatti. On the contrary, he criticized both men for their "lack of historical sense" and for their conservatism. (The term "conservative," one notes, has degenerated into a negative epithet; in many circles, to describe something or someone as "conservative" is simply a politicized way of signaling one's disapproval.) Distinguishing between the "battle-ridden neoconservatism" of Mr. Podhoretz and the "more charming" conservatism of President Giamatti, Professor West wondered whether the "dynamism" championed by President Giamatti didn't at bottom merely represent "the recovery of high-brow classical humanism." He can rest easy on that score, I think, even if it must be admitted that, in comparison with Professor West's vision of the humanities, President Giamatti's does seem conservative.

To my mind, however, the real clue to Professor West's view came with his celebration of the incorporation of the New Left into the university. Among other things, he championed the New Left for creating "combat zones" that could challenge the entire ethos of bourgeois humanism that stands behind the humanities as traditionally conceived. And taking issue with Mr. Podhoretz's severe criticism of the intellectual, moral, and political effects of the New Left, Professor West described writers like Herbert Marcuse and the post-World War II French Marxists as "the best of Western civilization."

Now, it is worth pausing for a moment over Professor West's identification of Herbert Marcuse and the "French Marxists" as representatives of "the best of Western civilization." Just what do these individuals stand for? What have they contributed to furthering the fundamental principles of the humanities? Consider Louis Althusser, one of the most influential among the French Marxists whom Professor West admires. In an interview that he gave in 1968, this example of the "best of Western civilization" explained that he had come to philosophy through his attempt to "become a Communist militant" during and after World War II. Having finally understood that "philosophy is fundamentally *political*"—more specifically, that it is a tool of "class struggle"—Althusser also realized that "it was not easy to resist the spread of contemporary 'humanist' ideology, and bourgeois ideology's other assaults on Marxism." Being an intellectual, a philosopher, made things especially difficult, he confided: "Proletarians have a 'class instinct' which helps them on the way to proletarian 'class positions.' Intellectuals, on the contrary, have a petty-bourgeois class instinct which fiercely resists this transition." Most would agree, however, that Althusser succeeded rather well in overcoming the specified resistance, even if he finally fell prey to "contemporary humanist ideology" when he confessed to murdering his wife in 1980. In any case, it is quite clear that Althusser's view of intellectual life is deeply inimical to the ideal of disinterested scholarly inquiry, an ideal that is at the heart of the humanist tradition.

Then there is Marcuse. One could turn to any number of his works for an introduction to his view of the value of the humanities—to the "Political Preface" that he added to the 1966 edition of *Eros and Civilization,* for example, where he calls for a thorough-going revolt against "the political machine, the corporate machine, the cultural and educational machine" of "affluent Western society." What he calls for, in short, is a revolt against just those political, social, and intellectual traditions that define the humanistic endeavor. But perhaps the best précis of Marcuse's thinking about such matters is to be found in his notorious 1965 essay, "Repressive Tolerance." Unable to deny that modern Western democracies offer their citizens an unparalleled degree of personal and political liberty, Marcuse is nevertheless able to denounce the West as essentially "totalitarian" by the simple device of declaring its brand of liberty "repressive" and a product of "false consciousness." (What a versatile tool of obfuscation the notion of "false consciousness" has been, utterly exempt from subservience to mere "empirical reality"!) Indeed, he offers a simple formula for distinguishing between the "repressive tolerance" that expresses itself in the real world in such phenomena as freedom of speech and freedom of assembly and the "liberating tolerance" that would seem to occur chiefly in his imagination: "Liberating tolerance," he writes, "would mean intolerance against movements from the Right, and toleration of movements from the Left."

In brief, then, what Marcuse wants is "not 'equal' but *more* representation of the Left," and he blithely sanctions "extralegal means if the legal ones have proved to be inadequate." In one of the more extraordinary passages of the essay, Marcuse admits that "extreme suspension of the right of free speech and free assembly is indeed justified only if the whole of society is in extreme danger," but continues immediately to note that

> I maintain that our society is in such an emergency situation. . . . Different opinions and "philosophies" can no longer compete peacefully for adherence and persuasion on rational grounds: the "marketplace of ideas" is organized and delimited by those who determine the national and the individual interest. In this society, for which the ideologists have proclaimed the "end of ideology," the false consciousness has become the general consciousness—from the government down to its last objects.

There is no escape, apparently—unless of course one happens to be blessed, as Marcuse believed himself to be, with the "true consciousness" that allows one to penetrate such nearly universal mendacity.

It is in the context of such passages from Professor West's intellectual heroes, I believe, that we must understand the conception of freedom that underlies his view of the humanities. Like his heroes, Professor West finds the "ideology of pluralism" suspect because it "domesticates" radical thought. And like them, too, he questions the traditional "bourgeois" notion of the citizen as a "bearer of rights." Instead, he lobbies for an idea of citizenship that would incorporate "collective action," that would "undermine the liberal protection of rights" in favor of a more encompassing ideal. In response to an objection from Mr. Podhoretz, Professor West admitted that the New Left faced the "temptation" to nihilism and totalitarianism. But he did not seem to think the temptation very serious, and stressed the promise of freedom over such obstacles. Given the record of utopian thinking in this century, however, Oscar Wilde's boast that he could resist anything but temptation seems perhaps less a piece of wit than a solemn admonition.

❧

Since the second session of Yale's symposium on the humanities and the public interest had sought to dispose of this traditional rationale for the humanities, it seemed only appropriate that the final session should address itself to the question of formulating a new rationale for its discredited predecessor. The session was moderated by Professor Brooks, and featured presentations by Jonathan Culler, professor of English and comparative literature at Cornell University, and Vincent Scully, professor of the history of art at Yale. Responding to Professors Culler and Scully were Carolyn G. Heilbrun, professor of English at Columbia University, and J. Hillis Miller, professor of English and comparative literature at Yale.

Professor Culler began by criticizing the traditional rationale for the humanities as "universalist" and "foundationalist." The pretension to be "universalist," he said, was primarily a political consideration: the humanities as traditionally conceived had presumed to speak universally to the human condition, but had in fact represented a narrow "white male" viewpoint. The attempt to be "foundationalist" involves epistemological considerations: the humanities had pretended to provide a foundation for both thought and values, but radical criticism in the last decades had exposed the fictional, and ideologically motivated, ground of that pretense. Professor Culler did not, however, attempt to formulate the new rationale for the humanities that he demanded, but merely offered a list of "divided imperatives" that he thought the humanities ought to heed. The list was fairly vague, even banal, unfortunately—the humanities ought to "assume unity" but also assert the value of other cultures, and so on—though it was full of appropriately combative rhetoric and wonderful sounding, Nietzschean proclamations like his suggestion that thought really becomes valuable "only when it is extreme."

As an example of the kind of retrograde thinking he disparaged, Professor Culler cited a letter he had recently received from a dean at St. John's College in Annapolis, Maryland, inviting him to lecture there. St. John's offers a traditional "great books" curriculum—tailored to include classic developments in modern science and mathematics—and the dean, explaining the nature of the curriculum, described it as based on the "greatest books" of the Western tradition. This Professor Culler and his audience found quite risible, for after all what did the good dean from St. John's mean by the "greatest books"? Only books written by "white Western males before 1900," of course, something that for Professor Culler seemed to demonstrate how parochial—not to say ethnocentric and sexist—his correspondent's notion of education must be. (For the record, one does read women authors and beyond 1900 at St. John's.) Professor Culler never really specified his own idea of a good college curriculum. But one can bet that it wouldn't be "ethnocentric"—indeed, it's not even clear that it would be anthropocentric, since Professor Culler wondered in passing whether a view of the humanities based exclusively on a study of mankind wouldn't be guilty of "speciesism."

Mercifully, Professor Culler did not pursue this absurdity, though it was taken up by Vincent Scully, who began his talk by suggesting that what we needed was not so much a new rationale for the humanities as a new rationale for "animality." Professor Scully then treated us to a slide show that opened, as such slide shows must, with a picture of the snow shovel Marcel Duchamp presented as a work of art in 1915. What won't be taken as a work of art today, Professor Scully reflected, and then went on to share with his audience a number of other truly novel ideas: that the movies and television have emerged as the dominant style of modern life, for example, or that the artist must be "open-minded, pluralistic, poised for surprise." One began to understand why Professor Scully is most successful in a lecture hall full of undergraduates: when entertainment with a dash of edification about the wonderfulness of art is the goal, one needn't worry about the details.

Carolyn Heilbrun began her response on a melancholy note by observing that even now, even at a symposium on the humanities at Yale in 1986, she was the only woman on the panel. And I was surprised, I must confess, that Professor Brooks could have made this blunder. Surely he must have known that such a discrepancy in numbers would be held up for criticism. And as an academic administrator, he must also have known that the important thing in such situations is not to get the appropriate speakers for the occasion but to assemble a panel with the correct ethnic, social, and sexual mix. In any case, Professor Heilbrun went on to note that, though she was also the oldest person on the panel, it was the symposium's youngest representatives, Professors Culler and West, who spoke for her. She, too, believed that college should "teach us to be dissatisfied" and that thought is really valuable only when it is extreme. In addition, as the panel's official feminist, she also told us that it is the questions that women can ask about the canon that are the important questions. Why only women can ask them, or indeed, what the important ones might be, she didn't really say. Nevertheless, one got a pretty good idea of the kind of thing she had in mind when she criticized Professor Scully for presenting Michelangelo's depiction of the creation of man as representative of the human condition. After all, both God and Adam were—well, there's no getting around it; they were male, and how universal can that be?

After all this, J. Hillis Miller cannot be blamed for failing to add much to the discussion; by this time, the fashionable positions had all been staked out. Professor Miller has proved himself an expert at creatively adapting fashionable positions, however, and in his talk he adroitly elaborated on several of the day's themes. Above all, he warned against attempting simply to reimpose the traditional canon and proposed, as a kind of compromise, a curriculum in which canonical works would be read alongside "non-canonical" ones. What seemed crucial to him—and this was an idea that appealed to a good number of speakers that day—was not so much the teaching of particular texts or subjects as the teaching of "reading" in general.

The session, and the symposium, ended with a few comments and questions. Two comments in particular stuck with me. The first was Professor Heilbrun's assertion that our reading of texts is inescapably "ideological." And the second was Professor Brooks's concluding observation that, because the humanities are "inherently subversive," the recent developments in the academy that people like Secretary Bennett and Mr. Podhoretz bemoan ought actually be taken as signs of health. Together, the comments seemed to me to epitomize the proceedings in New Haven that day, and it may be well to conclude by considering them in a bit more detail.

The idea that all reading is "ideological" has gained great currency in literary studies in recent years. Among other things, it implies that we are imprisoned by our point of view, that our language, our social or ethnic background, or our sex inescapably condition the way we understand things. But are we so imprisoned? Granted that such contingencies *influence* our point of view, do they finally determine it? "Ideologies," as Hannah Arendt observed years ago, are "isms which to the satisfaction of their adherents can explain everything and every occurrence by deducing it from a single premise." In this sense, she notes, an ideology differs from a simple opinion "in that it claims to possess either the key to history, or the solution for all 'riddles of the universe,' or the intimate knowledge of the hidden universal laws which are supposed to rule nature and man." Yet it is precisely this sort of distinction that the contention that all reading is ideological dismisses. It dismisses, in other words, the crucial distinction *between* a point of view and an ideology, between an individual perspective on the world—which as a perspective is open to challenge, accommodation, correction—and an *idée fixe*. All in all, what we might call the universalization of ideology underscores the truth of Northrop Frye's observation that "it is a curious tendency in human nature to believe in disillusionment: that is, to think we are nearest the truth when we have established as much falsehood as possible."

And in this context, since Matthew Arnold was invoked, whether as friend or foe, by practically every speaker at the Yale symposium, it is worth mentioning that in "The Function of Criticism" Arnold identifies "disinterestedness" as the chief mark of responsible criticism. Now in describing criticism as "disinterested," Arnold did not mean that it presumes to speak without reference to a particular point of view—though critics of the idea often so caricature it. Rather, he meant a habit of inquiry that keeps "aloof from what is called 'the practical view of things' . . . [b]y steadily refusing to lend itself to any . . . ulterior, political, practical considerations about ideas." In modern terms, Arnold looked to criticism to provide a bulwark *against* ideology, against interpretations that are subordinated to essentially political interests. Of course, the ideal of such disinterested criticism is rejected by many contemporary critics as naïve (or worse), though it is not at all clear whether the criticism they practice is more astute than Arnold's or, alas, only more ideological.

Arnold is also useful in appreciating the oft-voiced contention that education ought to instill "dissatisfaction" or, to use Professor Brooks's more dramatic formulation, that the humanities are "inherently subversive." Such sentiments were so widely shared at the Yale symposium that it was almost taken for granted that the function of education is not to impart knowledge but to subvert, to excite "dissatisfaction." Behind this idea is a deep suspicion of authority, a suspicion that, in fact, would have us collapse the distinction between authority and authoritarianism. Yet it is a nice question whether the humanities can survive without recognizing the authority of tradition. It is indeed for this reason that, in "The Literary Influence of Academies," Arnold praised the willing "deference to a standard higher than one's own habitual standard in intellectual matters" as the result of a "sensitiveness of intelligence." And thus it is, too, that Hannah Arendt suggested that "conservatism, in the sense of conservation, is of the essence of the educational activity, whose task is always to cherish and protect something." "The real difficulty in modern education," Arendt wrote,

> lies in the fact that, despite all the fashionable talk about a new conservatism [Arendt was writing in 1958], even that minimum of conservation and the conserving attitude without which education is simply not possible is in our time extraordinarily hard to achieve. There are very good reasons for this. The crisis of authority in education is most closely connected with the crisis of tradition, that is with the crisis in our attitude toward the realm of the past. . . . The problem of education in the modern world lies in the fact that by its very nature it cannot forgo either authority or tradition, and yet it must proceed in a world that is neither structured by authority nor held together by tradition.

"Neither structured by authority nor held together by tradition"—in the end, this would seem to describe the goal of the "new rationale" for the humanities as envisioned at Yale. And of course the real casualties are the students and junior faculty, who often haven't the foggiest notion of the value of the tradition they have been taught to disparage. The senior faculty are at least old enough to recognize what it is they are abandoning. Champions of the "new rationale" like to pretend that they are merely thinking more critically than the tradition had allowed. In fact, though, they have as often as not degenerated from criticism to nihilism. Indeed, the whole situation reminds one of nothing so much as of Turgenev's portrait of the nihilist Bazarov in *Fathers and Sons*:

> "A nihilist," said Nikolai Petrovich. "That comes from the Latin *nihil*—*nothing*, I imagine; the term must signify a man who. . . who recognizes nothing?"
>
> "Say—who respects nothing," put in Pavel Petrovich, and set to work with the butter again.
>
> "Who looks at everything critically," observed Arcady.
>
> "Isn't that exactly the same thing?" asked Pavel Petrovich.
>
> "No, it's not the same thing. A nihilist is a person who does not take any principle for granted, however much that principle may be revered."

The humanities had once striven to inculcate the ability to think critically, that is, to enable one to discriminate between ideology and a point of view, between legitimate authority and authoritarianism, between genuine freedom and its tyrannical parody. The "new rationale" propounded at Yale would have us believe that thinking critically is undistinguishable from Bazarov's nihilism.

Why the West?

(1988)

William J. Bennett

This address by U.S. secretary of education William J. Bennett at Stanford University on April 18, 1988, responded to the university's escalating curriculum battles during the previous year and the rising number of faculty members who found the study of "Western civilization" either narrow or odious. The Bennett address brought long-simmering issues of academic content and multiculturalism into the political arena, where they stayed for the remainder of the decade.

Stanford's decision to alter its Western Culture program has been much in the news lately—and deservedly so. For what happens at Stanford has significance for the rest of American higher education, and the central question underlying the debate here is under debate on other campuses across the country. So in the spirit of free and frank discussion, let me begin my remarks by offering my candid judgment about what has happened here.

My judgment is this: Stanford's decision of March 31 to alter its Western Culture program was not a product of enlightened debate, but rather an unfortunate capitulation to a campaign of pressure politics and intimidation. For evidence of this, let me briefly turn to the sequence of events as I understand it from press accounts and from individuals here at Stanford.

The Western Culture program was established in 1980. By all accounts, the program was immensely popular with both faculty and students—in fact, a good many students considered it their most worthwhile academic experience at Stanford. In the spring of 1986, a small but very vocal group of students called on the university to abolish the program. In its place, they proposed a course that would emphasize the "contributions of cultures disregarded and/or distorted by the present program." This marked the beginning of a steady stream of charges against the existing course, against the supporters of the existing course, and against the Western tradition that sustained the existing course—charges of racism, sexism, imperialism, elitism and ethnocentrism.

The Stanford administration appointed a task force to evaluate the program. The group's preliminary report—which was to become the basic working document for the "Cultures, Ideas and Values" (CIV) course that replaced Western Culture—prompted a great deal of discussion and debate among faculty and students alike. What is unfortunate is that one side of the debate was, in certain subtle and not so subtle ways, discouraged from making its case. Supporters of the proposal were encouraged to air their views, and they did so frequently and forcefully—in the papers, at rallies, and during demonstrations. Last spring some members of the so-called Rainbow Agenda student group occupied President [Donald] Kennedy's office for five hours and released a set of ten demands, one of which was the adoption of the task force proposal. So far as I know, no one was punished or even censured for this occupation. When, however, opponents of the proposal ventured words of criticism, they were publicly taken to task by the administration for reacting too hastily or harshly.

Last fall, a faculty senate subcommittee met to consider the CIV proposal. While the meeting was in progress, students disrupted the proceedings, chanting, "Down with racism, down with Western Culture, up with diversity." One participant in the interruption was quoted as saying, "The [subcommittee] was getting a bit timid and we wanted them to be well aware of the dedication to changing the Western Culture program." The subcommittee got the message and sent the proposal on to the faculty senate for prompt consideration.

The faculty senate deliberated, discussed, and amended the CIV proposal at several meetings. But at the meeting of March 31, there was a heightened sense of urgency. By this point the issue had been publicized extensively in the press, and many simply wanted to get it over with. The proponents of CIV demanded that the matter be brought to a swift and certain conclusion. Amendments proposed by the faculty senate's steering committee that would have shifted CIV to a more Western orientation were unacceptable, they said. President Kennedy urged the senate not to allow the prospect of a "best" proposal to undermine its chances of adopting a "very good" one.

Why was it so necessary for the senate to make its decision on that particular day? More important, why was it so necessary for the senators to accept the proposal without the steering committee's amendments? The answer to this may be found in the answer to my next question: Why were there 200 angry CIV supporters waiting outside the meeting room?

These supporters were apparently ready to disrupt the meeting if a vote on a particular amendment went the "wrong way." "We would have walked in. We would have interrupted," a student leader was quoted as saying.

Many more instances, much more evidence could be adduced. But this much is clear: CIV was primarily a political, not an educational decision. The tactics of intimidation that were employed throughout the debate's two-year history not only brought about CIV's success; they were—and they continue to be—central to CIV's meaning. The cultivation and promotion of "diversity" is held up as the primary goal of CIV, but its supporters have done much to discourage free and open debate of the issue. In the end, CIV stands as the political product of a political process.

There have been attempts to portray CIV as a minor pedagogical change—a slight alteration in a single Stanford freshman requirement. Indeed, at first blush, the new course has an air of intellectual respectability to it. The plan for CIV contains the language of something intellectually promising—it talks about "diversity," "self-understanding," and "the common intellectual experience." But the fact is that the core reading list of 15 significant works in Western philosophy and literature has been thrown out. Instead, CIV instructors will decide year by year what the content of the course will be. And following the guidelines set down on March 31, the instructors must include works by "women, minorities, and persons of color," and at least one work per quarter that explicitly addresses the issues of race, gender, or class. Does anyone doubt that selecting works based on the ethnicity or gender of their authors trivializes the academic enterprise? Does anyone really doubt the political agenda underlying these provisions?

The events of the past two years at Stanford, therefore, serve as a striking example of what Allan Bloom has called the "closing of the American mind." In the name of "opening minds" and "promoting diversity," we have seen in this instance the closing of the Stanford mind. Observing the events from close by, the distinguished American philosopher Sidney Hook has written of the situation here that he regards "as far more significant than the ultimate constitution and fate of the course in Western culture, the manner in which the discussion at Stanford has so far been conducted . . . " Professor Hook finds that manner of discussion deeply troubling for American higher education. And so do I.

Life of course will go on. In fact, now that the debate appears to be over, one can predict what is likely to happen. First, I believe, Stanford will be praised by like-minded institutions and individuals for being "forward-looking," "progressive," and "innovative." Second, other universities that make a habit of imitating Stanford will decide that they too should change their programs in the same or similar ways. Third, Stanford will continue to prosper. Some alumni will be uneasy about what has happened here, but only a few of them will withhold their support from the university on that account. Fourth, I suspect that this will be only the beginning—the first of many chapters. Having been so effective in this instance, the tactics of intimidation will be used again. The methods that succeeded in pushing CIV through the faculty senate have shown that intimidation works—that intimidation *can* take the place of reason. The loudest voices have won, not through force of argument, but through bullying, threatening, and name-calling. That's not the way a university should work.

Fifth and finally, Stanford will be harmed—though perhaps not visibly, perhaps not for a while—by these recent events. I say not visibly because many of those who deplore what has transpired here will not say so publicly. They know that speaking out against CIV will invite charges of racism—an utterly false but highly damaging accusation. To his credit, President Kennedy recently spoke out against such name-calling, such McCarthyism of the left. But the name-calling, having been tolerated for so long, is not likely to cease. For now the defenders of Western culture will mostly confine themselves to talking quietly with one another about what has happened. But they know what they know, and others around the country know it too: that for a moment, a great university was brought low by the very forces which modern universities came into being to oppose—ignorance, irrationality, and intimidation.

Our universities should oppose these forces because our universities are the bearers, the transmitters, of Western civilization. And above all else, Western civilization stands and should stand for the claim that the life of the mind can and should prevail over ignorance, irrationality, and intimidation. That is why it is ironically appropriate that the issue on which Stanford capitulated was whether a course in Western civilization should be included in the freshman curriculum. The issue of the merits of the course came to stand for the issue of the merits of Western civilization as a whole. Let me therefore now briefly address the core issue under debate at Stanford, an issue of significance to American higher education in general: Why the West?

Why must we study, nurture, and defend the West? I'll give you four reasons. First, because it is ours. It is the culture in which we live and in which most of us will continue to live, whether our grandparents are African or Asian, Hungarian or Mexican, Muslim or Shinto. Our institutions and ideals—our schools and universities and their great, still honored traditions, our churches and synagogues, our government and laws, even our notions of friendship and family—have all acquired their shape and significance through the course of Western history, largely though not exclusively through the European experience. To be sure, China, India, Africa, and other societies and cultures have made contributions to our institutions and ideals. Where contributions have been made, they must be acknowledged. Where new contributions emerge, they must be included. Historically, this has in fact been the standard Western practice: Western civilization is strong in part because it is open—it studies and learns from others.

The second reason we must study the West is that it is good. It is not all good. There are certainly great blots on its record. In the story of Western civilization, there are volumes of injustices great and small, of sins, omissions, and errors. Nevertheless, still, the West has produced the world's most just and effective system of government: the system of representative democracy. It has set the moral, political, economic, and social standards for the rest of the world. To quote Allan Bloom, "Our story is the majestic and triumphant march of two principles: freedom and equality." And those principles now define no less than a universal standard of legitimacy.

This leads me to the third reason—the reason that Western civilization's critics seem to have entirely missed: the West is a source of incomparable intellectual complexity and diversity and depth. Western civilization is emphatically *not* an endorsement of a particular "party line." On the contrary, the West's long history of self-critical dialogue is one of its greatest strengths. Since the time of Socrates, what has distinguished the West is its insistence, in principle, on the questioning of accepted ways and beliefs—its openness to the appeal to nature, to use Socratic terms, as opposed to mere convention. It is true that the West has often failed, beginning with the death of Socrates, fully to live up to this principle—but the principle has always animated the Western experience.

The point for contemporary higher education is this: The classics of Western philosophy and literature amount to a great debate on the perennial questions. To deprive students of this debate is to condemn them to improvise their ways of living in ignorance of their real options and the best arguments for each. In the tradition of Peter Abelard, our civilization offers a great *sic et non* on the human condition. Consider the point/counterpoint of Western thought. On the ends of government, whom do we follow—Madison or Marx? On the merits of the religious life—Aquinas or Voltaire? On the nobility of the warrior—Homer or Erasmus? On the worth of reason—Hegel or Kierkegaard? On the role of women—Wollstonecraft or Schopenhauer? The study of Western civilization is not, then, a case for ideology; it is a case for philosophy and for thoughtfulness. It considers not only the one hand, but the one hand *and* the other—and, just as often, the third and fourth hands as well. Those who take the study of the West seriously end up living a variety of different lives and arriving at a diversity of opinions and positions. And for this diversity, in the West as nowhere else, there is unparalleled tolerance and encouragement.

Indeed, some of the West's greatest teachers and statesmen are those who have participated most vigorously in this continual process of dissent, discussion, and redirection. In our time, this tradition is well exemplified by the Rev. Martin Luther King, Jr. The Rev. King immersed himself in the writings of the great philosophers: "From Plato to Aristotle," as he wrote, "down to Rousseau, Hobbes, Bentham, Mill and Locke." These great thinkers—these *Western* thinkers—helped teach and inspire Rev. King to tear down the ugly injustices of Jim Crow and to bring us closer to the dream of freedom and equality for all men and women.

It is true that the Rev. King was also inspired by the example of a non-Westerner—Gandhi. We should give credit where credit is due, and we should study Gandhi's thought and deeds, as we should study the thought and deeds of others from outside the West. But I would add that in this case, when we study Gandhi, we shall see that Gandhi was himself very much indebted to such Western philosophers as Henry David Thoreau, and to such Anglo-American traditions as the rule of law. So even in studying Gandhi's East, one cannot escape the West. Now, of course, nothing stops Stanford from requiring a course in traditions of thought other than the West; indeed much commends such an idea. But such an idea in no way diminishes the importance, the necessity, of studying the West.

Each year since becoming Education Secretary, I've been invited to the Martin Luther King Center to deliver an address marking the Rev. King's birthday. And each year, I speak of how the Rev. King drew strength and purpose from his education, an education in the Western intellectual tradition. Last year, at Stanford, the Rev. King's birthday was marked by Jesse Jackson leading a group of students in the now famous cry: "Hey, hey, ho, ho, Western Culture's got to go." Just a week earlier, I had been at the King Center in Atlanta talking about the Rev. King's self-proclaimed debt to Western thought. Either the Rev. King was right, or the Rev. Jackson is right. I'll stand with King.

This brings me to my final reason for studying and protecting the West and its unique tradition of open discourse and philosophic inquiry: we must do so because the West is under attack. Oftentimes the assault comes from outside the West, but sometimes, sadly, it comes from within. Those who attack Western values and accomplishments do not see an

America that—despite its imperfections, its weaknesses, its sins—has served and continues to serve as a beacon to the world. Instead, theirs is an America hopelessly tainted—tainted by racism, imperialism, sexism, capitalism, ethnocentrism, elitism, and a host of other "isms." You're probably familiar with such rhetoric—it has been used over and over again as a justification for the abolition of the Western Culture program here at Stanford. As one member of the Stanford community has said: "The Western Culture program gives intellectual justification to sexism, racism, and national chauvinism." So, the assertion goes, by diminishing the study of the West in our colleges and universities, we can make an important step toward ridding the world of these unholy "isms."

I would remind those critics that it is Western civilization that has taught much of the world about the evils of "sexism, racism, and national chauvinism." Indeed, it is the West that has given us the very language used to attack the West here at Stanford. After all, where do the concepts of rights, equality, and, yes, diversity come from? It is in the West, it is from the West, that we have learned—over time, through struggle, after bloodshed—to stand squarely behind liberty and equality for all people. An honest study of the West will provide the reasons for its protection. But how are we to protect the West if we set about systematically robbing ourselves of opportunities to know and study it?

Let me therefore speak to Stanford students: Study the West, study it well and thoughtfully, and build on that study as you continue your education. In saying "study the West," I don't mean study *only* the West. Of course not. But if what I said here tonight is even partly true, the West is worthy of your study.

Let me close with a quote from William James. Speaking at a Founders' Day celebration on this campus in 1906, James set forth his vision for Stanford's "ideal destiny."

> Can we not, as we sit here to-day, frame a vision of what [Stanford] may be a century hence, with the honors of the intervening years all rolled up in its traditions? Not vast, but intense; . . . a place for . . . training scholars; devoted to truth; radiating influence; setting standards. . . .

Now, almost "a century hence," we can ask whether Stanford has lived up to James's vision. For the moment, in this instance, I believe it has not. But it is not too late. Stanford can turn the events of the past two years to its advantage by rejecting sloganeering and political pressure. In so doing, Stanford would be true to its purpose as, in James's words, a place devoted to truth and setting standards.

Bennett Misreads Stanford's "Classics"
(1988)

Stephen R. Graubard

The national response to the Stanford speech was swift. Bennett's calculated maneuver provoked distress and pique among humanities professors and other cultural custodians then extolling "diversity." This opinion piece that appeared in the *New York Times* a few days after the speech combined standard academic complaints with standard airs of condescension. Unlike many of his critics, however, Bennett realized that the controversy was more than a quibble over a few books.

Secretary of Education William J. Bennett, who has done so much to encourage exaggerated rhetoric, recently traveled to Palo Alto, Calif., to take on Stanford University. In a speech, he claimed the university had been "brought low by the very forces which modern universities came into being to oppose—ignorance, irrationality and intimidation."

Such harsh words, in a civil society, must have been induced by an extraordinary occurrence. In fact, they were principally provoked by the Faculty Senate's decision to create a new course—Cultures, Ideas and Values—replacing an eight-year-old Western Culture course, which had required freshman students to read selections from 15 "classic texts."

The readings in the new course, which begins in September 1989, will include only six such selections—from the Bible, Plato, St. Augustine, Machiavelli, Rousseau and Marx. In addition, professors are asked to assign works by "women, minorities and persons of color." This last requirement, Secretary Bennett complains, can only "trivialize" the academic enterprise.

Why is Mr. Bennett so agitated? First, he views the new course as an attack on his concept of a pristine Western civilization. In his opinion, any course that exchanges required readings in 15 "great books" for six can only be inferior. Without waiting to learn what additional texts professors may choose to assign, he is certain that they will not be as good as those used these last eight years.

Knowing Stanford's reputation, realizing the publicity he stands to gain in certain political quarters from condemning the faculty for "unfortunate capitulation to a campaign of pressure politics and intimidation" by radicals, he uses Washington rhetoric that is admirably suited to a political candidacy but inimical to intellectual discourse. I must ask: Why should a faculty of a pre-eminent university so neglect its reputation, so evade its teaching responsibilities as to succumb to unspecified pressures, instituting a program that is manifestly inferior?

Nonetheless, the charge has been made—and in Washington a charge, however spurious, often suffices: It serves as a two-minute item on the television news, and for a politician that is gravy. Surely, the charge would never have been made, and the Secretary would never have gone on the attack, had he not believed that his opinion is shared by others who are convinced that the so-called elite universities are irresponsible and craven.

In recent years, Mr. Bennett and others of like mind have propagated the idea that "standards" in our universities have been falling and that they themselves, as the guardians of "tradition," must mount the barricades to combat this vice and error. In their picaresque drama, those who view the matter differently are barbarians, know-nothings, unregenerate leftists—the detritus of the terrible 1960s—who now pander to unfortunate, ill-educated progeny—a student rabble both feared and fawned over. This travesty misses the point that American universities collectively are the best in the world—that the more outstanding, appreciated individually, are remarkable as teaching institutions and centers of research.

Yet in a televised "debate" with Donald Kennedy, Stanford's president, Secretary Bennett created the illusion that conditions of a very different kind prevail. He made much of Stanford's dropping Dante from required readings, seeing this as proof of the decline of higher education and of a belief in the "classics." In fact, the concept of a "classic" is substantially more complex than his citing of an author's name—known to millions—may suggest.

In 1908, Charles William Eliot, president of Harvard, assembled the great writings of ancient and modern literature and published them as the Harvard Classics—the famous "five-foot shelf"—which were intended to "enrich, refine and fertilize" the mind. Considered today, president Eliot's modern-fiction selections, with their concentration on certain English and American novels, are dated and seem almost quaint. The point is that views change about what constitutes a "classic" that ought to be taught, and why.

It is not nearly as obvious as Mr. Bennett implies that a new course in Cultures, Ideas and Values must be inferior to what was offered under the rubric of Western Culture. Obviously, an able faculty will carry out intelligently and responsibly what it has decided is a useful curriculum experiment—and, if it fails, changes undoubtedly will be made.

This is not to say that colleges and universities are immune to narrow ideological or political pressures—that none exist at Stanford. But these were not the forces that made curriculum changes seem appropriate and reasonable there. The glory of our university system is that curriculum reformations occur regularly, that many have taken place in the last half century, that different institutions—all self-governing—have selected different curriculum paths, and that all this has happened without the stentorian interventions of Federal appointees.

The supreme irony of today's so-called debate is that if Western civilization can be characterized by a single attribute, it is its historic refusal to remain static, to accept tradition as inviolable. Choices among "classics" will always have to be made. There can never be a short list that will satisfy all criteria of importance. It ought to be taken for granted that these choices, when made at a distinguished university such as Stanford, will reflect professional judgment about what a course is intended to achieve and what readings should be assigned to realize those purposes.

There may be sound educational principles that recommend substituting Mary Wollstonecraft for John Stuart Mill and Ralph Ellison for Sir Walter Scott. These are not "equivalents," and only a mind paralyzed by yesterday's values rather than actively engaged by today's problems will demand that they be weighed on some mythical scale to determine their cultural worth. A decision to alter an eight-year-old course at a major university ought not to be made a matter of cosmic importance—particularly if the attack on that decision serves mostly to deflect attention from other crucial educational issues that America ought to face now.

Allan Bloom and E. D. Hirsch: Educational Reform as Tragedy and Farce
(1988)

Helene Moglen

Moglen's violent critique of Allan Bloom, E. D. Hirsch, Jr., and William J. Bennett, which first appeared in a publication of the Modern Language Association, reflected the passion—and indignation—of the academic left as its programs and initiatives faced increased scrutiny and criticism.

Cultural literacy is usually discussed by educators as a straightforward curricular problem, a relatively simple matter of textual choices. Underlying such discussions, however, are a number of deeply rooted assumptions about the nature and value of cultural diversity: about race and class and gender; about nationalism and transnationalism; about individual development and social coherence; about pedagogical strategies and the relation of students to teachers. From the perspective that seems now to dominate institutional relations and practices on all educational levels, cultural diversity is a social disease for which cultural literacy is the appropriate cure: the imposition of a common culture on a pluralistic student body through, on the one hand, the teaching of standard English and mechanical skills and, on the other, the celebration of canonical texts that represent a great tradition that is essentially Western white, middle-class, and male. This point of view has achieved considerable attention and support with the recent publication of E. D. Hirsch, Jr.'s *Cultural*

Literacy: What Every American Needs to Know and Allan Bloom's *The Closing of the American Mind.* Both Hirsch and Bloom take a dim view of the current state of education: Hirsch in the elementary schools, Bloom in the university. Both advocate a retreat from the precipice into an Edenic past when students were god-like in the range of their knowledge, the extent of their aspirations, and the simple elegance of their homogeneity. While both authors have defined quite different projects for themselves—Hirsch is a relentless pragmatist, Bloom an uncompromising idealist; Bloom structures his educational critique as tragic vision while Hirsch offers a program for reform that reads as farce—both are enormously valuable in their unintentional revelation of the ideological underpinnings of the New Right agenda.

In *Cultural Literacy,* Hirsch presents a modest proposal for educating children by discouraging thought. His goal is wonderfully clear and the process he outlines for achieving it is equally straightforward: all obstacles are swept away by the force of his central purpose. Hirsch sees himself as one of the "nation builders" for whom "fixing the vocabulary of a national culture is analogous to fixing a standard grammar, spelling and pronunciation." He has organized "the basic information needed to thrive in the modern world" into a "national vocabulary": a sixty-three-page list of proper names, words, and phrases that have their referents in popular culture, history, geography, and science. Hirsch hopes that these words and phrases, described alternatively as "facts," "core information," "background information," and "content," will be organized into a sequenced curriculum by public leaders, publishers, and "distinguished educators" (presumably university faculty members and administrators rather than mere teachers, for whom Hirsch seems to have little respect).

As a modest proposer, Hirsch does not aspire unrealistically on behalf of the children whom he would accommodate to our postmodern society; they do not, after all, have to possess knowledge—only its appearance. He assures his reader that he is not advocating a list of books that every child should be forced to read and that he rarely even specifies titles that they must learn; instead he presents words, vague descriptive references that need only to be "hazily remembered" to be effectively used, since "haziness is a key characteristic of literacy and cultural literacy." An unabashed and uncompromising pragmatist, Hirsch is always clear about his priorities: socioeconomic pressures that have earned the concern of some educators are put aside because they are resistant to treatment, and the "complex problem of how to teach values in American schools" is not allowed to "distract attention from [the] fundamental duty to teach shared content." Because Hirsch defines all "facts" (alternatively "content" and "information") as "objective," he can credit claims that his list is partial but will have nothing to do with the argument that it is necessarily biased—that it is political, as all canonical choices must be, in the principles of inclusion and exclusion that it employs and in the ideological commitments that it represents. The stubborn naïveté of his positions enables him to remain oblivious to the contradiction inherent in his statement that "[a]though our public schools have a duty to reach widely accepted cultural values, they have a duty not to take political stands on matters that are subjects of continuing debate." He does not find it necessary to ask by whom and why some cultural values are accepted, nor does he perceive the dialectical relation between acceptance and debate.

Like Dickens's Gradgrind, of whom he often seems a parody, Hirsch would guarantee the teacher's neutrality by making her or him a blind functionary of her or his own curriculum: in Dickens's words, "a kind of cannon loaded to the muzzle with facts," prepared to blow the students "clear out of the regions of childhood in one discharge." Nor does Hirsch understand what Dickens saw so clearly; that children are, in this sense, canonproof, neither passive observers of their own lives nor empty vessels waiting to be filled; that they are active participants, possessed of their own needs and desires, capable also of resistance. Motivation has no place in Hirsch's system. It is erased along with the teacher, socioeconomic realities, familial circumstances, writing, imagining, and thinking. Hirsch does not ask what will make those who are subject to his system wish to memorize his list of facts, what will make them willing to take, and struggle to pass, the "general knowledge examinations" that would "exert a normalizing effect" on the curriculum that he recommends. By making "abstract skills" (which, according to Hirsch, provide the core of the current curriculum) and "substance" oppositional, reducing substance to his index of facts, and designating memorization as the only significant cognitive activity, Hirsch effectively eliminates any reflective and interactive process from his educational method. If his system were to be taken seriously and adopted—and it must be remembered that Hirsch has friends in high places, some of whom have written the blurbs printed on his bookjacket—it would certainly ensure "the trivialization of cultural information" which Hirsch himself acknowledges as a "near certainty." It would also make it virtually impossible for schools to accept, as their central project, literacy not merely defined in Hirsch's terms as the capacity to read the daily newspaper but rather defined as the ability to read the daily newspaper knowledgeably, reflectively, analytically, and critically.

Of course, the children who would survive Hirsch's ordeal of cultural literacy would be similar to those who have always surmounted the obstacles that educators have put in children's paths. They would be the same students that Allan Bloom would wish to subject to his system: "The kind of young persons who populate the twenty or thirty best universities"; those "of comparatively high intelligence, materially and spiritually free to do much of what they want in the few years of college they are privileged to have. . . those who will have the greatest moral and intellectual effect on the nation." In other words, those "bright" students who are white, middle-class, and preferably, male, who flocked to Ivy League institutions in the mid-fifties when, according to Bloom, "no universities were better than the best American universities in the things that have to do with a liberal education." As Hirsch looks back nostalgically to a halcyon nineteenth-century past before lower-school education was compulsory and universal, when the student body was relatively homogeneous, values unambiguous, and the curriculum traditional, Bloom locates the golden age some time before open admissions and affirmative action, before feminism and women's studies, before black studies and black power. It was then that he was able to teach Plato and Aristotle to the adoring young men who sat at his feet, as he himself had sat at the feet of his great teachers at the University of Chicago, and as young men had once sat at the feet of Socrates.

In *The Closing of the American Mind* Bloom has written autobiography as educational and intellectual history. In the story he tells, the flowering of the American university coincides with his own coming of age as an intellectual, a philosopher, and a teacher of great books. At the age of fifteen he discovered what would become for him a permanent refuge from bourgeois culture when he entered the University of Chicago and began to travel "the road of learning that leads to the meeting place of the greats." Once he had himself become a high priest in the exalted order of philosophers, he delivered to awed neophytes the revealed meanings of the sacred texts. His curriculum, which also defines the central argument of his book, provided a critique of the moral, intellectual, and political tradition of the West from its birth in Socratic idealism and its belief in abstract reason as the greatest human good, through its transformation into the pragmatism of the Enlightenment with its valorization of practical reason and its bourgeois assertion of men's rights, to its final debasement by Nietzsche, whose "agonized atheism" led to a cultural and intellectual relativism that initiated the crisis of modernity. Whatever response Bloom's students and colleagues might have had in the fifties to his reading of the decline of Western civilization, they apparently felt some sympathy for his conviction that "[m]en may live more truly and fully in reading Plato and Shakespeare than at any other time, because then they are participating in essential being and are forgetting their accidental lives." Their sympathy is not, after all, surprising. The attractions of the ivory tower were enhanced at that time by the threat of McCarthyism and the stark polarities of cold-war politics. The sputnik crisis validated an elitist approach to education that linked excellence and national purpose, making it clear, in Bloom's words, that "survival itself depended on better education for the best people."

The loss of paradise and the fall of Allan Bloom came in the next decade. With the "Nietzscheanization of the Left" in the sixties—the relativization of belief and thought as ideology—accidental lives were assigned by many a higher value than essential being. In "a time of unmitigated disaster for the universities" students, before so docile, questioned mainstream social and academic values and hierarchical structures: forms of aestheticism and idealism that rationalized social conflict and contradiction; alienating pedagogical practices; apartheid at home and a war of oppression abroad. Marginalized faculty members, who had previously known their places, became insurrectionists: they included not only junior faculty members who identified with their students but also blacks and women who demanded stronger institutional voices, greater representation in the curriculum, and a deauthorization of canons. Most reprehensible, in Bloom's judgment, were his own colleagues at Cornell who capitulated to the demands and the threatened violence of black students. Even now, Bloom reads the anger, confusion, intellectual struggle, and emotional pain of that period as a personal betrayal that he projects as social, moral, and intellectual apocalypse. He had and has only scorn for that emergent social consciousness, which he continues to consider petty: "The imperative to promote equality, stamp out racism, sexism and elitism (the peculiar crimes of our democratic society), as well as war, is overriding for a man who can define no other interest worthy of defending." Defending as his higher interest "participation in essential being," Bloom regards attempts to eradicate inequity not merely as irrelevant but as antithetical to his purpose. To maintain as dominant the curriculum that he values, to choose from the "best" his own coterie of students, to protect from threat the manly virtues that he so admires, he would return not only the university but the society in which it functions to that pastoral moment in which white male privilege was sustained by a force of shadow laborers who did not insist that others should take note of the oppressive conditions in which they lived their accidental lives.

Throughout the book, Bloom's strategy is to essentialize the traditional values and practices he approves: those that he sees as subversive of old hierarchical orders he deplores as "unnatural." It is not surprising, therefore, that he views affirmative action programs, initiated to redress historical wrongs, as hypocritical and necessarily unsuccessful attempts to veil what he calls "natural" racial inferiority: "Affirmative action now institutionalizes the worst aspects of separatism. The fact is that the average black student achievements do not equal those of the average white students in the good universities, and everybody knows it." Since Bloom does not credit the significance of social influence on academic achievement, he believes performance expresses innate ability exclusively and he categorically rejects white bias as a factor in the alienation of black students in the academy. "It would require a great deal of proof to persuade me that [white students] remain subtly racist," he says; on the contrary, he knows that they "are rather straightforward in such matters." If blacks have "remained indigestible" despite the fact that they have been welcomed into the university, their own "shame" and "resentment" are responsible: shame at their own incapacities and resentment that whites are in a position to do them favors. "They are victims of a stereotype," Bloom acknowledges, adding "but one that has been chosen by black leadership." His conclusion is that "affirmative action (quotas), at least in universities, is the source of what I fear is a long-term deterioration of the relations between the races in America."

Just as Bloom finds civil rights activism ultimately responsible for racism, he finds feminism fundamentally responsible for sexism: "The new interference with sexual desire is more comprehensive, more intense, more difficult to escape," he observes, "than the older conventions, the grip of which was so recently relaxed." According to Bloom, it is because of this "new interference" that feminist harpies have found it possible to define man's natural (and apparently neutral) sexual passion as rape, sexual harassment, and child molestation, making innocent men feel anxious as well as guilty. "Not founded on nature," the women's movement has been responsible for corrupting the young, trivializing and de-eroticizing sexuality, and ruining the vitality of the classic texts. Worst of all, it has been responsible for suppressing modesty, which Bloom sees as the natural female virtue, the bedrock of the double standard and the sexual division of labor, the indelible sign and guarantee of female inferiority. (Women, apparently, are modest because they are ashamed of their physical "difference" from men—that infamous "lack" with which we are all familiar—as blacks are ashamed of their intellectual "difference" from whites.) Bloom speaks with all the anxious misogyny of the late Victorian patriarch when he observes:

> It is one thing. . .to want to prevent women from being ravished and brutalized because modesty and purity should be respected and their weakness protected by responsible males, and quite another to protect them from male desire altogether so that they can live as they please.

In Bloom's judgment it is intolerable for women to live as they please, to think as they please, to have sex when and with whom they please: in short, to be equal to men. It is also intolerable for them, therefore, to flee the home that is supposed to be the focus of domestic bliss. "The decomposition of [the family] bond is surely America's most urgent social problem," he tells us, as he mourns the transformation of the family from its nineteenth-century incarnation as a "sacred unity," the "little polity," into its shattered contemporary form that creates "the slight deformity of the spirit" that he is wonderfully able to detect in students with divorced parents. Most instructive is the transparency of Bloom's protest against the feminist threat to phallicism, in all its personal, sexual, social, economic, and nationalistic forms:

> And here is where the whole business turns nasty. The souls of men—their ambitious, warlike, protective, possessive character—must be dismantled in order to liberate women from their domination. Machismo—the polemical description of maleness or spiritedness, which was the central *natural* passion of men's souls in the psychology of the ancients . . . was the villain, the source of the difference between the sexes. . . . It is indeed possible to soften men. But to make them "care" is another thing, and the project must inevitably fail.

"Machismo" is indeed revealed to be the defensive and insecure inventor—not the essential counterpart—of female modesty, as it is the inventor of all the qualities that mark the threatened "other" as inferior. It is fundamentally his "machismo," then, that Bloom wishes to affirm at any cost, with the Western tradition that is, in his judgment, its expression and justification. He has written his book in its defense.

Both Hirsch and Bloom argue in behalf of reason, and both demonstrate the correctness of Bloom's assertion that "[r]eason transformed into prejudice is the worst form of prejudice." In their efforts to construct scaffolding to support their fundamentally unstable positions, both prove themselves adept at bending logic to accommodate bias. Both reject the centrality of interpretation in cognitive and educative processes and remain oblivious to the intensely subjective nature of their own beliefs: Hirsch in the incontrovertible integrity of "facts," Bloom in the absolute status of "truth." Both maintain a naïve confidence in the retrievability of authorial intention, although each effectively defines himself as a high priest to whom the function of revelation appropriately belongs. Both isolate texts from historical and social contexts, never acknowledging the ideological assumptions that determine their own positions. Both are fundamentally disrespectful of students: Hirsch simply denies their subjectivity altogether, seeing them as empty vessels to be filled with the scraps of information he selects; Bloom attacks everything from their taste in music to their mindless egalitarianism to their "niceness," which, in his judgment, is "not particularly moral or noble." Each is interested in a generic student who fits the contours of his own theoretical position and political purpose. Both reject difference, therefore—racial, ethnic, even personal—Hirsch by urging social appropriation, Bloom by advocating exclusion. *Cultural Literacy* and *The Closing of the American Mind* stand as persuasive indictments of their own educational philosophies: the outrageous reductionism of one and the unabashed prejudice of the other; the illogicality of their authors' arguments in behalf of reason; the inhumane nature of their advocacy of the humanities; not least of all, their definitions of learning as unreflective accommodation to professorial and social authority.

A significant alternative to the conservative agendas that both books offer is represented by academic programs and theoretical perspectives grounded in the two pivotal events of the late sixties and early seventies to which Bloom refers with so much scorn: the admission into the university of a heterogeneous, often poorly prepared student population, which necessitated a new emphasis on literacy education, and the demands of women and minority faculty members for all forms of institutional representation and expression. These faculty members, who had either chosen or been relegated to the ghettos of writing programs and women's and ethnic studies departments, accepted the task of educating students who had been marginalized and disempowered: students who had little sense of social or intellectual entitlement and believed neither in the authority of their own judgments nor in the validity of their experience. The worlds that had been constructed for them by the educational systems by which they had been processed—the "facts" that they had been taught, the canonical traditions that had been introduced to them as theirs, even the language that they had been assumed to speak—had effectively silenced them while encouraging them to develop strategies of alienated survival.

In programs now defined as theirs—programs in which they were the subjects, not the objects, of study—teachers worked to engage them as self-conscious readers and writers of themselves and their societies, able to identify their own personal and collective biases at the same time that they became adept at interpreting verbal, visual, and social texts in their cultural and historical contexts. Feminist theory, colonial and ethnic discourse theory, and literacy theory provided many with ways of exploring the social, psychological, and historical relations of reading and writing from decentered perspectives, so that they could see how interpretive, methodological, and theoretical practices are influenced by the politics of gender, race, nationality, and class. For some, poststructuralist methodologies proved effective tools for radical interrogation, when experientially applied. Student semioticians read the everyday images with which they were presented as projections of belief systems that had shaped their conscious and unconscious desires. Apprentice deconstructionists brought to the surface those assumptions previously disguised in oppositional and categorical modes of thought in order to decode the ways in which their own material lives and consciousnesses had been structured by dominant ideologies invisible before. Together, these varied theoretical and methodological approaches illuminated the underlying processes of canon formation, suggesting in behalf of which interests canonization takes place and in defense of which needs and biases canons are preserved, resisted, deformed and transcended. Through their self-critical interactions with texts and traditions, students came to see how the power of discursive systems moves in many complex, intersecting, conflictual, and often contradictory ways: ways that they could not only grasp but could subvert and change, once their own locations—and possible relocations—in those systems had been defined. Finally, from the pedagogical practice followed in feminist, ethnic "minority," and writing classrooms, there emerged a relational model that encouraged the reconceptualization of hierarchical structures that had previously been perceived as necessarily inflexible and inevitably oppressive. As the authority of the text had to be recognized only to be deconstructed in the interests of an expansive, comparative perspective that called itself constantly into question, so too was the authority of the instructor questioned, along with that of the diverse interpretive communities that formed in shifting patterns of alliance and opposition in response to the personal, cultural, and political meanings that were identified. In this collaborative project, authority derived from depth of insight, breadth of learning, and authenticity of experience was shared and its directionality changed in a process that strove to be fundamentally interactive.

Of course, these theoretical assumptions and pedagogical practices are the very ones that E. D. Hirsch and Allan Bloom have so vociferously deplored, against which William Bennett has so passionately declaimed. It is clear that however the conservative critiques are cast—whether they are, like Hirsch's, offered in the form of farce or, like Bloom's, written as personal tragedy or, as Bennett's, presented with all the grandeur of epic— the stakes are high, and there is much on both sides to be lost and gained. It is also clear that the New Right has been able to craft an organization appropriate to its aspirations and its purpose. In the opinion of many, Bloom and Hirsch speak powerfully for its agenda. It remains now for those groups born of the strife of the sixties and seventies and working largely until now in relative isolation to begin to know themselves and one another as part of a remarkable coalition that has its roots and its future in movements that are not only national but global: movements of colonized peoples, feminists, and literacy workers, all committed to enlightened self-consciousness and radical social change.

Battle of the Books
(1988)

James Atlas

Atlas's review of university-based exchanges over the "literary canon" appeared in the *New York Times Magazine,* an effort to explain rising campus turbulence and the changing content of the humanities. Atlas asserted: "The questioning of authority that's such a pervasive theme in criticism now is a theoretical version of the battles that were fought on campuses 20 years ago—with real police."

The philosopher George Santayana was once asked which books young people should read. It didn't matter, he replied, as long as they read the same ones. Generations of Eng. lit. majors in American colleges followed his advice. You started with the Bible, moved briskly through Beowulf and Chaucer, Shakespeare and Milton, the 18th-century novel, the Romantics, a few big American books like "The Scarlet Letter" and "Moby-Dick"—and so on, masterpiece by masterpiece, century by century, until you'd read (or browsed through) the corpus. Occasional disputes broke out, reputations flourished and declined. T. S. Eliot smuggled in the 17th-century metaphysical poets, Malcolm Cowley promoted Faulkner, there was a Henry James revival. For the most part, though, the canon was closed: You were either on the syllabus or off the syllabus.

It was in the academic journals that I first noticed the word *canon.* Originally, it referred to those works that the church considered part of the Bible; now, apparently, it had a new meaning. *PMLA*, the journal of the Modern Language Association, proposed a future issue on "the idea of the literary canon in relation to concepts of judgment, taste and value." This spring, the Princeton English department held a symposium on "Masterpieces: Canonizing the Literary."

Canon formation, canon revision, canonicity: the mysterious, often indecipherable language of critical theory had yielded up a whole new terminology. What was this canon? The books that constituted the intellectual heritage of educated Americans, that had officially been defined as great. The kind of books you read, say, in Columbia's famed lit. hum. course, virtually unchanged since 1937: Homer, Plato, Dante, Milton . . . The masterpieces of Western civilization. The Big Boys.

In the academic world, I kept hearing, the canon was "a hot issue." "Everything these days has to do with the canon," one of my campus sources reported. Then, early this year, a flurry of articles appeared in the press. "From Western Lit to Westerns as Lit," joked the *Wall Street Journal* in a piece about some English professors down at Duke University who have been teaching "The Godfather"—book and movie—"E.T." and the novels of Louis L'Amour. An article in *The New York Times*, "U.S. Literature: Canon Under Siege," quoted a heretical brigade of academics who were fed up with hierarchies of literary value.

Why should Melville and Emerson dominate the syllabus? argued renegade professors from Johns Hopkins and Northwestern, Queens College and Berkeley. What about Zora Neale Hurston, a hero of the Harlem Renaissance? What about Harriet Beecher Stowe? "It's no different from choosing between a hoagy and a pizza," explained Houston Baker, a professor of literature at the University of Pennsylvania. (Did he mean that all literature, like all junk food, was essentially the same?) "To hell with Shakespeare and Milton, Emerson and Faulkner!" retorted Jonathan Yardley in *The Washington Post*, setting a high standard for the debate. "Let's boogie!"

By the end of March, when Stanford University announced plans to revise the series of Western culture courses it required of freshmen, eliminating the core list of classics and substituting works by "women, minorities and persons of color," what began as an academic squabble had burgeoned into a full-blown Great Books Debate. Comp. lit. and humanities professors, Afro-American specialists, historians, college administrators and government spokesmen entered the fray. All over the country, editorials appeared decrying the sorry developments at Stanford, where last year students on a march with Jesse Jackson had chanted, "Hey, hey, ho, ho, Western culture's got to go."

Days after the new course was unveiled, William J. Bennett, the Secretary of Education, showed up in Palo Alto, Calif., to deplore the university's decision. Speaking before an overflow crowd, Bennett expressed contempt for the faculty senate that had voted for the change. "The West is the culture in which we live," Bennett asserted. "It has set the moral, political, economic and social standards for the rest of the world." By giving in to a vocal band of student radicals, "a great university was brought low by the very forces which modern universities came into being to oppose: ignorance, irrationality and intimidation."

Bennett's polemic ignored the fine print. Instead of dealing with 15 "classic texts," students would read the Old and New Testaments as well as the works of five authors: Plato, St. Augustine, Machiavelli, Rousseau and Marx. The other works assigned would concentrate on "at least one non-European culture," with "substantial attention to issues of race, gender and class." No one was proposing to "junk Western culture," insisted Stanford's president, Donald Kennedy. The point was simply to reflect "the diversity of contemporary American culture and values."

Never mind. For Bennett, what happened at Stanford was another opportunity to rehearse one of his favorite themes: the decline of the West. In 1984, as chairman of the National Endowment for the Humanities, he published a report titled "To Reclaim a Legacy," which decried the influence of the 1960s on higher education in America, working in the obligatory reference to Matthew Arnold's famous definition of culture as the best that has been thought and said.

The trouble with this "Matthew Arnold view of literature and culture," as Gerald Graff, a professor at Northwestern University and one of the more reasoned commentators on the debate, observes, is that there never was any consensus about the best that has been thought and said—or, for that matter, why the West should have a corner on the high culture market. The idea of literature as a fixed and immutable canon—the Great Books, the Five-Foot Shelf—is a historical illusion. "Canon-busting is nothing new," Graff says. "There have always been politics. Teaching Shakespeare instead of the classics was a radical innovation."

So why is this debate over the canon different from all other debates? The fierce arguments about Socialist Realism that raged among American intellectuals in the 1930s and 40s were a lot more acrimonious. As for what's literature and what isn't, the critic Leslie Fiedler was anatomizing the cultural significance of Superman decades ago. What's different is who's doing the debating. A new generation of scholars has emerged, a generation whose sensibilities were shaped by intellectual trends that originated in the 60s: Marxism, feminism, deconstruction, a skepticism about the primacy of the West. For these scholars, the effort to widen the canon is an effort to define themselves, to validate their own identities. In the 80s, literature is us.

⁊⁊

On the shelves in Jane Tompkins's office at Duke are rows of 19th-century novels; she is one of the few who read them now. Her book

"Sensational Designs: The Cultural Work of American Fiction 1790-1860" is a brilliant exhumation of what she considers lost masterpieces, the history of a different American literature from the one I read in college in the 1960s. Writers like Charles Brockden Brown, Harriet Beecher Stowe and Susan Warner still deserve an audience, Tompkins argues with considerable persuasiveness. If they're no longer read, it's because our values have changed. The way to read these books is from the vantage of the past. Only by reconstructing the culture in which they were written and the audience to whom they were addressed can we learn to appreciate their intrinsic worth and see them for what they are: "man-made, historically produced objects" whose reputations were created in their day by a powerful literary establishment. In other words, the Great Books aren't the only books.

Tompkins is one of the jewels in the crown of Duke's English department, which in the last few years has assembled a faculty that can now claim to rival any in the country. Attracted by salaries that in some cases approach six figures and a university willing to let them teach pretty much whatever interests them, the new recruits compose a formidable team: Frank Lentricchia, the author of "After the New Criticism" and other works, Fredric Jameson, probably the foremost Marxist critic in the country; Barbara Herrnstein Smith, president of the Modern Language Association, and Tompkins's husband, Stanley Fish, chairman of the department. (Duke is known in academic circles as "the Fish tank.")

Canon revision is in full swing down at Duke, where students lounge on the manicured quad of the imitation-Cotswold campus and the magnolias blossom in the spring. In the Duke catalogue, the English department lists, besides the usual offerings in Chaucer and Shakespeare, courses in American popular culture; advertising and society; television, technology and culture.

Lentricchia teaches a course titled "Paranoia, Politics and Other Pleasures" that focuses on the works of Joan Didion, Don DeLillo and Michel Foucault. Tompkins, an avid reader of contemporary fiction—on a shelf in her office I spotted copies of "Princess Daisy" and "Valley of the Dolls"—is teaching all kinds of things, from a course on American literature and culture in the 1850s to one called "Home on the Range: The Western in American Culture."

Tompkins talks about her work with a rhetorical intensity that reminded me of the fervent Students for a Democratic Society types I used to know in college. Like so many of those in the vanguard of the new canonical insurrection, she is a child of the 60s and a dedicated feminist. In her book "Sensational Designs," she recounts how she gradually became aware of herself as a woman working in a "male-dominated schol-arly tradition that controls both the canon of American literature and the critical perspective that interprets the canon for society." The writers offered up as classics didn't speak to Tompkins; they didn't address her own experience. "If you look at the names on Butler Library up at Colum-bia, they're all white males," she notes one afternoon over lunch in the faculty dining hall. "We wanted to talk about civil rights in the classroom, to prove that literature wasn't a sacred icon above the heat and dust of conflict."

The English literature syllabus, Tompkins and her colleagues on other campuses discovered, was a potential instrument of change: "This is where it all came out in the wash." By the 1970s, Afro-American depart-ments and women's studies majors had been installed on college campus-es across the land. Books on gender, race, ethnicity poured from the university presses. Seminars were offered in Native American literature, Hispanic literature, Asian-American literature. "It wasn't only women we'd neglected," says Marjorie Garber, director of English graduate studies at Harvard University. "It was the whole third world."

The ideology behind these challenges to the canon is as unambigu-ous as the vanity plates on Frank Lentricchia's old Dodge: GO LEFT. Pick up any recent academic journal and you'll find it packed with articles on "Maidens, Maps and Mines: the Reinvention of Patriarchy in Colonial South Africa" or "Dominance, Hegemony and the Modes of Minority Dis-course." The critical vocabulary of the 1980s bristles with militant neolo-gisms: *Eurocentrism, phallocentrism, logophallocentrism.* (Why not *Euro-phallologocentrism?*) "This is not an intellectual agenda, it is a political agenda," Secretary of Education Bennett declared on the "MacNeil/Lehrer News-Hour" the night after his Stanford speech.

Why should a revolutionary curricular struggle be happening at a time when radical politics in America is virtually extinct? Walk into any classroom and you'll find the answer. Enormous sociological changes have occurred in American universities over the last 20 years; the ethnic profile of both students and faculty has undergone a dramatic transformation.

There's a higher proportion of minorities in college than ever before. By the end of this century, Hispanic, black and Asian-American undergrad-uates at Stanford may well outnumber whites. Their professors, many of whom were on the barricades in the 60s, are now up for tenure. "It's a demographic phenomenon," Jane Tompkins says. "There are women, Jews, Italians teaching literature in universities. The people who are teach-ing now don't look the way professors used to look. Frank Lentricchia doesn't look like Cleanth Brooks."

I had never seen Cleanth Brooks, the eminent Yale professor emeritus, but I could imagine him striding across campus in a conservative gray suit and neat bow tie—not at all the way Frank Lentricchia looks. The photograph on the book jacket of "Criticism and Social Change" shows a guy in a sports shirt, posed against a graffiti-scarred wall—"the Dirty Harry of contemporary critical theory," a reviewer in *The Village Voice* called him.

In person, Lentricchia is a lot less intimidating. I found him mild-mannered, easygoing, and surprisingly conventional in his approach to literature. Standing before his modern poetry class in a faded blue work-shirt open at the neck, he made his way through "The Waste Land" just the way professors used to, line by line, pointing out the buried allusions to Ovid and Dante, Marvell and Verlaine. His work is densely theoretical, yet there's nothing doctrinaire about it. What comes through is a devotion to the classics that is more visceral than abstract. "I'm interested in social issues as they bear on literature, but what really interests me is the main-line stuff, like Faulkner," he says after class, popping open a beer—no sherry—on the porch of his comfortable home in the nearby town of Hillsborough. "I'm too American to be a Marxist."

One afternoon I talk with Stanley Fish, the chairman of Duke's English department, in his newly renovated office in the Allen Building. Fish has on slacks and a sports jacket, but he doesn't look any more like Cleanth Brooks—or my image of Cleanth Brooks—than Frank Lentricchia does. He's never been comfortable with the T. S. Eliot tradition, he says, though he's one of the leading Milton scholars in America. Now 50, Fish is maybe a decade older than the generation of radical scholars who came of age in the 60s; but like many of them, he discovered his vocation largely on his own. "You come from a background where there were no books, the son and daughter of immigrants," he says. In such a world, Milton was a first name.

For American Jewish writers who grew up in the Depression, the art critic Clement Greenberg once noted, literature offered "a means of flight from the restriction and squalor of the Brooklyns and Bronxes to the wide open world which rewards the successful fugitive with space, importance and wealth." Making it in those days meant making it on others' terms: in this case, the terms established by tradition-minded English departments dominated by white, Anglo-Saxon Protestants, which even in the 1940s looked with skeptical distaste upon the Jewish assistant professors who were trying to storm the gates.

Diana Trilling has written movingly about the humiliation her celebrated husband, Lionel, suffered at the beginning of his career, when he was briefly banished from Columbia by the English department on the grounds that he was "a Freudian, a Marxist and a Jew." There was nothing subversive about Trilling's ambition; for him, as for Jewish critics like Philip Rahv and Harry Levin, literature was an escape from ethnic identity, not an affirmation of it.

Fish and his radical colleagues are no less ambitious. They, too, aspire to "space, importance and wealth," but on their own terms. Frank Lentricchia has a swimming pool in his backyard. In his work, though, he writes openly and with unashamed ardor, in the autobiographical fashion of the day, about his Italian-American origins, his grandfather in Utica, his working-class Dad. "To become an intellectual from this kind of background means typically to try to forget where you've come from," he writes in "Criticism and Social Change." It means becoming "a cosmopolitan gentleman of the world of letters, philosophy and art." That's not Lentricchia's style. For the scholars of his generation, it's no longer a matter of proving their claim on literature; that struggle has been won. What they're demanding now is a literature that reflects their experience, a literature of their own. "Assimilation is a betrayal," says Fish. "The whole idea of 'Americanness' has been thrown in question."

In a way, this was what the debate at Stanford was about. "If you think we are talking about a handful of good books you are mistaken," Bill King, a senior and president of the university's Black Student Union, declared in an eloquent speech before the faculty senate. "We are discussing the foundations of education in America and the acceptance of Euro-America's place in the world as contributor, not creator." Why had he never been taught that Socrates, Herodotus, Pythagoras and Solon owed much of what they knew to African cultures in Egypt, or that "many of the words of Solomon" were borrowed from the black Pharaoh Amen-En-Eope? Where, in the great scheme of things, were *his* people to be found?

Yet "opening up the canon," as the effort to expand the curriculum is called, isn't as radical as it seems. It's a populist, grassroots phenomenon, American to the core. What could be more democratic than the new "Columbia Library History of the United States," which incorporates Chippewa poems and Whitman's "Song of Myself," Mark Twain and Jay McInerney? There are chapters on Afro-American literature, Mexican-American literature, Asian-American literature, on immigrant writers of the 19th century and slave narratives of the Civil War. "There isn't just one story of American literature," says Emory Elliott, chairman of Princeton's English department and the volume's general editor. "Things are wide open."

❧

No group has been more assiduous in the effort to institutionalize new canonical discoveries than the feminists. Gynocriticism, the study of women's literature, is a flourishing academic field. Catalogues list English department courses in "Feminism, Modernism and Post-Modernism," "Shakespeare and Feminism," "Feminist Theory and the Humanities." Margaret Williams Ferguson of Columbia University teaches a course on "Renaissance Women of Letters"—Christine de Pisan, Mary Sidney, Aphra Behn. "This is just the tip of the iceberg," says Harvard's Marjorie Garber. "These aren't just oddities or curiosities, but major writers."

But the feminist enterprise is more than a matter of introducing works by women into the curriculum, or "mainstreaming." Men and women, it is now believed, have different responses to literature. What is needed, says Princeton's Elaine Showalter, one of the most articulate feminist critics around, is a "defamiliarization of masculinity," "a poetics of the Other"—a critical methodology that addresses gender and sexual difference. On campus bulletin boards I saw notices for lectures on "Coming Unstrung: Women, Men, Narrative and Principles of Pleasures"; "Men's Reading, Women's Writing: Canon-Formation and the Case of the 18th-Century French Novel"; "Abulia: Crises of Male Desire in Freud, Thomas Mann and Musil."

Lit. crit. in the 80s is like child-raising in the 80s: Both sexes share the burden. Lentricchia's work on Wallace Stevens attempts to sort out the poet's attitude toward his own masculinity—to "feminize" his image. At Harvard, Marjorie Garber is at work on a book about "cross-dressing" that discusses Sherlock Holmes, Laurie Anderson, old movies. "There's a lot of work to be done on cross-dressing," she says. Her most recent book is "Shakespeare's Ghost Writers: Literature as Uncanny Causality." "I'll sell you a copy," she offers. "I have a whole box of them." I put down my $14 and read it on the shuttle back to New York.

Garber has written a shrewd, idiosyncratic book, full of curious lore and lively speculation about hidden sexual motifs in Shakespeare's plays. But isn't the focus somewhat narrow? "They're looking for things to write," says Garber's colleague Walter Jackson Bate, the great biographer of Keats and Samuel Johnson. "You can't write the 40th book on the structure of 'Paradise Lost.'" Bate is convinced that the humanities are in "their worst state of crisis since the modern university was formed a century ago—and that specialization is the cause. "The aim and tradition of literature is to give, if possible, the *whole* experience of life."

The idea that literature should reflect our unique identity is "the new academic shibboleth," Gertrude Himmelfarb, a historian and highly visible proponent of the traditional curriculum, objected last month on the Op-Ed page of *The New York Times*. "It used to be thought that ideas transcend race, gender and class, that there are such things as truth, reason, morality and artistic excellence, which can be understood and aspired to by everyone, of whatever race, gender or class." Now we have democracy in the syllabus, affirmative action in the classroom. "No one believes in greatness," Bate says mournfully. "That's gone."

All these "texts" that are being rediscovered, republished, "revalorized"—the sermons and spinsters' diaries, the popular fiction of 1850: Are any of them neglected masterpieces? Jane Tompkins makes a persuasive case for the merits of Susan Warner's "The Wide, Wide World" (reissued last year in paperback by the Feminist Press), and it *is* a powerful book. The story of a young woman orphaned and exiled to bullying relatives in Scotland, Warner's novel portrays an experience of physical and spiritual renunciation that was obviously familiar to its 19th-century audience. The writing is energetic and vivid, and the humiliations endured by the heroine recall the trials of Lily Bart in Edith Wharton's "The House of Mirth" or Dreiser's "Sister Carrie." Only how do you know whether a book is "good" or not? Who decides and by what criteria? There are no universals, Tomkins insists: "It is the context—which eventually includes the work itself—that creates the value its readers 'discover' there." The critic is only part of the story.

What the Duke critics discovered was "the historicization of value," says Stanley Fish. It's not that texts have no literal meaning, as the deconstructors who dominated literary studies in the 1970s believed; they have "an infinite plurality of meanings." The only way that we can hope to interpret a literary work is by knowing the vantage from which we perform the act of interpretation—in contemporary parlance, where we're coming from.

Barbara Herrnstein Smith, a power at Duke and a specialist in matters canonical, has written the definitive text on value relativity. "Contingencies of Value," to be published this fall by Harvard University Press, is an exasperating book, especially in the first chapter, where Smith goes on about her life as a professor, and claims to be so close to Shakespeare's sonnets that "there have been times when I believed that I had written them myself." Still, for all her confessional posturing, her self-professed "monstrous" immodesty, Smith is on to something. What is taste? What do we experience when we contemplate a work of art? Like Fish, Smith is less interested in the status of a given work than in how that status is established. Who decides what's in and what's out? Those who possess "cultural power." What is art? Whatever the literary establishment says it is.

Smith's recent work is, among other things, a shrewd polemic against "high-culture critics" intent upon "epistemic self-stabilization" (that is to say, maintaining the status quo). Just who are these critics? A tribe of "non-acculturated intellectuals," "post-modern cosmopolites," "exotic visitors and immigrants." In other words, professors. The vanguard of this new professoriate has transformed the landscape of contemporary literature. Many of them are tenured; they publish books. So why do they cultivate an image of themselves as literary outlaws? Frank Lentricchia isn't the only heavy academic dude around. D. A. Miller, a professor of comparative literature at Berkeley, has adorned his latest book with a photograph that mimes Lentricchia's notorious pose on the back of "Criticism and Social Change"—biceps rippling, arms folded across his chest like Mr. Clean.

Lentricchia's new book is titled "Ariel and the Police." Miller's is "The Novel and the Police." Both are ostensibly works of literary criticism—Lentricchia is writing largely about William James and Michel Foucault; Miller about the Victorian novel—but their real subject is the repressive nature of society, power and the containment of power, how our culture "polices" us. "Where are the police in 'Barchester Towers' (1857)?" Miller asks in a chapter on Trollope. Where, indeed? They're "literally nowhere to be found. . . ." But not so fast. Their very absence is significant, Miller claims, proof that Victorian England was a repressed society. The novel, then, is a form of concealment as well as of disclosure. Its truths are latent, murky, undeclared. Miller's own aim as a critic is to "bring literature out of the classroom and into the closet."

What's going on here? Reading between the lines, one begins to get the message. The questioning of authority that's such a pervasive theme in criticism now is a theoretical version of the battles that were fought on campuses 20 years ago—with real police. "The new epistemology—structuralism, deconstruction—provided the interpretive framework for challenging the canon," says Tompkins. "It's out in the hinterlands now. It's everywhere."

How will the New Canonicity—to coin a term—affect the way literature is taught in America? What will students in the next generation read? It would be presumptuous to guess. But at least the debate has focused public attention on books—not an easy thing to do. "It's an issue that's made literary studies suddenly vital and exciting," says Gerald Graff. The struggle over who belongs in the canon and what it means is more than a literary matter, Tompkins asserts. "It is a struggle among contending factions for the right to be represented in the picture America draws of itself."

From

The Storm Over the University

(1990)

John Searle

In his review of several books on the state of higher education, University of California, Berkeley, philosopher John Searle took a cool and balanced view of mounting discord on campuses. The result was a remarkably clear line of thought about the state of the nation's colleges and universities—and exposition of the ideological contests troubling them.

I cannot recall a time when American education was not in a "crisis." We have lived through Sputnik (when we were "falling behind the Russians"), through the era of "Johnny can't read," and through the upheavals of the Sixties. Now a good many books are telling us that the university is going to hell in several different directions at once. I believe that, at least in part, the crisis rhetoric has a structural explanation: since we do not have a national consensus on what success in higher education would consist of, no matter what happens, some sizable part of the population is going to regard the situation as a disaster. As with taxation and relations between the sexes, higher education is essentially and continuously contested territory. Given the history of that crisis rhetoric, one's natural response to the current cries of desperation might reasonably be one of boredom.

A few years ago the literature of educational crises was changed by a previously little-known professor of philosophy at the University of Chicago in a book implausibly entitled *The Closing of the American Mind: How Higher Education Has Failed Democracy and Impoverished the Souls of Today's Students*. To me, the amazing thing about Allan Bloom's book was not just its prodigious commercial success—more than half a year at the top of *The New York Times*'s best-seller list—but the depth of the hostility and even hatred that it inspired among a large number of professors. Most of Bloom's book is not about higher education as such, but consists of an idiosyncratic, often original, and even sometimes profound—as well as quirky and cranky—analysis of contemporary American intellectual culture, with an emphasis on the unacknowledged and largely unconscious influence of certain German thinkers, especially Weber and Nietzsche.

Why did Bloom's book arouse such passion? I will suggest an explanation later in this article, but it is worth noting that Bloom demonstrated to publishers and potential authors one thesis beyond doubt: it is possible to write an alarmist book about the state of higher education and a long-winded title and make a great deal of money. This consequence appears to provide at least part of the inspiration for a number of other books, equally alarmist and with almost equally heavy-duty titles, for example *The Moral Collapse of the University, Professionalism, Purity and Alienation,* by Bruce Wilshire; *Killing the Spirit: Higher Education in America,* by Page Smith; *Tenured Radicals: How Politics Has Corrupted Our Higher Education,* by Roger Kimball; and *The Moral and Spiritual Crisis in Education: A Curriculum for Justice and Compassion in Education,* by David E. Purpel.

One difficulty with the more alarmist of these books is that though they agree that the universities are in a desperate state, they do not agree on what is wrong or what to do about it. When there is no agreement not only on the cure, but on the diagnosis itself, it is very hard to treat the patient. Another weakness of such books is their sometimes hysterical tone. There are, indeed, many problems in the universities, but for the most part, they tend to produce silliness rather than catastrophe. The spread of "poststructuralist" literary theory is perhaps the best known example of a silly but noncatastrophic phenomenon. Several of these books try to describe current threats to intellectual values. How serious are these threats? Right now we can't tell with any certainty because we can't yet know to what extent we are dealing with temporary fads and fashions or with long-term assaults on the integrity of the intellectual enterprise.

I think the best way to enter this discussion is by examining at least briefly the current debate about the status of what is called the "canon" of the best works in our civilization, and what part the canon should play in the education of undergraduates. . . .

Consider what would have been taken to be a platitude a couple of decades ago, and is now regarded in many places as a wildly reactionary view. Here it is: there is a certain Western intellectual tradition that goes from, say, Socrates to Wittgenstein in philosophy, and from Homer to

James Joyce in literature, and it is essential to the liberal education of young men and women in the United States that they should receive some exposure to at least some of the great works in this intellectual tradition; they should, in Matthew Arnold's over-quoted words, "know the best that is known and thought in the world." The arguments given for this view—on the rare occasions when it was felt that arguments were even needed—were that knowledge of the tradition was essential to the self-understanding of educated Americans since the country, in an important sense, is the product of that tradition; that many of these works are historically important because of their influence; and that most of them, for example several works by Plato and Shakespeare, are of very high intellectual and artistic quality, to the point of being of universal human interest.

Until recently such views were not controversial. What exactly is the debate about? The question is more complex than one might think because of the variety of different objections to the tradition and the lack of any succinct statement of these objections. For example, many African Americans and Hispanic Americans feel left out of the "canon," and want to be included. Just as a few years ago they were demanding the creation of ethnic studies departments, so now they are demanding some representation of their experiences and their point of view as part of the general education of all undergraduates. This looks like a standard political demand for "representation" of the sort we are familiar with in higher education. If the objection to the "canon" is that it consists almost entirely of works by white males, specifically white males of European (including North American) origin, then there would appear to be an easy and common-sense solution to the problem: simply open the doors to admit the work of talented writers who are not white, or not male, or not European. If, for example, the contribution of women in literature has been neglected, there are plenty of writers of similar stature to Jane Austen, George Eliot, and Virginia Woolf who can be added.

Some of the opponents of the tradition will accept this reform, but most of the authors of *The Politics of Liberal Education* [a collection of essays resulting from a conference sponsored by Duke University and the University of North Carolina] would not, and you will have misunderstood the nature of the dispute if you think that it can be resolved so simply. The central objections to the tradition are deeper and more radical, and they go far beyond the mere demand for increased representation. What are these objections?

To approach this question, I have selected the proceedings of the North Carolina conference not because they contain any notable or original ideas—such conferences seldom do—but because they express a mode of literary and political sensibility that has become fairly widespread in some university departments in the humanities and is characterized approvingly by some of the participants at the conference as "the cultural left." I doubt that "the cultural left" is a well-defined notion because it includes so many altogether different points of view. It includes 1960s-style radicals, feminists, deconstructionists, Marxists, people active in "gay studies" and "ethnic studies," and people of left-wing political persuasion who happen to teach in universities. But on certain basic issues of education these groups tend to agree. In describing the North Carolina conference in his concluding statement Richard Rorty writes:

> Our conference has been in large part a rally of this cultural left. The audience responded readily and favorably to notions like "subversive readings," "hegemonic discourse," "the breaking down of traditional logocentric hierarchies," and so on. It chortled derisively at mentions of William Bennett, Allan Bloom, and E. D. Hirsch, Jr., and nodded respectfully at the names of Nietzsche, Derrida, Gramsci, or Foucault.

Whether or not Rorty is justified in using the label, the views expressed show a remarkable consensus in their opposition to the educational tradition and in their hostility to those who, like Bloom, have supported a version of the tradition. Here are some typical passages:

Mary Louise Pratt, a professor of comparative literature at Stanford, writes,

> Bloom, Bennett, Bellow, and the rest (known by now in some quarters as the Killer B's) are advocating [the creation of] a narrowly specific cultural capital that will be the normative *referent* for everyone, but will remain the *property* of a small and powerful caste that is linguistically and ethnically unified. It is this caste that is referred to by the "we" in Saul Bellow's astoundingly racist remark that "when the Zulus have a Tolstoy, *we* will read him." Few doubt that behind the Bennett-Bloom program is a desire to close not the American mind, but the American university, to all but a narrow and highly uniform elite with no commitment to either multiculturalism or educational democracy. Thus while the Killer B's (plus a C—Lynne Cheney, the Bennett mouthpiece now heading the National Endowment for the Humanities) depict themselves as returning to the orthodoxies

of yesteryear, their project must not be reduced to nostalgia or conservatism. Neither of these explain the blanket contempt they express for the country's universities. They are fueled not by reverence for the past, but by an aggressive desire to lay hold of the present and future. The B's act as they do not because they are unaware of the cultural and demographic diversification underway in the country; they are utterly aware. That is what they are trying to shape; that is why they are seeking, and using, national offices and founding national foundations.

Pratt laments "the West's relentless imperial expansion" and the "monumentalist cultural hierarchy that is historically as well as morally distortive" and goes on to characterize Bloom's book as "intellectually deplorable" and Bennett's *To Reclaim a Legacy* as "intellectually more deplorable." In the same vein, Henry A. Giroux, a professor of education at Miami University of Ohio, writes:

> In the most general sense, Bloom and Hirsch represent the latest cultural offensive by the new elitists to rewrite the past and construct the present from the perspective of the privileged and the powerful. They disdain the democratic implications of pluralism and argue for a form of cultural uniformity in which difference is consigned to the margins of history or to the museum of the disadvantaged.

And according to Henry Louis Gates, Jr., a professor of English at Duke:

> The teaching of literature [has become] the teaching of an aesthetic and political order, in which no women and people of color were ever able to discover the reflection or representation of their images, or hear the resonance of their cultural voices. The return of "the" canon, the high canon of Western masterpieces, represents the return of an order in which my people were the subjugated, the voiceless, the invisible, the unrepresented, and the unrepresentable. Who would return us to that medieval never-never land?

Anybody who has been to such a conference will recognize the atmosphere. It is only within such a setting that Bloom and Hirsch (one a professor of philosophy in Chicago, the other a professor of English in Virginia) can seem (to people who are themselves professors somewhere) to exemplify "the privileged and the powerful."

One of the conferees, Gerald Graff of Northwestern, writes: "Speaking as a leftist, I too find it tempting to try to turn the curriculum into an instrument of social transformation." He goes on to resist the temptation with the following (italics mine): "But I doubt whether the curriculum (*as opposed to my particular courses*) can or should become an extension of the politics of the left."

It turns out that he objects to politicizing the entire curriculum not because there might be something immoral about using the classroom to impose a specific ideology on students, but because of the unfortunate fact that universities also contain professors who are not "leftists" and who do not want their courses to become "an extension of the politics of the left"; and there seems to be no answer to the question, "What is to be done with those constituencies which do not happen to agree . . . that social transformation is the primary goal of education." What indeed?

I said earlier that it was difficult to find a succinct statement of the objections to the educational tradition made by the so-called cultural left, but this is largely because the objections are taken for granted. If you read enough material of the sort I have quoted, and, more importantly, if you attend enough of these conferences, it is easy to extract the central objection. It runs something like this: the history of "Western Civilization" is in a large part a history of oppression. Internally, Western civilization oppressed women, various slave and serf populations, and ethnic and cultural minorities generally. In foreign affairs, the history of Western civilization is one of imperialism and colonialism. The so-called canon of Western civilization consists in the official publications of this system of oppression, and it is no accident that the authors in the "canon" are almost exclusively Western white males, because the civilization itself is ruled by a caste consisting almost entirely of Western white males. So you cannot reform education by admitting new members to the club, by opening up the canon; the whole idea of "the canon" has to be abolished. It has to be abolished in favor of something that is "multicultural" and "nonhierarchical."

The word "nonhierarchical" in the last sentence is important and I will come back to it. In the meantime I hope I have given enough of the arguments from those who oppose the traditional conceptions of liberal education to make it clear why the dispute cannot be resolved just by opening up the club to new members, and why it seems so intractable. Even if the canon is opened up, even if membership in the club is thrown open to all comers, even after you have admitted every first-rate woman writer from Sappho to Elizabeth Bishop, the various groups that feel that they have been excluded are still going to feel excluded, or marginalized. At present there are still going to be too many Western white males.

The actual arguments given often speak of improving education, but the central presuppositions of each side are seldom explicitly stated. With few exceptions, those who defend the traditional conception of a liberal education with a core curriculum think that Western civilization in general, and the United States in particular, have on the whole been the source of valuable institutions that should be preserved and of traditions that should be transmitted, emphatically including the intellectual tradition of skeptical critical analysis. Those who think that the traditional canon should be abandoned believe that Western civilization in general, and the United States in particular, are in large part oppressive, imperialist, patriarchal, hegemonic, and in need of replacement, or at least of transformation. So the passionate objections that are made by the critics to Allan Bloom often have rather little to do with a theory of higher education as such. (This is unfortunate, because there is plenty to object to in Bloom's book on purely educational grounds—for example, its failure to give sufficient attention or value to the study of history and its blindness to the achievements of contemporary analytic philosophy.) Their objection to the educational tradition is intended to make a political point about the nature of American society.

There is a certain irony in this in that earlier student generations, my own for example, found the critical tradition that runs from Socrates through the *Federalist Papers,* through the writings of Mill and Marx, down to the twentieth century, to be liberating from the stuffy conventions of traditional American politics and pieties. Precisely by inculcating a critical attitude, the "canon" served to demythologize the conventional pieties of the American bourgeoisie and provided the student with a perspective from which to critically analyze American culture and institutions. Ironically, the same tradition is now regarded as oppressive. The texts once served an unmasking function; now we are told that it is the texts which must be unmasked.

More puzzling than the hatred of Bloom is the hostility shown to E. D. Hirsch, Jr. After all, Hirsch's central idea is that it would be desirable for American schoolchildren to be taught a common body of knowledge, a set of elementary facts and concepts that Hirsch calls "cultural literacy." (Among the texts and ideas he believes should be "explained in depth" are, for example, the Bill of Rights, *Don Quixote,* and ecology.) It is hard to imagine how anybody could object to such an innocuous proposal for improving education in the grade schools and high schools. However, even this is greeted with rage; indeed, only Bloom and Bennett arouse more anger than Hirsch in these polemics. In a savage attack, Barbara

Herrnstein Smith quotes Hirsch as saying that his project of cultural literacy will result in

> breaking the cycle of illiteracy for deprived children; raising the living standards of families who have been illiterate; making our country more competitive in international markets; achieving greater social justice; enabling all citizens to participate in the political process; bringing us that much closer to the Ciceronian ideal of universal public discourse—in short, achieving the fundamental goals of the Founders at the birth of the republic.

To this project, she responds:

> Wild applause; fireworks; music—*America the Beautiful;* all together, now: *Calvin Coolidge, Gunga Din, Peter Pan, spontaneous combustion.* Hurrah for America and the national culture! Hurrah!

Why the hysterical tone of opposition? Herrnstein Smith reveals her own preoccupations when she says that Hirsch is "promoting a *deeply conservative view of American society and culture* through a rousing populist rhetoric" (my italics). But of course there is no reason at all why students who become familiar with the range of facts and ideas compiled by Hirsch should not arrive at "radical" or "liberal" or other positions.

But what about the question of intellectual excellence? The very ideal of excellence implied in the canon is itself perceived as a threat. It is considered "elitist" and "hierarchical" to suppose that "intellectual excellence" should take precedence over such considerations as fairness, representativeness, the expression of the experiences of previously underrepresented minorities, etc. Indeed, in the recent debate at Stanford about the course in Western civilization, one of the arguments against the traditional curriculum (quoted with approval by Pratt) went as follows:

> A course with such readings creates two sets of books, those privileged by being on the list and those not worthy of inclusion. Regardless of the good intentions of those who create such lists, the students have not viewed and will not view these separate categories as equal.

I find this an amazing argument. One obvious difficulty with it is that if it were valid, it would argue against any set of required readings whatever;

indeed, any list you care to make about anything automatically creates two categories, those that are on the list and those that are not.

One curious feature of the entire debate about what is "hegemonic," "patriarchal," or "exclusionary" is that it is largely about the study of literature. No one seems to complain that the great ideas in physics, mathematics, chemistry, and biology, for example, also come in large part from dead white European males. Historians of science have been showing how talented women were discouraged throughout modern history from pursuing scientific careers. But I have not heard any complaints from physics departments that the ideas of Newton, Einstein, Rutherford, Bohr, Schrödinger, etc., were deficient because of the scientists' origins or gender. Even in history of philosophy courses—as opposed to general education courses—there is little or no objection to the fact that the great philosophers taught in these courses are mostly white Western males, from Socrates, Plato and Aristotle through Frege, Russell, and Wittgenstein.

No doubt literature articulates the variety of human experience in ways that are unlike those of the sciences, but that is not enough by itself to explain the selective attitude that causes the humanities to be treated so differently from the sciences. To understand this difference you have to understand a second fundamental, but usually unstated, feature of the debate: in addition to having political objections to the United States and Europe, many members of the cultural left think that the primary function of teaching the humanities is political; they do not really believe that the humanities are valuable in their own right except as a means of achieving "social transformation." They (apparently) accept that in subjects like physics and mathematics there may be objective and socially independent criteria of excellence (though they do not say much about the sciences at all), but where the humanities are concerned they think that the criteria that matter are essentially political. The argument goes: since any policy in the humanities will inevitably have a political dimension, courses in the humanities might as well be explicitly and beneficially political, instead of being disguised vehicles of oppression. These points are often stated in a kind of code. (In the code, to be "monumentalist" is to treat some works as if they were monuments, and to be "hierarchical" is to think that some works are better than others; I think "critical" used to mean vaguely Marxist as in some versions of "critical legal studies" but now it appears just to mean politically radical, as "critical pedagogy.")

For example, after having told us that "the most important questions facing both the liberal arts and higher education in general are moral and political" and that the university "is a place that is deeply political" Henry Giroux tells us the following about how we should teach "the canon":

How we read or define a "canonical" work may not be as important as challenging the overall function and social uses the
notion of the canon has served. Within this type of discourse,
the canon can be analyzed as part of a wider set of relations that
connect the academic disciplines, teaching, and power to considerations defined through broader, intersecting political and
cultural concerns such as race, class, gender, ethnicity, and
nationalism. What is in question here is not merely a defense of
a particular canon, but the issue of struggle and empowerment.
In other words, the liberal arts should be defended in the interest of creating critical rather than "good" citizens. The notion of
the liberal arts has to be reconstituted around a knowledge-
power relationship in which the question of curriculum is seen
as a form of cultural and political production grounded in a radical conception of citizenship and public wisdom.

He concludes that this transformation of our attitudes toward the tradition
will link the liberal arts to "the imperatives of a critical democracy."

Notwithstanding its opaque prose, Giroux's message should be clear:
the aim of a liberal education is to create political radicals, and the main
point of reading the "canon" is to demythologize it by showing how it is
used as a tool by the existing system of oppression. The traditional argument that the humanities are the core of a liberal education because of
the intrinsic intellectual and aesthetic merits and importance of the
works of Plato, Shakespeare, or Dante is regarded with scorn. Giroux
again:

The liberal arts cannot be defended either as a self-contained
discourse legitimating the humanistic goal of broadly improving the so-called "life of the mind" or as a rigorous science that
can lead students to indubitable truths.

So the frustrating feature of the recent debate is that the underlying
issues seldom come out into the open. Unless you accept two assumptions, that the Western tradition is oppressive, and that the main purpose
of teaching the humanities is political transformation, the explicit arguments given against the canon will seem weak: that the canon is unrepre-
sentative, inherently elitist, and, in a disguised form, political. Indeed if
these arguments were strong ones, you could apply them against physics,
chemistry, or mathematics.

From the point of view of the tradition, the answers to each argument are fairly obvious. First, it is not the aim of education to provide a

representation or sample of everything that has been thought and written, but to give students access to works of high quality. Second, for that very reason, education is by its very nature "elitist" and "hierarchical" because it is designed to enable and encourage the student to discriminate between what is good and what is bad, what is intelligent and what is stupid, what is true and what is false. Third, the "tradition" is by no means a unified phenomenon, and properly taught, it should impart a critical attitude to the student, precisely because of the variety and intellectual independence of the works being taught, and the disagreements among them. Fourth, of course the humanities have a political dimension at least in the sense that they have political consequences; so does everything else. But it does not follow from the fact that there is a political dimension to the humanities—as there is to music, art, gastronomy, and sex, as well as mathematics, philosophy, and physics—that the only, or even the principal, criteria for assessing these efforts should be political ones.

PART VI

The Movement of Culture

From

After Virtue

(1981)

Alasdair MacIntyre

This conclusion to MacIntyre's philosophy book drew much scholarly attention for its original inquiry into the future—and its final, ominous prediction. Here MacIntyre reiterates the impact of Nietzschean convictions on mass morality and modern thinking. At the time this book was written, the German philosopher's unparalleled significance on twentieth-century thought and feeling was seldom considered among intellectuals or cultural observers, a state of affairs that would change during the eighties.

Nietzsche *or* Aristotle? The argument which leads to that question had two central premises. The first was that the language—and therefore also to some large degree the practice—of morality today is in a state of grave disorder. That disorder arises from the prevailing cultural power of an idiom in which ill-assorted conceptual fragments from various parts of our past are deployed together in private and public debates which are notable chiefly for the unsettlable character of the controversies thus carried on and the apparent arbitrariness of each of the contending parties.

The second was that ever since belief in Aristotelian teleology was discredited moral philosophers have attempted to provide some alternative rational secular account of the nature and status of morality, but that all these attempts, various and variously impressive as they have been, have in fact failed, a failure perceived most clearly by Nietzsche. Consequently Nietzsche's negative proposal to raze to the ground the structures of inherited moral belief and argument had, whether we have regard to everyday moral belief and argument or look instead to the constructions of moral philosophers, and in spite of its desperate and grandiose quality, a certain plausibility—unless of course the initial rejection of the moral tradition to which Aristotle's teaching about the virtues is central turned out to have been misconceived and mistaken. Unless that tradition could be rationally vindicated, Nietzsche's stance would have a terrible plausibility.

Not that, even so, it would be easy in the contemporary world to be an intelligent Nietzschean. The stock characters acknowledged in the dramas of modern social life embody all too well the concepts and the modes of the moral beliefs and arguments which an Aristotelian and a Nietzschean would have to agree in rejecting. The bureaucratic manager, the consuming aesthete, the therapist, the protester and their numerous kindred occupy almost all the available culturally recognizable roles; the notions of the expertise of the few and of the moral agency of everyone are the presuppositions of the dramas which those characters enact. To cry out that the emperor had no clothes on was at least to pick on one man only to the amusement of everyone else; to declare that almost everyone is dressed in rags is much less likely to be popular. But the Nietzschean would at least have the consolation of being unpopularly *in the right*—unless, that is, the rejection of the Aristotelian tradition turned out to have been mistaken.

The Aristotelian tradition has occupied two distinct places in any argument: first, because I have suggested that a great part of modern morality is intelligible only as a set of fragmented survivals from that tradition, and indeed that the inability of modern moral philosophers to carry through their projects of analysis and justification is closely connected with the fact that the concepts with which they work are a combination of fragmented survival and implausible modern inventions; but in addition to this the rejection of the Aristotelian tradition was a rejection of a quite distinctive kind of morality in which rules, so predominant in modern conceptions of morality, find their place in a larger scheme in which the virtues have the central place; hence the cogency of the Nietzschean rejection and refutation of modern moralities of rules, whether of a utilitarian or of a Kantian kind, did not necessarily extend to the earlier Aristotelian tradition.

It is one of my most important contentions that against that tradition the Nietzschean polemic is completely unsuccessful. The grounds for saying this can be set out in two different ways. . . . Nietzsche succeeds if all those whom he takes on as antagonists fail. Others may have to succeed by virtue of the rational power of their positive arguments; but if Nietzsche wins, he wins by default.

He does not win. [A] rational case . . . can be made for a tradition in which the Aristotelian moral and political texts are canonical. For

Nietzsche or the Nietzscheans to succeed that case would have to be rebutted. Why it cannot be so rebutted is best brought out by considering a second way in which the rejection of Nietzsche's claims can be argued. Nietzschean man, the *Übermensch,* the man who transcends, finds his good nowhere in the social world to date, but only in that in himself which dictates his own new law and his own new table of the virtues. Why does he never find any objective good with authority over him in the social world to date? The answer is not difficult: Nietzsche's portrait makes it clear that he who transcends is wanting in respect of both relationships and activities. Consider part of just one note (962) from *The Will to Power.* "A great man—a man whom nature has constructed and invented in the grand style—what is he? . . . If he cannot lead, he goes alone; then it can happen that he may snarl at some things he meets on the way. . . he wants no 'sympathetic' heart, but servants, tools; in his intercourse with men he is always intent on *making* something out of them. He knows he is incommunicable: he finds it tasteless to be familiar; and when one thinks he is, he usually is not. When not speaking to himself, he wears a mask. He rather lies than tells the truth: it requires more spirit and *will*. There is a solitude within him that is inaccessible to praise or blame, his own justice that is beyond appeal."

This characterization of "the great man" is deeply rooted in Nietzsche's contention that the morality of European society since the archaic age in Greece has been nothing but a series of disguises for the will to power and that the claim to objectivity for such morality cannot be rationally sustained. It is because this is so that the great man cannot enter into relationships mediated by appeal to shared standards or virtues or goods; he is his own only authority and his relationships to others have to be exercises of that authority. But we can now see clearly that, if the account of the virtues which I have defended can be sustained, it is the isolation and self-absorption of "the great man" which thrust upon him the burden of being his own self-sufficient moral authority. For if the conception of a good has to be expounded in terms of such actions as those of a practice, of the narrative unity of a human life and of a moral tradition, then goods, and with them the only grounds for the authority of laws and virtues, can only be discovered by entering into those relationships which constitute communities whose central bond is a shared vision of and understanding of goods. To cut oneself off from shared activity in which one has initially to learn obediently as an apprentice learns, to isolate oneself from the communities which find their point and purpose in such activities, will be to debar oneself from finding any good outside of oneself. It will be to condemn oneself to that moral solipsism which constitutes Nietzschean greatness. Hence we have to conclude not only that Nietzsche does not win the argument by default against the Aristotelian tradition, but also, and perhaps more importantly, that it is from the perspective of that tradition that we can best understand the mistakes at the heart of the Nietzschean position.

The attractiveness of Nietzsche's position lay in its apparent honesty. When I was setting out the case in favour of an amended and restated emotivism, it appeared to be a consequence of accepting the truth of emotivism that an honest man would no longer want to go on using most, at least, of the language of past morality because of its misleading character. And Nietzsche was the only major philosopher who had not flinched from this conclusion. Since moreover the language of modern morality is burdened with pseudo-concepts such as those of utility and of natural rights, it appeared that Nietzsche's resoluteness alone would rescue us from entanglement by such concepts; but it is now clear that the price to be paid for this liberation is entanglement in another set of mistakes. The concept of the Nietzschean "great man" is also a pseudo-concept, although not always perhaps—unhappily—what I [have] called a fiction. It represents individualism's final attempt to escape from its own consequences. And the Nietzschean stance turns out not to be a mode of escape from or an alternative to the conceptual scheme of liberal individualist modernity, but rather one more representative moment in its internal unfolding. And we may therefore expect liberal individualist societies to breed "great men" from time to time. Alas!

So it was right to see Nietzsche as in some sense the ultimate antagonist of the Aristotelian tradition. But it now turns out to be the case that in the end the Nietzschean stance is only one more facet of that very moral culture of which Nietzsche took himself to be an implacable critic. It is therefore after all the case that the crucial moral opposition is between liberal individualism in some version or other and the Aristotelian tradition in some version or other.

The differences between the two run very deep. They extend beyond ethics and morality to the understanding of human action, so that rival conceptions of the social sciences, of their limits and their possibilities, are intimately bound up with the antagonistic confrontation of these two alternative ways of viewing the human world. This is why my argument has had to extend to such topics as those of the concept of fact, the limits to predictability in human affairs and the nature of ideology. . . .

My own conclusion is very clear. It is that on the one hand we still, in spite of the efforts of three centuries of moral philosophy and one of sociology, lack any coherent rationally defensible statement of a liberal individualist point of view; and that, on the other hand, the Aristotelian tradition can be restated in a way that restores intelligibility and rationality to our moral and social attitudes and commitments. But although I take the weight and direction of both sets of arguments to be rationally compelling, it would be imprudent not to recognize three quite different kinds of objection that will be advanced from three quite different points of view against this conclusion.

. . . A motley party of defenders of liberal individualism—-some of them utilitarians, some Kantians, some proudly avowing the cause of liberal individualism as I have defined it, others claiming that it is misinterpretation to associate them with my account of it, all of them disagreeing among themselves—are likely to offer objections . . .

A second set of objections will certainly concern my interpretation of what I have called the Aristotelian or classical tradition. For it is clear that the account I have given differs in a variety of ways, some of them quite radical, from other appropriations and interpretations of an Aristotelian moral stance. And here I am disagreeing to some extent at least with some of those philosophers for whom I have the greatest respect and from whom I have learned most (but not nearly enough, their adherents will say): in the immediate past Jacques Maritain, in the present Peter Geach. Yet if my account of the nature of moral tradition is correct, a tradition is sustained and advanced by its own internal arguments and conflicts. And even if some large parts of my interpretation could not withstand criticism, the demonstration of this would itself strengthen the tradition which I am attempting to sustain and to extend. Hence my attitude to those criticisms which I take to be internal to the moral tradition which I am defending is rather different from my attitude to purely external criticisms. The latter are no less important; but they are important in a different way.

Thirdly there will certainly be a quite different set of critics who will begin by agreeing substantially with what I have to say about liberal individualism, but who will deny not only that the Aristotelian tradition is a viable alternative, but also that it is in terms of an opposition between liberal individualism and that tradition that the problems of modernity ought to be approached. The key intellectual opposition of our age, such critics will declare, is that between liberal individualism and some version of Marxism or neo-Marxism. The most intellectually compelling exponents of this point of view are likely to be those who trace a genealogy of ideas from Kant and Hegel through Marx and claim that by means of Marxism the notion of human autonomy can be rescued from its original individualist formulations and restored within the context of an appeal to a possible form of community in which alienation has been overcome, false consciousness abolished and the values of equality and fraternity realised. My answers to the third type of criticism need to be spelled out a little further. They fall into two parts.

The first is that the claim of Marxism to a morally distinctive standpoint is undermined by Marxism's own moral history. In all those crises in which Marxists have had to take explicit moral stances—that over Bernstein's revisionism in German social democracy at the turn of the century or that over Khruschev's repudiation of Stalin and the Hungarian revolt in 1956, for example—Marxists have always fallen back into relatively straightforward versions of Kantianism or utilitarianism. Nor is this surprising. Secreted within Marxism from the outset is a certain radical individualism. In the first chapter of *Capital* when Marx characterizes what it will be like "when the practical relations of everyday life offer to man none but perfectly intelligible and reasonable relations" what he pictures is "a community of free individuals" who have all freely agreed to their common ownership of the means of production and to various norms of production and distribution. This free individual is described by Marx as a socialised Robinson Crusoe; but on what basis he enters into his free association with others Marx does not tell us. At this key point in Marxism there is a lacuna which no later Marxist has adequately supplied. It is unsurprising that abstract moral principle and utility have in fact been the principles of association which Marxists have appealed to, and that in their practice Marxists have exemplified precisely the kind of moral attitude which they condemn in others as ideological.

Secondly . . . as Marxists move towards power they always tend to become Weberians. Here I [am] of course speaking of Marxists at their best in, say Yugoslavia or Italy; the barbarous despotism of the collective Tsardom which reigns in Moscow can be taken to be as irrelevant to the question of the moral substance of Marxism as the life of the Borgia pope was to that of the moral substance of Christianity. None the less Marxism has recommended itself precisely as a guide to practice, as a politics of a peculiarly illuminating kind. Yet it is just here that it has been of singularly little help for some time now. Trotsky, in the very last years of his life, facing the question of whether the Soviet Union was in any sense a socialist country, also faced implicitly the question of whether the categories of Marxism could illuminate the future. He himself made everything turn on the outcome of a set of hypothetical predictions about possible future events in the Soviet Union, predictions which were tested only after Trotsky's death. The answer that they returned was clear: Trotsky's own premises entailed that the Soviet Union was not socialist and that the theory which was to have illuminated the path to human liberation had in fact led into darkness.

Marxist socialism is at its core deeply optimistic. For however thorough-going its criticism of capitalist and bourgeois institutions may be, it is committed to asserting that within the society constituted by those institutions, all the human and material preconditions of a better future are being accumulated. Yet if the moral impoverishment of advanced capitalism is what so many Marxists agree that it is, whence are these resources for the future to be derived? It is not surprising that at this point Marxism tends to produce its own versions of the *Übermensch*: Lukacs's ideal proletarian, Leninism's ideal revolutionary. When Marxism does not become Weberian social democracy or crude tyranny, it tends to become Nietzschean fantasy. One of the most admirable aspects of Trotsky's cold resolution was his refusal of all such fantasies.

A Marxist who took Trotsky's last writings with great seriousness would be forced into a pessimism quite alien to the Marxist tradition, and in becoming a pessimist he would in an important way have ceased to be a Marxist. For he would now see no tolerable alternative set of political and economic structures which could be brought into place to replace the structures of advanced capitalism. This conclusion agrees of course with my own. For I too not only take it that Marxism is exhausted as a *political* tradition, a claim borne out by the almost indefinitely numerous and conflicting range of political allegiances which now carry Marxist banners—this does not at all imply that Marxism is not still one of the richest sources of ideas about modern society—but I believe that this exhaustion is shared by every other political tradition within our culture. . . . Does it then follow more specifically that the moral tradition which I am defending lacks any contemporary politics of relevance and more generally that my argument commits me and anyone else who accepts it to a generalised social pessimism? Not at all.

It is always dangerous to draw too precise parallels between one historical period and another; and among the most misleading of such parallels are those which have been drawn between our own age in Europe and North America and the epoch in which the Roman empire declined into the Dark Ages. None the less certain parallels there are. A crucial turning point in that earlier history occurred when men and women of good will turned aside from the task of shoring up the Roman *imperium* and ceased to identify the continuation of civility and moral community with the maintenance of that *imperium*. What they set themselves to achieve instead—often not recognising fully what they were doing—was the construction of new forms of community within which the moral life could be sustained so that both morality and civility might survive the coming ages of barbarism and darkness. If my account of our moral condition is correct, we ought also to conclude that for some time now we too have reached that turning point. What matters at this stage is the construction of local forms of community within which civility and the intellectual and moral life can be sustained through the new dark ages which are already upon us. And if the tradition of the virtues was able to survive the horrors of the last dark ages, we are not entirely without grounds for hope. This time however the barbarians are not waiting beyond the frontiers; they have already been governing us for quite some time. And it is our lack of consciousness of this that constitutes part of our predicament. We are waiting not for a Godot, but for another—doubtless very different—St. Benedict.

The Worship of Art
(1983)
Tom Wolfe

In a material world, Wolfe argued, the art museum was the new cathedral where spiritual hungers were satisfied. Wolfe's comedic tour de force had a serious underlying premise—that for the culturally ambitious, works of art had become objects of devotion and that art was "the new religion of the educated classes."

Let me tell you about the night the Vatican art show opened at the Metropolitan Museum of Art in New York. The scene was the Temple of Dendur, an enormous architectural mummy, complete with a Lake of the Dead, underneath a glass bell at the rear of the museum. On the stone apron in front of the temple, by the lake, the museum put on a formal dinner for 360 souls, including the wife of the President of the United States, the usual philanthropic dowagers and corporate art patrons, a few catered names, such as Prince Albert of Monaco and Henry Kissinger, and many well-known members of the New York art world. But since this was, after all, an exhibition of the Vatican art collection, it was necessary to include some Roman Catholics. Cardinal Cooke, Vatican emissaries, prominent New York Catholic laymen, Knights of Malta— there they were, devout Christians at a New York art world event. The culturati and the Christians were arranged at the table like Arapaho beads: one culturatus, one Christian, one culturatus, one Christian, one culturatus, one Christian, one culturatus, one Christian.

Gamely, the guests tried all the conventional New York conversation openers—real estate prices, friends who have been mugged recently, well-known people whose children have been arrested on drug charges, Brits, live-in help, the dishonesty of helipad contractors, everything short of the desperately trite subjects used in the rest of the country, namely the weather and front-wheel drive. Nothing worked. There were dreadful lulls during which there was no sound at all in that antique churchyard except for the pings of hotel silver on earthenware plates echoing off the tombstone facade of the temple.

Shortly before dessert, I happened to be out in the museum's main lobby when two Manhattan art dealers appeared in their tuxedos, shaking their heads.

One said to the other: "Who *are* these *unbelievable people?*"

But of course! It seemed not only *outré* to have these . . . these . . . these . . . these *religious types* at an art event, it seemed sacrilegious. The culturati were being forced to rub shoulders with heathens. That was the way it hit them. For today art—not religion—is the religion of the educated classes. Today educated people look upon traditional religious ties—Catholic, Episcopal, Presbyterian, Methodist, Baptist, Jewish—as matters of social pedigree. It is only art that they look upon religiously.

When I say that art is the religion of the educated classes, I am careful not to use the word in the merely metaphorical way people do when they say someone is religious about sticking to a diet or training for a sport. I am not using "religion" as a synonym for "enthusiasm." I am referring specifically to what Max Weber identified as the objective functions of a religion: the abnegation or rejection of the world and the legitimation of wealth.

Everyone is familiar with the rejection of the world in the ordinary religious sense. When I worked for the *Washington Post*, I was sent into the hills of West Virginia to do a story about a snake-handling cult—or I should say religion, since a cult is nothing more than a religion whose political influence is nil. The snake-handling religion is based on a passage in Mark in which Jesus, in the Upper Room, tells his disciples that those who believe in him will be able to "handle snakes" and "come to no harm." At the services, sure enough, there is a box or basket full of snakes, poisonous snakes, right before your eyes, and their heads poke out from the lid and you can see their forked tongues. Snake-handling thrives only in mountain areas where the farmlands are poor and the people scrape by. The message of the preachers usually runs as follows: "Oh, I know that down there in the valley they're driving their shiny cars, yes, and smoking their big cigars, unh hunh, and playing with their fancy women, unh hunh, oh yes. But you wait until the Last Days, when it comes time to kiss the snake. *You* will ascend to the right hand of God and live in His Glory, and they will perish." There you have the religious rejection of the world.

Today there are a few religions that appeal to educated people—Scientology, Arica, Synanon, and some neo-Hindu, neo-Buddhist, and neo-Christian groups—but their success has been limited. The far more common way to reject the world, in our time, is through art. I'm sure you're familiar with it. You're on the subway during the morning rush hour, in one of those cars that is nothing but a can of meat on wheels, jammed in shank to flank and haunch to paunch and elbow to rib with people who talk to themselves and shout obscenities into the void and click their teeth and roll back their upper lips to reveal their purple gums, and there is nothing you can do about it. You can't budge. Coffee, adrenaline, and rogue hate are squirting through every duct and every vein, and just when you're beginning to wonder how any mortal can possibly stand it, you look around and you see a young woman seated serenely in what seems to be a perfect pink cocoon of peace, untouched, unthreatened, by the growling mob around her. Her eyes are lowered. In her lap, invariably, is a book. If you look closely, you will see that this book is by Rimbaud, or Rilke, or Baudelaire, or Kafka, or Gabriel García Márquez, author of *One Hundred Years of Solitude*. And as soon as you see this vision, you understand the conviction that creates the inviolable aura around her: "I may be forced into this rat race, this squalid human stew, but I do not have to be *of* it. I inhabit a universe that is finer. I can reject all this." You can envision her apartment immediately. There is a mattress on top of a flush door supported by bricks. There's a window curtained in monk's cloth. There's a hand-thrown pot with a few blue cornflowers in it. There are some Paul Klee and Modigliani prints on the wall and a poster from the Acquavella Galleries' Matisse show. "I don't need your Louis Bourbon bergères and your fabric-covered walls. I reject your whole Parish-Hadley world—through art."

And what about the legitimation of wealth? It wasn't so long ago that Americans of great wealth routinely gave 10 percent of their income to the church. The practice of tithing was a certification of worthiness on earth and an option on heaven. Today the custom is to give the money to the arts. When Mrs. E. Parmalee Prentice, daughter of John D. Rockefeller Sr. and owner of two adjoining mansions on East Fifty-third Street, just off Fifth Avenue, died in 1962, she did not leave these holdings, worth about $5 million, to her church. She left them to the Museum of Modern Art for the building of a new wing. Nobody's eyebrows arched. By 1962, it would have been remarkable if a bequest of that size had gone to a religion of the old-fashioned sort.

Today it has reached the point where there is a clear-cut hierarchy of museum bequests. Best of all is to found a new museum with your name on it, such as the Hirshhorn Museum in Washington, named for Joseph H. Hirshhorn, whose collection of modern art is the core of the museum's holdings. Next best is endowing a new wing, such as the new wing at the

Museum of Modern Art. Next best, a big gallery on the first floor with sunlight; next best, other galleries on the first floor. Then you go up to the second floor, with the sunny corner rooms in front the first pick, and the rooms in the rear next best; then upward to the third floor, and the fourth until there are no more upper floors and you are forced to descend into the cellar. Today it is not unusual to be walking along a basement corridor of a museum and come upon what looks like the door to a utility room with a plaque on it reading: "The E. Runcey Atherwart Belgian Porcelain Cossack Collection."

When the new Metropolitan Opera House was built, there were so many people eager to pour money into it that soon every seat in the orchestra had its own little plaque on the back reading "Sheldon A. Leonard and Family," or whatever. That was nothing more than the twentieth-century version of a traditional religious practice of the seventeenth and eighteenth centuries, when every pew in the front half of the main floor of the church had its own plaque on the back with the name of the family that had endowed it—and sat in it on Sunday. At the Opera House, when they ran out of seats in the orchestra, they went into the lobbies. People endowed columns. And when I say columns, I'm not talking about columns with stepped pediments or fluted shafts or Corinthian capitals with acanthus leaves. I'm talking about I-beams, I-beams supporting the upper floors. When they ran out of columns, they moved on to radiator covers and water fountains.

There was a time when well-to-do, educated people in America adorned their parlors with crosses, crucifixes, or Stars of David. These were marks not only of faith but of cultivation. Think of the great homes, built before 1940, with chapels. This was a fashionable as well as devout use of space. Today those chapels are used as picture galleries, libraries, copper kitchens, saunas, or high-tech centers. It is perfectly acceptable to use them for the VCR and the Advent. But it would be in bad taste to use them for prayer. Practically no one who cares about appearing cultivated today would display a cross or Star of David in the living room. It would be . . . *in bad taste*. Today the conventional symbol of devoutness is—but of course!— the Holy Rectangle: the painting. The painting is the religious object we see today in the parlors of the educated classes.

There was a time, not so long ago, when American businesses gave large amounts of money to churches. In the Midwest and much of the South, areas dominated by so-called Dissenting Protestants, if any man wished to attain the eminence of assistant feed-store manager or better, he joined the Presbyterian or the United Brethren or the Lutheran or the Dutch Reformed church in his community. It was a sign of good faith in every sense of the term. It was absolutely necessary. Businesses literally prayed in public.

Today, what American corporation would support a religion? Most would look upon any such thing as sheer madness. So what does a corporation do when the time comes to pray in public? It supports the arts. I don't need to recite figures. Just think of the money raised since the 1950s for the gigantic cultural complexes—Lincoln Center, Kennedy Center, the Chandler Pavillion, the Woodruff Arts Center—that have become *de rigueur* for the modern American metropolis. What are they? Why, they are St. Patrick's, St. Mary's, Washington National, Holy Cross: the American cathedrals of the late twentieth century.

We are talking here about the legitimation of wealth. The worse odor a corporation is in, the more likely it is to support the arts, and the more likely it is to make sure everybody knows it. The energy crisis, to use an antique term from the 1970s, was the greatest bonanza in the Public Broadcasting Service's history. The more loudly they were assailed as exploiters and profiteers, the more earnestly the oil companies poured money into PBS's cultural programming. Every broadcast seemed to end with a discreet notice on the screen saying: "This program was made possible by a grant from Exxon," or perhaps Mobil, or ARCO. The passing of the energy crisis has been bad news for PBS. That resourceful institution would do well to mount an attack on real estate ventures, money-market funds, low-calorie beer, flea collars, antihistamines, videodisc racks, pornographic magazines, or some other prosperous enterprises. One of the pornography *jefes*, Hugh Hefner, has given his Chicago headquarters, known as the Playboy Mansion, worth an estimated $3 million, to the Chicago Art Institute. It is safe to predict that other pornographers will seek—and with some success—to legitimize their wealth by making devout offerings upon the altar of Art. To give the same offerings to a church would make them look like penitent sinners.

As you can imagine, this state of affairs has greatly magnified the influence of the art world. In size, that world has never been anything more than a village. In the United States, fashions in art are determined by no more than 3,000 people, at least 2,950 of whom live in Manhattan. I can't think of a single influential critic today. "The gallery-going public" has never had any influence at all—so we are left with certain dealers, curators, and artists. No longer do they have the servant-like role of catering to or glorifying the client. Their role today is to save him. They have become a form of clergy—or clerisy, to use an old word for secular souls who take on clerical duties.

In this age of the art clerisy, the client is in no position to say what will save him. He is in no position to do anything at all except come forward with the money if he wants salvation and legitimation.

Today large corporations routinely hire curators from the art village to buy art in their behalf. It is not a mere play on words to call these people curates, comparable to the Catholic priests who at one time were attached to wealthy European families to conduct daily masses on their estates. The corporations set limits on the curators' budgets and reserve the right to veto their choices. But they seldom do, since the entire purpose of a corporate art program is legitimation of wealth through a spiritually correct investment in art. The personal tastes of the executives, employees, clients, or customers could scarcely matter less. The corporate curators are chiefly museum functionaries, professors of art, art critics, and dealers, people who have devoted themselves not so much to the history of art as to the theories and fashions that determine prestige within the art world—that village of 3,000 souls—today, in the here and now.

Thus Chase Manhattan Bank hired a curator who was a founding trustee of the scrupulously devout and correct New Museum in New York. IBM hired a curator from the Whitney Museum to direct the art program at its new headquarters in New York. Philip Morris, perhaps the nation's leading corporate patron of the arts, did IBM one better. In its new headquarters in New York, Philip Morris has built a four-story art gallery and turned it over directly to the Whitney. Whatever the Whitney says goes.

For a company to buy works of art simply because they appeal to its executives and its employees is an absolute waste of money, so far as legitimation is concerned. The Ciba-Geigy agricultural chemical company started out collecting works of many styles and artists, then apparently realized the firm was getting no benefit from the collection whatsoever, other than aesthetic pleasure. At this point Ciba-Geigy hired an artist and a Swiss art historian, who began buying only Abstract Expressionist works by artists such as Philip Guston and Adolph Gottlieb. These works were no doubt totally meaningless to the executives, the employees, and the farmers of the world who use agricultural chemicals, and were, therefore, a striking improvement.

If employees go so far as to protest a particular fashionable style, a corporation will usually switch to another one. Corporations are not eager to annoy their workers. But at the same time, to spend money on the sort of realistic or symbolic work employees might actually enjoy would be pointless. The point is to be acclaimed for "support of the arts," a phrase which applies only to the purchase of works certified by the curates of the art village. This was quite openly the aim of the Bank of America when it hired a curator in 1979 and began buying works of art at the rate of 1,000 a year. The bank felt that its corporate image was suffering because it was not among those firms receiving "credit for art support."

The credit must come from the art clerisy. It is for this reason that IBM, for example, has displayed Michael Heizer's *Levitated Mass* at its outdoor plaza at Madison Avenue and Fifty-sixth Street. The piece is a 25-foot-by-16-foot metal tank containing water and a slab of granite. It is meaningless in terms of IBM, its executives, its employees, its customers, and the thousands of people who walk past the plaza every day. Far from being a shortcoming, that is part of *Levitated Mass*'s exemplary success as a spiritual object.

It is precisely in this area—public sculpture—that the religion of art currently makes its richest contribution to the human comedy. A hundred years ago there was no confusion about the purpose of public sculpture. It glorified the ideals or triumphs of an entire community by the presentation of familiar figures or symbols, or alternatively, it glorified the person or group who paid for it. The city where I grew up, Richmond, Virginia, was the capital of the Confederacy during the Civil War. After the war, Robert E. Lee ascended to the status of a saint in the South, and above all in Richmond. In 1888, a six-story-high statue of Lee on his horse was commissioned. In 1890, when it arrived by boat up the James River, the entire city turned out and went down to the harbor. The men of Richmond took off their seersucker jackets and rolled up their sleeves and, by sheer manpower, hauled the prodigious figures of Lee and his horse Traveller up a two-mile slope to the crest of Monument Avenue, where it now rests. Then they stepped back and cheered and wept. Such was the nature of public sculpture a century ago.

Other public sculpture, as I say, was created simply for the glory of whoever paid for the building it stood in front of. My favorite example is the statue of James Buchanan Duke of the American Tobacco Company that stands in the main quadrangle of the Duke University campus. He's leaning debonairly on his walking stick and has a great round belly and a jolly look on his face and a cigar in his left hand. The statue just comes right out and says: "He made a lot of money in tobacco, he gave you this place, he loved smoking, and here he is!"

That, too, was the nature of public sculpture up until World War II. Shortly before the war, the Rockefeller family erected a monument to itself known as Rockefeller Center, a great building complex featuring two major pieces of sculpture (and many smaller sculptures and bas-reliefs). One, at the skating rink, is a gilt statue of Prometheus, rampant, by Paul Manship. The other, on Fifth Avenue, is Lee Lawrie's highly stylized rendition of Atlas supporting the globe. The use of mythological imagery was typical of public sculpture at the time, and the local meaning was clear enough: the Rockefellers and American business were as strong as Atlas and Promethean in their daring.

But what did the Rockefellers commission in the way of public sculpture *after* World War II? The Rockefellers' Number One Chase Manhattan Plaza was the first glass skyscraper on Wall Street. Out front, on a bare Bauhaus-style apron, the so-called plaza, was installed a sculpture by Jean Dubuffet. It is made of concrete and appears to be four toadstools fused into a gelatinous mass with black lines running up the sides. The title is *Group of Four Trees*. Not even *Group of Four Rockefellers*. After all, there *were* four at the time: David, John D. III, Nelson, and Laurance. But the piece has absolutely nothing to say about the glory or even the existence of the Rockefellers, Wall Street, Chase Manhattan Bank, American business, or the building it stands in front of. Instead, it proclaims the glory of contemporary art. It fulfills the new purpose of public sculpture, which is the legitimation of wealth through the new religion of the educated classes.

Six years after Number One Chase Manhattan Plaza was built, the Marine Midland Bank building went up a block away. It is another glass skyscraper with a mean little Bauhaus-style apron out front, and on this apron was placed a red cube resting on one point by Isamu Noguchi. Through the cube (a rhombohedron, strictly speaking) runs a cylindrical hole. One day I looked through that hole, expecting at the very least that my vision would be led toward the board room, where a man wearing a hard-worsted suit, and with thinning, combed-back hair, would be standing, his forefinger raised, thundering about broker loan rates. Instead what I saw was a woman who appeared to be part of the stenographic pool probing the auditory meatus of her left ear with a Q-Tip. So what is it, this red cube by Noguchi? Why, nothing more than homage to contemporary art, the new form of praying in public. In 1940, the same sculptor, Noguchi, completed a ten-ton stainless steel bas-relief for the main entrance of Rockefeller Center's Associated Press building. It shows five heroic figures using the tools of the wire-service employee: the Teletype, the wire-photo machine, the telephone, the camera, and the pad and pencil. It is entitled *News*. Noguchi's sculpture in front of the Marine Midland building is entitled *Rhombohedron*. Even a title suggesting that it had anything to do with American banking would have been a gauche intrusion upon a piece of corporate piety.

No doubt some corporations find it convenient not to have to express what is on their minds, nor to have to make any claims about being Promethean or Atlas-like or noble or even helpful in any way. How much easier it is, surely, to make a devout gesture and install a solemn art icon by Jean Dubuffet or Isamu Noguchi or Henry Moore. Noguchi's solid geometries, lumps, and extruded squiggles, and Moore's hard boluses with holes in them, have become the very emblems of corporate devoutness.

This type of abstract public sculpture is known within the architectural profession, sotto voce, as the Turd in the Plaza school. The term was coined by James Wines, who said, "I don't care if they want to put up these boring glass boxes, but why do they always deposit that little turd in the plaza when they leave?"

We are long since past the age when autocrats made aesthetic decisions based on what *they* wanted to see in public. Today corporations, no less than individuals, turn to the clerisy, saying, in effect, "Please give us whatever we should have to certify the devoutness of our dedication to art."

If people want to place Turds in the Plaza as a form of religious offering or prayer, and they own the plazas, there isn't much anybody else can do about it. But what happens when they use public money, tax money, to do the same thing on plazas owned by the public? At that point you're in for a glorious farce.

The fun began with a competition for the Franklin Delano Roosevelt memorial. In 1955 Congress created a commission, which called in a jury composed of art curates, headed by an orthodox Bauhaus-style architect named Pietro Belluschi. By 1955 this seemed natural enough. In fact, it was a novel step, and an indication of the emerging power of the art clerisy. In the case of the Lincoln Memorial, completed in 1922, Congress appointed a commission, and the commission solicited entries from only two men, Henry Bacon and John Russell Pope, both classicists, and chose Bacon. To make sure that the Jefferson Memorial, completed in 1947, would match the Lincoln Memorial, another congressional commission chose Pope. In the case of the Roosevelt memorial—a project initiated just eight years after the completion of the Jefferson Memorial—neither Congress nor the public could figure out what hit them.

As soon as the idea of building a memorial was announced, every American who had lived through the Depression or World War II could envision Roosevelt's prognathous jaw and his grin with more teeth than a possum and his cigarette holder cocked up at a forty-five-degree angle. So what did they get? The jury selected a design by a devout modernist sculptor named Norman Hoberman: eight rectangular white concrete slabs— some of them as high as 200 feet. That was it: homage not to Franklin

Roosevelt but to—of course!—Art. The Roosevelt family and Congress were nonplussed at first and, soon enough, furious. The press named the slabs Instant Stonehenge. Congress asked to see the designs of the other five finalists. But there was nothing to choose from. All five designs were abstract. To this day no Roosevelt memorial has been built, even though the project remains officially alive.

This *opéra bouffe* has been repeated with stunning regularity ever since. Our own period has been especially rich, thanks in no small part to the General Services Administration's Art-in-Architecture program and the Veterans Administration's Art in Public Places program, under which the federal government in effect gives the art clerisy millions of tax dollars for the creation of public sculpture.

In 1976, the city of Hartford decided to reinforce its reputation as the Athens of lower central midwestern New England by having an important piece of sculpture installed downtown. It followed what is by now the usual procedure, which is to turn the choice over to a panel of "experts" in the field—i.e., the clerisy, in this case, six curators, critics, and academicians, three of them chosen by the National Endowment for the Arts, which put up half the money. So one day in 1978 a man named Carl Andre arrived in Hartford with thirty-six rocks. Not carved stones, not even polished boluses of the Henry Moore sort—rocks. He put them on the ground in a triangle, like bowling pins. Then he presented the city council with a bill for $87,000. Nonplussed and, soon enough, furious, the citizenry hooted and jeered and called the city council members imbeciles while the council members alternately hit the sides of their heads with their hands and made imaginary snowballs. Nevertheless, they approved payment, and the rocks—entitled *Stone Field*—are still there.

One day in 1981, the Civil Service workers in the new Javits Federal Building in Manhattan went outside to the little plaza in front of the building at lunchtime to do the usual, which was to have their tuna puffs and diet Shastas, and there, running through the middle of it, was a wall of black steel twelve feet high and half a city block long. Nonplussed and, soon enough, furious, 1,300 of them drew up a petition asking the GSA to remove it, only to be informed that this was, in fact, a major work of art, entitled *Tilted Arc*, by a famous American sculptor named Richard Serra. Serra did not help things measurably by explaining that he was "redefining the space" for the poor Civil Service lifers and helping to wean them away from the false values "created by advertising and corporations." Was it his fault if "it offends people to have their preconceptions of reality changed"? This seventy-three-ton gesture of homage to contemporary art remains in place.

The public sees nothing, absolutely nothing, in these stone fields, tilted arcs, and Instant Stonehenges, because it was never meant to. The public is looking at the arcana of the new religion of the educated classes. At this point one might well ask what the clerisy itself sees in them, a question that would plunge us into doctrines as abstruse as any that engaged the medieval Scholastics. Andre's *Stone Field,* for example, was created to illustrate three devout theories concerning the nature of sculpture. One, a sculpture should not be placed upon that bourgeois device, the pedestal, which seeks to elevate it above the people. (Therefore, the rocks are on the ground.) Two, a sculpture should "express its gravity." (And what expresses gravity better than rocks lying on the ground?) Three, a sculpture should not be that piece of bourgeois pretentiousness, the "picture in the air" (such as the statues of Lee and Duke); it should force the viewer to confront its "object-ness." (You want object-ness? Take a look at a plain rock! Take a look at thirty-six rocks!)

Public bafflement or opposition is taken as evidence of an object's spiritual worthiness. It means that the public's "preconceptions of reality" have been changed, to use Serra's words. When George Sugarman's sculpture for the plaza of the new federal courthouse in Baltimore was protested by both the building's employees and the judges, Sugarman said: "Isn't controversy part of what modern art is all about?" These are devout incantations of the Turbulence Theorem, which has been an article of faith within the clerisy for the past forty years. It was originally enunciated by the critic Clement Greenberg, who said that all great contemporary art "looks ugly at first." It was expanded upon by the art historian Leo Steinberg, who said that the great artists cause us "to abandon our most cherished values." In short, if a work of art troubles you, it's probably good; if you detest it, it's probably great.

In such a situation, naturally you need expert counsel: i.e., the clerisy. The notion of "the art expert" is now widely accepted. The curators of programs such as Art-in-Architecture and Art in Public Places are contemptuous of the idea that politicians, civic leaders, or any other representative of the public—much less the people themselves—should determine what sculpture is installed in public. The director of the Art-in-Architecture program, Donald Thalacker, once said: "You go to a medical expert for medical advice; you go to a legal expert for advice about the law. . . . Yet when it comes to art, it seems they want the local gas station attendant in on things." This is a lovely piece of nonsense—as anyone who sought to devise a licensing examination for an art expert or, for that matter, an artist, would soon discover. An "art expert" is merely someone who understands and believes in the tastes and values of the tiny art village of New York.

The public is nonplussed and, soon enough, becomes furious—and also uneasy. After all, if understanding such arcana is the hallmark of the educated classes today, and you find yourself absolutely baffled, what does that say about your level of cultivation? Since 1975, attendance at museums of art in the United States has risen from 42 million to 60 million people per year. Why? In 1980 the Hirshhorn Museum did a survey of people who came to the museum over a seven-month period. I find the results fascinating. Thirty-six percent said they had come to the museum to learn about contemporary art. Thirty-two percent said they had come to learn about a particular contemporary artist. Thirteen percent came on tours. Only 15 percent said they were there for what was once the conventional goal of museumgoers: to enjoy the pictures and sculptures. The conventional goal of museumgoers today is something quite different. Today they are there to learn—and to see the light. At the Hirshhorn, the people who are interviewed in the survey said such things as: "I know this is great art, and now I feel so unintelligent." And: "After coming to this museum, I now feel so much better about art and so much worse about me."

In other words: "I believe, O Lord, but I am unworthy! Reveal to me Thy mysteries!"

Ethics Without Virtue

(1984)

Christina Hoff Sommers

By the eighties new forms of moral education had surfaced in schools, emphasizing individual choice in ethical matters. Some progressive educators acted as
school-based missionaries of sixties-style social justice. Others ridiculed "old
bags of virtues"; in the spirit of counterculture, they applauded relativism, self-
referential thinking, the wisdom of the young, and their own moral awareness.

What do students in our nation's schools do all day? Most of them
are clearly not spending their time reading the classics, learning math, or studying the physical sciences. It is likely that,
along with photography workshops, keeping journals, and perhaps learning about computers, students spend part of their day in moral education
classes. But these classes are not, as one might expect, designed to
acquaint students with the Western moral tradition. Professional theorists
in schools of education have found that tradition wanting and have
devised an alternative, one they have marketed in public schools with
notable success.

A reform of moral education is not a task to be undertaken lightly.
The sincerity and personal integrity of the theorist-reformers is not at
issue, but their qualifications as moral educators is a legitimate subject of
concern. The leaders of reform do not worry about credentials. They are
convinced that traditional middle-class morality is at best useless and at
worst pernicious, and they have confidence in the new morality that is to
replace the old and in the novel techniques to be applied to this end. In
1970 Theodore Sizer, then dean of the Harvard School of Education, co-
edited with his wife Nancy a book entitled *Moral Education.* The preface set
the tone by condemning the morality of "the Christian gentleman," "the
American prairie," the McGuffey *Reader,* and the hypocrisy of teachers who

tolerate a grading system that is "the terror of the young." According to the Sizers, all of the authors in the anthology agree that "the 'old morality' can and should be scrapped."

. . . One gains some idea of the new moral educators from the terminology they use. Courses in ethics are called "values clarification" or "cognitive moral development"; teachers are "values processors," "values facilitators," or "reflective-active listeners"; lessons in moral reasoning are "sensitivity modules"; volunteer work in the community is an "action module"; and teachers "dialogue" with students to help them discover their own systems of values. In these dialogues the teacher avoids discussing "old bags of virtues," such as wisdom, courage, compassion, and "proper" behavior, because any attempt to instill these would be to indoctrinate the student. Some leaders of the new reform movement advise teachers that effective moral education cannot take place in the "authoritarian" atmosphere of the average American high school. The teacher ought to democratize the classroom, turning it into a "just community" where the student and teacher have an equal say. Furthermore, the student who takes a normative ethics course in college will likely encounter a professor who also has a principled aversion to the inculcation of moral precepts and who will confine classroom discussion to such issues of social concern as the Karen Ann Quinlan case, recombinant DNA research, or the moral responsibilities of corporations. The result is a system of moral education that is silent about virtue.

The teaching of virtue is not viewed as a legitimate aim of a moral curriculum, but there is no dearth of alternative approaches. From the time the values education movement began in the late nineteen sixties, its theorists have produced an enormous number of articles, books, films, manuals, and doctoral dissertations; there are now journals, advanced degree programs, and entire institutes dedicated exclusively to moral pedagogy, and for the past several years, teachers, counselors, and education specialists have been attending conferences, seminars, workshops, and retreats to improve their skills in values-processing. At present, two opposing ideologies dominate moral education: the values clarification movement, whose best-known proponent is Sidney Simon of the University of Massachusetts School of Education; and the cognitive moral development movement, whose chief spokesman is Lawrence Kohlberg, a professor of psychology and education, and director of the Center for Moral Education at Harvard.

Values clarification, according to Sidney Simon, is "based on the premise that none of us has the 'right' set of values to pass on to other people's children." Its methods are meant to help students to get at "their own feelings, their own ideas, their own beliefs, so that the choices and decisions they make are conscious and deliberate, based on their own value system." The success of the values clarification movement has been phenomenal. In 1975 a study from the Hoover Institute referred to "hundreds perhaps thousands of school programs that employ the clarification methodology" and reported that ten states have officially adopted values clarification as a model for their moral education programs. Proponents of values clarification consider it inappropriate for a teacher to encourage students, however subtly or indirectly, to adopt the values of the teacher or the community. In their book, *Readings in Values Clarification,* Simon and his colleague Howard Kirchenbaum write:

> We call this approach "moralizing," although it has also been known as inculcation, imposition, indoctrination, and in its most extreme form brainwashing. Moralizing is the direct or indirect transfer of a set of values from one person or group to another person or group.

The student of values clarification is taught awareness of his preferences and his right to their satisfaction in a democratic society. To help students discover what it is that they genuinely value, they are asked to respond to questionnaires called "strategies." Some typical questions are: Which animal would you rather be: an ant, a beaver, or a donkey? Which season do you like best? Do you prefer hiking, swimming, or watching television? In one strategy called "Values Geography," the student is helped to discover his geographical preferences; other lessons solicit his reaction to seat belts, messy handwriting, hiking, wall-to-wall carpeting, cheating, abortion, hit-and-run drivers, and a mother who severely beats a two-year-old child.

Western literature and history are two traditional alienating influences that the values clarification movement is on guard against. Simon has written that he has ceased to find meaning "in the history of war or the structure of a sonnet, and more meaning in the search to find value in life." He and his colleagues believe that exposure to one's cultural heritage is not likely to be morally beneficial to the "average student."

> Because values are complex and because man's thoughts and accomplishments are both abundant and complicated, it is difficult to recommend that the average student rely on this approach. It takes substantial mental stamina and ability and much time and energy to travel this road. While the study of our cultural heritage can be defended on other grounds, we would not expect it to be sufficient for value education.

The values clarification theorist does not believe that moral sensibility and social conscience are, in significant measure, learned by reading and discussing the classics. Instead Simon speaks of the precious legacy we can leave to "generations of young people if we teach them to set their priorities and rank order the marvelous items in life's cafeteria."

. . . The student has values; the values clarification teacher is merely "facilitating" the student's access to them. Thus, no values are taught. The emphasis is on *learning how,* not on *learning what.* The student does not learn that acts of stealing are wrong; he learns how to respond to such acts.

The values clarification course is, in this sense, contentless. As if to make up for this, it is methodologically rich. It is to be expected that an advocate of values clarification emphasizes method over content in other areas of education, and indeed he does. Many handbooks, strategies, board games, and kits have been developed to help teachers adapt the methods of values clarification to such subjects as English, history, science, math, and even home economics and Spanish. Values clarification guides for girl scout troops and Sunday school classes are also available, as well as manuals to assist parents in clarifying values at the dinner table.

Simon and his colleagues explain that it is useless and anachronistic to teach the student at a "facts level." In a history lesson on the Constitution, for example, the teacher is advised not to waste too much time on such questions as where and when the Constitution was drawn up. Undue attention should also not be given to the "concepts level," where, for example, the teacher discusses the moral origins of the Bill of Rights. When the learning of subject matter is unavoidable, Simon and his colleagues recommend that it be lifted to a higher and more urgent level where students are asked "you-centered" questions, such as, "What rights do you have in your family?" Or, "Many student governments are really token governments controlled by the 'mother country,' i.e., the administration. Is this true in your school? What can you do about it?" And, "When was the last time you signed a petition?"

The classical moral tradition will not be revived by the practitioners of values clarification. Indeed, it is, in their eyes, an alien tradition that is insensitive to the needs and rights of the contemporary student.

ᕗᕳ

Lawrence Kohlberg, the leader of the second major movement in moral education, shares with values clarification educators a low opinion of traditional morality. In his contribution to Theodore and Nancy Sizer's anthology, *Moral Education,* he writes, "Far from knowing whether it can be taught, I have no idea what virtue really is." Kohlberg's disclaimer is not a Socratic confession of ignorance; he considers the teaching of traditional virtues to be at best a waste of time and at worst coercive. Like Sidney Simon, he, too, uses the language of conspiracy to characterize the American educational system. He refers often to the "hidden curriculum" and insists that the teacher must not be "an agent of the state, the church, or the social system, [but] rather . . . a free moral agent dealing with children who are free moral agents." Kohlberg cites as an example of covert indoctrination a teacher who yelled at some boys for not returning their books to the proper place. "The teacher would have been surprised to know that her concerns with classroom management defined for her children what she and her school thought were basic values, or that she was engaged in indoctrination." Kohlberg and his disciples are currently busy transforming some of the best school systems in the country into "just communities" where no such indoctrination takes place.

Kohlberg's authority derives from his cognitive developmental approach to moral education. Following John Dewey, Kohlberg distinguishes three main stages of moral development (each of which is partitioned into a higher and lower stage, making six in all). The first stage is called the premoral or preconventional reward/punishment level. In the second stage morals are conventional but unreflective. In the third stage moral principles are autonomously chosen on rational grounds. Kohlberg's research applies Piaget's idea that the child possesses certain cognitive structures that come successively into play as the child develops. According to Kohlberg, the latent structures are a cross-cultural fact of cognitive psychology. Kohlberg's more specific thesis on the unfolding of the child's innate moral propensities has received a great deal of deserved attention. The literature on Kohlberg is controversial, and it is far too early to say whether his ideas are sound enough for eventual use in the classroom. Kohlberg himself has urged and already put into practice pedagogical applications of his ideas.

From the assumption of innateness, it is but a short step to the belief that the appropriate external circumstances will promote the full moral development of the child. It then becomes the job of the educator to provide those circumstances "facilitating" the child to his moral maturity. The innate structures are essentially contentless, and Kohlberg and his followers do not think it is the job of the moral educator to develop a virtuous person by supplying the content—that is, the traditional virtues. To do that would be, in Kohlberg's contemptuous phrase, to impose on the child an "old bag of virtues." Kohlberg and his associate Moshe Blatt remark in the *Journal of Moral Education:*

Moral education is best conceived as a natural process of dialogue among peers, rather than as a process of didactic instruction or preaching. The teacher and the curriculum are best
conceived as facilitators of this dialogue.

. . . Brookline High School in Massachusetts provides a particularly
sad example of the way the new ideologies can penetrate a fine high
school. The school administration has been taken over by Kohlbergians
who, with the help of federal funds, are trying to turn it into a "just community." To this end the governance of the school has been given over to
the entire school community—students, teachers, administrators, secretaries, and janitorial staff. To make the process work smoothly, not all students are invited to the weekly "town meetings," just their representatives.
But, because many of the two thousand or so students are indifferent,
many student representatives are self-appointed. And a big problem is that
most of the teachers do not attend (nor, of course, do tired secretaries and
maintenance workers).

I attended one meeting with thirty students, five teachers, two student visitors from Scarsdale who are working with Kohlberg and studying
the Brookline program in hopes of using it in New York, and two observers
from the Carnegie-Mellon Foundation, who were there to investigate the
possibility of making a film about the Brookline experiment for public television. The kids who participated in the meeting were charming and articulate and the Carnegie-Mellon people were clearly pleased, and they will
make their film. Like many educational experts who admire the Brookline
town meetings, these observers are probably unaware that many of the
teachers feel harassed and manipulated by the Kohlberg administration. So
far, the participants in the town meetings—who are mostly teenagers exercising more power than they will ever be granted in college or graduate
school—have voted to rescind a rule against Walkman radios on campus, to
prohibit homework assignments for vacation periods, to disallow surprise
quizzes, and they have instituted a procedure for bringing teachers who
give tests or assignments that are too demanding before a "Fairness
Committee." One teacher told me that the students had never asked for the
powers they now enjoy. According to the teacher, the school authorities
handed these powers over to students "for their own good." Just communities are Kohlberg's answer to the oppression exercised by established
authority. Evidently, Kohlberg sees no need to question his assumption
that established authority is intrinsically suspect. In any event, it is ironic
that now, when teachers with authority are so rare, educational theorists
like Kohlberg are proposing that authority itself is the evil to be combated.

Ralph Mosher, a Harvard-trained Kohlbergian, is the chief education-al consultant to the Brookline High School. In his anthology he writes the following about the standards that had been in place:

> Moral education, all the more powerful because it is "hidden," is embedded in the tacit values of the curriculum and the school. For example, the most worthy/valued student in Brookline High School is the one who achieves early admission to Harvard on a full scholarship. How few can accomplish this is obvious. Yet teachers, counselors, and parents put great, albeit subtle, pressure on the many to do likewise. . . . What the research [in moral education] has attempted to do is to make some schooling more just.

Mosher's attitude is instructive. Ideals, it seems, are not goals to aim for. They must be attainable by the majority of students. If any goals are set up, they must be ones to which most students can realistically aspire. For Mosher, vigilance against superimposing a hidden agenda with elitist bias is the order of the day.

Kohlberg's ideas have taken hold in the better schools, where one can still find a fair number of parents who can afford to hold attitudes against elitism. Should the public schools of Brookline, Cambridge, or Scarsdale fail to provide the education necessary for admission to the best colleges, those parents have recourse to some fine private schools in the neighborhood. In the meantime they can indulge the unexceptional con-cept of a just community, whose egalitarian character is welcomed by those who find themselves uncomfortably well-fixed, particularly after the radical views they held in the halcyon sixties.

The values clarification and cognitive development reformers are well aware that they are riding a wave of public concern about the need for an effective system of moral education. Thus Mosher writes:

> [A] high proportion of Americans (four of five in recent Gallup Polls) support moral education in the public schools. What the respondents mean by moral education is, of course, moot. Probably the teaching of virtues such as honesty, respect for adults, moderation in the use of alcohol/drugs, sexual restraint and so on. . . . Educators would have to exceed Caesar's wife not to capitalize on an idea whose time appeared to have come.

This last remark about capitalizing on the parent's desire for higher moral standards is disarmingly cynical. Naturally the public wants its "old bag of virtues," but educational theorists such as Mosher are convinced that giving the public what it wants is ineffective and unjust. The traditional moralists have failed (witness Watergate), so now it's their turn. Mosher's attitude to the benighted parents is condescending. No doubt for Mosher and Kohlberg, the morally confident leaders of the reform movement, theirs is the right kind of elitism.

The deprecation of moralizing common to values clarification and cognitive development theory has been effective even in those schools where the reforms have not yet penetrated. Increasingly nowadays, few teachers have the temerity to praise any middle-class virtues. The exception is the virtue of tolerance. But, when tolerance is the sole virtue, students' capacity for moral indignation, so important for moral development, is severely inhibited. The result is moral passivity and confusion and a shift of moral focus from the individual to society.

The student entering college today shows the effects of an educational system that has kept its distance from the traditional virtues. Unencumbered by the "old bag of virtues," the student arrives toting a ragbag of another stripe whose contents may be roughly itemized as follows: psychological egoism (the belief that the primary motive for action is selfishness), moral relativism (the doctrine that what is praiseworthy or contemptible is a matter of cultural conditioning), and radical tolerance (the doctrine that to be culturally and socially aware is to understand and excuse the putative wrongdoer). Another item in the bag is the conviction that the seat of moral responsibility is found in society and its institutions, not in individuals.

The half-baked relativism of the college student tends to undermine his common sense. In a term paper that is far from atypical, one of my students wrote that Jonathan Swift's "modest proposal" for solving the problem of hunger in Ireland by harvesting Irish babies for food was "good for Swift's society, but not for ours." All too often one comes up against a grotesquely distorted perspective that common sense has little power to set right. In one discussion in my introductory philosophy class, several students were convinced that the death of one person and the death of ten thousand is equally bad. When a sophomore was asked whether she saw Nagasaki as the moral equivalent of a traffic accident, she replied, "From the moral point of view, yes." Teachers of moral philosophy who are not themselves moral agnostics trade such stories for dark amusement. But it appears that teachers in other disciplines are also struck by the moral perversity of their students. Richard M. Hunt, a professor of government at Harvard University, gave a course on the Holocaust to one hundred Harvard undergraduates. In the course he was disturbed to find that a majority of students adopted the view that the rise of Hitler and the Nazis was inevitable, that no one could have resisted it, and that in the end no one was responsible for what happened. Hunt's teaching assistant remarked to him, "You know, I think if some of our students were sitting as judges at the Nuremberg trials, they would probably acquit—or at least pardon—most of the Nazi defendants." Professor Hunt has dubbed his students' forgiving attitude toward the past "no-fault history."

It is fair to say that many college students are thoroughly confused about morality. What they sorely need are some straightforward courses on moral philosophy and a sound and unabashed introduction to the Western moral tradition—something they may never have had before. But few teachers will use that tradition as a source of moral introduction: the fear of indoctrination is even stronger in the colleges than it is at primary and secondary schools. In a recent study of the teaching of ethics prepared by the Hastings Center, a well-respected institute for the study of ethical questions, the authors write:

> A major concern about the teaching of ethics has been whether and to what extent it is appropriate to teach courses on ethics in a pluralistic society, and whether it is possible to teach such courses without engaging in unacceptable indoctrination.

And elsewhere in the same report:

> No teacher of ethics can assume that he or she has a solid grasp on the nature of morality as to pretend to know what finally counts as good moral conduct. No society can assume that it has any better grasp of what so counts as to empower teachers to propagate it in colleges and universities. Perhaps most importantly, the premise of higher education is that students are at an age where they have to begin coming to their own conclusions and shaping their own view of the world.

It would, however, be altogether incorrect to say that the colleges are ignoring moral instruction. The spread of moral agnosticism has been accompanied by an extraordinary increase in courses of applied ethics. Philosophy departments, isolated and marginal for many years, are now attracting unprecedented numbers of students to their courses in medical ethics, business ethics, ethics for everyday life, ethics for engineers, nurses, social workers, and lawyers. Today there are dozens of journals and conferences, hundreds of books and articles, and—according to the Hastings Center—eleven thousand college courses in applied ethics.

The new interest in applied ethics is itself a phenomenon to be welcomed. Public discussions of controversial issues will surely benefit from the contributions of philosophers, and the literature of applied ethics should be read by anyone who seeks a responsible understanding of topical issues. In reading the anthologies of applied ethics, a student encounters arguments of philosophers who take strong stands on important social questions. These arguments often shake a student's confidence in moral relativism. Nevertheless, the literature of applied ethics, like the literature of values clarification and cognitive moral development, has little or nothing to say about matters of individual virtue. The resurgence of moral education in the college thus reinforces the shift away from personal morals to an almost exclusive preoccupation with the morality of institutional policies. After all, most students are not likely to be involved personally in administering the death penalty or selecting candidates for kidney dialysis; and, since most will never do recombinant DNA research, or even have abortions, the purpose of the courses in applied ethics is to teach students how to form responsible opinions on questions of social policy. A strong ethical curriculum is a good thing, but a curriculum of ethics without virtue is a cause for concern.

The applied ethics movement in the universities started in the late nineteen sixties when philosophers became interested once again in normative ethics. Between 1940 and 1968 ethics had been theoretical and methodologically self-conscious, to the relative neglect of practical ethics. A large number of philosophers emerged from the sixties eager to contribute to national moral debates. But like Simon, Kohlberg, and their followers, these philosophers were suspicious and distrustful of moralizing and deeply averse to indoctrination. It is no small feat to launch a powerful and influential movement in normative ethics without recourse to the language of vice and virtue and a strong notion of personal responsibility, but that is exactly what is being attempted. The new university moralists, uncomfortable and ideologically at odds with the discredited middle-class ethic, are making their reform movement succeed by addressing themselves, not to the vices and virtues of individuals, but to the moral character of our nation's institutions. Take a look at almost any text used today in college ethics courses—for example, *Ethics for Modern Life,* edited by R. Abelson and M. Friquegnon, *Today's Moral Problems,* edited by R. Wasserstrom, or *Moral Problems* by J. Rachels—and you will find that almost all of the articles consist of philosophical evaluations of the conduct and policies of schools, hospitals, courts, corporations, and the United States government.

Inevitably the student forms the idea that applying ethics to modern life is mainly a question of learning how to be for or against social and institutional policies. Appropriately enough, many of the articles sound like briefs written for a judge or legislator. In that sort of ethical climate, a student soon loses sight of himself as a moral agent and begins to see himself as a moral spectator or a protojurist. This is not to deny that many of the issues have an immediate personal dimension. They do, but the primary emphasis is not on what one is to do as a person but on what one is to believe as a member of society—in other words, on ideology and doctrine rather than on personal responsibility and practical decency.

The move to issue-oriented courses is hailed as a move back to the days when moral instruction played a significant role in education. Nothing could be further from the truth. Where Aristotle, Aquinas, Mill, and Kant are telling us how to behave, the contemporary university moralist is concerned with what we are to advocate, vote for, protest against, and endorse. Michael Walzer has compared the applied ethics movement to the scholarly activities of the Greek Academicians, the Talmudists, and the medieval Casuists. The comparison is inept, for those earlier moralists were working in a tradition in which it was assumed that the practical end of all moral theory was the virtuous individual. The ancient sophist, with his expertise in rhetoric and politics, is a more convincing analogue to the teachers of issue-oriented ethics, who find little time for the history of ethical theory with its traditional emphasis on the good and virtuous life. One may therefore be wary of the widespread enthusiasm for the "exciting new developments" in the teaching of ethics. Especially misleading is the frequent observation that the revival of interest in practical ethics is a great advance over the earlier preoccupation with evaluative language (meta-ethics). Admittedly the preoccupation with meta-ethics that characterized the teaching of ethics a decade ago left the student undernourished by neglecting normative ethics. But, in all fairness, neither students nor teachers were under any illusion that meta-ethics was the whole of ethics. Today the student is learning that normative ethics is primarily social policy. This being so, moral action should be politically directed; the individual's task is to bring the right civic institutions (the true moral agents) into place. The student tacitly assumes that ethics is not a daily affair, that it is a matter for specialists, and that its practical benefits are deferred until the time of institutional reform.

The result of identifying normative ethics with public policy is justi-fication for and reinforcement of moral passivity in the student. Even problems that call for large-scale political solutions have their immediate private dimension, but a student trained in a practical ethics that has avoided or de-emphasized individual responsibility is simply unprepared for any demand that is not politically or ideologically formulated. The stu-dent is placed in the undemanding role of the indignant moral spectator who needs not face the comparatively minor corruptions in his own life.

. . . For social-minded reformers, justice is the principal virtue, and social policy is where ethics is really "at." The assumption is that there is an implicit conflict between the just society and the repressive morality of its undemocratic predecessors. An extreme version of this theme is presented in a little book edited by Trotsky, *Their Morals and Ours,* with its searing attack on the "conservative banalities of bourgeois morality." For Trotsky, of course, social reform requires revolution, but his indictment of the hypocrisies and "brutalities" of "their morals" must sound familiar to the Kohlbergians. The fate of those societies that have actually succeeded in replacing personal morality with social policy is the going price for ignoring the admonition of Max Weber: "He who seeks salvation of the soul—of his own and others—should not seek it along the avenue of politics."

Victims All?

(1991)

David Rieff

More radical than multiculturalism, Rieff argued in this essay, was the recovery movement, for it elevated nearly every person to the special status of the sufferer. Among the educated and affluent in the eighties, self-actualization became a cynosure of spiritual health. Increasingly, this process seemed to require atonement and recovery. "Proponents of recovery do not think in group terms," Rieff concluded. "They claim that virtually everyone in the country is, in some essential sense, a victim—a victim, mostly, of abusive parents."

I magine a country in which millions of apparently successful people nonetheless have come to believe fervently that they are really lost souls—a country where countless adults allude matter-of-factly to their "inner children," who, they say, lie wounded and in desperate need of relief within the wreckage of their grown-up selves. Imagine the celebrities and opinion-makers among these people talking nightly on TV and weekly in the magazines not about their triumphs but about their victimization, not about their power and fame but about their addictions and childhood persecutions.

Imagine that this belief in abused "inner children" dragging down grown-up men and women has become so widespread as to exert considerable influence over the policies of such supposedly practical bodies as corporations, public hospitals, and boards of education—which, in turn, have taken to acting as if the greatest threat facing their various constituencies is a nexus of addictions and other self-destructive "behaviors," ranging from alcoholism and drug addiction to the more nebulous, if satisfyingly all-encompassing, category of "co-dependency," a term meaning, in essence, any reliance for one's sense of self on the opinion of someone else, someone more often than not plagued by his or her own addiction. One would be imagining a place, then, where nearly *everyone* is identified—is identifying himself or herself—as some sort of psychological cripple.

In this country, it is taken for granted that no blame for these addictions or dependencies can be assigned to those who exhibit them. Terms such as "character," "weakness," and "individual responsibility" are no longer deemed appropriate. Those who drink too much, take drugs, or destroy themselves (and their co-dependents) in other ways suffer either from a disease (like alcoholism) or from difficulties that are the direct, ineluctable result of the faulty upbringing to which they had been subjected as children.

A desperate creed, and yet this country is not—as, upon hearing it, an outsider might have had reason to suppose—on anything approaching its last legs. It has neither been bombed by fighter aircraft so technologically advanced as to be undetectable to its air defenses nor has its morale been unhinged by the rigors of prolonged triple-digit inflation, an austerity program imposed by the World Bank, the emigration of its skilled professionals, or inter-communal savagery. To the contrary, here is a country that, although scarcely without its difficulties, remains one of the richest countries on earth, indeed one of the richest places the world has ever known.

There is even good argument to be made that the most salient thing about this country is not its apprehension of decline, but, rather, how many people from all over the less-favored reaches of the globe seem willing to risk anything to pull up stakes and immigrate here—and, having arrived, to fill with reasonably good grace all those dirty, humiliating, low-paying jobs that native-born workers have grown unwilling to perform.

In any event, those drawn to the idea of their wounded "inner child" are doing pretty well. Many have life stories that hew to what has long been the country's favorite narrative about itself: rags to riches. But now there has developed a new narrative: from addiction, through discovery of the "inner child," to recovery. In this country, this is the story men and women are increasingly telling themselves and one another. The country is the United States of America, circa 1991.

❧

Most public-minded Americans would agree that there is a crucial debate going on just now, the resolution of which will have a deep impact on the character of our society. I am referring to the debate over "political correctness." President Bush, perhaps because he has always had a keen eye for inflammatory domestic symbols, has joined the chorus of voices that have dubbed the "P.C./multiculturalism" debate the most significant domestic argument about ideas in decades. At the same time, like the professors and pundits on both sides of the issue, he has been silent about the meaning of that much larger and, in terms of money and mass appeal, more influential enthusiasm that is usually referred to as the twelve-step, or recovery, movement.

This is not to underestimate the importance of political correctness. Certainly, on university campuses, however vociferously and disingenuously the militants themselves continue to deny it, the teaching of the humanities has largely been hijacked, replaced by the factitious cant of deconstructionism and Third World apologetics, or, as its proponents, with their flawlessly tin ears, prefer to call it these days, "postcoloniality." Yet the fact remains that for every literature department that has been taken over by one or another of the vying ethnic and intellectual particularisms that pass for thinking in the contemporary academy, there are likely to be at least two new books preaching the message of recovery edging their way onto the national bestseller lists, not to mention the innumerable twelve-step chapters being formed every month in cities and suburbs all over the country.

Nevertheless, for intelligent Americans with no direct experience of these groups, the recovery movement is news from the fringe, trivial and evanescent. And it is a safe bet that books bearing such titles as *Healing the Child Within; Lost in the Shuffle: The Co-dependent Reality; The Road Less Traveled; Children of Trauma: Rediscovering Your Discarded Self;* and *Choice-Making for Co-dependents, Adult Children and Spirituality Seekers* will never be held up by some Republican officeholder caught in a tight race against a liberal challenger the way the works of leading radical multiculturalists are likely to be during the 1992 campaign. Nor are authors like John Bradshaw, Robert Subby, Scott Peck, Sharon Wegscheider-Cruse, or Ann Denis likely to find themselves excoriated as threats to Western civilization.

On the face of things, however, it is by no means immediately obvious why this should be so. Indeed, the claims that the recovery movement routinely makes for itself seem far more radical and infinitely more destabilizing of "establishment" values than even the most picturesque pronouncements of the campus radicals. When, for example, John Bradshaw, one of the recovery movement's leading figures, insists that "soul-murder is the basic problem in the world today," and then goes on to assert that everything about the way people live in modern America—not their lifestyle so much as their "death style," as Bradshaw puts it—confirms its essentially pathological character, he is going a great deal further than those who content themselves with demonstrating for the transformation of university humanities curricula.

Even when it comes to those assumptions that the recovery movement shares with radical multiculturalism, it is almost invariably within the context of recovery that they are presented in their most extreme form. Both movements deny the value of any important distinction between the personal and the political; but where the multiculturalists, however much their politics too may be based on feelings, at least try to hold on to certain political categories, the recovery people are interested only in their subjective selves. When *they* say the personal is the political they really mean it.

That the recovery psychotherapists are more radical than the academic multiculturalists becomes most clear when one examines the politics of victimhood, a centerpiece of both movements. In P.C. circles, this idea is inherently self-limiting in the sense that if the concept of oppression is to make any kind of sense, the situation of the various groups of victims—be they blacks, Hispanics, women, or gays—must be opposed to that of an oppressor group—these days, straight white males. Proponents of recovery do not think in group terms. They claim that virtually everyone in the country is, in some essential sense, a victim—a victim, mostly, of abusive parents. Moreover, the recovery advocates say they have the statistics to back up this sweeping assertion. "What we're hearing from experts," John Bradshaw confidently told an interviewer not long ago, "is that approximately 96 percent of the families in this country are dysfunctional to one degree or another."

Small wonder, then, that for the recovery movement only a complete transformation of American society will do. Unlike the demands made by even the most extreme multiculturalists, which mostly boil down, for all the apocalyptic verbiage in which they come wrapped, to calls for various sorts of linguistic affirmative action, the goals of the recovery movement appear to be authentically millennial. Even the gravest of the specific ills the movement wants to remedy—the physiological and psychological addictions, as well as what, more broadly, recovery writers often characterize as "chronic inner pain"—are no more than symptoms of the larger spiritual crisis, and their redress is only the first step toward some larger spiritual awakening. As Bradshaw has put it, "I believe there are moments of great readiness in collective human consciousness . . . I think if we were to use a new Jungian archetype to characterize our time it would be the wounded child . . . and so if we change parent-child relationships, we can change history."

⁓

It is, perhaps, the use of this sort of pop-psychological language that has led American intellectuals and academics to underestimate the recovery movement. There is nothing new about recovery except the packaging, they tend to say, insisting that the search for "inner children" and such are only the latest in that long series of enthusiasms for self-improvement to which Americans have been drawn since at least the middle of the nineteenth century. They admit that Bradshaw's books sell millions of copies but go on to remind you that neither the turn-of-the-century French psychotherapist Emile Coué nor Aimee Semple McPherson, whose revivals attracted thousands in the 1920s, did too badly themselves.

There is no denying that the "self-help" ethos is anything but new. Indeed, few Americans, no matter how European they may fancy themselves to be, live untouched by the conviction that they can change almost anything about themselves if they really want to do so. For Americans, self-creation has from the beginning been the essential act. The great American stories, from James Fenimore Cooper to Philip Roth, are about busting free, finding some way of shucking off the bonds of family and tradition, not so much with the purpose of winning the freedom to *be* oneself as out of the conviction that only the act of lighting out for the territories ensures that one will ever *become* oneself.

This old myth of the frontier is part of the story, of course. If spiritual quests have always been described as journeys, rarely has the spatial element had such resonance as in the American version. When the recovery writer Sharon Wegscheider-Cruse calls one of her books *Learning to Love Yourself: Finding Your Self-worth,* the echoes of the California state motto, born of the Gold Rush—Eureka ("I Have Found It")—are still audible. But even the noise of those spiritual covered wagons is, in the end, less compelling than another entrenched American idea, that of "know-how." The point of all these self-help books—of the entire recovery movement—is to give someone interested the *means* to recover. The very phrase "twelve-step program" is telling enough, as is the frequency with which a successful recovery book is soon accompanied by a "workbook" of some kind. Thus, John Bradshaw writes a book on the "inner child," but just down the shelf from it in most bookstores is Cathryn L. Taylor's *Inner Child Workbook: What to Do With Your Past When It Just Won't Go Away.* Sometimes, the same author produces both works. Melody Beattie's *Codependent No More* sold almost 2 million copies when it appeared in 1987. Three years later, Ms. Beattie was back on the bestseller list with *Codependents' Guide to the Twelve Steps.*

It seems that, given the proper tools, success is all but a sure thing. The recovery gurus may occasionally pause to insist that "working a program," to use the argot of the movement, can be a grueling business. But, for the most part, the tone is relentlessly upbeat. In the section of his book *Lost in the Shuffle* called "Recovery Hints and Reminders," Robert

Subby writes of the year or two he expects it will take an addict to kick his or her habit. "These will not be years spent in drudgery and self-denial, but they will be years filled with learning a new way of life, building healthy relationships and laying the foundation for self-actualization." The tone is so artisanal that one wonders how Dr. Subby resisted the urge to just come out and say *pouring* the foundation. But when the promise is self-transformation, getting off dope or booze, no matter how essential, must indeed come to seem like little more than a kind of karmic renovation project.

And it is striking to what degree the American embrace of the how-to and the American apprehension of the psychological can be reconciled within the context of the idea of recovery. Alienated we may be but, whether it's on the floor of the health club or in one of John Bradshaw's co-dependency workshops where people pay hundreds of dollars a day to interact with their "inner children," often represented by toy animals they hold in their hands—frogs, usually, or teddy bears—it's all in the know-how.

※

The direct antecedent of all the twelve-step groups is not hard to identify. As almost every recovery writer makes clear, the movement derives its method and its inspiration from Alcoholics Anonymous. Many recovery books begin with impassioned accounts of their authors' alcoholism and their eventual discovery of the twelve steps through which they found a way out of their misery at a moment when they were convinced that all was lost. To understand how addiction and recovery have become our central metaphors—addicted to cocaine, the wrong kind of men, TV, gas guzzlers; recovering from too much sex, too little leisure, welfare dependency, the Vietnam syndrome—one first needs to look at AA.

Certainly it would be difficult, in any event, to overstate the influence that AA has exerted over mainstream American life since its formation in the 1930s, the outgrowth of a chance encounter in Akron, Ohio—every AA member learns this story; it is the organization's Genesis—between Bill Wilson, a stockbroker from New York City who had recently stopped drinking but was desperately afraid that he was on the verge of taking it up again, and the alcoholic Akron physician Bob Smith, who lives on in AA lore as Doctor Bob, a man who had tried everything but had never succeeded in remaining sober for very long. Not only has the so-called Big Book of the organization sold millions of copies since its first edition was published in 1939 but the millions of members who have belonged to AA over the decades have been followed by millions more who have been to at least one AA meeting sometime in their lives.

In retrospect, AA at its founding seemed like one of the responses offered by a white, Protestant, small-town America despondent over the failure of Prohibition. Passed in 1919, the Volstead Act was ignominiously repealed in 1933, and with its passing went any serious hope of legally mandated temperance. Of course, AA was no more a conscious expression of these changed circumstances than the turning inward that art historians discern in Biedermeier furniture was a thought-out response to the failure of political liberalism in Central Europe in the early nineteenth century. That said, like Biedermeier, AA can be partly understood as such a turning inward. Instead of political action, AA followed its spiritual progenitor, the early-twentieth-century Oxford Group, in preaching a species of personalized moral rearmament. Individual AA members would accomplish what political action had failed to: They'd do away with booze. In the process, a "social problem" was transformed into a "disease" over which alcoholics insisted they had no control.

It is interesting that so many of the recovery advocates speak of their own political involvement during the 1960s. Indeed, some write of that period so nostalgically that it is hard not to feel they are looking for their "inner decade" as much as their "inner children." "For me," writes Lucia Capacchione, author of *Recovery of Your Inner Child,* "the sixties were about marriage, family, and artistic achievement. On the larger level they were also about human rights, and I helped fight Johnson's War on Poverty as a Head Start director. By the decade's end, the Women's Movement was fully launched. Like many of my sisters, I was juggling a number of roles, i.e., wife, mother, artist, and educator. Then, one day, the bottom dropped out as the seventies began . . ."

To the followers of recovery, the lesson of their activism during the Sixties is that those political involvements were either, as Bradshaw once put it, "not genuine . . . a mood-altering trip"—in other words, yet another form of co-dependency, this time on revolution—or else simply premature. Most would angrily deny that their absorption in what they sometimes call "ego work" represents any abdication of social responsibility. "You can't go to work in the social order unless you've healed the wound (of your inner child)," Bradshaw has said.

Of course, many of these ideas were commonplace in the Sixties as well. What else, when all is said and done, is all this talk in recovery circles about the primacy of the emotional over the rational, the instinctual over the repressed, and the spontaneous over the deliberate, if not a New Age gloss on the wilder assertions of a Wilhelm Reich or an R. D. Laing— the transliteration into Middle American terms of that catchphrase of May '68, "the imagination to power"? But whereas, in the now much-maligned

Sixties, there was always at least a tension between the impulse to heal oneself and the impulse to heal the world, the recovery movement is in no doubt as to which choice is the right one. In recovery, one returns not to first principles but to the "inner child," the most private self. In this, recovery is fully the product less of the decade during which many of its adherents were young than of the Reaganite Eighties. When John Bradshaw replies to a question from an interviewer about how he sees the obligations adults owe their aging parents by declaring flatly that "we didn't come into this world to take care of Mom and Dad," he is, wittingly or not, recapitulating the Reagan-Bush approach when confronted by the problems of the frail and vulnerable in American society. The message, whether psychological or political, is that there are no civic, no social obligations, only private ones.

It will be obvious that Bradshaw is not a man to shrink from extremes. For him, not only are the personal and the political one and the same but so are the historical and the psychological. Borrowing liberally from the work of the Swiss child psychoanalyst Alice Miller, he argues that Nazism was the direct result of Hitler's having been abused as a child. Hitler, too, it would seem, was a victim. "Hitler," Bradshaw writes, "was re-enacting his own childhood, using millions of innocent Jews as his scapegoats." Small wonder, then, that Bradshaw and those who accept his arguments believe that recovery work is far more important than any more conventional social activism. As Bradshaw puts it, "Hitler and black [sic] Nazism are a cruel caricature of what can happen in modern Western society if we do not stop promoting and proliferating family rules that kill the souls of human beings."

More than anything else, it is this bleak, totalizing view of the world that distinguishes the message of most recovery books from that contained in the other self-help volumes with which they share space on bookstore shelves and bestseller lists. The message is not Coué's "every day, in every way, I'm getting better and better," or Norman Vincent Peale's "power of positive thinking," or even Eric Berne's rather more tentative "I'm okay, you're okay." These authors offered little direct criticism of society in those books. Contrast their messages with John Bradshaw's unyielding assertion that "our family life is killing the souls of human beings" and his recommendation that since "most families are dysfunctional because our rules for normalcy are dysfunctional. . . . The important issue is to find out what species of flawed relating your family specialized in. Once you know what happened to you, you can do something about it."

And the one thing that all the recovery writers insist upon is that, whether an individual remembers it or not, *something did happen.*

According to Dr. Charles Whitfield, one of the most successful recovery writers, only between 5 and 20 percent of Americans grew up "with a healthy amount and quality of love, guidance and other nurturing. . . ." The rest—and, unsurprisingly, most recovery writers favor Dr. Whitfield's lower figure for those raised in healthy homes—did not receive anywhere near enough of the aforementioned psychic nutrients to successfully "form consistently healthy relationships, and to feel good about themselves and what they do." If the result is not a substance addiction like drink or drugs it is likely to be a "process" addiction taking the form of either too much interest in some activity or too much reliance on some other person or thing for an individual's sense of identity—the dreaded co-dependency.

In their book *Adult Children: The Secrets of Dysfunctional Families,* John and Linda Friel provide a list of recovery groups—an incomplete list, they advise—that maps (or begins to) the contours of contemporary American addiction and victimhood. Beginning with AA, the Friels go on to note Al-Anon (the organization founded as a sort of ladies' auxiliary to AA, in the period when it was all male, to help the wives—later, more ecumenically, any loved one—of alcoholics), Alateen, Al-Atot, Narcotics Anonymous, Cocaine Anonymous, Overeaters Anonymous, Bulimics/Anorexics Anonymous, Sexaholics Anonymous, Sex Addicts Anonymous (the recovery movement is full of mysteriously fine distinctions), Adult Children Anonymous, Adult Children of Alcoholics, Gamblers Anonymous, Spenders Anonymous, Smokers Anonymous, Debtors Anonymous, Fundamentalists Anonymous, Parents Anonymous, Child Abusers Anonymous, Workaholics Anonymous, Shoplifters Anonymous, Pills Anonymous, and Emotions Anonymous.

Whew! And, of course, such a list is infinitely expandable. For if there is really not all that much difference between working too hard and abusing your children (and the Friels' decision to place them side by side suggests that, in the recovery context, there really isn't), then any conduct that can be engaged in enthusiastically, never mind compulsively—from stamp collecting to the missionary position—would be one around which a recovery group could presumably be organized.

And new categories are, indeed, cropping up all the time. The biggest growth sector seems to have been in the co-dependency area. Cocaine Anonymous has begot Co-Anon; Narcotics Anonymous, Nar-Anon; Overeaters Anonymous, a slim O-Anon; and Sex Addicts Anonymous, Co-Sa. But there are plenty of wholly new addictions to recover from as well, including at their different ends of the tragedy scale Incest Survivors Anonymous, which is ghastly and self-explanatory, and Recovering Couples Anonymous, which is mysterious and turns out to mean a kind of group family therapy in which couples can figure out how to stay together. As Melody Beattie puts it in her *Codependents' Guide to the Twelve Steps*, the goal of RCA is "mutual interdependence," which, it seems, is not to be confused with co-dependency. The list goes on and on, and it is clear that the next decade will give rise to any number of new subsets of the victimized, the impaired, and the addicted.

It is interesting to chart just how a new group of victims is located. To take but one example, in 1983 Janet Geringer Woititz write a book called *Adult Children of Alcoholics*. It was turned down by most mainstream publishers and, at first, was sold almost entirely by mail order. Within four years, however, Woititz's book had not only gotten onto the *New York Times* bestseller list, eventually selling more than 2 million copies, but it had spawned a movement, the National Association for Children of Alcoholics, a magazine, *Changes*, and a whole new category within that larger grouping that Herbert Gravits and Julie Bowden, authors of *Recovery: A Guide for Adult Children of Alcoholics*, call the 96 percent of the population who are "children of trauma." But after the magazine and the movement and the database, could the spin-off be far behind? Of course not. In 1988, Ann Smith, the director of a Pennsylvania family services clinic, published *Grandchildren of Alcoholics: Another Generation of Co-dependency*. "My apologies," she writes, "for introducing another 'label.' I know of no other way to bring this group of people out of hiding and into recovery."

Here I must declare an interest. Being the adult grandchild of an alcoholic—one is not supposed to hide these facts in the land of the free and the home of the autobiography—I naturally scrutinized Ms. Smith's book with particular care. But while it is never safe to underestimate the power of repression, I must report that I just don't see it. I was surprised to learn that the first characteristic Ms. Smith identifies in people like me is a "distorted family image." This turns out to mean "seeing only the good in [one's family]." Now, this is not a trait associated either with my family or, I would submit, that of many other writers. Oh well. The second category is "self-blaming." It may be old-fashioned to say this, but would that it were so. The rest of Ms. Smith's list is scarcely more revealing. I had been "outed," it seemed, for no purpose. Indeed, I have been more shaken up by a trip to a Broadway fortune-teller.

❧

Of course, it may be that I simply do not know which addiction or co-dependency I have. There are, after all, so many to choose from. This is presumably why so many of the recovery books on the market include endless questionnaires and checklists through which the reader can take a reading on his or her emotional situation. The categories are, to put it charitably, broadly phrased. In *Bradshaw On: The Family*, for example, the author offers a checklist for what he calls "adult children of dysfunctional families"; i.e., his readers, not to say the American people as a whole. "See if you identify yourself in several of the following traits," he writes. "If you do, it's likely that you are co-dependent and are carrying your family dysfunction." These traits turn out to include such harmless aspects of temperament as "inveterate" dreaming and keeping "secrets." There is even the fearsome trait "avoids depression through activity," which, particularly if one is prey to severe depression, hardly seems like such a bad idea.

Dr. Charles Whitfield's "Recovery Potential Survey" in his *Healing the Child Within* is, if anything, even more all-encompassing. Indeed, it is hard to see how, given the way Dr. Whitfield has defined childhood trauma, *any* reader could feel exempt. The questions in the survey range from relatively benign queries like "Do you seek approval and affirmation?" through the more ominous "Do you respond with anxiety to authority figures and angry people?" (here one wants to ask, With or without a firearm in their hands?) to the merely bathetic, as in that old self-help standby "Do you find it difficult to express your emotions?" And, of course, the whole thing is rigged. It turns out that in Dr. Whitfield's system of grading even one answer of "occasionally" (never mind "often" or "usually") means that the respondent stands in considerable need of having his or her inner child tended to. And just to make sure that those who have not admitted to any such feelings aren't let off the hook, Dr. Whitfield is quick to point out that if the reader answers "mostly 'Never,' you may not be aware of some of your feelings." Checkmate.

For people like Whitfield and the other recovery writers to insist that we are all victims is pretty much the same thing as asserting that no one is a victim. Either way, the civic voice is muffled, if not blotted out; it is up to you or to me, but not we. Of course, such an outbreak of self-pity among the affluent classes as recovery has spawned all but ensures that the real victims in American society—those who will never be affluent enough or have enough free time to work it out with their "inner children"—will not get the attention that is the necessary first step to any improvement in *their* lives.

Meanwhile, resources as well as attention are lavished on "inner children." Bradshaw writes in *Homecoming: Reclaiming and Championing Your Inner Child* that he found he had to balance the demands of his new celebrity with his obligations to his "inner child" and so "chose some things that my inner child likes. For the last few years, we always fly first class."

The recovery writers insist that nearly everyone in the United States has been the victim of some instance of child abuse. One would think that if a term like "child abuse" is to have any real meaning, it must be limited to some variant of sexual violation or battery. The recovery movement would have it otherwise. They talk of mental abuse, of parents abusing their children by "invalidating their experiences," even of abusers who thwart "the child's spirituality," to quote Charles Whitfield. So much for life in its full, honest imperfection.

In recovery workshops, as well as at home in the living room, recovery workbooks opened, people are encouraged to try to get in touch with that "inner child" and discern, through a dialogue with it, whether he or she was abused: "Memory work," it is called. One might reasonably ask if someone moved to do such memory work were not, in some way, predisposed to uncover evidence of abuse—some explanation of their addiction or emotional unhappiness. But this is not a question to be entertained. Steven Farmer writes in his book *Adult Children of Abusive Parents,* "No matter how abuse is defined or what other people think, you are the ultimate judge: If you think you were abused, you were. If you're not sure, you probably were."

What matters is the story that you arrive at. Thus, to imagine is to make it so, or, as the title of an anthology of postwar American women writers would have it, "We are the stories we tell." Bradshaw's story is, as he says in *Homecoming,* that we are "divine infants in exile," a nation of E.T.'s desperate to come home. And it seems that increasing numbers of Americans are beginning to agree with him.

But *are* we the stories we tell? During the period that I was reading little but recovery books, I kept remembering an encounter I had seen once on television between reporters and the grieving father of one of the passengers killed when Sikh terrorists blew up an Air India flight over the Irish Sea in 1985. The weeping father had been shown coming out of the makeshift morgue that the Irish police had set up in a small coastal village, and no sooner had he done so than he was surrounded by the hacks who bombarded him with questions. "What are you going to do?" one called out. To which, with astonishing dignity, the man replied simply, "Do? What do you expect me to do in this dirty world?"

The point that he was trying to make through his sobs was precisely the one that the recovery movement is most anxious to deny. Life may be whatever story you invent in a Bradshaw seminar, but only very affluent, very cut-off people could persuade themselves, at least once they have "returned home," that this is really the way things are. A quick way of seeing just how specific the recovery idea is to prosperous Americans in the late twentieth century is to think how preposterous it would seem not only to a man whose daughter had just been killed by a terrorist bomb, or someone who was hungry, but to someone, anyone, in Croatia, the Soviet Union, or South Africa. It is a safe bet that they are more worried about what will befall their real children than what has befallen their inner children. It is a measure of the continued economic success of the United States that so many of its citizens could be so buffered from the real harshness of the world that they can spend their time anatomizing the state of their own feelings and speculating, often deep into middle age, about whether or not their parents always behaved as well as they should have.

In most of the world, though, people's thoughts are elsewhere. Beyond our innocent shores, it is understood that the past is not always knowable and never recuperable, that there is sometimes nothing to be done, and that reality conforms neither to our desires nor to our schemes, psychic or material. There is chance, and fate, and tragedy.

Of course, it is true that there is a group within the population who often do not know this or believe it. We call them children, and while we may envy them their ignorance, and their belief in the potency of their own wishes, we know that they are under a false impression. We also know, or should, that however much we may feel nostalgia for our childhood, there is no going back, no reprieve from adulthood, which is to say from consciousness. That is the splendor and misery of being an adult, a condition from which we should not want to and, more to the point, cannot recover.

THE EIGHTIES

From
Culture Wars
(1991)

James Davison Hunter

What the press had deemed the culture wars grew out of competing moral systems, each with its own private and public philosophy, said Hunter. Each had its own foundations of ethical authority, one theological and the other constitutional. Americans were finding it increasingly difficult to understand the language and assumptions of their fellow citizens, in Hunter's view, as they were increasingly animated by dissimilar moral premises.

The central dynamic of the cultural realignment is not merely that different public philosophies create diverse public opinions. These alliances, rather, reflect the *institutionalization and politicization of two fundamentally different cultural systems*. Each side operates from within its own constellation of values, interests, and assumptions. At the center of each are two distinct conceptions of moral authority—two different ways of apprehending reality, of ordering experience, of making moral judgments. Each side of the cultural divide, then, speaks with a different moral vocabulary. Each side operates out of a different mode of debate and persuasion. Each side represents the tendencies of a separate and competing moral galaxy. They are, indeed, "worlds apart."

As a consequence of this mutual moral estrangement, concessions on many policy matters become a virtual impossibility. The abortion debate exemplifies this most poignantly, particularly in the voices of those who care most passionately about the outcome. No one on the pro-life side of this controversy doubts that "God's gift of life begins at conception." How do we know this? "The Bible clearly states that life begins at conception." Thus, the Old and New Testament texts are copiously cited. But what is more, modern science also demonstrates that there is life in the womb. After all, "The unborn child has a beating heart at 24 days, brain waves and unique fingerprints at 43 days, a complete skeleton and reflexes at 6 weeks," and so on. Abortion, therefore, could never be anything else than "killing of innocent life." For this reason, "the abortion of the 22 million fetuses between 1973 and 1988" is nothing short of "mass genocide." The moral choice, then, is clear: one is, as a Methodists for Life brochure put it, "either for life or against life; for Jesus or against Jesus."

The moral logic is fundamentally different on the pro-choice side of the controversy. Arguments also grounded in theological and scientific insight show that there is "an important distinction between potential life and actual life" and that fetuses "are not of equal moral value with actual persons." After all, "The biblical characterization of human being is that of a complex, many-sided creature with the god-like ability and responsibility to make choices. The fetus hardly meets those characteristics." On this side too, as the Religious Coalition for Abortion Rights makes clear, abortion is a religious issue. Not only do different faith traditions hold different theological and philosophical beliefs about "personhood," they also hold different ideas about when abortion is morally justified. The bottom line, according to the Religious Coalition for Abortion Rights and other progressive groups, is simply this: "If abortion is a religious issue, and religious theologies differ, and each denomination counsels its members according to its own theology, wouldn't a law prohibiting abortion violate religious liberty? Exactly. . . . The issue of abortion is a crucial test of religious liberty—one of the cornerstones of democracy."

The reality of politics and public policy in a democracy is, for better or worse, compromise born out of public discussion and debate. But such discussion would seem to be unattainable when the moral language employed by opposing sides is so completely antithetical. One can easily imagine an Evangelical Protestant, charismatic Catholic, Hasidic Jew, or a Mormon asking rhetorically: "How can murder be a First Amendment right?" One could also imagine a liberal Protestant, liberal Catholic, Reform Jew, or secularist asking just the opposite: "How can the exercise of basic First Amendment rights be called murder?" Political resolution seems sociologically impossible when the moral language for talking about mutual problems is so contrary.

This problem is also crystallized within the debates about homosexuality. For the orthodox communities, homosexuality is "the zenith of human indecency"—a sin "so grievous, so abominable in the sight of God that he destroyed the cities of Sodom and Gomorrah because of [it]." For most progressivists, homosexuality is "not unscriptural" but simply an alternative sexual lifestyle; one other way in which loving relationships can be expressed, Once again each employs a fundamentally different moral vocabulary to understand this behavior. For one side, homosexuality is sin; for the other, homosexuality is "just one type of human behavior"—the only sin is the "sinful discrimination against lesbians and gay men." As a consequence, any mutually agreeable resolution of policy, much less cultural consensus, is almost unimaginable.

Virtually the same moral impasse has been reached in discussions about war, inequality, pornography and obscenity, euthanasia, the use of fetal tissue for medical research, and other controversies. All of these disputes, as Alasdair MacIntyre has described them, are characterized by an "interminable character." True, not all of these issues are equally polarizing. Nevertheless, the existence of common moral ground from which to build and resolve differences appears to be equally elusive in every case.

The moral arguments on either side of these disputes appeal with equal facility to the evidence of science (as, for example, in discussions about human biology), the precedents (or lack of precedents) from social history, and the legitimations of theology and biblical textual analysis. At least from a lay person's point of view, the logic of the competing claims is equally rigorous. But in the end, whether concerned with abortion, homosexuality, women's rights, day care, or any other major moral or political issue of the day, the tools of logic and the evidence from science, history, and theology can do nothing to alter the opinions of their opposition. Because each side interprets them differently, logic, science, history, and theology can only serve to enhance and legitimate particular ideological interests. The willingness or unwillingness of opposing groups to have a "dialogue" about their differences is largely irrelevant. Even a spirit of compromise maintained by either side would be irrelevant. *In the final analysis, each side of the cultural divide can only talk past the other.*

The orthodox and progressivist impulses provide the foundations not only for competing moral visions, then, but for competing dogmas. This is true because what both sides bring to this public debate is, at least consciously, non-negotiable. What is ultimately at issue, then, are not just disagreements about "values" or "opinions." Such language misconstrues the nature of moral commitment. Such language in the end reduces morality to preferences and cultural whim. What is ultimately at issue are deeply rooted and fundamentally different understandings of being and purpose.

To put this in the terms proposed by the French sociologist Emile Durkheim, what is ultimately at issue are different conceptions of the sacred. For Durkheim, the sacred was not necessarily embodied in a divine or supernatural being, the sacred could be anything that was viewed as "set apart" and "exalted"; anything that provided the life-orienting principles of individuals and the larger community. To know the nature of the sacred in each moral community is to know the source of their passion, the wellspring of their fervor. The reality, as Durkheim pointed out, is that communities cannot and will not tolerate the desecration of the sacred. The problem is this: not only does each side of the cultural divide operate with a different conception of the sacred, but the mere existence of the one represents a certain desecration of the other.

ֆ֎

Needless to say, this cultural realignment has tremendous historical significance. Few would disagree that the rise of Christianity as a world religion between the first and third centuries, and the success of the Protestant Reformation in the sixteenth century created the most fundamental cultural divisions in the history of Western civilization: those that divide Christian from Jew and Protestant from Catholic. . . . [T]he historical effect of these divisions was not only "religious" or cultural but manifestly and irrefutably political as well. They have been at the root of centuries of prejudice and discrimination. They have been at the heart of social strife and even war.

But if the organizing principle of American pluralism is shifting in the direction described here—so that progressively oriented Protestants, Catholics, Jews, and secularists share more in common with each other culturally and politically than they do with the orthodox members of their *own* faith tradition (and vice versa)—then the practical effects of the birth of Christianity and the Reformation have, at least in the U.S. context, become both politically and culturally defunct.

If the organizing principle of American pluralism has shifted in these ways, then, it is because another world-historical "event" has become paramount. Yielding to the temptation of hyperbole, it could be said that the politically relevant divisions in the American context are no longer defined according to where one stands vis-à-vis Jesus, Luther, or Calvin, but where one stands vis-à-vis Rousseau, Voltaire, Diderot, and Condorcet, and especially their philosophical heirs (including Nietzsche and Rorty). The politically relevant world-historical event, in other words, is now the secular Enlightenment of the eighteenth century and its philosophical aftermath. This is what inspires the divisions of public culture in the United States today.

This, of course, is a caricature of our situation. Virtually everyone, nowadays, is influenced by the profound philosophical reorientation of the Enlightenment with its rejection of otherworldly "superstitions" and its emphasis on societal progress through human mastery over nature and rational judgment. Even the most Bible-believing Evangelical, the most Rome-bound Catholic, and the most observant Orthodox Jew has been influenced in subtle even if unacknowledged ways. What really divides our culture is the matter of priority—the sources upon which different moral communities rely *most* in establishing their own sense of right and wrong. Clearly there are people at each extreme, particularly those who act as voices for opposing communities. There are also . . . many people somewhere in the middle, who draw in varying degrees from both Enlightenment and biblical sources of moral understanding. . . . Still, as a historical event, the Enlightenment has become an increasingly promi-nent source of division in American public life. The division is certainly "religious" or cultural, but it has unmistakable political consequences too. Already these have begun to take expression as new forms of prejudice, discrimination, social strife, and political conflict.

Drawing by R. Chast from the *New Yorker,* 1991

Index

Permissions Acknowledgments